John Todd –
Six decades of footy

Brian Dawson

Published by Cambridge Publishing – a division of Cambridge Media
17 Northwood Street
West Leederville WA 6007 Australia
Tel: (08) 9382 3911   Fax: (08) 9382 3187
Web: www.cambridgemedia.com.au

Text copyright © Brian Dawson 2004

This book is copyright. Apart from any fair dealing for the purposes of private study, research, criticism or review, as permitted under the Copyright Act, no part may be reproduced in any form without written permission of the publisher. Every effort has been made to comply with requirements for reproducing copyright material. The author and publisher are happy to rectify any inadvertent omissions at the earliest opportunity.

National Library of Australia cataloguing data

Dawson, Brian

John Todd – Six decades of footy

ISBN 0-9579343-3-5

1. Sport, Australian rules
2. Biography
3. West Australian history

Special editorial assistance provided by Alan East

Designed by Ceridwen Clocherty

Cover photos

Front cover: John after the 1982 grand final (main picture), at State training in 1959 (top thumbnail), coaching South Fremantle in 1966 (middle thumbnail) and coaching West Coast in 1988 (right hand thumbnail).

Back cover: The banner for John's last game as a coach, August 2002.

John Todd – Six decades of footy

Brian Dawson

The name John Todd has been synonymous with WA football for six decades. For the 47 years from 1955 to 2002, he was involved as a player or coach; no-one has seen the game evolve like he has while remaining a part of it.

In his first season in 1955 as a 17-year-old, he won the Sandover Medal, the youngest winner in the award's 84 year history in open competition. In the same year, he became the youngest player to represent Western Australia when he played against South Australia.

Then, in 1956, in only his 28th league game, he severely injured his left knee; an injury that should have ended his career, as surgery to repair a torn anterior cruciate ligament (as practised today) was not then available. However, he refused to accept that his career was over and, with great perseverance and discipline over the next 10 years, he added another 104 league games, earning another two club fairest and best awards and playing 12 more matches for the State, earning All-Australian selection in 1961 as a member of the victorious WA carnival side.

In 1959, aged 20, he was appointed captain-coach of South Fremantle, the youngest senior coach in WA football history. When he retired as the league's oldest ever coach in 2002, he had amassed 721 games, easily the most in WA. He has coached sides to six premierships, more than any other WA coach since the final four system was adopted in 1931, taking three different clubs to the ultimate success – East Fremantle in 1974, a Swan Districts hat trick in 1982-83-84, again at Swans in 1990 and then back home at South Fremantle in 1997.

He coached the West Coast Eagles to their first final in 1988 and took the State to successive Australian championships in 1983-84; that year he also coached the first official Australian side to tour Ireland, winning the composite Gaelic rules series 2-1. He is by far the most decorated coach in WA football history.

This sporting biography traces John Todd's career as a player and coach – from his childhood obsession with football to be *"the greatest player the game has ever seen"*, through the devastating period of his knee injury and how he strove to return and play the game that was his life, and on to his many coaching triumphs (and low points) spread over five decades. The book looks at his coaching philosophies and records his thoughts on the great players he has seen over this time. The enormous changes in football that he has witnessed first hand are briefly discussed by reviewing how WA football was in the 1950s, '60s, '70s, '80s and '90s and he looks at where the sport might head in the 21st century.

Author's note

Left to his own devices, John Todd would not have bothered with a book about his career in football. Despite being an integral and influential figure in WA football for almost the past 50 years – a time span surpassed by no-one – he is content to downplay his involvement, declaring it to be *"no big deal"*.

He was finally sold on the idea on the basis that the history of WA football from the 1950s onward would also be covered so that the kids of today could know something of the game from these times, particularly prior to 1987, when the West Coast Eagles joined the expanded VFL (now AFL). He was also very keen to ensure that all of the people who assisted him in his playing and coaching careers received due recognition in the book, so that *"it wasn't just about me, as I couldn't have done it without their help"*.

Hopefully this book will do justice to these various purposes, and he now seems genuinely pleased that his story has been written, as, if nothing else, *"my grandchildren will be able to read about me, much better than I could remember it to tell to them"*.

Brian Dawson
February, 2004

About the author

Brian Dawson grew up as an avid Swan Districts supporter, but was too young to see or remember the 1961-63 premierships. His first contact with John Todd came in 1977, when he was coached by John at Swans. At the time, he was studying physical education at the University of Western Australia, so from 1977-81 he combined playing and working at Swans as John gave him an opportunity to be one of his fitness advisors. After again missing the triple premiership years of 1982-84 (by playing with Perth FC), he returned to Swans in 1985 as a selector and fitness coach, roles he maintained until 1987.

When John took over at West Coast in 1988 he was taken along as the fitness coach, a position which he held for the next 13 years. In 2002 he returned to Swans as an assistant coach, working closely with John in his final year of coaching.

By day, when not involved with football, he is an Associate Professor in sports science and exercise physiology in the School of Human Movement and Exercise Science at the University of Western Australia. He is also retained as a sports science and research consultant by the West Coast Eagles.

Acknowledgements

The number of people who have contributed their time, energy, opinions and memories to the writing and production of this book are too numerous to all list here. However, some deserve to be acknowledged for their special assistance.

John's family – mother Doris, brother Bill, sister Diane, wife Meryl and daughters Debbie and Kylie – were ever helpful and special credit must go to Doris for her wonderful foresight in keeping scrapbooks detailing John's career over nearly 40 years.

At the clubs he either played with or coached, many people gave freely of their time to help with the checking of records and reflections on John's time there. At South Fremantle, Brian Ciccotosto and Ben Condon; at East Fremantle, Merv Cowan, Tony Micale and Bob Uittenbroek; at Swan Districts, John Cooper, Bob Manning and Bill Walker; and at West Coast, Bob Manning and Trevor Nisbett all provided valuable information and assistance on multiple occasions.

At the Western Australian Football Commission, the access to WAFL records and archives and general assistance provided by Grant Dorrington and Clint Roberts was greatly appreciated, also the interest and enthusiasm shown for the project by Neale Fong. Football historian Dave Clement was also called many times to provide or verify factual information, which he was always able to do.

Ray Wilson at *The West Australian* and Wally Foreman at the ABC both provided valuable advice and critical review of some early drafts, which was a great help.

Finally, to Joan Williams for her cheerful acceptance of, and skill in deciphering, many hundreds of hand written pages and typing them into a coherent Word document, which ended up as this book.

Editing

Special recognition is required for Alan East, who made a great contribution through his careful and skilled editing of the final version.

Contents

Forewords 6

The 1940s
Chapter 1   Growing up: School or football? 9

The 1950s
Chapter 2   Joining South Fremantle 19
Chapter 3   A Sandover at 17 25
Chapter 4   Wrecking a knee 33
Chapter 5   Finding a way back 45
Chapter 6   Would you like to coach South Fremantle? 59
Chapter 7   Football in the 1950s 69

The 1960s
Chapter 8   Battling on 75
Chapter 9   Time to retire 91
Chapter 10 A coach again 103
Chapter 11 Football in the 1960s 117

The 1970s
Chapter 12 Coaching the enemy 125
Chapter 13 A premiership at last! 137
Chapter 14 Off to Bassendean 155
Chapter 15 Football in the 1970s 169

The 1980s
Chapter 16 Close, but not quite 177
Chapter 17 After 19 years, another hat trick 189
Chapter 18 Coaching the Green and Gold 211
Chapter 19 The Eagles land (but without JT) 217
Chapter 20 Highs and lows in the VFL 229
Chapter 21 Football in the 1980s 247

The 1990s
Chapter 22 Bouncing back 259
Chapter 23 Heading back home (twice) 267
Chapter 24 Football in the 1990s and the new millennium ...279
Chapter 25 A football legacy 287

Epilogue 297

Foreword

I first saw John Todd play football in the 1954 WAFL reserves grand final for South Fremantle. At the tender age of 16 years, he kicked seven goals from a half-forward flank, announcing himself as a future champion. Never in my wildest dreams did I imagine that at some future time, I would establish a football connection with this young man that would prove to be something special for us both. Some 23 years later, in 1977, John Todd was appointed league coach of the Swan Districts Football Club, one year after my election as president. I believe, even now, that this appointment was to become a defining moment in both of our lives.

Right from the start, controversy was evident. John's appointment was not unanimous and came only after I had exercised my casting vote in his favour. This was the start of a roller-coaster ride of emotion, controversy, loyalty and passion that was to take our club to many final round appearances. These included four premierships (three in succession), a defeat of Collingwood in Melbourne, the sending of a reserves team to the same city to play an Escort Cup semi-final against Richmond and subsequent disqualification from that VFL night competition. I enjoyed it all.

For Toddy, it saw him serve as WA State of Origin coach, All-Australian coach against the Irish, the Eagles VFL coach and finally the wonderful achievement of having coached more than 700 WAFL/VFL games. Quite rightly, he has gained many honours along the way – the WA Hall of Champions induction, life membership of the WA Football Commission, the Order of Australia Medal and the naming of the John Todd Entrance at Subiaco Oval.

I sincerely hope this book gives a real insight into John Todd, the man, so that some of the myths and criticisms surrounding him as a coach will be dispelled forever. On being appointed coach of Swans he told me, *"I will coach the players to not only get the team into the finals, but also make them mentally tough enough to WIN when they get there"*.

It was through his almost obsessive drive to produce the necessary mental toughness in his players that the fertile ground for criticism levelled at him was created, not only from players who couldn't cope with it (he did not want them in any case), but also from the media 'giants' who never really understood his coaching philosophy and psychology.

His unflinching commitment to the cause and his tremendous passion for the game and the club brought him into conflict with many people, so much so it was very much a case of love him or hate him. There were no half measures in his relationship with others. Those who love him, know him; those that hate him do not. Despite his wonderful record of achievement for all to see, some will neither forgive him nor try to understand him. John Todd is a football legend by any measure and has long left his critics lamenting in his wake.

By his own success, he has lifted an average footballer-turned-administrator to a level of recognition that I probably do not deserve. I thank God for my long association with the master coach and the man. We had our moments but, on reflection, all have been worthwhile. His generosity to me, my family and those in need will live with me for the rest of my days. Even more, until my last breath and without reservation, he will be my friend.

Enjoy the book.

John Cooper, OAM, ASM, JP

Foreword

John 'The Nose' Todd has been known to me since 1955. As a one-eyed Bulldog supporter, I marvelled at JT's skills, was devastated by his knee injury, enthralled by his knee brace and thrilled by his kicking into Souths forward line to my hero, John Gerovich.

As a coach, Toddy was tough. He was unfair, demanding, ruthless, innovative and tactically ahead of his time. To coach six premierships with three different clubs is unique and, together with his 1955 Sandover Medal win, this made him very special in WAFL (I still can't say WAFC) history.

I never played against Toddy, but my assessment of him as a boy and by listening to the old timers, is that he was obviously a rare talent. His pursuit of excellence put him at loggerheads with many – did he have a chip on his shoulder? Probably not, he just had no respect for administrators – all rubbish. Toddy loved our game and hated young men wasting their talent or others wasting time and space. Todd had no regard for big names and one and all had to fit into the team plan – as he showed when he coached the Australian team.

He brought a plan and discipline to the West Coast Eagles. He sorted out who wanted to play and who would pay the price to be successful, and he strengthened them mentally, including the board and the administrators.

'Nose' – you and Meryl have enriched our great game, adding colour, controversy and skill, as well as collecting premierships and well-deserved honours along the way.

Good fishing.

An old adversary – Mal Brown

The Champion (Player)

John Todd – the name brings back the speed and grace

As he created his own time and space

The fascination and the crowd's devotion

His unique blend of poetry in motion.

Gerry Cohen, Carine, WA

The 1940s

Chapter 1
Growing up: School or football?

John's mother Doris, remembering his early childhood:

"He could dropkick a football really well at the age of three".

"I sometimes thought he was a bit wacky, the way he would train for hours on his own".

John Todd was born in Manjimup, in the South West of Western Australia, on May 21, 1938. However, the family home was in Deanmill, a small, sleepy timber town 5km down the road from the larger regional centre of Manjimup and it was there John lived until he was seven.

While Deanmill has probably never been home to more than a 1000 people at any one time, it can proudly claim to have produced more than its fair share of champion footballers. In a remarkable coincidence, John lived six doors from the home of Ross Hutchinson (later Sir Ross) who enjoyed great success as a player and coach in the 1930s and '40s. They are the only two WA coaches to take three different clubs to premierships since the Page finals system was introduced in 1931 [1]. Other footballers of note who grew up in Deanmill were Ray (Lizard) Richards, who played with John both in the timber town's streets and in the South

John with mother Doris and grandmother Lucy, in 1940, aged 20 months.

---

1. Sir Ross Hutchinson – East Fremantle (1937), West Perth (1941) & South Fremantle (1947-48).
    John Todd – East Fremantle (1974), Swan Districts (1982-83-84 and 1990) & South Fremantle (1997).

Fremantle teams of the 1950s; Jack Murray, the great Swan Districts ruckman of the 1930s and '40s; 1950s Perth stalwart Charlie Skehan and 1960s and '70s East Perth forward Gary Bygraves, who all represented Western Australia.

John's mother Doris was the daughter of Charlie and Lucy Hindes, long-time residents of the region, with Charlie a Deanmill pioneer, having helped clear land to establish the townsite in the early 1900s. As a teenager, Doris was a talented hockey player who represented the district in Country Week championships. She was friendly with Gwen Hutchinson (Ross' sister), who went on to play hockey for Australia and Doris fondly recalls how the hockey team would travel to games up to 30km away to towns like Pemberton and Bridgetown in the back of open trucks – the same method of transport used for the Saturday night dances. John describes his mother as *"having a very determined streak"* and there is little doubt this characteristic was passed on to her son.

John's father, Bill, was a tree feller and sleeper cutter in Deanmill, working long hours and finding little time for play with John, even on days when he wasn't working. He died in 1971 and John remembers him as a *"man's man"* and *"not exactly a family man"*. They never really *"clicked"* and even when John was a child, they weren't close. However, this didn't seriously impact on his childhood and he holds no ill-feeling towards his late father. Doris was well aware of the distance between John and his father, and was over-protective of him as a result. He has always been very close to his mother, who has been his greatest ally, taking immense pleasure from his sporting involvement.

Life was tough in Deanmill in the early 1940s. The War saw many of the town's men, including Bill Todd, join the armed forces; food rationing was in force and commodities were scarce and, while the Todds weren't a rich family, they got by with little complaint. There was a great community spirit, which helped offset the relative isolation and lack of luxuries.

Much of John's early upbringing was done by his grandparents, Charlie and Lucy, as Doris worked as a cook at the local hospital and hotel to provide extra income. It mattered little to young John, who thrived in the small town and only has happy memories of Deanmill, always looking forward to holiday visits when the family moved to Fremantle after the War. Charlie worked as the 'sanitary man' for the town and John regularly accompanied him as he collected pans from the houses, taking them into the bush where they dug long trenches in the solid earth to bury the waste. The transport was horse and cart, with just two motor cars in town. Charlie (and his big draught horse) was a popular Deanmill figure, with everyone knowing him as 'mate' and they soon got to know the small, skinny boy along for the ride.

John remembers that the sanitary run wasn't easy work – *"The pans were heavy, the smell terrible, the earth hard to dig and there were lots of snakes who didn't enjoy trenches being dug in their neck of the woods"*; he has maintained a strong dislike of snakes ever since. However, the job provided regular contact with the townsfolk, which they both enjoyed. It was also John's introduction to horses, which Charlie fostered by offering John one shilling and three pence every Saturday to act as his 'runner' from home to the Deanmill boarding house to place a bet with the SP bookie who operated there. John didn't mind this job at all and was soon picking out his own fancies and placing bets! These innocent beginnings led to a lifelong interest in horses and John has part-owned and raced several thoroughbreds, finding a day at the races a pleasant escape from the pressures of football.

John remembers often rising before dawn to accompany Bill and the other tree fellers into the bush for the day. While the men cut timber from sunrise to sunset, John and his mates caught marron in the dams and creeks, or trapped rabbits and possums. The marron and rabbits were a useful additional source of food for the dinner table and a day in the bush was an adventure not to be missed. John also became aware of how hard the work was – *"There were no mechanical aids or machinery, everything was done by hand. The big logs were hauled by draught horses and cut to size by the men working in pairs with a crosscut saw. The railway sleepers were cut with an axe and the men usually kept at it for the whole day without a lunch break"*. Witnessing this backbreaking work may have perhaps reinforced John's own personal work ethic; certainly in both his football and his employment as a butcher, John was never afraid of putting in long hours and extra effort to improve himself. Sadly, he sees little of this attitude in society today – *"In the main, young people, instead of persevering when things get tough, give up too easily, preferring the easy way out"*.

When John wasn't on the sanitary run, placing bets with the SP bookie or chasing marron and rabbits, he was playing football. His first introduction to the game was probably through his uncle, Ron Hindes (Doris' younger brother), who made the 1938 State Schoolboys football team as a 14-year-old – a feat later emulated by John. Ron was a keen footballer and often took John to the Deanmill school grounds where he kicked for goal and honed his skills while little John, only two or three years old, 'foxed' the ball for hours at a time. Doris often went as well or, if she walked past the school, she invariably found the boys engrossed in their game, with John showing no signs of fatigue. Doris has no doubt that the time John spent playing football with Ron at such an early age sparked his passion for the game – by the age of three *"John could drop kick really well"*.

Ron can't remember ever seeing John without a football in his hand once he began to walk. However, Ron never tried to coach John, he merely *"played football with him"* and John simply observed and copied his kicking and marking skills. One of their favourite games was kicking the ball through the doorway of a timber shed from various angles. Errant kicks often brought the woodpile tumbling down, which incurred the wrath of Bill and/or Doris. Ron, as the much older boy, normally bore the brunt of their displeasure, but having to re-stack the woodpile was no deterrent. John readily acknowledges that the time Ron spent with him at that early age was important to his future development as a player. Ron continued his interest in John's career through to senior ranks and also played three league games himself with East

John with grandfather Charlie, on the 'sanitary run' in Deanmill in the early 1940s.

Perth in 1947; the War had interrupted his career and also cost him a little finger when a block and tackle crushed his hand.

John's first football – and his only one until he was about nine – was a bundle of old socks tied up with string. The Todd family budget was tight, but this made little difference to young John, who took his 'football' everywhere and practised incessantly. In fact, the socks worked in his favour as he could play inside the house as well as outside without causing too much damage. Doris recalls the day John was making up a new 'football' and, as he cut off the excess string with a knife, the upward action slashed his nose quite badly. However, it wasn't enough to keep him quiet for the day. After Doris applied some plaster to the nose, he was quickly outside and into a game. With no spare money for boots (he got his first pair in high school), John played barefoot, as did most boys in town, even in games played for the Deanmill Primary School. John never saw these things as obstacles or setbacks and never felt hard done by; his passion for the game remained undiminished.

When Uncle Ron was not around, John played football by himself or with any older boys who would let him join in. Ray Richards was several years older (they later played together at South Fremantle) and he had a few mates who kicked around regularly, including Charlie Skehan. The sanitary run was a focal point and at 2pm on Fridays, Charlie Hindes would stop at the school to collect the sanitary pans; Richards and Skehan often wagged school to accompany Charlie and little John into the bush to empty them. Charlie was happy to have them along as he could sit and read the newspaper while the young boys dug the trenches!

Richards had his own football, having saved up six months' worth of rabbit skins to buy one, so, despite their age difference, they became good friends through their love of having a kick. Richards recalls that John simply *"always wanted to play footy"* and *"practised everything"*. He has fond memories of kick-to-kick in Deanmill's main street, a gravel road, which often lasted until 9pm when the moon was full and there was no school the next day. Richards was happy to let John into their games, if only because as the smallest and youngest, he would fox the ball when it went 'out of bounds'. However, John recalls the time when they were kicking in the street and Richards jumped a fence to fetch the ball and landed on a broken bottle, almost severing a big toe! Luckily, Doris was close by and dressed the wound and took him to hospital. No permanent damage was done and Richards was soon back in the street kicking with John.

In his early years, John also spent a lot of time with his cousin Roger Gates, who was the same age and they enjoyed many hours around the timber mill, with all its nooks and crannies providing an excellent place for war games. Roger's father Frank had made some wooden rifles and the boys pretended they were the Mill security who, in actual fact, patrolled with wooden guns – with real guns in short supply, the army at that time did much training and drill work with wooden replicas, as did the civilian home guard. In their war games, John and Gates were usually (by choice) the *"bad guys"*, with John playing Mussolini often enough to earn the nickname 'Muzzo' – courtesy of Richards, who saw a similarity in the size and shape of John's nose and that of the Italian dictator – while his cousin was often Hitler. 'Muzzo' stuck with John as his Deanmill nickname and even on return visits after moving to Fremantle, the townspeople and his mates often greeted him in this way.

Chapter 1 – Growing up: School or football?

It's tempting to think that John's fierce competitive instincts and desire to succeed were honed by competing for a kick against older and bigger boys from a young age, but the truth is much more basic. It is simply that, from a young age and certainly while living in Deanmill, John resolved to become the greatest player to ever play the game – *"I firmly believed I was meant to be an athlete and football was the game I had been put on earth to play"*. If this sounds a little presumptuous and arrogant, then that may fit the typical public impression of the man, but the facts are that, as a young boy, John programmed his mind and trained his body to achieve this goal. He reasoned that lots of people had the ability to be good footballers, but not all would have the dedication and desire to make the best of their ability. Sacrifices needed to be made and he would gladly make them in order to achieve his goal. Any adversity encountered along the way would simply increase the hunger to succeed and make the mind stronger. So, by the War's end in 1945, which was to be the Todds' last year in Deanmill, John had already embarked on his journey to become the best player the game had ever seen. Even in the summer months, when other kids were playing cricket, John could be found running around the school grounds or nearby paddocks kicking his football for hours at a time.

After the War, Bill Todd didn't relish the prospect of returning to tree felling, so he switched to the Fremantle wharf; it was with great sadness that Doris and John left Deanmill and the country life. Doris had lived her whole life in Deanmill and was leaving her parents, while John had made his last sanitary run with Charlie and placed his last bet with the SP bookie. He knew he would miss the bush life – the marron, rabbits and horses – and the free and easy lifestyle they enjoyed in the country, despite their financial struggles. However, he was consoled by one important fact – he knew he could play footy anywhere, city or country, so the move wouldn't put his football goals at risk.

The family moved into a one bedroom self-contained flat on the top floor of the Johnson family's boarding house in Quarry Street, Fremantle and, while it was planned as a temporary stay, the Todds spent almost 4 years there. The family now numbered four, with Bill junior born in 1944, so there was little room to play football inside the flat – and with an extra mouth to feed, there was rarely any spare money. John, aged seven, started at the East Fremantle Primary School and, more importantly, soon found an oval not far from home, in Queen Victoria Street. Initially, Doris often ran around with John at the oval while he kicked his sock footy, but it didn't take him long to seek out kids keen on football. He met up with Don Stewart, who lived two doors down, and Ray 'Oscar' Howard, who both had footballs and enjoyed a kick. John would later rove with Stewart in South Fremantle's league side, while Howard played 157 league games with East Fremantle – and many against his two childhood partners.

The transition from country to city life for the Todds went smoothly and, while Doris and John missed the bush, they settled easily into Fremantle and found the Johnsons friendly landlords. Bill's wharf job was better than tree felling, although it didn't pay a lot more, and John was content at East Fremantle primary. Times were tough in the post-war years, with rationing of many commodities still in place and ends hard to meet. Their flat, while convenient for work and school, was cramped for four people, so they looked for a larger house as soon as possible. However, saving for this proved slow and difficult.

In 1949 the family moved from Quarry Street into temporary accommodation in the Melville Camps, which had been set up near the wharf to house people returning from the War. There was more room, indoors and outside, and the Todds spent 18 months there. John switched to the White Gum Valley Primary School where he caught the eye of Jack Lacey, a teacher who happened to be Ross Hutchinson's brother-in-law. Lacey took an interest in John's football development, passing on advice about various skills – he had no doubt that this youngster had the makings of a league footballer. Doris recalls Lacey visiting their house when John was about 12-years-old and telling her how good a player he was. At this stage, Doris didn't really know much about her son's ability, simply believing that *"he was a bit wacky, the way he would train for hours on his own"*. Doris knew Lacey other than as a teacher because of her friendship with the Hutchinson family, so she took notice of his opinion about John, which may have been important for keeping the peace at home and putting her at ease about his future prospects.

The family moved to a State Housing Commission home in Carrington Street, Hilton Park and, with the Hilton Park Oval across the road, Doris never had to look far for John – *"... you just couldn't keep him off the oval, he was there all the time playing football"*. The house also had a backyard and, as John now had a real football, he was invariably out there until after dark kicking and handballing at targets strung from the clothesline, trees or the fence. It had been pointed out to him, perhaps by Lacey, that it was important to be skilled on both sides of the body, so he would throw the ball in the air, catch it and turn to kick or handball at the targets. He was a natural left-footer, so he concentrated on his right side in these drills. The targets were old tyres, kerosene tins or wooden boxes and, if he missed, then a fence picket, a window or a louvre stood a good chance of suffering! Doris was thankful for her understanding neighbours as they never complained when the fence lost pickets, which was quite often. John also played imaginary games with himself – *"I had my own league, complete with weekly fixtures and a premiership table which I kept up to date with the results of that day's game"*.

Even in the house, the football was rarely out of his hands. He would bounce the ball as he walked through the house, throw it from hand to hand and try to control it behind his back and around his body. Other practice drills involved controlling the ball in one hand as his arm moved in an arc from above his head to his knee, where a quick change of hands would occur before repeating the movement on the other side of his body. Naturally, he slept with his football! Doris also remembers John reading in bed with one hand holding a book or a comic, while the other twirled the ball above his head. Bill (Jnr), who shared the bedroom with John, remembers watching him kick the ball to himself while lying on his back in bed. It never hit the floor. While the ball was banned from the dinner table, probably the only other place it didn't go with him was into the bath.

John settled in well at White Gum Valley primary, but he and Doris knew he was no scholar as he generally found school boring, but he certainly enjoyed the sport lessons, morning recess and lunchtime, which all naturally involved football! It was not so much that he found the work too hard, he simply lacked motivation and had no interest in it. He found school a nuisance, something that got in the way of his football and as a result he was prone to 'wag' school regularly so he could spend more time on the oval developing his game. Even at the age of 10 or 11, John had a tremendous self-belief and harboured no doubts that he would make it into league ranks and be a great player. School was one of the sacrifices that had to be made to achieve his goals; he felt he didn't need school because it wasn't going to take him where he knew he was going. Therefore, little homework was done and many Monday mornings at school began with John lining up for the cane for failing to submit the required work. However, John was no trouble at school (when he turned up) and generally his teachers allowed some latitude with his schoolwork because he was a likeable kid.

Even though he lacked some aptitude for education, he had a marvellous appetite for sport. Apart from football, where he was easily White Gum's best player, he was also a good cricketer and sprinter, regularly winning the 100-yard dash in school athletic carnivals. His sprinting prowess was largely natural talent, but also in part due to his dedication to football. To make sure he was fast, agile and light on his feet, with good balance, technique and rhythm when running, John joined the Fremantle Athletics Club and trained under Don Gillan, who coached some of WA's best sprinters. He progressed so much in his sprinting that, when John was 16, Gillan asked Doris whether he could train him to run in the Stawell Gift, Australia's most famous professional foot race... but football prevailed.

Professional running was quite big in Australia and there were regular meetings in city and country areas; John remembers attending several pro races at Leederville Oval, tagging along with John and Tommy Bottrell. John was a good sprinter and won many professional races. Tommy was also no slouch, although not quite as successful, and would later join South Fremantle as a trainer, forging a 50 year career at the Bulldogs, where he saw John's career take off. Gillan was also a trainer at Souths, so he was able to witness first-hand the fruits of his labour with regard to John's speed and agility. John thoroughly enjoyed the summer athletics training but, interestingly, and in complete contrast to the strong self-belief he had with football, he was a *"bundle of nerves"* whenever it came to a race, often experiencing cold sweats and dry retches. He cannot explain why he reacted that way for athletic competition, as he never felt like that before any football matches. As a consequence, John hated competing and preferred to just train for athletics simply to help his football.

Moving to the city also put John in contact with the league football environment at an earlier age than if he had remained in Deanmill; this reinforced his passion for the game. Bill and Doris were strong South Fremantle supporters and Bill regularly attended matches at Fremantle Oval, with John and his football tagging along. Doris didn't see too many games but listened to the radio broadcasts. John cannot recall who South played in the first league game he saw, but says it was a *"step in the process"* towards the goals he had set himself. He had no desire to be anywhere else. He liked what he saw at Fremantle Oval and knew that was where he was meant to be.

When Souths played away, he generally went to the Hilton Park Oval and played an imaginary game against their opponents for that day. His idol was Steve Marsh, the great South Fremantle rover and winner of the 1952 Sandover Medal, and John kept a scrapbook of pictures and press cuttings about him; he was thrilled to eventually play alongside him in 1955, when he made his league debut at 16. John also had a lot of admiration for Bobby Skilton, the champion South Melbourne rover who won Brownlow Medals in the VFL in 1959, '63 and '68. John had never met Skilton, but knew of him mainly through the *Sporting Globe*, which John read every week. Skilton was a champion schoolboy footballer and about the same age as John, so he followed his progress with interest because he saw that it paralleled his own development. He may have even seen it as competition from afar, which provided a challenge and a yardstick by which to chart his own progress.

During his primary school years, John usually had two games a week, one for the school and one for the Hilton Park juniors on the weekend. He first played in the under-13s in 1950 and soon started winning both club and association fairest and best awards. However, he had won his first best player trophy as an 11-year-old when representing the Warren Association in a carnival in Donnybrook in 1949. The carnival coincided with a family trip back to Deanmill, so John was 'recruited' to play for the team. On returning home, Doris asked John *"if he got a kick"*, which would become her standard question to him over the years. John proudly said *"yes"* and revealed the trophy hidden under his coat. Both mother and son were very pleased.

In 1951 John started high school at Fremantle Boys', where the sportsmaster was Jerry Dolan who, along with John Leonard and Haydn Bunton (Jnr), were overtaken by John in 1997 as WA's most successful coaches. Dolan won five senior premierships – at East Fremantle (1930, '33, '45 and '46) and East Perth (1936) – and also took Old Easts to a premiership in the 1943 underage competition.

While Dolan was now retired from league coaching, his eye for talent remained intact and he quickly noted the new boy's ability. He told John to ask his mother to get him a pair of boots, which they duly acquired; Doris thinks maybe Dolan himself organised them. John had never worn boots before and recalls them being two sizes too big! Doris thought he looked like Donald Duck as he was only small and lightly framed with these great big boots on the end of his skinny legs. Too big or not, the boots stayed with John for a few years and he had little difficulty making the transition from bare feet. Dolan coached the school team and exerted a strong influence on John. John knew of his coaching record of 17 years with East Fremantle and East Perth, never once missing the finals, so he was keen to learn as much as possible from him. John remembers that Dolan had a habit of pretending to read a newspaper when watching a game and gave the impression of only being semi-interested, but would later recount in great detail specific parts where you had made errors, before then explaining how to rectify the deficiencies.

In one school game John kicked 13 points and afterwards Dolan simply told him to practise his goal-kicking, so together they went to the oval and spent the next three hours kicking for goal. John didn't mind that, of course; he probably would have done it anyway. But it again demonstrated to him that you had to put in extra time to improve yourself. Sadly, John laments the fact that today's players shy away from doing extra training to improve their skills – *"It would be almost unheard of for a current player to spend an extra few hours by himself practising his skills after a bad game, yet golfers for example, think nothing of hitting 200 balls after a poor round"*.

As had been the case at White Gum Valley primary, the Fremantle Boys' team was much stronger with John in it. However, he still felt the same way about school and continued to play hookey when it suited him. John feels certain Dolan was instrumental in preventing him from being expelled on at least one occasion, primarily because of his sporting talents. In what Doris remembers as the *"most trouble he ever got into at school"*, John once wagged it for a whole week, leaving home in the morning nice and clean and returning in the afternoon absolutely filthy. His explanation was that they had done blacksmithing at school and hence the dirt on his clothes and skin! However, he had spent the days swimming in the river and playing football – this went on for a week before someone informed Doris, who was embarrassed to admit to the teachers that she hadn't realised John was wagging it. She also credits Dolan with saving him from expulsion. While it may not have made much difference to John in the long run if he had been expelled, in the short-term it could have cost him the chance to make the State Schoolboys team, as he was now under notice due to his form with Fremantle Boys.

John duly made the 1951 Schoolboys side as a 13-year-old, the squad's youngest member – he recalls being *"all feet"*, wearing size eight boots and weighing a strapping 7st 9lbs! The side had a number of players who would graduate to league ranks – Len Pavy (East Perth), Colin Hebbard (West Perth), Bill Towers (Perth) and Les Mumme (Claremont) among them. Also in the team was Barry Shepherd, who went on to captain WA in the Sheffield Shield and play Test cricket for Australia. The Schoolboys carnival was in Melbourne in August and not only gave John his first State guernsey, but provided his first trip out of WA and his first flight on an aircraft.

The team did well, beating New South Wales and South Australia, with John playing well as a rover or in the centre. The final against Victoria was only 10 minutes old when John was knocked unconscious and carried from the field by none other than Captain Blood – the late Jack Dyer, the great Richmond ruckman and coach of the 1930s and '40s. Richmond was host club to the WA side and *The West Australian* newspaper later reported that, after coming to, John received a rub down in the change rooms from Bill Morris, the Tigers captain. John avoided any serious injury, but his absence didn't help WA's cause as they went down by 22 points. Later, he was awarded the 'most courageous player' trophy for WA for the carnival.

Doris was naturally thrilled with John's trophy, but concerned about her son's size and the risk of injury by playing football. While she had little doubt he was good enough to play in representative teams, his slight build was always a concern, especially when playing against older kids – him being knocked unconscious obviously added to her fears. However, John had no such concerns. The incident was not given a second thought and he thrived on the challenges football provided. He arrived home full of excitement and proudly produced a gold watch he had bought as a present for Doris, being mindful that she and Bill (Snr) had saved for weeks to pay for the trip and provide some spending money. Doris was suitably touched and surprised, but also remembers that her head started to spin as she had counted on John bringing some of the money home to help with next week's food expenses! John's sister Diane had recently been born and money was tighter than usual for the Todd family; while Doris appreciated the gift, she recalls thinking that you couldn't eat a gold watch! In any case, the family survived and the gold watch still rates as one of her most cherished possessions.

The Schoolboys carnival only served to whet John's appetite for football and he set himself the goal of making the team again the next year. The training sessions at the Hilton Park Oval and in his backyard

1951 – State schoolboy, 13 years and 7st 9lbs.

grew in intensity and little Bill Todd (Jnr) was now old enough to help out and fox the ball. Now at high school and older, John stayed at the oval for longer, often returning home after dark. The practice games with his mates also became more competitive – one such exercise involved kicking high, awkward balls to the other player, who had to mark in his hands only; chest marks were not permitted. A dropped mark earned a penalty lap of the oval, or you had to sit out of the game until someone else made a mistake. Another practice game involved kicking the ball (by either foot) backwards and forwards to each other to see how many times it could be done before a mistake occurred; again attracting a penalty for errors. While these practice games were fun, they were hotly contested and no-one, least of all John, wanted to lose – he saw them as an excellent way of practising his skills. John's athletic talents also saw him in line for selection in the State Schoolboys cricket team in 1951. While he enjoyed playing the game, compared to football his heart *"simply wasn't in it"* and in the end he avoided selection by deliberately going to the wrong oval. The trial was being held at the WACA Ground, but he went to Perth Oval instead.

John had little trouble making the 1952 Schoolboys team and, as only one of two second year players, he was an easy choice as captain. The carnival was in Perth and the team was rated a reasonable chance to topple the Victorians, who virtually had a mortgage on the trophy as the champion junior State. The Vics had a much bigger schoolboy population to draw from than any other State and, much like their senior team, had dominated interstate competition for years. From the WA team, players who went on to become well known in league ranks were Norm McDiarmid (West Perth) and East Perth duo Kevin McGill and Laurie Kennedy.

The carnival was hit with the last minute withdrawal of South Australia and New South Wales, leaving only Victoria, Queensland, Tasmania and WA to contest the title. With the absence of SA, the other major football State, it was expected that WA and Victoria would contest the final; this duly happened as both sides had little trouble recording victories over Tasmania and Queensland. The final was tight, but WA finished the better to prevail by nine points, preserving a perfect 'home' record after winning previous carnivals in Perth in 1929 and 1947. John was the popular pick as WA's best player, with a brilliant four-quarter effort in the centre. To complete a victorious weekend, the next day he led Hilton Park to an easy 40 point win over South Fremantle in the grand final of the under-15s competition – his fourth game in eight days.

As captain of the team and one of its best players, John received some press attention and was written up in *The Daily News* as the week's 'sporting personality'; one of the paper's regular columns. In it John expressed a desire to become a butcher and to play league football for South Fremantle. What attracted him to butchering he isn't sure, but the article was noted by Wally Doust, an avid South Fremantle fan who ran a butcher's shop in Fremantle. He already had a current South player, Don Wares, working as a butcher and added another (potential) player to his staff by offering John an apprenticeship. It didn't take long for John to accept the offer as school held little attraction, particularly now that he would be too old for next year's State Schoolboys team. So, with the consent of Doris and Bill, John left school at the age of 14 to start a career as a butcher. However, there is no doubt that his football career remained No. 1 in his life.

While he enjoyed the work and never shirked any obligations in favour of football (he never wagged work!), his progress towards becoming the greatest player the game had ever seen was unaffected by leaving school and continued on, full steam ahead.

The 1950s

Chapter 2
Joining South Fremantle

John, explaining the reason for training himself so hard in his early years:

"You can't get back the lost time at a later age".

The Todd family lived in Carrington Street, Hilton Park, in the heart of South Fremantle territory, so there was never any doubt about which of the Fremantle clubs John would join. South knew they had a champion on the way. Apart from playing State Schoolboys, John won the fairest and best award for the combined East Fremantle-South Fremantle under-16 competition in 1952, a feat he would repeat in 1954 in the under-18s. With their great rover Steve Marsh nearing the end of his career, South had a ready-made replacement. South had been the most successful team of the previous 10 years, winning premierships in 1947, '48, '50, '52, '53 and '54, and had stayed at the top of the table despite losing players of the calibre of Jack (Corp) Reilly, Lenny Crabbe, Doug Ingraham, Clive Lewington (who took over as coach in 1950 from Ross Hutchinson), Don Wares and Harry Carbon through retirement. These greats had been replaced mainly by young players and the club had little doubt that John was next in line.

Starting work as a butcher meant there was no time for football during the day, so this simply meant more training in his backyard of an evening. Work was hard, carrying and cutting carcasses, and the hours were long; often starting at 4am and going through to 5.30-6pm. But he remained relentless in his attitude to be the best – *"I felt that if I was training while others were relaxing or sleeping, then I would have to be better than them and mentally stronger as well".*

This work and training regime left little time for socialising as John couldn't afford late nights with early starts and he needed to preserve his energy. This was just another sacrifice that had to be made to achieve his goals and he willingly made it. John had to make a choice with his friends – some wanted to go out and party and he didn't and, despite a good deal of peer pressure, he stood firm, accepting the fact that he would lose friends as a result – *"I felt some of them perhaps wanted to see me fall short of my goals, because they knew they wouldn't make it to league ranks themselves, so I did become selective in who I knocked about with".*

John had always been happy in his own company so he never felt lonely, despite only having a small circle of close friends. He and his mates spent time at the beach in the summer and regularly attended the Friday night cycling races at Fremantle Oval, which had a banked track around the arena until 1969. They got to know well the girls who played with the Fremantle Hockey Club and many had also joined the Fremantle Athletics Club, so John met up with most of them through athletics training.

John also spent more time at Fremantle Oval, watching training as well as games and asking questions of South Fremantle star players whenever an opportunity presented itself. He may have left school, but his football education was just gathering speed and he was always prepared to listen when the topic was football. He remembers Harry 'Hobart' Carbon, the great South rover who retired after the 1952 season, explaining the importance of being correct on both sides of the body so defenders couldn't easily force him onto the 'wrong' side and produce a poor disposal. This reinforced the point made a few years earlier by Jack Lacey. Carbon was a great example of a double-sided player, so much so that John felt it wasn't obvious whether he was a right or left footer. This soon became a goal of John's, to get his own skills to the point where you couldn't tell which side was dominant. Again, his right side, which by now was pretty good, came in for extra practice in the backyard.

Carbon was only too pleased to give John advice, as he knew something of his ability, having first seen him play in 1952 when, while recovering from a broken foot, he had watched the State Schoolboys carnival at Fremantle Oval. His first sighting of John always stuck in his mind. At the opening bounce, John roved the knock, evaded an opponent, took one step and sent a mighty punt kick downfield to score a point. Carbon was immediately impressed, as was Jack Dyer, who was talent scouting for Richmond and had seen John play in the 1951 carnival. In Carbon's view, John's only weakness as a player was his right side, so he reminded him of the need to practise his disposal skills on his non-preferred side at every opportunity.

John was very impressed by the talent of Bernie Naylor, Souths champion full-forward who, sadly, retired in 1954, the year before John burst onto the scene – a perfect Todd stab pass onto the chest of a fast leading Naylor would have been a sight to behold. Naylor always practised kicking for goal at training from about 40 metres out, a comfortable distance for a man with such a good kick. Night after night, John remembers watching the ball sail through *"goal post high"* as Naylor put in extra time on his game. Eventually, John asked why he didn't kick from further out – *"Bernie explained that, as full-forward, it was his job to kick goals when he got the ball, otherwise he was letting his team-mates down after they had worked hard in defence and midfield to get the ball to him. His responsibility was to be the finisher of the game and, to do this well, he needed to be a long and accurate kick for goal. Accuracy was all about balance, rhythm and timing and these things were best developed closer to goal where distance wasn't a problem. But the trick was to kick the ball through the goals, not just at the goals, so when forced to shoot from further out, you didn't sacrifice your timing and rhythm by striving for extra distance in the kick".*

To further improve his kicking for goal, Naylor generally practised into the wind, rather than with it, to develop extra control in his kicking action. Naylor still holds the record for the most goals kicked by a player in a WA league game, 23 goals (from 25 shots) against Subiaco in 1953. Later in the same season he kicked 19 goals in a derby; his record season's tally of 156 goals was only bettered by Subiaco's Austin Robertson (Jnr) in 1968. Naylor developed the habit of kicking a torpedo with the lace of the ball on the side, as he felt this gave the ball better stability in flight and allowed it to cut into the breeze better when kicking into a wind. John revelled in hearing advice like this and would immediately try such things out for himself.

He remembers Naylor as a *"true professional"* and considers that *"the forwards of today would do well to practise the way Bernie did, as generally their conversion rate is very poor. They simply don't put in the time necessary to improve this area of their game"*.

South had many other great players who made an impression on John. The Bulldogs were in their 'golden era', winning premierships in 1952, '53 and '54, and, with John's boyhood idol Marsh winning the Sandover Medal in 1952, the scrapbook had a lot of new entries. He thought so highly of Marsh because of his skill, courage and tenacity for the ball and these traits were already obvious in John's game. In addition, centre-half-forward Laurie Green was an outstanding talent, according to John. He was only 5ft 10in tall (177cm), which was small for a key forward, but quick and agile. Sadly, he only played 99 games before premature retirement because of a kidney injury. John also recalls marvelling at Des Kelly, the South ruck-rover or half-back who, in the 1952 grand final, turned the game with a withering solo run from defence into attack to goal, after which South lifted and came back to win. Eric Eriksson, Frank Treasure and Lenny Crabbe were other talented players who impressed John with their skill and determination, demonstrating what it took to become a successful footballer.

Apart from the players, John also loved the 'feel' of the place – *"It was like family, like home, you never wanted to leave. The team had a great camaraderie; they trained and played hard, but were also great mates"*. The team bond that made South the best was obvious to John, even at his young age, and he wanted to be a part of it. He fondly remembers on Sunday mornings at Fremantle Oval being one of the many supporters who went there to see their idols relax after the previous day's game. Naylor would often sing a few ditties and the story-tellers in the group would warm to their task after a few beers and delight the crowd with varied yarns and tales. To John, this was indeed his home away from home and he looked forward expectantly to joining South when his junior days were over. However, his call up came a little earlier than he expected.

In 1954 John again won the district fairest and best award as a 16-year-old in the under-18s, despite only playing nine games out of 14 because of a hand injury suffered at work when he sliced open his right thumb and severed the tendon. Initially the wound was just stitched, but the loss of function in the thumb became obvious and surgery was necessary to re-attach the tendon to the bone. He polled top votes in seven games and was voted third-best in the other two, an impressive record for a youngster still eligible to play in the competition for another year. The junior competition finished a few weeks before the league season, but with South in with a chance to win their third premiership in a row, John was happily spending more time at Fremantle Oval. South had finished third on the table, but gathered momentum in the finals with comfortable wins over Perth and West Perth to earn a grand final berth against arch-enemies East Fremantle. A derby grand final had Fremantle abuzz, with Wally Doust's butcher shop adorned with red and white balloons and streamers. South reserves had qualified for the grand final and, as further evidence of the club's dominance, were also seeking their third successive premiership.

One evening in the middle of the week there was a knock on the Todd's front door – and there stood Lewington, Souths league coach, and club vice-president Bill Collins, who had come to ask John to play for the reserves team in the grand final. A sudden 'epidemic' of chicken pox had swept through the club and a number of players were doubtful starters. Naturally, John readily agreed to play, but Doris was firmly against the idea, believing that, at 16, he was too young and too small to be pitted against men. She said no and, despite the best efforts of the two South men, she wouldn't budge. John was aghast and pleaded with Doris to let him play – a *"war of words"* and a fiery battle of wills ensued over the next 24 hours. Lewington knew John was more than ready to play at reserves level and was back the next day to try and get Doris around. Marsh, now the reserves coach, and Colin Potts, the captain, also called to speak to John and Doris, who recalls that Lewington was polite and courteous and very persuasive so that she eventually relented, against her better judgment. She feared that because of his small frame, he would be easily hurt or knocked out, as had happened in the Schoolboys carnival. She knew her son had no fear on the football field, but she also knew he was good enough to play. Having watched him train relentlessly over the past 10 or more years to make himself into a footballer, she was mindful that it was what John deserved. So, with her heart in her mouth, she told Lewington that John could play if they really needed him. Years later Doris has only one regret about changing her mind – she didn't ask for a reserved seat at the match. She was forced to stand on the steps of the old Subiaco grandstand, holding three-year-old Diane as she watched the game.

The South reserves also called up another talented junior, John Gerovich, and John could hardly wait for Saturday to come around, especially as he would be coached by his idol. Their opponents were Perth, who had lost players to the league side for an earlier semi-final and were now ineligible. This balanced up the South losses due to chicken pox; the teams looked evenly matched and a close contest was expected. However, South kept Perth goal-less in the first quarter while they kicked 6.7, so the match was virtually over at the first change.

Playing off a half-forward flank, John started brilliantly, with two goals in the first term. He got better as the game progressed, finishing with seven majors as South recorded an easy 70 point victory. He was the unanimous choice as best-afield and Marsh remembers John's game as *"poetry in motion"*. For Ray Richards, it simply confirmed his opinion of how good John was, having watched him play regularly for the Hilton Park juniors, while Ron Hindes, who followed his career closely, thinks it was the best game he ever saw John play. Carbon remembers it as an *"incredible performance"* and still marvels at the skill John displayed in one passage where he kicked a *"daisy cutter"* stab pass to a team-mate, which had to be inch perfect as there was a man blocking the right side and the boundary line on the left. John's pass found its mark.

Marsh also recalls that, despite his youth and great form from the start, John didn't particularly like playing off a half-forward flank and wasn't backward in saying so. At each quarter-time break, John would politely say – *"Mr Marsh, I know I can play even better in the centre or as a rover"*. At three-quarter-time, with the game well in hand and needing to go and strip for the league match, Marsh gave in and told John to *"rove the forward line"*, which he duly did and added another two goals.

After the game, John received hearty congratulations from the South committeemen and supporters and experienced a side of football he hadn't seen before. As was common then, a collection was made among those present and John was handed *"a substantial amount of money"* as a reward for his great game. For an apprentice butcher earning £2 a week, he received the equivalent of many weeks' wages for playing the game he simply loved; being paid to play football was not something he had ever thought about.

The South league team was also successful, notching a hard-fought but, in the end, comfortable victory over Old Easts, with Charlie Tyson winning the Simpson Medal, and Naylor, in his last game, posting seven goals. Fremantle Oval played host to loud and long victory celebrations that night as Bulldogs supporters and members toasted a hat trick of premierships for both the league and reserves teams.

South had one more match to play for the season – against VFL side Carlton on an end-of-season trip to Perth – and the sporting pages in Perth's newspapers were full of two things. Firstly, Marsh had hurt a wrist in the grand final, so there was speculation he may have played his last game for South, as he had hinted about retirement. Secondly, John was reported to have received an attractive offer from Richmond to move to Victoria in 1955. Jack Dyer, who had first noticed John in the 1951 State Schoolboys carnival when he had carried him from the ground after he was knocked out, had kept in touch. The Richmond scouting network had kept Dyer informed about John's progress and word quickly got back to Melbourne about the seven goal reserves' grand final debut – Richmond offered to set John up in a butcher's shop in Melbourne if he moved to Victoria. Some reports lamented the possible loss of John to WA football before he had even played a senior game, while others urged South Fremantle to quickly secure his services, especially as there was the possibility that Marsh would retire, with John the logical replacement.

While John was honoured to receive the Richmond offer, South and the newspapers had little to worry about. In the 1950s it was rare for a player to shift interstate unless it was a family move or a work transfer. Still 16 and half-way through his apprenticeship, John gave the offer little consideration. His connection to South had only been strengthened by his call up to play reserves and he had no desire to play for any other club. He had spent most of his life preparing himself to be the best player the game had ever seen and he couldn't see himself starting his career in anything other than a red and white jumper. He felt his reserves effort had set him up for next season and he was ready to make his mark on the game.

~

In the history of WA football, it's doubtful if any other player has been so single-minded in the pursuit of greatness and success as John Todd. Perhaps Graham (Polly) Farmer, Bill Walker and Barry Cable are three who showed similar characteristics in the post-war era, although whether they devoted themselves to the game the way John did from a tender age is debatable. In his pursuit of excellence, John left no stone unturned; he trained relentlessly on his skills all year round and took up athletics to assist his running and his football. He willingly sacrificed his social life (and some friends) because his priority was football. One of his favourite explanations for training himself so hard and regularly was that *"you can't get back the lost time at a later age"*.

It's interesting to compare his skills training as a young child with current theories on skill development and performance. Professor Bruce Abernethy, from the University of Queensland and a leading expert on motor skill learning, believes that the more time a child spends in *"unstructured play activities"* where skills are practised over and over again, but in a fun situation, then the better the skill development is likely to be. He cautiously suggests that up to 10,000 hours over several years might be necessary to develop really good skilled movements. There is no doubt John achieved this and more. His 'target practice', the imaginary backyard games and the kicking and marking contests at the oval with his mates, where making an error led to a penalty, fit perfectly with the notion of unstructured play activities. In total, he certainly accumulated many more than 10,000 hours of practice time.

Other sporting examples spring to mind here. Don Bradman spent much of his youth hitting a golf ball rebounding off a corrugated iron water tank with just a cricket stump and Steffi Graf was hitting forehands over a tennis net at the age of two. John was kicking drop-kicks at the age of three. He believes all real sporting champions have a tale to tell of dedication and determination to achieve their goals and mostly this occurred at an early age. So many people have the ability to be wonderful athletes, but you cannot reach the top by natural ability alone. To be the best you can possibly be, you need to be very dedicated and make sacrifices. And preferably start young.

In his latter years as a coach, John would lament the poor skill levels of many players at Swans and South. He has no doubt that *"while the game has got faster at AFL level and footballers are full-time players and making a career within the game, the skills in general haven't improved as you would expect"*. In the modern jargon, 'turnovers' and 'missed targets' occur much too frequently and he feels that these errors are due to a poor player skill level, rather than the increased speed of the game. John firmly believes the reason for the skill deficiencies of today's footballers is rooted in the way society has changed – *"In the 1990s, computer games, pinball parlours and, worst of all, TV viewing, took up too much leisure time for kids. It's a rare sight nowadays to see kids kicking a football in the park. In the 1940s, '50s and '60s it was simply 'what you did.' Technology had not advanced sufficiently to offer the range of leisure time pursuits that kids have today"*.

Consequently, the 10,000 hours the experts believe are needed to develop a good skill level are never achieved. Indeed, some kids today would be lucky to accumulate anywhere near 10,000 hours of exercise in total across any number of sports in their formative years. Technology has also made for a *"soft"* society in John's view – *"When things become difficult, it's more the norm for people to give up and simply do something else, rather than persist and persevere to solve the problem themselves. Hard work and sacrifice are too often ignored as the ways to overcome difficult situations and these attitudes are present in all parts of society, including sport"*. While many kids still dream of becoming a star footballer (as John did in his day), the environment in the 21st century makes this harder to achieve than in the 1940s, '50s and '60s. Society today doesn't respect or reward the type of single-minded pursuit of success which John displayed in his youth. While youngsters might aspire to make it to the AFL, perhaps only a very few are prepared to 'pay the price' to make themselves into one of the best players the game will ever see.

Chapter 3
A Sandover at 17

The Football Budget, commenting (prophetically) on John's first league game in 1955:

> "Young John Todd, without being spectacular, played useful football. He is too 'open' when going through packs and he will need to cover up more to escape serious injury".

After playing so well in the 1954 reserves grand final, John knew he was ready for league football; his summer training sessions went longer than before and he was excited at the prospect. What he had experienced on grand final day had left an indelible mark and he was hungry for more. South coach Clive Lewington knew John was ready and had him earmarked as part of the team for the coming season – the only problem was to convince Doris. While naturally thrilled with John's reserves game, Doris was still concerned about him playing against men, given that he was a skinny, lightly-framed 11st (70kg) boy who wouldn't turn 17 until May. She felt he should stay with the juniors for another year and develop his body before tackling league football. However, she also had no doubts that John was good enough. So, while John trained in the summer heat, Lewington, Bill Collins and other members of the South Fremantle committee were again trying to convince Doris that John should play. John knew his mother didn't want him to join South just yet, but he had no qualms – he could hardly wait for 1955 to arrive.

~

South were pre-season flag favourites despite the retirements of Bernie Naylor, Des Kelly and Laurie Green, with John Gerovich seen as a replacement for Naylor in front of goal. However, the club was further rocked by the unexpected 'retirement' of their great rover Steve Marsh, who had asked for an advance (£500) against his Provident Fund money so he could purchase a block of land to build a house. The club refused, saying they didn't have spare money for this purpose. The WANFL rules decreed that players could collect their Provident Fund if they were out of the game as at June 30, so this is what Marsh decided to do. In the 1950s football payments were small – up to a few pounds a game – and many players only earned a basic wage in their employment, so funding a house was difficult. South refused to relent, so Marsh 'retired', albeit temporarily. John found this very strange as he wasn't privy to the reasons – "*I was bitterly disappointed at the prospect of not playing with my idol that I had followed for so many years*". Perhaps South felt John was ready to step straight into the roving position that Marsh had made his own for many years, as they gave him Marsh's No. 7 jumper for the practice matches. John was naturally thrilled to wear Marsh's number and his pre-season form was good, kicking four goals and being rated best on ground against West Perth at Leederville Oval. However, South lost all their practice games, prompting some suggestions that the golden era was over.

John was duly selected for the opening league game at home against East Perth, who had named John Watts at centre-half-back for his first game. John has no special memories of the match other than South won a close contest by a few goals. He wore the No. 10 guernsey as the club decided to mothball Marsh's No. 7 in the expectation he would play later in the season. John started on a half-forward flank and spent time roving, as Lewington worked a three-way switch with Barry White (who kicked nine goals) and Colin Boot. The next week *The Football Budget* said about John's debut – *"Young John Todd, without being spectacular, played useful football. He is too 'open' when going through packs for the ball and he'll need to cover up more to escape serious injury"*. These words would prove prophetic as early as the next game and, sadly, in a year's time, would be shown to be absolutely correct.

The second game was a traditional derby at East Fremantle Oval and it was a match befitting the occasion – a hard, slogging encounter with little separating the teams. John played well, but collected several hard knocks and, after a heavy clash in the last quarter, he was carried from the ground semi-conscious, reducing South to 17 men for the last 15 minutes. Still, they clung to a slender lead until, with about 30 seconds remaining, East Fremantle rover Ray French pounced on a loose ball and kicked truly to see Old Easts home by four points.

At the Todd household that night Doris was regretting her decision to allow John to play. Not yet 17, this was the third time he had been knocked unconscious and she was concerned about him suffering permanent injury by playing against strong, mature men when he was so light and young. She had not seen the incident, as she chose not to watch John play for this very reason, and so the 1954 grand final is one of the few games Doris ever saw him play, other than juniors. However, she knew she had no chance of stopping John from playing now that he had started, so she simply implored him to watch out for himself better on the field. John thought little of the clash and saw it as just another part of the game, although he admits to playing with almost reckless abandon early in his career. This stemmed from his desire to be the best player to ever play the game and, as such, he went for *"everything"* without any regard for his physical well-being. He was regularly lauded for his courage right through junior ranks and it was now a natural part of his game; the possible consequences of any reckless acts were never considered. John was also in awe of no-one; such was his self-belief and desire to display his talents, that he was never intimidated by an opponent.

After the fourth game, against Claremont at Fremantle, Harry Carbon asked him who he had just played on. John had kicked five goals, but had no idea who his opponent had been. Carbon remembers John's *"matter of fact"* response when told that he had just played on (and beaten) Don Idle, a State player and one of the best half-back flankers in the game. It wasn't that John didn't respect his rival; he was simply so focused on his own game he didn't have time to worry about his immediate opponent. Plus, he was having great fun and living his dream by playing league football for South; at this stage, studying the opposition was not a major priority.

Over the next month, which included the 'double fixture' on June 4-6 when teams played on the Saturday and the Monday, John continued in good form, celebrating his 17th birthday on May 21 in round five by kicking five goals against Subiaco. He had been joined in the league team by the 16-year-old Gerovich, who showed early flashes of brilliance at centre-half-forward; in his fourth and fifth games, when moved to full-forward, he had hauls of seven and eight goals as South scored impressive wins over Swan Districts and East Perth. It seemed as though South had found a new Naylor.

The State team to play Victoria and South Australia on tour was to be announced after the June 6 Foundation Day round and most critics thought John should be picked; the only reservation being his age, having just turned 17. His form could hardly be ignored. After eight games, he led *The Daily News* Footballer of the Year Award, polling votes in both games over the long weekend. The next day *The West Australian* reported that John had become the youngest player ever picked to represent WA (which he remains to this day), surpassing Ern Henfry, who was now coaching Perth and had been approaching 18 when picked for a State game some years before.

Also making the side from South were Ray Richards, Ray Crawford and White. Perth's Charlie Skehan was also included – the three boys who, 10 years earlier, were kicking a football barefoot on a gravel road in Deanmill had come a long way. Richards recalls that as the team assembled at the airport for a chartered flight, Doris gave him a stern lecture about looking after John, emphasising that he had only just turned 17 and was *"still a boy"*. Richards naturally promised to look after John, but forgot to mention this to Jack Sheedy. Both John and Sheedy were left out of the side to play Victoria. Heavy rain had turned the MCG into a quagmire and the selectors were loathe to expose John's light frame to a hard, slogging physical game. Sheedy, an old hand at football trips, took John downtown to show him *"the other side of the game"* which was an educational experience for John, who quips that he *"went out aged 17 and came back 27"*.

He struck up a good relationship with Sheedy, which may have benefited John in a big derby later in the season. John can still remember grabbing the ball and turning out of a pack to find Sheedy bearing down on him and, in his own words, *"I was as open as a swinging gate"*. However, Sheedy applied a fairly tame tackle and, as he pinned John, he whispered *"You're valuable on the field son, not off it"*. John has absolutely no doubt Sheedy could have *"ironed him out"* with a perfect shirtfront (which Sheedy was notorious for doing), but gave the young player a lucky break. To this day, John remembers the incident and, as a coach, has related it many times to his players. Blind reckless courage, while always admirable, didn't make for a long career, as John can vouch for. Sheedy, for the record, went on to play 338 games.

After losing to Victoria by 29 points, WA travelled to Adelaide to play SA, with John coming into the team as a rover. He started in a blaze of glory, kicking two of WA's first three goals, but didn't add to his tally, playing a useful, but unspectacular game. After leading by 13 points at three-quarter-time, WA could only add three points in the last term, while the Croweaters kicked four goals to win by nine points.

While John was absent on State team duties, South beat West Perth at Fremantle to launch an 11 match winning streak, taking it to the top of the table and outright favourite for the flag, even though arch rivals East Fremantle finished second on the same number of wins. Souths stocks were further boosted in round 13 when Marsh returned after his self-imposed exile – John was ecstatic to finally play alongside his idol. Marsh's return meant less time on the ball for John, but while Marsh was short and strictly a rover, John was taller, nudging 5ft 10in (177cm) and could play in a forward role. In fact, for Marsh's return game against Perth at the WACA Ground, John was named at centre-half-forward. With White, who had made the State team, and Stewart, also in his first season, South now had four of the best rovers going around, and fitting them all in without upsetting team balance was a constant juggling act for coach Lewington.

1955 – The youngest player ever to play for WA. As cartoonist Paul Rigby saw it (The Daily News).

As South went from strength to strength, John did likewise with good form and regular goals. Despite working long hours at the butcher shop, John's appetite for football remained insatiable and he worked on his game in every spare minute. The league team trained on Tuesday and Thursday nights and John was generally first on the track and last off it, often being ordered into the rooms by Lewington or Carbon. Although a knee injury had forced Carbon's retirement in the 1953 pre-season, he still trained with the team and John often sought him out for extra work, with Carbon constantly challenging John to improve his right foot kicking skills, which he saw as his only weakness.

Naylor was coaching the South reserves, training on Monday and Wednesday nights, with the 'seconds' more separate from the league side in the 1950s than in recent times. However, John saw this as a perfect opportunity for further training and, with Naylor's blessing, ran with the reserves regularly until Lewington restricted him from doing so. Even then, John would still be at the club on Mondays and Wednesdays watching them train and lamenting the fact he wasn't allowed to join them.

Lewington was certainly impressed with John's work ethic and desire to better himself, but feared the 17-year-old could burn himself out by finals time, so he also gave John the occasional night off training in a bid to keep him fresh and injury free. However, this tactic proved a miserable failure because, when told to go home, John would grab his football and head to the Hilton Park Oval and then his backyard, where he had set up some lights and train by himself, or with his brother Bill – and for much longer than if he had stayed at Fremantle Oval. Lewington soon wised up to this and kept John at training, but would sometimes send him in early, which happened often enough for Marsh to dub John the *"cottonwool kid"*. John never felt tired and hated being sent in early and often pleaded with the coach to let him stay out. Even on Sundays, after playing the day before, John could be found at junior matches where he would kick the ball around with his mates and then watch the Fremantle Ex-Scholars play, with more kick-to-kick as the game went on. While he was happy with his form for South, there was no hint of complacency; there was still much to learn and improve upon and the fact that he was already playing league football did nothing to change this.

The week after Marsh's return, John was up to his usual tricks – in the second quarter against Swans at Bassendean he collided head-on with burly full-back Tim Barker and was carried from the ground unconscious. After recovering in the South change rooms and despite sporting an inch-long gash on his forehead and having no memory of the game, he complained about being taken off. As there was no interchange in this era, he could take no further part in the match. Doris, listening at home on the radio, heard the call of the clash and waited anxiously for Frank Fuhrmann, the South president, to get a message broadcast over the radio saying John was OK; something Fuhrmann had arranged with Doris to do if ever John was injured. It was a small concession to ease Doris' conscience and, as this was John's second knock out for the season, she was very worried about his health and still regretting her decision to let him play league football. John's uncle Ron Hindes was at the game and took him home that night, but remembers little of the incident other than John was feeling sore and sorry. However, John was back on the field next week to play East Perth. There was never any doubt about him playing, with the almost mandatory week off after concussion, as is the norm these days, not in force in the 1950s. In most press reports about John's football in 1955, there were two recurring themes – his great skill and talent mixed with his tendency to leave himself *"wide open"*.

In mid-August, South Australia visited Perth for matches on Saturday and Tuesday, with local fixtures suspended for the weekend. John retained his place in the State side and started the first game as No. 1 rover, finishing as probably WA's best in their narrow win. He was equal second with SA's Jim Taylor in the Simpson Medal voting, behind Fos Williams, the unanimous choice as best-afield. Three days later, a close-fought struggle saw WA claw its way to a 13 point lead at the last change, only to fade and lose by three points. John kicked two goals and was listed in WA's best six, but was more effectively held in check by the SA defenders than on the Saturday. Graham Farmer was acknowledged as WA's best with a tireless performance in the ruck.

After the break for the State fixtures, South continued winning and round 18 saw them beat Claremont by 74 points to celebrate Marsh's 200th league game. The next week, third-placed Perth were outclassed by 54 points at Fremantle Oval and, in the last game of the regular season, Swans were completely over-run, with South winning by a mammoth 160 points. Gerovich kicked an incredible 11.12, taking 23 marks and having the amazing total (for a full-forward) of 30 kicks, while John kicked five goals in what was little more than a training run. The press hailed the team as the *"greatest premiership certainty"* since World War II and it seemed that the golden era was far from over. However, Lewington went to great pains to get the players to ignore the flattering press statements, as he was concerned the team may have peaked too soon. Having just qualified for its sixth second semi-final appearance since 1945, South had two weeks to prepare for a tilt at its fourth successive premiership, a feat last achieved by its arch enemy, East Fremantle, in 1928-31.

On the Wednesday night after the last qualifying game, John was planning to take his girlfriend, Mary Robinson, to the movies in Fremantle, but he changed his mind at the last minute and stayed home to listen for the result of the Sandover Medal count being conducted at league headquarters. He hadn't given the medal, or his chances of winning it, much thought, even though newspaper polls rated him as a likely winner. He had finished third in *The Daily News* Footballer of the Year Award, behind Farmer, who took the £100 prize, and John Hyde, the former Geelong player and now Claremont captain-coach. The other popular fancy was Perth rover Dick Walker, who had an excellent season roving to Merv McIntosh, the Sandover medallist of the past two seasons. In the 1950s the medal count was behind closed doors with no players invited, making it a far cry from the lavish televised counts which began in the 1970s. The count wasn't broadcast, with the results generally announced in the 9 o'clock news and the next day's papers reporting in greater detail.

The Todds had no telephone, so John's decision to wait at home and listen for the result left him 'standing up' his girlfriend Mary. He, Bill (Jnr) and Doris sat listening for the 9pm news, with John's nervous waiting helped only by his twirling a football from hand to hand. When it was announced that John had indeed won the medal, Doris recalls that he jumped up off the floor and shouted that he had won *"it"*. She hadn't been paying that much attention and was forced to quietly enquire as to exactly what he had just won!

Well-wishers soon started calling at the house as the news spread, with Lewington, Collins and league captain Frank Treasure among the first to arrive and offer their congratulations. The noise woke the rest of the house, forcing Bill Todd (Snr) to get up and find out what the commotion was about. Doris remembers feeling somewhat embarrassed that she had nothing to offer them to drink (other than cold water), as there was no beer in the fridge, nor wine or sherry in the pantry. John excused himself and ran down Carrington Street to Mary's house, where she was asleep after not being impressed at being stood up for the pictures. John woke her and explained that he had just won the Sandover Medal, which he felt was a pretty decent excuse for not coming over earlier! Apparently, Mary was a little cool at first, but soon forgave John and celebrated with him.

The next day a column by Len Owens in *The Daily News* was headed *"Todd's win has no equal"* and his victory established records which still stand today. While not the only player to win the medal in his first season (Claremont's Sammy Clarke in 1933 and South's Frank 'Scranno' Jenkins in 1937 also achieved this feat), he remains the youngest winner of the Sandover (in open competition) and the youngest winner of the fairest and best award in any of the three major football States. He achieved this in a team that topped the table and therefore had many other good players likely to capture votes, whereas the other 'first season' Sandover medallists played in struggling teams. John polled votes in half of the games he played – 10 out of 20 – demonstrating remarkable consistency for a first year player. His 25 votes comprised six first votes, three seconds and one third, and he won by four votes from Farmer, with Greg Cox (Swans) third on 17 votes. He became South's fifth Sandover medallist and their third since the end of the War, emulating the wins of both his coach (Lewington in 1947) and his idol (Marsh in 1952). When presented with the medal, John thanked his team-mates and reserved a special tribute for Carbon for all his assistance.

In 1955, the final four comprised South, Old Easts, Perth and West Perth, in a lop-sided season where the finalists had been decided for several months, with only the placings in question. Ray Scott (West Perth) headed the goal-kicking with 81, the first time in six years the winner had not kicked 100 goals or more. John finished fifth with 49 goals (and 59 points), while fellow rovers White and Stewart notched 49 and 47 goals respectively, with Gerovich kicking 66 goals to finish third. Perth had a comfortable 22 point first semi-final win over West Perth, but most scribes considered them incapable of matching either South or East Fremantle.

The second semi-final derby was expected to be hotly-contested, but most pundits felt South would have the edge because of their brilliant roving quartet. Old Easts had injury problems, with rover Jim Conway (who would later coach Claremont to the 1964 flag) doubtful, but they triumphed by 19 points in a tough, hard-fought contest in wet conditions. They were superbly led by captain Sheedy, in tandem with Conway (who showed no signs of his hip injury) and 18-year-old Ray 'Oscar' Howard, who John had met on arriving in Fremantle 10 years earlier. While John was one of South's better players, he was under constant pressure and the effectiveness of his disposals was down by his usual standards.

Sandover Medal night 1955 – being congratulated at home by South Fremantle vice president Bill Collins (left) and coach Clive Lewington.

On the Friday before the preliminary final, John was paid a visit at work by Constable Charlie Skehan, now stationed in Fremantle and one of Perth's leading players. They reminisced about their childhood days in Deanmill as they posed for a photograph for *The West Australian*. The next day they lined up in opposing sides and it was generally expected that South would prevail, as most thought the previous week's loss was an aberration, perhaps caused by the wet weather. But big Perth ruckman Merv McIntosh soon wielded a huge influence and Perth led by seven points at quarter-time, a lead they extended to three goals by half-time. Although not out of the game, the signs didn't look good for South, as many of their stars, John included, were strangely quiet. In the third quarter, Perth scored six goals to South's two to open up a 44 point lead. South were staring at two consecutive finals losses after 11 previous wins, but they dug deep and kicked three goals in four minutes to bring the crowd alive. Perth rover Harry 'Doc' Meredith sent a perfect drop kick through the goals to steady the Redlegs, but South refused to die and when Marsh set up John with a beautiful pass and he kicked truly, the difference was only 12 points. However, Perth were not to be denied and when the final bell sounded they had won by 10 points. South, the *"greatest premiership certainties"*, had been bundled out, showing again that anything can happen in finals football when the stakes are high. Marsh was South's best and John finished with a knee injury, later reported to be a *"trapped cartilage"*, which would have prevented him playing in the grand final the next week anyway.

As was the practice in this era, John was advised to spend a few days in bed to rest the knee, but he was at the club later that week to be announced winner of the AW Walker Medal for South's fairest and best player, polling 65 votes to win from White on 49. John's win paralleled his Sandover success and that of Lewington and Marsh, who had also won the trophy in their Sandover Medal winning year. He also won an award from Rowleys, the local electrical goods retailer, as South's best player, which was worth considerably more than the £18 he was paid for his first season.

On grand final day, as the reigning Sandover medallist, John was a guest of the league and tossed the coin to start the game. He watched from the president's box in the members' stand, in the company of the Governor Sir Charles Gairdner and other dignitaries. From there he saw one of the all-time classic grand finals unfold as Perth, desperate to break a 48 year premiership drought and farewell favourite son McIntosh on a winning note, produced a magnificent second half. They turned a six goal half-time deficit into a gripping two point victory, hitting the front for the first time just minutes from the end. John watched spellbound as the drama unfolded and was awestruck by the emotion displayed by the Perth players and supporters when the siren signalled their win. He knew then that any number of Sandover Medals or fairest and best awards could not come close to the feeling produced by winning a flag. He was green with envy but, sadly, tossing the coin would be the closest he ever got to playing in a league grand final.

Chapter 4
Wrecking a knee

John's mother Doris remembering the time of his knee injury:

"It was like a death in the family".

Steve Marsh on John:

"... without the knee injury, there is no doubt he would have been the greatest player ever seen".

After his Sandover Medal win, John suddenly found himself 'public property' and he was both surprised and amazed at the requests for media interviews and community appearances, as well as opportunities for newspaper and radio advertisements. Gibson's barley sugar, probably the favourite sweet of the time, were quick to get John to advertise their product, as were several other businesses, particularly Fremantle firms. As a boy of just 17, John remembers finding all of this hard to cope with; by his own admission, he was a fairly shy person who didn't enjoy the limelight. While he was thrilled to win the Sandover, he couldn't understand why this had suddenly catapulted him to stardom and singled him out for so much attention. He viewed his success simply as an early reward for the time and effort he had put in to try and make himself a great player. John felt he was just starting out on the journey and there was a long way to go and more improvements to be made before he would achieve his ultimate goal.

While the 1955 season had certainly whet his appetite, he had no feelings of satisfaction or contentment about his football and never once felt he had *"arrived"*. It seemed to him that many people felt he had already reached the pinnacle of his career by winning the Sandover, but he knew this was not the case, so he soon began to restrict his public engagements and media requests. He also took the view that, for self-protection, he had to develop a more confident manner to camouflage his natural shyness, such was his discomfort when thrust into the public eye. Therefore, at the tender age of 17, he rightly or wrongly decided that a touch of calculated arrogance was the best way for him to handle these situations, so he consciously worked on developing a brash and confident manner, which probably typifies how he has been regarded by many media and football followers over the past 40 years. John agrees that he can be a *"Jekyll and Hyde"* character and, as a consequence, people don't quite know how to take him. Many readily accept the image so often portrayed by the media – loud and aggressive and someone who doesn't suffer fools. However, few people realise that this persona only came about as a means of coping with unwanted public and media attention at a young age and those close to him know that this characterisation really doesn't fit the man at all.

~

One effect of the publicity surrounding the reigning Sandover medallist was to make him realise that the expectations for 1956 were going to be far greater than in his first year. In

1955, he was a promising junior recruit, with no special pressures placed on him by coach Clive Lewington or the team. However, he could see this changing. Opposition teams would now pay him more physical attention and South would expect more from him. The 'second year blues' theory was active in the 1950s and John was determined not to be a victim. He saw all this as a further challenge and resolved to have an even better season, setting himself to make the State team again and give himself a realistic shot at a second Sandover Medal. He planned to train even harder over summer, but in November his injured left knee, which was hurt in the preliminary final, was still swollen and sore and he was unable to run. The 'trapped cartilage', as it was initially diagnosed, had not responded to rest and was showing no signs of improvement.

Privately, some South officials were expressing concern about John's playing future and, in some desperation, the club sent him to Kalgoorlie-Boulder to be treated by Kris Martinovich, a well-known chiropractor whose sons Ted, Chris and Ivan were later to practise the same form of manipulative therapy in Fremantle. Kris was well regarded, both in football and horse racing circles, as he often treated equine as well as human athletes with success. Kris apparently saw little wrong with John's knee, giving it a quick manipulation to free the 'trapped cartilage' and suggested that two more weeks of rest would probably fix it. John was pleased with this assessment and was confident of starting training in December.

After leaving Kris, John tasted some of the seedy side of Kalgoorlie life, as the accompanying South officials had headed to one of the illegal two-up schools, which were already firmly entrenched as part of WA's Goldfields folklore. The games operated in clandestine locations around Kalgoorlie and John has memories of driving along bush tracks on the outskirts of town before a simple arrow, painted on an old tin can, indicated the way to go. John was amazed by what he saw – a big crowd of men all holding fistfuls of pound notes and making more noise than a derby crowd as they barracked for a head or a tail. He remembers spotting Jim Schrader, the well-known trotting trainer and reinsman, holding the biggest pile of money he had ever seen. But by the time they left the game, it was all gone!

Medical science in the 1950s was a far cry from today, where the injury would have been definitively diagnosed by a magnetic resonance imaging (MRI) scan. However, the 'trapped cartilage' was probably close to the truth and it's likely John had torn or pinched part of the cartilage. These are injuries which often take weeks to resolve, especially without the physiotherapy and/or surgical treatments now available. In early December, after resting for another two weeks, John tested the knee with a beach run and reported no problems, announcing that he planned to give it a thorough test by playing Mercantile Association cricket the next week. Lewington and the rest of South Fremantle collectively breathed a sigh of relief, while John quietly and methodically stepped up his training programme. He combined beach runs at Leighton and athletics with Don Gillan, with lots of football workouts at Hilton Park, either by himself or with his younger brother Bill.

~

In the 1950s football pre-season training usually started 10-12 weeks before the first game, which was generally scheduled for the last weekend of April. Most players took part in summer sport – mostly cricket, although a few did athletics, which meant that football training didn't start until late January or early February and was generally twice a week, avoiding the main cricket training nights. Training generally started a few weeks before the annual club reunion, when trophies from the previous season were presented. The Fremantle Town Hall was the traditional venue for South and, on February 22, John was presented with both the Sandover and Walker Medals, while Steve Marsh received life membership for reaching 200 games with the club.

By the time Lewington marshalled his troops for the coming season, John had been hard at it for two months and the results were plain to see. In March, Len Owens, in *The Daily News*, headlined *"Todd's form points way to another medal"* and his report continued – *"If pre-season form and exuberance is any guide, John Todd is already on the way to winning his second Sandover Medal. He is setting his team-mates such a merry pace at training that South officials have almost had to hold him in check. The young champion has apparently thrown off the knee injury many thought would end his career. At Fremantle Oval he has been showing all the amazing energy and enthusiasm for football that characterised his tireless training last season. No-one at Fremantle trains faster. Todd is among the first on the field and rarely leaves voluntarily when the training session is ended".*

By the time the practice matches began in April, John was in superb touch. He was named South's best player in all their practice games, which they won convincingly, leading most pundits to nominate them again as premiership favourites. After the 1955 finals fade-out, the players were eager to make amends. South had suffered some losses – captain Frank Treasure had gone to the Eastern States for the year and vice-captain Charlie Tyson had switched to Subiaco as captain-coach. However, on the credit side, the club had regained the services of big ruckman Norm Smith, who had missed the 1955 season with a shoulder injury and carbuncles. The club was buoyed by the return of Smith, who had played over 100 league games and represented the State, as they felt the lack of a big strong ruckman had cost them, particularly in the preliminary final when Merv McIntosh had set Perth on the road to victory. One of South's strengths was its roving division, with Marsh, Barry White, Don Stewart and John regarded as the best small man brigade in the competition – having a top-line ruckman to feed and protect them would aid the team. Big things were expected of John Gerovich in his second year, with a century of goals not beyond him in a full season. There was a reasonable degree of expectation and optimism about the 1956 season, with Marsh elected by the players to take over the captaincy, with John Colgan as his deputy.

South recorded hard-fought wins in games against Claremont and Perth, with John named in the best, but he was first to admit that his opening games hadn't been as good as he would have liked, so he applied himself even harder at training. Lewington threw John the challenge of moving from rover and half-forward to the centre, a switch John relished as he saw the opportunity to be in the action more often. South were playing West Perth at Fremantle and rival centreman Don Marinko had received glowing praise over the first two rounds. The game was played in wet and slippery conditions, but this did little to dull John's brilliance, exploding out of his mini form slump to completely outplay Marinko, finishing with 30 kicks to be best-afield as South recorded a 29 point win. Austin Robertson (Snr), reporting in *The Daily News*, said of John, *"His handling of the wet ball was the best I have seen in WA"*. John was more satisfied with his game than he had been for the previous two weeks and was happy with his new position; he looked forward to playing many more games in the centre.

The next week was the first Fremantle derby for the season and the whole city was talking in expectation of a great tussle. South were unbeaten after three rounds and Old Easts had lost once, upset by Swan Districts at Bassendean, so both teams were in good form at the top of the premiership ladder. However, the game promised more than just the contest between the two sides. There was much anticipation about the clash of the respective centremen, with John's game against West Perth suggesting he should play centre in the State team for the Australian championships in Perth in June. His derby opponent was Ray Sorrell, who had burst onto the league scene with some dazzling displays after joining Old Easts in 1956 straight from junior ranks and who had featured in their best players in every game. Sorrell was also a left footer, so there was much debate in Fremantle about which of the *"young lefties"* would win the centre battle on Saturday.

However, the much-anticipated contest, both in regard to the teams and the centremen, proved to be something of a let down, largely due to John's exploits. He maintained his blistering form to be the unanimous choice as best on ground in South's 34 point win. In the second quarter alone, he racked up nine marks and 15 kicks to outpoint Sorrell, who was replaced in the centre by Alan Preen. This move made little difference to John, who finished with 15 marks and 35 kicks in what Len Owens described as *"... the most electrifying display by a centreman I can remember"*. He further added – *"... it would be a mistake to use him in any other position in the State team. Judged on Todd's performance, neither Jack Clarke, of Victoria, nor Lindsay Head, of South Australia, could subdue him in the big championship games"*. This was high praise indeed, as both Clarke and Head were acknowledged as champions and were experienced campaigners in State football. However, fate would soon step in to deny football followers the opportunity to see John clash with these stalwarts.

John celebrated his 18th birthday by taking the lead in *The Daily News* Footballer of the Year Award, polling top votes in his last two games, with Sorrell, who led after the first three matches, Marsh and Tyson two points behind. He was also named in a squad of 25 players for the carnival, being one of six South Fremantle players selected. Charlie Skehan and Ray Richards were again picked; the three young boys from Deanmill had all kept pace with each other. Barring injury, there would be no changes to the squad, which included East Perth regular centreman Tom Everett, so there was continued press speculation on where John would (or should) line up for the State team.

John continued his good form in the centre and South recorded hard-fought victories by 13 and five points over Subiaco and Swans. For the Swans game on the June 4 Foundation Day holiday, John had to shrug off the effects of a large boil on his left knee, which prevented him from training and working during the week. He was also involved in two heavy clashes which left him groggy, but he refused to leave the field and played the game out. These clashes were a result of two things – the Swans players were endeavouring to 'slow' John down with physical pressure and his 'blind' courage and desire to 'go for everything' was again to the fore.

Both daily newspapers carried columns about him, raising concerns for his longevity in the game given his unbridled exuberance for the contest and scant regard for his own welfare. With the important Australian championship looming, it was felt he had to *"wise up"* and change his style because *"... these Victorians have scant respect for brilliance if it threatens to destroy their supremacy. They believe a man who leaves himself wide open is inviting a hit. He must learn to curb his enthusiasm, keep his eyes and ears open and use better judgement when hurling himself into packs"*. And further – *"... Todd, in his sheer exuberance, seems to be taking too literally the football dictum that you must never take your eyes off the ball. For his own*

Chapter 4 – Wrecking a knee

protection, he must keep an eye out for the 'charger' and to roll with the bumps he can't avoid". While John read these articles, they didn't strike a chord with him – he simply shrugged off the heavy bumps as 'part of footy' and, if anything, was more prone to chastise himself for not being agile enough to avoid the clash. He was playing football the only way he knew how and was having a lot of fun doing it, so a conscious change of style was out of the question. Doris also read the articles, the tone of which had been raised many times before, and she was deeply worried about how John would fare in the championships, especially against the Victorians, who she regarded as *"bully boys"*. However, there was nothing she could say or do about the situation, so she quietly hoped for the best, trusting that John would not suffer any serious injury, particularly to his head.

South's last game before the championships was against East Perth at Perth Oval. Jack Sheedy had been recruited from East Fremantle to captain-coach the Royals, who had won four of their six games and were fancied to upset South, whose recent form had been patchy, despite remaining unbeaten. It was a big day for East Perth as they officially opened their new Perth Oval grandstand and clubrooms, built at a cost of £108,000 and deemed to be the equal of any such facilities in the country. It was East Perth's golden jubilee (50th) season and the match against South had been designated the 'golden jubilee game' to coincide with the opening of their new premises – a big crowd was in attendance. For South, Marsh was forced to watch from the grandstand because of a toe injury, but East Perth were at full strength, with Graham (Polly) Farmer in outstanding form, and expected to pose big problems for the Bulldogs.

The game lived up to the occasion, being a tough and tight affair from the opening bounce. South double-teamed Farmer at centre bounce-downs, preventing him from getting first hands on the ball, so the South small men, with John leading the charge (two goals in the first quarter), were picking up plenty of possessions. Richards, at full-back for South, remembers thinking that John was having a *"blinder"*, but early in the second quarter it all came to a sudden end. A high ball came John's way, but just out of his reach to mark. He got a finger on the ball, turning back into the pack behind him, leaving his left leg anchored on the ground and, as he tried to push off, the pack collapsed across him, with his leg bearing the brunt of the impact. John knew straight away that *"it was bad"* and feared he had broken his leg which, as it turned out, would have been a better result.

Marsh, Richards, Harry Carbon and Ron Hindes could all see the collision coming. Marsh was closest to the incident as it happened almost right in front of him and he recalls thinking how unnecessary it was – *"John shouldn't have gone for the mark, but let it go over his head and read the crumbs off the pack"*. Carbon, Hindes and Richards all agreed that going for the mark was *"almost suicidal"*. Richards could see that John was going to get crunched as the kick went over his head and remembers thinking *"Oh, geez, what's Doris going to say"*. John's memory of the incident matches these observations. He concedes – *"I needn't have gone for the mark and, if I had my time over again, then I probably would have stayed on the ground. However, my decision to fly for the mark was a natural instinctive one; it was simply how I played the game. When you are young, it's easy to feel almost invincible and this is how I felt. It is hard to temper this when you're young, you just go for everything..."*.

Needless to say, John was carried from the ground and, for once, without any protest as he knew he had a serious injury. Bill Todd (Snr) went to the change rooms, but was denied entry by the South officials. South president Frank Fuhrmann knew Doris would be listening and he had a message put over the radio saying John was OK after the South trainers established that no bones were broken, but no-one had much idea about the type or severity of the knee injury. This was the norm for the era – trainers generally only had rudimentary first aid skills and any serious injuries were referred to hospitals or specialists for further medical attention. It was felt that John didn't need to go to hospital immediately, but would see a specialist on the Monday to determine the extent of the injury. So John hobbled outside on crutches to watch the second half and saw South's unbeaten run come to an end as East Perth got up in the last minute to win by a solitary point after Ted (Square) Kilmurray goaled with seconds to go. This result topped off an already *"bad day at the football"*.

At home that night the atmosphere was sombre as no-one knew how bad the injury might be and the championships were starting in five days' time. John knew his chances of playing were slim at best, but everyone tried to remain positive, although with little conviction. To distract himself, John went to the movies but, after sitting for a couple of hours, found that he couldn't straighten his leg out so he went home even more depressed. The next afternoon John checked into Fremantle Hospital and on Monday saw a specialist who gave him the grim news – he had suffered major ligament damage to his knee and the joint needed to be immobilised. The specialist couldn't be sure this would fix the injury, hinting that his career may be in jeopardy, but it was the best option available. If any of the knee ligaments had been torn off the bones or snapped by the force of the collision, then they would have the best chance of healing and re-attaching to the bones if given complete rest. Therefore, John's left leg was encased in plaster from hip to ankle, which is how it would remain for three weeks. He remained in hospital that night as the State selectors named replacements for the championship – Sheedy came in for John and John Gerovich for Kilmurray, who had suffered a fractured cheekbone against South.

On the Tuesday John left hospital on crutches and on Wednesday, South secretary Frank Harrison reported to *The West Australian* that there was *"... no sign of damage to ligaments, but there may be a slight internal injury"*. This demonstrated that even as far back as the 1950s, football clubs kept injury details 'in-house' and were content to feed the public half-truths or outright lies.

John was devastated. He was out of the championships and was going to miss many matches for South. His dream was on hold – and his prospects of a second Sandover Medal were dashed, with the records showing that he had polled six votes in the first six games. However, he considered he could get back for the finals and he refused to contemplate the specialist's comment that he might be finished. With his leg in plaster, he was forced off work, which Wally Doust, being a strong South supporter, understood. However, John was still an apprentice and on junior wages (about £2 a week) so Doris went to Doust and argued (successfully) that John should receive adult wages while off work, as he had been injured playing senior football. John also received some injury compensation money from South, who had introduced a scheme that season where members and supporters were asked to 'adopt a player' to insure them against injury. For £4/10/- per person, league players were insured for loss of time and wages to the extent of £12/12/- a week for up to eight weeks and medical expenses not exceeding £25. Therefore, John was not out of pocket because of the injury, but actually received considerably more than for a normal three week period.

However, this was small compensation. For virtually the first time in his life, John was inactive and he absolutely hated it. His depression grew week by week as he couldn't work, kick a ball or train in any way. Watching WA and South Fremantle train and play only added to the agony, so he worked out his frustrations by helping coach the Hilton Park juniors. WA put up a spirited fight in the championships, but were eventually beaten by Victoria in the match to decide the carnival winners. Gerovich and Cliff Hillier were rewarded with All-Australian blazers and Farmer won the Tassie Medal for the best player in the championships. When the local fixtures resumed, South had many other regular league players missing with injury and they lost first-up to Claremont by 27 points, before recovering to beat Perth by 42 points.

As the days of forced inactivity dragged on, Doris recalls the changes in John. The frustrations saw him virtually withdraw from everything around the house – he was disinterested in what his brother and sister were doing and had little inclination to talk with anyone. Meal times were silent affairs as football, which normally dominated the conversation, was avoided. Attempts to brighten the mood by talking about other subjects invariably only lasted a few minutes and did nothing to alter John's sullen and surly demeanour. Doris felt awful and totally helpless and remembers this period as being *"like a death in the family"* such was her despair at seeing John as he was.

The removal of the plaster after three weeks did little to boost the spirits. John was aghast at the size of his leg, thinking it looked like *"a pencil"*, such was the wasting. He couldn't bend the knee fully or squat on his haunches. However, the specialist was not concerned about the shape and size of John's leg and matter-of-factly told him to build up the muscles. He offered no thoughts on how best to do this, leaving John to his own devices, as was typically the case in this era. Rehabilitation programmes and indeed any sort of follow-up after leaving hospital, particularly for sporting injuries, was unheard of in the 1950s, in stark contrast to the situation today.

Although dismayed by the contrast in size and strength between his right and left legs, at least with the plaster gone he could be active again. He returned to work and training, which lifted his spirits. He started a punishing daily programme of pre-dawn walking and jogging in the soft sand at Leighton Beach before work, which left the afternoons free for training at Fremantle Oval, riding a bicycle in the rooms and doing skills work on the oval by himself and with Carbon. He progressed to running in knee-deep water at the beach as well as on the sand and in the afternoons ran lap after lap of Fremantle Oval, always with a football in his hands. He refrained from kicking and after a week and a half of this training, he was pleased with the recovery of his leg. Although he had only run in straight lines, the knee felt good and he was optimistic about an earlier than expected return to football. However, his left thigh circumference was still a good inch (2.5cm) less than his right, so the early morning beach work continued.

The next Tuesday John surprised officials and delighted supporters at training by joining in with the senior squad. It was July 10, a mere 31 days after the golden jubilee game with East Perth. However, after looking good for about 30 minutes, John turned sharply to chase a loose ball and felt his knee buckle under him. He was carried from the oval, dashing hopes of a quick return to playing, but the initial despair subsided as two days later John put in a full day's work at the butcher's shop without any troubles. He was hopeful (but not over-confident), that the training 'hiccup' was only a minor setback and not related to the injury. His knee felt sore, similar to how it was at the end of 1955, but there was little swelling. He remained optimistic of returning before the finals and, after a few days of rest, resumed beach running and cycling to strengthen the muscles around the knee.

Three weeks later, he was back on the track. South were looking a little shaky, having won only three games in seven weeks and slipping to third spot. Having a fit John return to the side suddenly became an appealing prospect, but there was no pressure from Lewington for him to play, although some committeemen became understandably 'excited' when he appeared at training. John had an open mind about playing – he was content to see how he felt during and after training. He completed Tuesday's session without mishap and was in sparkling form on the Thursday night until, with about 10 minutes of training left, his left knee again gave way as he attempted a sharp turn, just as it had done before. If he had completed training he would have been selected for Saturday's game, but instead the papers reported – *"Todd breaks down again; out for year"*.

While John wasn't ready to concede this just yet, the second setback certainly knocked his confidence and put him in a real quandary about whether to attempt a further comeback or rest up and prepare for 1957. Most newspaper scribes thought this should happen and the papers were full of reports that John, at 18 years of age, should protect his career by staying out of the game until the next year. There were articles criticising South for allowing him to train so soon after the initial injury, but officials pointed out that John, given his make-up, would have trained by himself elsewhere if he had not been permitted to train with the league side, so they reasoned it was better to have him train at the club where they could keep an eye on him.

This second breakdown sent John spiralling back into depression. His season had been severely disrupted, if not prematurely finished, and the dream was being taken away despite all his efforts to strengthen the knee. Doris and Bill (Snr) watched despairingly as John tried to cope with the frustration and disappointment caused by the injury and, while they would have preferred John to sit out the rest of the season, in some desperation they asked South to arrange for another visit to Martinovich. South agreed, not only because John was the key to their premiership chances, but they wanted him to get through this difficult period and play many more games, not necessarily just in 1956.

South committeeman Bill Holt accompanied John to Kalgoorlie and, for one of the few times in his life, John left home without any training gear. He met with Martinovich on Monday, August 20 and again the next day, after which Martinovich declared that John's knee was as good as fixed, as the problem had been a displaced kneecap, which was cutting off the blood supply to the joint. Manipulating the joint had corrected this problem and some hot poultice treatment restored the normal blood supply. To prevent the kneecap from slipping out of place, Martinovich taped a halfpenny coin to the outside of John's knee, ostensibly to keep the ligament in place, a remedy that John said made him feel *"... the richest footballer playing the game"*.

John was *"over the moon"*, especially when Martinovich said he would like to see him train to assess whether the hard grounds of Kalgoorlie would cause any undue soreness. John wasted no time in having his gear sent up to him and on Thursday he stripped with local side Mines Rovers, who were coached by Bill Colgan, the brother of Souths vice-captain, John. The session attracted many town folk, as word of John's appearance quickly spread. After running 10 laps of the oval at good speed, John asked for some match practice to test the knee thoroughly. Colgan was only too happy to oblige and arranged two sides. For almost an hour, the teams competed against each other with gusto, with John in the thick of the action. He weaved and propped his way around opponents with relative ease. But John remembers that he *"protected"* himself and his knee and didn't play as he would have for South. Martinovich examined the knee the following day and saw no reason why John shouldn't play next week against West Perth.

Back in Perth, John told the press that his leg *"felt as good as gold"* and while the gleam appeared back in his eye, he was, in fact, talking up his prospects, as he wasn't certain how the knee would stand up to the pressure of league football. South were buoyed by the news from Kalgoorlie and Martinovich's apparent success in treating the knee, but secretary Harrison sounded a note of caution, saying John would have *"to prove himself 100% fit before the club would consider playing him again"*.

Tuesday saw a big crowd at Fremantle Oval in the expectation of seeing John train and they weren't disappointed. After a searching warm up by himself, John joined the full training session and didn't miss a beat, leaving the crowd excited at the prospect of seeing him play on the coming Saturday. There was still plenty of press debate about the wisdom of John attempting to play again, with most pundits advising him to wait until 1957. He could see the logic of their argument of putting his career at risk for the sake of a few games and, after discussions with his family and South officials, he announced that he would not attempt to play again this season. *"My knee feels perfectly fit, but I've decided to give it every chance. I won't even train again this season"*, he told reporters. Generally, John (and South) were lauded for making the hard decision, although many club supporters were naturally disappointed. Coach Lewington backed the decision, saying *"... John could have 15 years of football ahead of him. None of us want to see him jeopardise that by playing so soon"*. Nevertheless, circumstances over the next five weeks would conspire to compel John to renege on this decision.

Since the re-match with East Perth on August 11, which South lost by 22 points, the Bulldogs had lost to Claremont, but with a 29 point win over Old Easts, they were third, but in danger of missing the double chance. In the last three rounds, South recorded impressive victories over West Perth, Perth and Swans to secure a second semi-final berth against East Perth, who were chasing their first premiership for 20 years to coincide with their golden jubilee year.

On the weekend of the first semi-final, John accompanied Bill (Snr) on a trip to Barton's Mill with a Fremantle wharf lumpers team, planning to act as umpire for the social game against the prison team. However, the team was one short, so John, with Bill's blessing, made up the numbers. Playing as a rover, he kicked six goals and thoroughly enjoyed himself, having no problems with his knee. Encouraged by this, he trained with South on the Tuesday. With his competitive urges stirring, the lure of playing finals football was hard to resist.

A crowd of over 500 people saw John train impressively as the team prepared for its showdown with the Royals. Rumours swept Fremantle that John would make a comeback, but he scotched these on the Thursday by again declaring that he would not play, despite being sorely tempted. When the team was released, John was not named, but South were forced to leave out centre-half-back Cliff Hillier, who had been hospitalised with appendicitis. It got worse when ruckman Eric Grose woke up on Friday with chicken pox and half-back Don Darcy had a bruised thigh, being replaced by State defender Ray Crawford, who was only half fit due to a thigh strain and had been originally left out of the team on Thursday. Things were desperate for South, so they asked John to play as a reserve. Naturally John didn't need to be asked twice and, after discussions with Doris and Bill (Snr) and Harrison, South named him as the 19th man. Marsh, who as captain also acted as a selector, was not privy to this decision and had argued against John playing when the matter was raised on the Tuesday. He was surprised to arrive home from the movies to find a note pinned to his front door which simply said – *"Todd's playing tomorrow"*. It was 16 weeks since the knee was first damaged and six weeks since Martinovich had performed his *"miracle cure"*.

In the pre-match warm up, John sought out Farmer to congratulate him on winning the Sandover Medal, bringing warm applause from the crowd. He then moved to the bench, which was a completely foreign position for him. At three-quarter-time, John replaced Crawford, whose suspect thigh had eventually given out. A close finish was expected, with South leading by 16 points, but East Perth were coming home with the breeze. John went to a wing and, the first time he went near the ball, he was pounced on by two Royals players, suffering a corked thigh. This slowed him down and he finished with just a few possessions as South were kept goal-less while the Royals kicked four goals to win by seven points. His return after four months on the sidelines and limited training was less than spectacular and, coupled with South's loss, made for a quiet night, although John was consoled to some degree by one thought – his now famous knee had stood up to match play and would not need to be the centre of attention for the press in the coming week.

He trained lightly due to the cork, but was never in doubt for a derby preliminary final against East Fremantle, who had accounted for Perth in the first semi. South's injury woes had not eased, with Hillier, Grose and Darcy again unavailable and Crawford unable to recover. In contrast, Old Easts had no injury problems and were rated a good chance to win through to the grand final. John was named at centre-half-forward for South, who were sufficiently encouraged by his one quarter of play to thrust him into the starting line-up. He was prominent early, scoring the opening goal, but Old Easts gradually got on top to lead by nine points at quarter-time. Five minutes into the second term, disaster struck South when Norm Smith was forced off with a pulled thigh muscle, leaving Brian Collins, who was already limping, as the team's sole ruckman. In virtually the next passage of play, Marsh sent a stab pass in John's direction, but it was misdirected and, as John propped on his left leg, the knee again buckled under the strain. He collapsed, holding his knee, and was carried from the ground, with an almost audible groan from the packed oval signalling that this time his season was certainly finished.

Despite losing two stars, South bucked the odds to win by 18 points, holding their derby rivals to a solitary goal in the last quarter as John was laid up in the change rooms cursing his wretched luck. At the minimum, he was facing a long rehabilitation over summer to fix the knee, but also wondered whether he would ever get the knee better after the third collapse. For the moment, his dream and his football life was in tatters – and he was still only 18 years of age.

For the grand final, Grose recovered from chicken pox, but with Hillier, Darcy and John unavailable, they were the underdogs, having lost to the Royals in their four encounters for the year. After a promising start, South slowly wilted and at the last change were 33 points behind; they eventually went down by 13 points after a gallant fight-back. John watched from the stands, but took little enjoyment from the match. He found it difficult to get swept up in the euphoria and emotion of grand final day, as he again had been denied the opportunity to play in one. He was uncertain what the future held for him, but was due to see a specialist within the next two weeks. For South, this marked the end of their golden era and they would not play in a grand final for another 14 years.

Over the next few weeks John saw several specialists. Most were quite blunt in their assessment – the knee kept buckling when real pressure was placed on it, such as when turning sharply, because the cruciate ligaments had been torn in the initial injury. Without intact cruciate ligaments, playing a game like football, which relied on agility for quick turns, was virtually impossible. Only one specialist, a Mr MacKellar-Hall, gave John any slight hope of continuing his career. While he agreed that the cruciate ligaments had been damaged, he said if John could learn to run only in straight lines and not jump for marks, then he might get by, but it was only a slim chance. His message was to avoid any sharp turns and keep one foot on the ground. He also felt that the cartilage in the left knee should be removed, as it probably had been damaged in the initial injury and on the three subsequent occasions when the knee gave way. Any cartilage tears would be slow or unlikely to heal and might 'catch' in the joint, causing the knee to lock up.

John wasn't thrilled at the idea of an operation as he knew of several players who had not been able to come back after knee cartilages had been removed. But he was boosted by learning that Haydn Bunton (Snr), the Fitzroy and Subiaco champion, had played several seasons after having a cartilage out. The cartilage was one thing, but the damage to the cruciate ligaments and the unstable nature of his knee was another and likely to prematurely end his career. At least MacKellar-Hall had given him a glimmer of hope, although he wasn't sure he (or anyone) could effectively play football without twisting and turning. He thought of all the training he had put in since he was about seven years old on improving his skill and agility on both sides of his body and he now saw it all counting for nought. His boyhood dreams were crashing down and he felt angry and betrayed. Understandably, he thought – *"Why is this happening to me when I've worked so hard on my game and I've only just begun. This should be happening to someone who isn't as good; isn't as dedicated..."*.

For several weeks he slipped into a mood of depression as black as the one caused by the initial injury, but eventually Doris provided the circuit-breaker. She was torn apart by seeing John like this, knowing that football was his life, but her determined streak eventually over-rode her other emotions. She fronted John and gave him a strongly-worded piece of her mind. In a cold and deliberate fashion she questioned his determination to overcome the injury, emphasising that – *"If you have the courage, you can get through this"*. John remembers this lecture as an important defining moment. He bristled at her suggestion that he may lack the resolve to push on and might give up, as no-one had ever previously questioned his determination, desire or courage. It was 'spot on' and got him back on track. Thoughts of self-pity were quickly cast aside, as were any suggestions of surrender.

In November, John saw Mackellar-Hall and had the cartilage removed from his left knee. He didn't know for sure that he could beat the injury, but he refused to accept the prognosis of the specialists without first giving it one hell of a shot.

~

It is tantalising to think of what might have been if John had played in the 1980s or later. If he had been starting his career then, his knee injury would have been managed much differently, given the advances in medical science. There is little doubt the June 9 collision ruptured John's anterior cruciate ligament, or ACL as it is commonly known. There is also a posterior cruciate ligament (PCL) in the knee joint, but the ACL is more important. Many footballers have torn or ruptured their PCL and, while they generally miss several weeks, the injury is not usually career threatening. The ACL is absolutely critical to the stability of the knee joint, particularly for Australian football, where cutting, propping, turning and weaving movements are needed. The ACL basically stops the lower leg from sliding forward off the upper leg (thigh) and also controls rotational movements of the knee joint. It is commonly damaged in landing from a jump (with a straight knee), in pivoting movements or, as in John's case, when a large external force or weight (such as a pack of players) is applied to the knee, forcing it beyond its normal range of movement.

In the modern era, many players with ACL tears have had a surgical reconstruction of the knee joint (where hamstring or thigh muscle tendons replace the ACL and restore stability to the joint) and, after a 6-12 month rehabilitation, returned to continue their careers. Players such as John Worsfold and Glen Jakovich (West Coast), Paul Kelly (Sydney), Paul Salmon (Essendon and Hawthorn), Shaun Rehn (Adelaide and Hawthorn) and David Schwartz (Melbourne) all had surgery to overcome ACL tears and then returned to play with distinction. In fact, Schwartz underwent three surgical reconstructions of the same knee in the mid-1990s, but played several more seasons without further mishap. He also attempted to play just four months after one reconstruction, but the knee gave way before half-time, buckling underneath him in the same way that John's did as he attempted a sharp turn.

Generally, 12 months of rehabilitation is required for the tendon graft to fully mature and the muscles to return to their normal strength. In particular, hamstring muscle strength is of great importance in the recovery from an ACL injury and, these days, a prime focus of the rehabilitation programme is to strengthen this muscle group. If John had had these medical options and knowledge available then, barring other serious injuries, he would have had the surgery and spent 12 months out of the game, but come back almost as good as new. He could certainly have played the 300 or more league games that he desperately wanted – and expected – to play. Had that been the case, football followers in WA and Victoria, where he would have eventually gone to play, could have enjoyed more than just fleeting glimpses of one of the best players the game would ever see.

Chapter 5
Finding a way back

Ray Richards remembering John's attempts to overcome the knee injury in 1957:

> "We knew he would find a way, we knew he wouldn't quit".

John himself recalling this period:

> "I was certain I could beat it, but it was a hard, lonely journey, I just had to work it out myself. It certainly helped in my coaching, because I could relate to adversity"!

John spent a week in hospital after having the cartilage removed from his left knee. It was pretty well shredded, so the operation was necessary, although it did nothing to solve the problem of the torn ACL. The week felt like a month to John, who hated being inactive and off work, so one night some mates organised to take him to the drive-in movies. With his leg in a brace from hip to ankle, they collected him from the ward, carried him across the hospital lawns to the car park and loaded him carefully into the back seat of John's old Hillman so he could keep his leg straight. Unfortunately, they neglected to tell the ward sisters they were taking John out, so when they returned they were met by a very irate matron who gave them all a good ticking off, including John.

John's leg was in the brace for about six weeks, twice as long as before, so when it was removed he was in no doubt about what the size and shape of his leg would be. Nevertheless, it was still an awful, sickening moment when he compared the withered left leg with the right. Once again, the specialist's advice was brief – build up the muscles was the sum total of the discussion, with no elaboration on how best to do this. Still, John was not unduly bothered. It was what he expected and he was mentally prepared for many early mornings at Leighton Beach, ploughing through the soft sand and knee-deep water. At least he was active again and returned to work, plus he had resolved to give the knee extra time before playing again, so he wasn't fixed on the start of the 1957 season. He reasoned it would take time to re-train himself to keep to straight lines as much as possible and not fly for marks, which was just as important as restoring strength to the muscles around the knee. He was certain he could beat the injury and was absolutely determined to play again. With the benefit of the hindsight of later years, John feels that what kept him going were his age, enthusiasm and his boyhood dream – to be the greatest player the game would ever see. If he had been 25 and played 100 games then he feels he may have accepted his fate, but at the age of 18 after only 30 senior games, he simply refused to concede that his career was over.

~

John slipped back into his routine of summer workouts but with a couple of striking differences. He was restricted to walking and cycling and consequently there were no football workouts at Hilton Park Oval. Every day he worked on the leg – pre-dawn walks at Leighton Beach, cycling to and from work and at the oval and some weights training at the Tattersall's Club in Perth. Being on his feet in the butcher's shop all day was both a help and a hindrance. Carrying large carcasses of meat in and out of the freezer probably helped build strength back into the leg, but it was hard work and there was a fine line between too much strain and a training effect. Often the knee got sore and swelled as a result of John's manual labours, so, to provide better support for his knee, John wore army boots; walking around in these helped build up his leg. He gradually lost his limp and, after about two months, the leg had recovered to be only about an inch smaller in circumference at the thigh than his right leg. The specialist gave him permission to start running, but only slowly and in straight lines.

There was much speculation about whether John would (or should) play in the coming season. He did little to help the situation and, in March, at the annual reunion and trophy presentations, he announced that he would coach the Hilton Park under-18s side and take a break from playing in 1957 to let the knee fully recover. A few days later, after no more than five weeks of (slow!) running, he won the Griff John Handicap 100 yard dash, an annual sprint race conducted by the club, usually in conjunction with the WA Amateur Athletic Association. In this race the South players ran in full team kit in tribute to Griff John, the club's founder and first secretary. No doubt because of his operation, John snuck under the guard of the handicapper and was given a generous nine yards as his mark and, with great speed out of the blocks, he won comfortably in 10.3 seconds, beating Pat Daly and Tony Parentich.

While this race was a straight line sprint, it gave John some heart; at least his speed was intact and the knee felt good. However, he knew there was still plenty of work to do in regard to how he could successfully return to playing the game, without putting the knee under extreme pressure. This required some changes in his style of play – he could only prop and turn on his right leg and had to curb his natural desire to fly for marks. This would take time and he was in no hurry, but the Griff John win gave him the confidence to start football training again.

~

As the season drew closer, South officials had another matter to be resolved. The club's favourite son, Steve Marsh, had defected to the enemy, being appointed captain-coach of East Fremantle. Marsh had been the only applicant for the South coaching position for 1957, as Clive Lewington was undecided about continuing, but maybe because of the 1955 dispute Marsh had with the club, the committee enticed Lewington back. Marsh was upset, but never considered leaving South until East Fremantle – for the first time in their history – offered the coaching job to an outsider. South reacted angrily, refusing a clearance. One committee member wrote to Marsh, expressing his disgust at the *"treachery"* and suggested that his life membership be revoked! South finally relented, but only on the Friday before the season opened and after being given three players, including Ron Doig, who went on to play State football, and a £300 fee by Old Easts. John was disappointed to see Marsh leave Fremantle Oval, as he had expected to play many more games with his former idol, rather than against him. He felt Marsh should have been given the coaching position. However, in a striking parallel, in the 1970s, John would also be accused of *"treachery"* by South when he was appointed coach of arch-rivals East Fremantle.

Chapter 5 – Finding a way back

As pre-season matches unfolded, South wasn't being touted as premiership fancies – the much-vaunted roving division having been reduced to just Barry White and newcomer Stan Badham in the absence of John, Marsh and Don Stewart, who also looked like missing the season with a leg injury. On the credit side, Parentich had established himself in the centre, where he won the Simpson Medal in the 1956 grand final loss, and former captain Frank Treasure had returned from Victoria to play one more season before retiring. South's practice match form was indifferent and most pundits felt the team might struggle to make the finals. In the season opener, new captain John Colgan led the side out and Des Miller played in the No. 10 guernsey, perhaps indicating that South were not expecting to see too much of John in 1957.

John's knee was holding up fairly well and running in straight lines was no problem. In his own time, either at the club or at Hilton Park, he cautiously tested some side-stepping movements, but only on his right leg. He also used an American knee brace provided by Subiaco president Bert Mills, who had obtained a similar brace from the Harlem Globetrotters basketball team in the USA to help star Lions rover Don Carter recover from the same injury. This generous act further fostered strong links between the two clubs which had been forged after the 1954 season, when South completed a hat trick of league and reserves premierships. Conscious of its depth in talent, South offered several reserves players to a struggling Subiaco to give them the chance of more league football. Such a move was rare in the 1950s, as players usually only swapped clubs to take up coaching positions. South cleared players like Peter Amaranti, Don Glass, Colin Hickman and Bill McGilvray and all became regular league contributors at Subiaco. Glass topped the league goal-kicking in 1957 and Amaranti became a centreman of note and one of John's toughest opponents over coming seasons. The gesture by Mills was a token of gratitude to South and was also motivated by a desire to help one of the State's brightest young stars avoid premature retirement.

The brace added to John's confidence, but it wasn't designed for a game like football and proved awkward at first, although there was never any doubt about John persisting with it. It weighed nearly two pounds and was made from a coarse material that rubbed the skin raw at the back of the knee. If wet, it held the water and probably doubled in weight, so running at speed became difficult and the leg tired noticeably compared to the right one. Still, it represented the way back for John, so he experimented with it at Hilton Park, away from the prying eyes of the press, and tried various ways of padding and taping his knee to protect the skin. By early May, he felt optimistic about playing again and completed three training sessions in a week at Fremantle Oval without mishap. His knee felt strong and his left thigh was almost the same girth as his right. He was well practised at propping on his right leg, although whether he would remember this in the heat of a match, only time would tell. The specialist cleared him to test the knee under match conditions, so it was just a question of which game.

After discussion with his parents, Lewington and others at the club, John decided to return via the lower grades, where the pressure and speed of the game would be less than in league football. He rang Harry Carbon, who was coaching South's thirds team and asked if he could play on the coming Saturday. Carbon immediately responded with *"You're mad – you're a Sandover medallist, they will try and kill you"*. John persisted and in round 5 on May 18, he ran out with the thirds team against Perth at the WACA Ground. This was the first year of the thirds competition and games were played at the alternate ground from the league fixture, so there were only a handful of spectators and no press on hand to witness John's comeback.

Early in the game John was heavily tackled from behind. He went to the ground and stayed down. Carbon remembers watching with his *"heart in his mouth"* as the trainers rushed to him, but breathed a sigh of relief when John slowly got to his feet and gingerly flexed his left knee, then slowly jogged back to his position. When the head trainer returned to the bench, Carbon told him that *"... if Todd goes down again, don't go near him"*. Carbon reasoned that he knew what John was feeling – the awful, sick, grating feeling of bone rubbing on bone you get after a cartilage is removed, as Carbon had experienced himself. Soon enough, John went down in a tackle and stayed on the ground, but got up without needing any trainers and, in Carbon's words, *"... never looked back"*. He now knew the feeling and realised this wasn't a sign that his knee was going to buckle under him. While he completed the game without mishap, John remembers *"my left leg feeling so tired and heavy (from the weight of the brace) that after half-time I spent long periods playing in a forward pocket, standing next to the goal posts"*.

The Football Budget reported that South officials were impressed with John's display in the thirds, quoting vice-president Bill Hughes as saying – *"... although he did not have the opposition to make him go at his top, Todd played in his old style and he played very well. However, he has yet to give his left knee a real test, twisting and turning at his top in match play"*. The club was receiving some criticism for letting John play again, but secretary Frank Harrison said John was not playing contrary to the advice of his specialists. He had been training with all his natural zest and that *"... his whole ambition is to play league football and the time must come for him to test the leg in a match, therefore he asked to play in the thirds"*.

The knee stood up well, although the brace had rubbed a large piece of skin away from the back of John's leg and Doris worked overtime to heal the sore. He stripped for the thirds for the next three games, managing to get reported against Claremont for disputing an umpire's decision. Found guilty, he received a severe reprimand from the Tribunal, as Harrison made a passionate plea for leniency. Under cross-examination from Tribunal chairman Wally Stooke, John admitted he had been upset by some decisions – *"I was heated. I was being belted about and the umpire was not giving me any protection"* was his forthright explanation. As Carbon had predicted, John was a target, but swallowing some pride and starting off in the lower grades was the right thing to do. It allowed John to find his feet again without undue game pressure, although the physical clashes and heavy tackling helped toughen up his body for league football. Perhaps the act of getting reported forced South's hand, as they may have felt the risk of injury might be no greater in the seniors. John was back in the league side the next week.

John was told by Lewington that he would be selected to play against Subiaco, but with Parentich well set in the centre and the roving division feeling the absence of Marsh, he would start in the forward pocket with an occasional run on the ball. John was confident he was ready to play senior football and, except for the raw patch of skin behind his knee, he had recovered well from the four thirds games he had played. Doris greeted the news of John's impending return to league ranks with a mixture of joy, relief and trepidation and redoubled her nursing efforts on the sore at the back of his knee.

Watching the teams run out for the clash must have been a bitter-sweet moment for Mills. The Subiaco president was no doubt pleased to see John in the No. 10 jumper, complete with his American knee brace, but would have despaired over the absence of Subiaco star rover Carter,

Playing with the knee brace in the late 1950s.
Ken Armstrong is the Perth player attempting the mark, Laurie Jinman is the South player behind him.

who had broken down again earlier in the season. While the brace provided extra support to the knee joint, particularly when twisting, it was no replacement for the ACL. In comparing his situation with Carter's, John believes he was able to make it back because he was a left footer, while Carter was a right footer. Both had hurt their left knees, which was John's preferred kicking leg, while for Carter it was his support, or platform, leg when kicking. John feels this difference was important and helped *"save me, because when bumped or tackled in the act of kicking my left leg was usually off the ground and not taking my body weight, whereas the reverse applied to Don and his suspect knee couldn't take the strain under physical contact"*. Carter never played again after the 1955 season, retiring in 1957 after 78 games, but has been honoured as one of Subiaco's greats by having a room in their clubrooms named after him.

For John, the game went well. After a slow start, he adapted to the faster tempo of league football and played his best in the last quarter when he spent time on the ball and kicked three of his four goals. However, it wasn't enough to get South over the line, as Subiaco were upset 24 point winners. The loss left South with five wins from nine games, but John was elated to be back in the league team. Some early nerves quickly disappeared and by the last quarter he was playing without any conscious thoughts about his knee. Except for the raw skin behind the knee, he pulled up well and looked forward to next week when South were up against league leaders East Perth.

The next Saturday was wet and Fremantle Oval a mudheap, but it made no difference to John. He relished the greasy conditions and was the popular pick as best-afield, kicking three goals as South upset the Royals to win by eight points. He was back in the headlines – Tom Hadfield's report in *The Daily News* said *"A roving Todd sets victory pattern"*, while Ron Davidson, in *The Sunday Times*, went further – *"John Todd the destroyer in great South win over East"*. His display was so good that, despite having only played two league games, Austin Robertson (Snr) called for his inclusion in the State squad to play Victoria in Perth the next weekend. However, when the squad was announced, John's name was missing, as the selectors, Frank Fuhrmann (Souths president), George Fogarty and George Moloney, resisted the temptation to play him on such a limited preparation. The WA team was one of the best selected since the 1947 championships, while the Victorian side was thought to be one of the weakest for many years.

John watched the game in a new role – he made his debut as a newspaper columnist for *The Sunday Times*. The Vics trounced WA 15.25 (115) to 6.12 (48), with Ted Whitten winning the Simpson Medal. John pulled no punches in his review, lamenting the poor disposal of the home side, their lack of backing up and the static nature of their play, which was in stark contrast to the Victorians. He wasn't shy at taking a crack at the coach, bluntly claiming that his South team-mate John Gerovich was wasted at full-forward, where he stayed for the entire game and suggested he should have been tried at centre-half-forward, where WA was well beaten. One wonders what the coach, none other than Lewington, thought of these forthright comments! At 19 years of age, John was already prepared to speak his mind.

As was the 1950s routine, there was a return game on the Tuesday. John's newspaper comments obviously didn't irk the selectors as he was added to the squad; up to six players were unavailable, including Reg Zeuner (Perth) and West Perth pair Brian Foley and Don Marinko who were granted permission to join their clubs on an Eastern States tour. While thrilled to be called up, John was worried about his lack of hard match play after just two senior games and, knowing how the tempo went up in State matches, he was concerned about his ability to run out four quarters. Believing that he needed some hard training to bring him up to the mark, he put himself through a punishing two hour session at Hilton Park Oval on the Tuesday morning of the game. Needless to say, when he ran out in the afternoon he felt tired and flat and had a poor match, managing to get knocked out in the last quarter after colliding heavily with an opponent. Therefore, his eagerly-awaited first State game against Victoria was certainly not one of his best and, with the considerable benefit of hindsight, he concedes that much of it was self-inflicted by his morning training session. It was not something he repeated later in his career, learning that coming up fresh for a game was vitally important, but it does reflect the strength of his desire about football. Concerned that he was not 'fit enough to play', his simple remedy was to train! WA fared a little better in the re-match, but the Victorians were untroubled to win, leaving no doubt their team was the equal of the 1956 championship-winning side.

John was listed as doubtful to play the next week due to concussion, but he shrugged off the knock and kicked three goals. It wasn't enough to prevent Swans recording their first win of the season by two points, leaving South on six wins and locked in a battle for fourth spot with Subiaco and West Perth. John continued in good form over the next month, kicking goals regularly, although the side struggled. In atrocious conditions against Claremont, he again relished the mud, putting in a best on ground performance which won him strong accolades from Austin Robertson (Snr), who wrote in *The Daily News* – *"In such conditions Todd starred. We saw not a fine weather champion hovering on the edge of the play waiting for the ball, but a grimly determined rover throwing himself into the fray as if he had never known injury; as if it were the grand final; as if his place in the team depended on that one game. Thrilled by his form against Claremont – he twisted, turned, absorbed bumps like a sponge, taxing his knee to the utmost and taking some incredible risks – I shed any doubts that here was the most brilliant and natural footballer seen in WA in 20 years. Watching him bewitch his rivals, I couldn't help thinking how narrowly football tragedy was averted"*.

Robertson, an avowed fan of John's, went on to say *"... though Todd never wavered in his belief that he would recover from the knee injury... probably this State has never known a player with such singleness of mind about football"*. He then speculated, judging by the strain John was placing on his knee, that he could probably throw away the American-style bandage as he appeared safe from a recurrence of the injury, although he did caution him not to do so. He finished by saying *"Without Todd, I wouldn't favour South to make the four. With him, they could even be a danger to East Perth"*. After such high praise, it was almost predictable that John's season would soon come to a shuddering halt.

Early in the first quarter of the next game, against Subiaco at Fremantle Oval, his left knee twisted awkwardly in a tackle and he was again stretchered from the ground. This was John's last game for the season and was also South's last win, beating Subiaco by 53 points before slumping to finish fifth and miss the finals for the first time since the end of the War.

John's initial despair was tempered when a doctor diagnosed a strained medial ligament, a common injury in football when a blow on the outside of the knee forces it to cave inwards and, therefore, had little to do with the ACL injury. At least he wasn't back to square one or facing a further knee operation. Including the thirds games and the State match, John had managed to string together 13 matches without being forced off the field because of knee problems until the Subiaco match. Not bad for a player who really should have been finished. With some luck and a lot of dedication, he had bucked the odds.

The knee brace had certainly helped stabilise the joint, although it caused plenty of grief as he and Doris and the South trainers battled to patch up the red raw skin. A crusty sore developed at the back of the knee, which often prevented him from training fully during the week, as whenever he straightened his leg, the scab would crack and bleed. Managing the sore became just part of a normal week for all concerned. John's sister Diane remembers the house as having an almost permanent smell of Mercurochrome, the antiseptic solution Doris applied to the raw skin.

Although it wasn't obvious to those who watched him, there were subtle, but important changes in the way he played which helped him get through. He mostly ran in straight lines and pivoted only on his right leg and, in tight situations, he fed the ball off with a quick handball, knocked it forward or produced a hurried kick to get out of trouble to avoid twisting and turning on his left leg. He curbed his natural desire to fly for marks, although in the heat of the contest there were certainly times when these modifications were forgotten and instinct took over. Reflecting on the early part of 1957, when he tentatively began to run again, John recalls that *"... I was certain I could beat it, but it was a hard, lonely journey. I just had to work it out myself. It certainly helped with my coaching, because I could relate to adversity"*. Ray Richards, who had known him the longest, had no doubts John would get through, given his make up and his unbridled desire and love for the game – *"We knew he would find a way, we knew he wouldn't quit. Each week we would watch the trainers patch up his knee, but he never once complained"*.

~

In the 1957 finals East Perth had a massive 86 point win over Perth in the second semi-final, while East Fremantle accounted for West Perth in the first semi. The preliminary final saw one of the most amazing finishes to a game in WA football history. Perth had dominated to lead Old Easts by 53 points at the last change, with Marsh, in his first season as captain-coach, virtually conceding the game over. He almost ignored his players at the break, saying *"... you've got yourselves into this mess; get yourselves out of it..."* before moving about 10 metres away from the huddle to sit forlornly on a medical box. Whether this was a masterful piece of coaching or not remains in the realms of footy folklore. Marsh doesn't think it was, but East Fremantle turned on a 10 goal last quarter to win by four points, but not before some wag in the crowd produced a convincing impression of the final siren, causing spectators to flood onto the oval with 40 seconds left on the clock. The umpires had to venture into the excited East Fremantle rooms to explain that the game hadn't finished and Marsh was forced to take the players back on to the oval. Needless to say, he packed the backline and there was no further score in the final chaotic seconds.

In the grand final lead-up, John received an SOS call from Marsh and Roy Corbett, the East Fremantle president. Their star centreman Ray Sorrell had wrenched his knee falling off a motor cycle and hadn't been able to play in the finals. They were desperate to give Sorrell every chance of playing against East Perth, not least because Royals centreman Tommy Everett was in great touch. So, on the Tuesday night, John walked onto East Fremantle Oval with his knee brace to speak to Sorrell, much to the surprise of the large throng of Old Easts supporters. However, after trying to fit the brace to Sorrell's right knee, they abandoned the attempt as John's brace was made for a left leg. Undeterred, John offered to come back on Thursday night, telling Sorrell how to strap and pad his knee to protect the skin around the joint. John returned with two braces, having contacted Mills to borrow the one used by Carter and, after showing Sorrell how to put it on, he then stripped and joined in with training.

Michael Throssell, reporting in *The Daily News*, said – *"By far the most impressive player at East Fremantle's final training run last night was John Todd"*. John thoroughly enjoyed himself, combining nicely with Marsh in passages of play reminiscent of their South days, but when he helped put Sorrell through a fitness test, the star's knee gave way when attempting to turn, putting him out of contention for Saturday's game.

In the grand final, East Perth were favourites to take out back-to-back flags, particularly with the absence of Sorrell, but they suffered a blow on the Thursday when Graham Farmer was bedridden with a particularly virulent dose of Asian 'flu. As late as 11am on the Saturday he was not expected to play, but he eventually stripped for the Royals, although he was clearly well below his best. In a tight struggle, Old Easts came from four goals behind at half-time to lead by eight points at the final break, with East Perth having a strong breeze in the last quarter. This time Marsh had plenty to say to his team[2] and they responded magnificently, scoring three goals to two to win by 16 points. John's former idol had struck gold in his first season as coach, but unfortunately it was with South's arch-enemy, not the red and whites.

John with Steve Marsh (middle) and Ray Sorrell, trying to help Sorrell overcome a knee injury in time to play in the 1957 grand final.

2. Steve Hawke's book *Polly Farmer* says Steve Marsh virtually ignored his team at the three-quarter-time break of the grand final. However, it actually happened in the preliminary final, confirmed by Marsh, who remembers the circumstances quite clearly.

The lead up to the 1958 season again saw South embroiled in player disputes, as had happened in 1957 with Marsh. Because of South's golden era and their glut of star players – in the mid-1950s they had 20 State representatives – the club was the first place rivals looked when searching for a new coach. In 1954, the now-retired Carbon coached Claremont; in 1956 Charlie Tyson was captain-coach of Subiaco and then, in 1957, Marsh defected to the enemy. After missing the finals, South accepted the need to re-build the team and took a hard line on players, especially stars wanting to leave. Captain Colgan had been offered the West Perth coaching job, but South refused his clearance application. As a 145 game player, Colgan was a seasoned footballer around whom South wanted to re-build the league team. Don Darcy, a young half-back with almost 30 games over the previous two seasons, had moved to Melbourne and signed with Footscray, but he had also been refused a clearance. Imagine the committee's despair when the news broke in late 1957 that John, at the tender age of 19, had been appointed playing-coach of Tasmanian football league side New Norfolk. To lose their brightest young star when he had seemingly just recovered from his knee problems was unthinkable.

The offer was too good for John to refuse – £500 to coach the team, his own butcher's shop and an additional £500 if New Norfolk won the flag. At South, match payments were a few pounds per game, even for established stars like John, so it represented a great football and business opportunity for a teenager. John informed South of the approach, saying he would only go for the 1958 season, giving an assurance that he would play with South in 1959. However, the rules of the game required a clearance not only from the player's club, but also the WANFL permit committee and in the 1950s there was no such thing as 'restraint of trade' to challenge their decision. The WANFL was reluctant to clear the State's best players across the border, as State football rivalry was intense, and the permit committee had rejected virtually all recent applications for clearances to Eastern States clubs unless it was satisfied that, first and foremost, it was a legitimate employment transfer or job opportunity. With the 1958 ANFC carnival in Melbourne in July, there was little chance of interstate clearance applications being received favourably by the WANFL.

John knew the rules and said – *"Everything depends on whether or not I receive a [WANFL] clearance. If my application is refused, I will not be able to accept the appointment"*. However, he thought he had a verbal agreement with South, made when he agreed to play in the 1954 reserves grand final, that he would be cleared to the Eastern States if he ever wanted to go. When the South committee refused his clearance application, with secretary Harrison explaining that *"... we felt Todd's best prospects were in WA"*, John immediately announced he would not play for South in 1958, as they had *"... gone back on a promise to me"*. He made good his threat, refusing to join South's pre-season training and withdrawing from the provisional State squad – even the lure of a carnival couldn't budge him at this stage. He didn't report for training and was dropped.

South officials made many overtures to John, but he continued to train alone at the beach and at Hilton Park and stayed away from the club. In March, with the pre-season games only a few weeks away, the impasse remained, despite South's best efforts at reconciliation. To further complicate the situation, Dr Ernie Manea (who would later become chairman of the WA Trotting Association), of the South Bunbury Football Club in the South West league, somewhat mischievously offered John a package of £35 per week to be playing coach and set up a butchering business in Bunbury. Manea said – *"We will not object if South Fremantle refuse to clear Todd, providing the club adequately compensates him for the lost opportunity"*, adding that they would not rule out legal action because *"Todd's unsound knee makes his football future doubtful and he deserves everything he can get"*. John had recently undergone an Army medical examination which, on the basis of his 'weak' left knee and 'flat feet', had exempted him from National Service training.

Still in no mood to negotiate with South, John put in a clearance application to South Bunbury, adding to the mischief by saying that *"... my knee is not sound and I feel I'm finished as a league footballer"*. South, not unexpectedly, were unimpressed with this development and refused the request, explaining that they simply couldn't afford to have league footballers leave their ranks because of their rebuilding programme.

The practice matches had started when John's tough stance began to soften and he told Austin Robertson (Snr) in *The Daily News* of his desire to *"fix things up"* and said he would play for South if negotiations proved satisfactory, putting the ball firmly back into the club's court. He never wanted to sit out of football, but was disappointed with South's refusal to clear him to New Norfolk, thereby breaking the promise made four years earlier, even though he fully expected the WANFL to reject the application in any case. While he would have gladly gone to Tasmania for the year, the South Bunbury offer was not taken seriously, but it helped make South squirm a bit more, which John didn't mind at all. Country football was not league football; he had just spent the worst year of his life getting over the knee injury and, with renewed confidence about his ability to stand up to the rigours of league footy, the coming season loomed as a great challenge. He had no desire to sit in the stands watching. South made their peace with John and he returned to training in the week leading up to the first game. The clearance saga had cost him the practice matches and some football training with the team, but had given him an early insight into the politics and workings of a football club and how people and words can be manipulated to suit a particular purpose. It certainly reinforced his long-held belief that, whatever the circumstances or the situation, you should *"... be honest, because then no-one walks away bitter"* – a creed which has typified both his playing and coaching career. The knowledge and experience gained from this episode would prove valuable in as little as 12 months' time, as he would again find himself the centre of controversy at South, when surprisingly offered the league coaching position.

~

Not much was expected of South in 1958, with the rebuilding process taking time and veterans Treasure and Norm Smith retiring. Colgan had returned after his clearance application to West Perth was rejected, but it cost him the captaincy, with Ray Richards named to skipper the side. John's return provided a much-needed boost; fellow rover Stewart had also returned after missing a season through injury, so the roving stocks looked healthier. However, disaster struck in the last practice game, when Gerovich badly dislocated a shoulder, putting him in hospital for a couple of weeks and out of the game for a few months. Ironically, the first game was against Subiaco, where Glass, the South Fremantle player cleared in 1955, had kicked 83 goals in 1957 to head the WANFL goal-kicking ladder.

After only two nights of training, John was named in the reserves, although he didn't play due to leg soreness. South lost by 27 points and Lewington and his fellow selectors had no hesitation in bringing John into the league side for the next game. Despite his limited preparation, he kicked three goals and was instrumental in turning the game for South as they kicked nine goals in the last quarter to come from behind and beat Claremont. Lewington opted to let John finish the game on the bench given his conditioning, but even with the game safe, he was not keen to leave the field and Don Gillan, John's athletics coach and also a trainer at South, had to chase him down the length of the oval to tell him to come off!

John continued in good form as his match fitness improved, topped off by his own extra training at Hilton Park. He was still wearing the American knee brace, but usually trained without it during the week to give the skin around his knee a chance to recover. The weekly routine of Doris and the South trainers trying to heal the sore at the back of the knee continued, but generally his ACL-deficient knee was standing up well to the pressures of league football. The medial ligament damaged in 1957 had also recovered well and the self-protection restrictions of only turning on his right leg and not flying for impossible marks were becoming almost automatic.

As the pundits forecast, South struggled, winning only two of their first six games leading into the Foundation Day derby. Then, as has so often been the case, the underdog rose to the occasion and upset the favoured team. East Fremantle were on a 15 game winning streak dating back to August 10, 1957, but, against the odds, South produced a blistering first quarter with the wind, kicking 11.8. Old Easts never recovered, losing by 39 points. John was in grand form, playing the first half as a rover before shifting into the centre and finishing with four goals. An interested spectator was Footscray coach Ted Whitten, who had flown to Perth to speak to South about a clearance for Don Darcy; he had no hesitation in declaring that John *"would walk into most VFL teams"* and appeared to be *"a natural for the centre position"*. The next week John lined up in the centre from the start and turned in another best on ground performance, as South romped to an easy 46 point win over Subiaco. Col Wilkinson's match report in *The Sunday Times* carried the headline *"Subiaco strikes an unbeatable Todd"*. John's form had people talking about a second Sandover Medal, as he led *The Daily News* Footballer of the Year Award after polling top votes in the last three games. With the return of Gerovich, the club was optimistic about a finals berth, but they had to play the next two matches without their State players.

The squad of 25 to play in the Melbourne carnival contained eight South players, with John joined by Cliff Hillier, Don Byfield, White, Parentich, Richards, Gerovich and Colgan. While this was a great honour for the players and the club, it spelt doom for South. They couldn't cover the loss of these players and duly lost their two matches. Top side East Fremantle had five players in the squad, East Perth and West Perth four and the rest only one each, so their depth was not so severely tested.

The WANFL had spared no expense in its quest for victory, with the squad training four times under lights at the WACA Ground with white footballs, as night games were to be played for the first time. The league chartered a plane to transport the players and officials to Victoria as *"a daylight trip will not weary the players like an overnight journey"*. They provided a new pair of boots for each player, complete with non-aluminium stops, which were banned in Victoria. WA started well, beating South Australia outside Perth for the first time in 31 years, with John revelling in the heavy conditions, kicking four goals and picking up three Tassie Medal votes. But a shock loss to Tasmania dented WA's championship chances; John copped a heavy knock on his shoulder in the second quarter forcing him from the ground, marking the end of his carnival as he missed games against the VFA and VFL. While WA easily accounted for the VFA, they were always behind against the Vics, losing by 19 points. The next week in *Football's postbag* in *The Football Budget*, WA's failure to match the Victorians was roundly lamented, with the view expressed that it was a case of professionals (Victoria) versus amateurs (WA and the rest of the footballing States). The WANFL had put a lot of time and money into the carnival challenge and was disappointed with the return.

John's shoulder injury recovered for him to play in the derby after the carnival, but Gerovich was missing, having bruised some ribs in the Victorian game. Old Easts five State players returned from Melbourne without any injuries and they avenged their first round defeat, winning by 19 points. A month later, South were still in the reckoning for a finals berth when they faced West Perth, who were sitting comfortably in second position.

Leading up to the game, John dropped a wooden chopping block onto his left foot at work, taking the nail off the big toe which later became infected. Unable to wear shoes for two days and forced to limp around, the South selectors were ready to take John out of the team on the Saturday morning, but he insisted on playing. Footballers in the 1950s were hardy souls and John made light of his injured foot, kicking six goals and leading South to an important 28 point win. After the game, South president (and selector) Frank Fuhrmann paid a glowing tribute to John's courage and determination in playing so well under considerable duress. South then upset Perth at the WACA Ground, leaving them only one game behind the Redlegs with three rounds to play. However, losses to East Perth and bottom side Swans (with John missing with a recurrence of his shoulder injury) put paid to their finals hopes.

The final game was a derby, but the build-up lacked the usual atmosphere as Old Easts were safe in the top two, while South was consigned to the bottom four. Most interest centred around John and East Fremantle ruck-rover Alan (Punga) Preen, as these two, along with East Perth's Ted Kilmurray, were the only players who could win *The Daily News* £100 Footballer of the Year Award. John was two votes ahead, but not certain to play, leaving the door open for Preen and Kilmurray if they could put in good performances. However, John did play and produced *"a blinder"* of a first half to help South to a good lead before a tongue lashing from Marsh woke Old Easts from their slumber and they swamped the Bulldogs to win by 34 points.

On the Sunday after the derby John won his second AW Walker Medal for the club's fairest and best and on the Monday he was confirmed as winner of *The Daily News* award, having polled two votes in the final match. He also won the Rowleys Footballer of the Year (a repeat of 1955), receiving a Philips radiogram, a Pope washing machine, an Elray electric stove, a Pinnock sewing machine, a Technics vacuum cleaner and a Hills Hoist clothesline. Doris was well-pleased! In addition, he was a favourite for the Sandover Medal, but only received seven votes, with Kilmurray winning on 20, from Preen on 15.

Despite his disappointing Sandover tally, John was happy with his other wins, which represented a good personal year of football, although he would have swapped them gladly for a finals berth. Marsh again asked John down to training in grand final week and he gladly accepted, getting a 'fix' of finals atmosphere. It was all part of his on-going football education and he lapped it up. He watched another epic grand final unfold as East Perth upset East Fremantle to win by two points after a tense last quarter. It was a season in which the Royals won everything – the flag, the Sandover Medal, two Simpson Medals (Farmer and Ned Bull for the carnival and grand final), the goal-kicking award (Bill Mose with 114) and the Rodriguez Shield for the overall champion club.

For his first full season back after the setbacks of 1956 and '57, John had played 17 games for South and two State fixtures, missing three matches with shoulder injuries and one because of his late start to the season. He kicked 36 goals, finishing as South's second-highest goal-kicker behind Stewart and had won a major media award. By any yardstick, it was a great season and the despair and disappointment of 1956 in particular had faded, although John still felt he was on borrowed time with his knee. Against considerable odds, he had made it back and, while those who knew him well could sense he wasn't quite the same player as before because of his inability to prop and turn both ways, as Marsh said *"... he was still a damn sight better than most"!*

A sobering moment for John also occurred this year. On a Friday night, his grandmother Lucy passed away, having spent the last few years of her life in a wheelchair after suffering a stroke. John was close to his grandparents, who had virtually raised him in the early years in Deanmill when Doris was working during the War. Lucy's death shook him greatly and he considered withdrawing from the game the next day. However, he eventually resolved to strip, wanting to play his *"best game ever"* as a tribute to his grandmother. Sadly, it didn't turn out as planned. After little sleep and being emotionally drained, he played his worst game of the year, as so often happens in these circumstances. As he explains – *"Often, after emotional upsets of this type, many players find themselves 'spent' as, not surprisingly, they can't keep the nervous energy under check"*. His grandfather Charlie lived for several more years and died after John had retired, but his passing was again a time of great sadness. John mourned the deaths of his grandparents much more than the demise of his father.

Chapter 6
"Would you like to coach South Fremantle?"

John, in 1999, recalling his first season as a coach, 40 years earlier:

"*I was a lunatic! I expected everyone to train the way I did*".

After missing the finals in 1958, South was desperate to arrest its slide and, despite public comments about the need to rebuild, the committee was concerned the side was stagnating and not improving as quickly as hoped. Clive Lewington had completed his ninth season as coach, the longest tenure in the club's history, but the view was aired that perhaps he had run his race and wasn't necessarily the right man to develop the young players. There was a feeling that he was too soft with the players and training was not hard enough. However, he was keen to continue; this left the committee caught between their desire for change and an obligation to a man who was one of their best players and the club's most successful coach, with four flags (1950, '52, '53, '54) and two other grand finals ('51, '56). After prolonged debate in the committee room at Fremantle Oval, it was decided that it was time for a change.

~

In early December, 1958 John was surprised to receive a visit at the Maypole butcher shop in High Street, where he was working, from South committeeman Ron Warren. Warren didn't beat around the bush – he asked if John was interested in coaching the league side in 1959. This came like a bolt out of the blue to the 20-year-old youngster with 55 games to his credit. While coaching at some point was certainly in his mind, particularly after his failed bid to coach New Norfolk, taking the reins at South at this stage wasn't something he had thought about and, besides, he wasn't aware the position was under review. As far as he was concerned, Lewington was the coach and John wasn't expecting any change. However, after the initial surprise of Warren's offer, he said he would be interested if the position became available. John had never lacked confidence in his own abilities and remembers thinking *"I can do this"*. He had never shied away from a challenge and saw this as the biggest of his short career. He took heart from the fact he had even been considered for the job at such a young age.

Why South thought John would be a good replacement for Lewington is unclear; certainly there were many more experienced players in the club. John Colgan was the most senior player, with 163 games, and had been forced to turn down the West Perth coaching position in 1958 when South refused to clear him, while Ray Richards, Don Byfield and Barry White were all approaching 150 games. It seems none of those players were approached about the job, with Richards, in fact, going to Claremont as playing coach in 1959. The club had settled on John, perhaps believing that, with a relatively young side, a young and enthusiastic coach would work – John clearly had great dedication and discipline. South might also have been protecting their interests, as John had already received one coaching offer, the New Norfolk proposal. With his second Walker Medal in four seasons, the smartest way to keep their best player was to appoint him coach, otherwise it seemed inevitable he would be poached by another club, as had happened with many of South's better players in the 1950s.

From John's point of view, the opportunity to coach South was a chance to further his football prospects. Despite a good 1958 season, he still felt he was on borrowed time as a player and, to stay in the game long-term, he knew he had to coach. The coaching role also represented a chance for some recompense for the £500 he had missed out on when unable to get a clearance to Tasmania. John also felt the club could have helped him more in 1956 and '57 when he was off work and battling to overcome the knee injury – certainly Doris was of this view. So the coaching job was a chance to get something back from the club that perhaps he had been denied. However, the monetary considerations were not a major attraction – he was interested because of the challenge. Football (and life) was about challenges and John thrived on them.

Lewington was informed that the club felt a playing coach was required because of the youth in the team and John was announced as the youngest coach in WA history[3] – a record which still stands today, matching that of his 1955 Sandover Medal win. Lewington, ever the gentleman, took his demise with good grace, saying – *"I can only wish Todd as much success as I had in my early years as coach"*. The 1959 season was one for playing coaches, as four other clubs had appointed new on-field leaders – Richards at Claremont; Percy Johnson had moved from Old Easts to Swan Districts; Don Marinko had replaced Ray Schofield at West Perth; and Tommy Everett had been recruited from East Perth by East Fremantle to replace Marsh, who had surprisingly stepped down after only two years. With Jack Sheedy still in charge of the Royals and Charlie Tyson at Subiaco, this left Ern Henfry at Perth as the sole non-playing coach.

~

Many South players most likely viewed John's appointment with some trepidation. Having watched him train over the years, they must have suspected they might be on the receiving end of a spartan pre-season – he certainly didn't disappoint. Training at Leighton Beach started on January 1, much earlier than normal, and the twice-weekly 6am sessions were a supplement to the rest of the training programme, which was organised by Bill de Gruchy, the well-known WA athlete and recent Empire Games representative. At John's request, he took the squad two nights a week and introduced them to the sessions that sprinters and middle-distance runners usually tackled, which was certainly different to their normal pre-season workouts. John was keen for de Gruchy to give the players more rhythm and balance in their running by improving their technique, as he felt he had gained enormous benefit from his work with Don Gillan at the Fremantle Athletics Club. John credited this training with improvements in his own stamina as he ran more efficiently and therefore wasted less energy.

3. Haydn Bunton (Jnr) was appointed coach of SA club Norwood in 1957 at age 19, which is the Australian record.

Training was definitely harder than it had been previously for most of the squad, although for John, who was accustomed to training like this in January, the main change was that he had to share the sand at Leighton with about 30 other players. He pushed the squad hard, urging them to improve their fitness to new levels, declaring that he wanted the fittest players in the league playing for South Fremantle.

After six weeks of beach and track sessions, training resumed at Fremantle Oval and the players saw footballs for the first time in the year. With most players completing at least some of the January workouts, John started with some hard ball-work sessions and singled out individual players for extra work if he felt they were behind the rest of the squad. One regular for the extra work was none other than Marsh, who was not quite ready to finish as a player and wanted to play one final season at South. He had not taken part in the early workouts, but turned up at Fremantle Oval in February indicating his desire to play. This caught the club and John by surprise, as it was generally thought that, rising 35 and with his best years behind him, Marsh had retired when he left East Fremantle. However, his 1958 form had been sound and he felt he was good for one more season.

While many at the club were pleased to see an experienced player of Marsh's calibre return, John was less so and consequently gave him no latitude on the training track, despite his veteran status. Whether this was because John was determined to have no favourites, or simply an example of the 'new broom' policy, Marsh recalls that John *"murdered me in pre-season and, after about six weeks, my 35-year-old knees decided enough was enough and I announced my retirement"*. John doesn't remember singling Marsh out, but both men agree there was a coolness between them; this was probably a reflection of John not wanting a recent and successful former coach on the scene, possibly intruding on his attempts to stamp his authority on the players. Still only 20 years of age, John recognised that one of his biggest tasks was to gain the respect and confidence of the senior players such as Colgan, Byfield, Hillier and Parentich. They were many years older and had played in the golden era, representing the State several times.

It is somewhat ironic that Marsh's career finished this way [4]. For so long he had been John's idol – the two had enjoyed a good relationship as team-mates at South and even as opponents when Marsh was coaching East Fremantle and had invited John to train with them during the finals. For John to suddenly find himself coaching his boyhood idol was not something either would have anticipated. However, any strain in their relationship was only short-lived and in later years they would successfully coach together at East Fremantle.

~

As the season drew closer, the match committee had many new players vying for selection and a few notable holes to plug. Assisting John with selection were former players and current committeemen Bill Collins and Don Smith and one-time club champions Dave Ingraham and Bernie Naylor, who also coached the reserves. John had no input into their appointments, but this was not uncommon for the era and it didn't faze him. In any case, he saw Collins as an ally and he got on well with the others. The club had lost defender Richards to Claremont and rover

---

4. In 1960 Marsh returned to East Fremantle as coach and mid-season he pulled on the boots for one game during an injury 'crisis', kicking two goals. The club urged him to play on, but he refused, thereby ending his career after 265 games.

Barry White had retired. High hopes were held for Jack Sumich, a State athlete who looked capable of filling a hole in the ruck, and youngsters Ron Bowe and Colin Beard, who showed promise in the practice matches. The side was short on experience and lacked a key defender and a key forward, so most pundits had South missing the four in their pre-season predictions.

However, at the club there was cautious optimism. John's disciplined approach had everyone very fit and if he and John Gerovich, who had managed only nine games in 1958, could have injury-free seasons, then a final four berth was not beyond the team. The two Johns were the keys to the team – if they were playing well, then so was South. It was the club's diamond jubilee (60th) season and many functions were planned, along with a return to finals action. John's coaching initiation was a talking point in Fremantle, with the opening match a derby, and plenty of supporters dropped by the butcher's shop in High Street to wish him well.

It was a stormy Saturday, with rain ominous as the game began and, surprisingly, despite winning the toss, Old Easts kicked against the strong breeze. South started well, with Byfield winning in the ruck, John playing superbly in the centre and Gerovich climbing all over Norm Rogers to take some brilliant high marks and post three of the team's seven goals for the term. The rain came and the breeze changed, but Old Easts narrowed the gap to three goals at half-time, with John playing as a loose man in defence. East Fremantle closed the gap to a point at three-quarter-time, aided by the absence of John, who left the ground midway through the term with a pulled thigh muscle. After a rousing address from their young coach at the break, South came home on the breeze to win by 17 points. Coaching from the bench, John had Byfield and Gary Scott alternating a kick behind the play and provide the impetus for the win.

There were quiet, but joyful scenes in the Todd household as the family celebrated John's first-up win as coach, although he was more concerned about treating his thigh in order to be fit for next week. John also had an attack of boils on his hip during the week and reluctantly left himself out of the team to play Swans at Fremantle, with the visitors winning a tight game by 17 points. John returned the next week, but suffered a recurrence of the thigh strain which kept him out for two more matches as South chalked up three wins from five starts before facing top teams Perth and East Perth. John was desperate to lead from the front; missing games with his knee injury had been bad enough, but now as coach he really felt the frustration of not playing, particularly as it was due to a simple muscle strain. Even at this early stage, he felt it was easier to coach from the bench, but he sorely missed playing and there was no doubt South was a better side with him on the ground. The South faithful believed John held the key to the form of their brilliant, but inconsistent goalsneak Gerovich, whose impact ebbed and flowed with John's presence. Certainly, with John on the ground, the quality of delivery into the forward line was much improved, which no doubt helped Gerovich's opportunities.

Perth held on grimly to win by 12 points and the next week South were outclassed by the unbeaten East Perth, with John celebrating his 21st birthday leading up to the game. The 60 point loss was their worst performance of the season and left them out of the four after the first round of fixtures. A finals berth in the diamond jubilee season seemed a long way off for the rookie coach.

~

After seven games at the helm, John felt more settled in his new role, though disappointed at not winning at least one more game. He was reasonably happy with the information being relayed to him from the bench via the trainers (there were no team runners in the 1950s) and how the side was being run by the rest of the match committee. In reality, John played much more than he coached. At 21, he still had youthful exuberance to burn and he was such an important player that his main contribution revolved around his match form. Don Smith mostly ran the bench and kept John informed of positional changes, but generally didn't seek or require John's approval for these switches. One problem John had was where best to play himself – in the centre or as a rover. Without White, the roving division was thin, with only Stewart established in this role. South's attack had also been hit-and-miss. Gerovich had kicked 23.19 and Stewart was next with 14.10, but the rest of the goals were spread thinly. There was a view around the club that John should rove and rest up forward to bolster the side's goal-scoring but, equally, he gave the side great drive from the middle, where *"you could really influence a game and quickly drop back behind the game when the situation called for it"*.

Parentich was an accomplished centreman and, if John played there, where else could Parentich be used? It was probably easier to coach from the middle, rather than as a rover, which further complicated the situation. In most games he had moved to the centre when the side needed a lift, after starting as a rover. He debated the situation many times with the match committee and sought the views of Harry Carbon as well, but came to no definite decision, taking each game as it came and reacting as the situation demanded. As for the rest of the team, the rucks were well established, with Byfield, Scott and newcomer Sumich all playing well and Pat Daly and Colgan consistent on the wings. Stewart was solid as a rover and Gerovich was dangerous, though inconsistent, up forward. Hillier was strong and reliable at centre-half-back and Parentich useful wherever he was played, but full-back, centre-half-forward and the pockets and flanks had young players rotating regularly as their form fluctuated.

~

The Foundation Day derby attracted a big crowd to Fremantle Oval and proved to be one of the games of the season and probably South's finest hour for the year. At half-time, Old Easts led 9.4 to 3.9, but the margin, exemplified by South's inaccuracy, belied the tough, hard-hitting nature of the contest. South produced a magnificent third quarter to kick six goals before Old Easts scored, setting up a classic derby finish. In a pulsating last quarter, with John brilliant in defence, Parentich on top of Ray Sorrell in the middle and Sumich playing the best game of his short career, South refused to wilt and eventually got home by 11 points, 12.17 (89) to 11.12 (78). That made it a perfect derby record for John and rekindled hopes of a finals spot; these were further boosted by a solid 25 point win over Swans at Bassendean. Remarkably, this was South's first win over Swans since early 1957, despite their lowly standing. John was best-afield, with Austin Robertson (Snr) reporting in *The Daily News* that *"... Todd's influence was colossal..."*. It was his best game of the season and South were now on five wins from nine starts, with the younger players showing new-found poise and assurance in their play.

There was renewed optimism as the team prepared for West Perth, who were currently bottom of the ladder, with only one victory, but the game was a disaster for South, as they slumped to a four goal defeat. The loss was characteristic of South over the past four seasons, who had dropped several games to teams below them on the ladder and John was livid, both during and after the game, giving the players a fearful tongue-lashing, suggesting they were mentally weak and complacent. He told them to expect to pay a price at Tuesday's training and he didn't disappoint them, serving up the hardest session of the year, as match practice and tackling drills dominated the workout.

However, John was not present as he was at Subiaco Oval for State training, so he left Naylor to conduct the session. With the State side away for two weekends, John wouldn't coach South. Joining him on the Eastern States tour for games against Victoria, Tasmania and South Australia were Byfield, Colgan and Gerovich, leaving a considerable hole in the line-up. Once again, Richards and Charlie Skehan made the side to keep a solid Deanmill representation in WA colours. Robertson had written in *The Daily News* that the two John's – Todd and Gerovich – held the key to WA's fortunes as the State side hoped to end a run of 13 consecutive losses against the Vics, having not beaten them since 1948 and never in Melbourne. He again implored John to protect himself better and *"... to be just a little less fearless"* in his endeavours to win possession, for fears that the Vics would pick him off and put him out of the game.

The Melbourne weather was unkind to the Sandgropers, as the rain bucketed down on the Friday; there had been just one wet Saturday in WA for the season. The MCG was a mudheap, although the rain stopped for the match, but the heavy conditions favoured the home side. Nevertheless, WA was quietly confident as the team boasted many famous names such as John Watts, Norm Rogers, Keith Harper, Les Mumme, Brian Foley, Graham Farmer, Sorrell, Gerovich and Todd. It looked to be a well-balanced combination.

To get a better look at the surface, WA coach George Moloney sent the side onto the ground early and John estimates the team had been in the middle for 15 minutes before the Victorians entered the arena. They then lined up for a photograph (John believes this was a deliberate ploy by the Vics), so when the game started, the WA players had been warming up for 20 minutes and had gone 'off the boil'. Not surprisingly, the Vics jumped them to lead five goals to one at the break, as the WA players struggled to keep their feet and handle the ball with any surety. The second quarter became a rout as Victoria piled on 11 goals, while WA could only manage two behinds to end the half 96 points down. Moloney reshuffled the side, but to no avail as the Vics added 15 goals to two in the second half to win by a mammoth 178 points, easily WA's worst drubbing in State football. For the winners, Ron Evans kicked nine goals, as did rovers Bobby Skilton (5) and Allen Aylett (4) between them. John roved and scored one of WA's three goals, along with Mumme and Gerovich.

In addition to the magnitude of the loss, the game is well remembered by John for the skills displayed by Skilton and Aylett in the boggy conditions. He and Mumme were virtually powerless to prevent them from taking the ball away from the centre, as Moloney's pre-match strategy of using Farmer's handballing skill to clear the ball from the congestion and give the rovers time to deliver it to the forwards with precision simply never had a chance. John and Mumme were instructed to run forward and wide at bounce-downs so Farmer could fire out a 20 metre handball to them running past, as he did so regularly for East Perth. However, Farmer was double-teamed by the Vics and was worked over physically, rarely getting clean possession. Skilton and Aylett swooped on the crumbs from the ruck contests and, with little pressure, consistently put the ball onto Evans' chest as he led out from goal, leaving full-back Watts in his wake. Watts became so tired of watching the ball go over his head (after the game he complained of a sore neck) that in the last quarter he actually helped the goal umpire wave the flags to signal another Victorian goal!

Chapter 6 – "Would you like to coach South Fremantle?"

After the match Mumme commented to John that he felt like he hadn't even played a game, such was the Victorian dominance and John remembers the clash as *"a really embarrassing performance"*. At a function that night the side was basically ignored and the players treated as outcasts as the Vics celebrated their record victory. The game had a lasting impression on John for several reasons. Firstly, he believes all players need a defeat such as this as it builds a steely resolve that *"it won't happen again"*. In his view, to be embarrassed by a personal or team performance should certainly see an immediate lift in attitude and desire if the player and the team has any heart and soul, as *"you just can't live with yourself"* and *"you can't wait for the next match to put things right"*. Secondly, the Victorians rotated their players through different positions, which wasn't the norm for this era and confused the WA players, who were not only concerned about keeping their feet in the slippery conditions, but were unsure as to who their immediate opponents were. As a rookie coach, John saw great merit in this tactic and, while it would be many years before this ploy became commonplace, he remembers this first experience of it and the significant confusion it caused the opposition. Thirdly, he was impressed by Skilton, who displayed enormous stamina on the heavy surface as he ran hard all day through the central corridor. Never still, he tracked the ball from defence to attack and back again with great anticipation and certainly made John work overtime trying to man up with him. This was John's first game against Skilton, whom he had been aware of since his schoolboy days from reports in *The Sporting Globe*. It came as no surprise to John when Skilton won the first of his three Brownlow Medals that year.

WA took on Tasmania in Hobart on the Tuesday and set out to regain some State pride. With John and Gerovich leading the charge, WA took the Tasmanians apart in the last quarter, kicking 11 goals to none to win by 59 points. Both kicked seven goals each and were popular choices as best-afield, with strong contributions from Farmer, Sorrell and Mumme. Having restored some State pride, the team flew to Adelaide, with John doubtful after rolling an ankle against Tasmania. He then went down with a severe attack of hives, which he attributed to a self-inflicted *"sugar overload... – with time on your hands, it's easy to over-eat because of boredom and I remember having plenty of milkshakes, chocolates and sweets on the Friday morning"*! In pain and unable to sleep, a doctor was summoned to the team hotel and, after an injection, John managed just three or four hours' sleep before the game. He told the selectors he was fit and took his place in the team, but after an indifferent display, he was replaced early in the last quarter as WA failed by two points to upset the Croweaters. The team headed home with a good deal of State pride restored, after the terrible beating received a week before in Melbourne.

Back in Perth, South was locked in a battle with Subiaco and West Perth for fourth spot, with East Perth, East Fremantle and Perth safe in the top three, while Swans and Claremont appeared out of contention. They were soon joined by the young Bulldogs, who lost to the top three sides in their next three matches. Against East Perth, John was forced from the ground with a jarred knee as the Royals maintained their unbeaten record with a 35 point win which virtually spelt the end of South's finals hopes. John was named in the State squad for the return matches against South Australia in Perth, despite not playing for two weeks, but was forced to withdraw from the squad to concentrate on getting fit for South's next game, a virtual final against West Perth, who had surged into contention for the final four. He called a special players' tea after Thursday's training, when he and president Frank Fuhrmann emphasised hopes that a finals berth could still be achieved in the diamond jubilee year.

The match was at Fremantle Oval and John declared himself fit to play, immediately boosting South's hopes. He started in the centre in dazzling form, picking up 16 kicks for the quarter and completely eclipsing West Perth captain-coach Marinko, who moved himself elsewhere in the second term. South led by 43 points, but their goal-front inaccuracy threw the Cardinals a lifeline as they led 11.11 to 6.2 (22 shots to eight) at the half, squandering their dominance.

The third quarter saw the match transformed. While John picked up 10 kicks, he was virtually powerless to halt the Cardinals comeback as they narrowed the gap to 14 points. At the break he implored his tiring team to find that *"bit extra"* or the finals would be out of reach, but big 'Blue' Foley, the West Perth ruckman who would later win the Sandover Medal for the season, dominated the quarter to see the Cardinals home by 11 points. Not having played for a month, John faded, failing to gain a kick, but leaving him with the remarkable statistic of 35 kicks for three quarters. John gave full credit to West Perth for their terrific comeback, but also saved a parting shot for the umpire, adding that *"... I have only one complaint and that is umpire Fitzpatrick's interpretation of the flick pass. Souths were penalised for using it all day, but East Perth get away with it every Saturday. Either we use it or forget it. There is a need for uniformity in umpiring"*. In later decades such criticism of an umpire would have attracted a heavy fine from the WANFL, but in the 1950s John got away with it, and the flick pass, which East Perth players such as Sheedy and Ted Kilmurray used expertly, was eventually outlawed in 1966.

The defeat ended South's slim final four chances and, with little left to play for, the side managed only one more win, against Claremont; this at least gave John a perfect record against his old friend from Deanmill, Richards. For the final three rounds of the season, John was again forced to coach from the bench, having copped a shirt-front against Subiaco from another former team-mate, Tyson, after dominating the game at centre. An x-ray confirmed a cracked collarbone, which capped off an injury-riddled season – a combination of muscle, knee and shoulder injuries had restricted him to 12 games for South. However, when he did play, his form was exceptional. Even the burden of coaching didn't affect his form – he finished equal sixth in the Sandover Medal, with 11 votes, and was fifth in South's Walker Medal, won by the dependable Hillier.

In the 1959 finals, fourth-placed Subiaco set records in blitzing Perth by 129 points after posting a third quarter score of 16.8. They took their brilliant form into the preliminary final and accounted for East Fremantle by 34 points after being 10 goals ahead at the last change. This set up an East Perth-Subiaco grand final, with the Lions sentimental favourites; it was their first finals outing since 1946 and they had not won a flag since 1924. However, with Farmer in devastating form to win the Simpson Medal, the Royals were too good, claiming their second premiership in a row and their third in four seasons.

~

There are few, if any, coaches in Australian football who can lay claim to being a senior coach 40 years after their coaching debut, so it is of interest to record how John remembers the 1959 season. He turned 21 during the year and had four injury-interrupted seasons behind him when he was surprisingly chosen to replace Lewington. While it never occurred to him at the time, he now considers that the appointment probably represented *"... a soft option by the South committee. Appointing a playing coach was a convenient way of letting Lewington down lightly, as he was (and still is) South's most successful coach. The committee was still hung over and giddy from the golden era of the 1950s and simply didn't have the balls to tell him...".* In John's view, this should have happened at the end of 1956, with Marsh getting the job, but the club chose to retain Lewington and simply drifted through '57 and '58 as a result.

In regard to his coaching debut, John is quite blunt in his assessment – *"I was too young, too immature and really, out of my depth. I was a lunatic, I expected everyone to train the way I did".* Forty years on, he says coaching is mostly about man management; knowing your players well and taking an interest in their lives, not just their football. Different individuals naturally require different approaches to get the best out of them, but he readily confesses there was little of that philosophy evident in 1959. As a wild mustang of 21, *"I was attempting to coach players who were several years my senior and far more experienced, with finals, premierships and State games under their belts".* Not that he had any major discipline problems with the senior players, but he probably didn't improve them either.

Parentich, in reflecting on John's first year, remembers a *"shy young man who found it difficult to talk to the group of players, struggling for words and avoiding eye contact"*[5]. Both he and Colgan, as senior players, had no problems with John, but felt almost embarrassed for him, agreeing that the committee put him in an awkward position by appointing him coach at such a young age. John concedes he was more of a player than a coach in this season; his best method of contributing to the team's performance was to play well, rather than coach with any special flair. While there were no major coaching blunders, there were also no coaching masterstrokes, although in the 1950s team tactics and strategies were nowhere near as prevalent as in latter eras. Players were specialists and played one or two positions at most and weren't shifted around too much, even if their opponents were on top. There was no interchange rule, so, even on a poor day, players usually stayed on the ground until three-quarter-time at least, unless forced off with injury.

South won eight games for the second season in a row and missed the finals for the third straight year, but there were some positive signs. In 1959 the team probably had an unhealthy reliance on the two Johns, but with Todd playing 12 games and Gerovich only kicking 45 goals from 17 matches, it was a poor return all round. However, a record 43 players were used in the league side and many fine players made their debut, such as Beard, Bowe, Sumich, Bob Bucat, Ron Doig and Murray McDonald, whereas in 1958 only 33 players were played and no rookies of note were blooded. While John doesn't recall specifically attempting to blood youngsters, he does remember feeling the burden of being one of two players who virtually carried the team. Missing games with injury was tough as he knew how important he was to the team, which is in no way a boastful comment, but simply the reality of the situation.

He ruefully remembers staunch South supporters Mick Read and Noel Conigrave, who ran a Friday night euchre school at the club. Given his injury problems, they would take bets from supporters on which quarter John would be injured in the next day. In terms of his later coaching, he quickly realised that two or three brilliant players couldn't bring team success. Also, team development was paramount and the team was always more important than the

---

5. In later years as a coach, these characteristics would almost become his trademarks, as many of his players would readily attest after 'copping a serve'!

individual; a philosophy that would become a hallmark of his coaching. While he has coached some brilliant players, they were never given extra latitude, with the team the priority – an attitude impressed on him in 1955 when Marsh sat out the first half of the season, but the side hardly missed a beat. *"I remember thinking that if you can win without Marsh, you can win without anyone"* and the point has never left him.

~

For coaching and playing in 1959, John was paid £300, which he put towards buying a block of land in Hilton Park, although this was not purchased until 1961. He had talks with the committee about continuing as captain-coach in 1960 and was keen to carry on, although he was aware of his limitations as a coach. He was not aware that South were speaking to anyone else about the coaching position, so it was with a mixture of surprise and disgust when he opened *The West Australian* one morning in December to read that Marty McDonnell, the former Footscray player, had been appointed non-playing coach for 1960. It would not be the only time he would learn of his dismissal from a coaching job by reading it in a newspaper.

Chapter 7
Football in the 1950s

The Prime Minister of Australia, Sir Robert Menzies, opening the 1958 ANFC championships:

"I make no apologies for my firm belief that Australian football is the greatest winter game devised by mortal man".

The 1950s remain South's most golden era, winning won four flags (1950, '52, '53, '54) and being runners-up twice ('51, '56) in seven seasons. In nearly 50 years since the 1954 triumph, the Bulldogs have added only three more premierships – 1970, 1980 and 1997 – which significantly pales by comparison to the 1950s. Their dominance fell away quickly after 1956, as retirements and defections to rival clubs saw the nucleus of the side severely eroded and the club missed the finals in 1957, '58 and '59. Their mantle as the best team in the league moved to Perth Oval and, under the leadership of Jack Sheedy, the Royals played in four grand finals in the late '50s, winning three flags and being runners-up once, to almost topple South as the team of the decade. Swans missed the finals for the whole of the decade; Claremont and Subiaco fared little better, playing in the finals only once; and West Perth, Perth and perennial finalists East Fremantle all won a flag each, but were denied further grand final glory by the dominance of South and East Perth. West Perth in particular suffered most in South's golden era, losing grand finals in 1952 and 53.

However, for John, the golden era slipped by without him. In his debut year of 1955, South lost the second semi and preliminary finals, after winning their previous 11 matches, and in 1956 his knee injury cost him a grand final berth.

~

League football in WA in the 1950s was in a healthy state, with attendances regularly reaching 500,000 or more. In 1959 the record was smashed as just over 700,000 people went to the footy. Income for the WANFL was around £60,000 pounds a year and in 1957 the clubs each received a dividend of between £3600-£3800. Clubs aimed for between 1000-2000 members, with badges sold for 10/- to £1. However, the footballers didn't make a great deal of money, with the majority of regular league players earning £20-£100 in total; a useful supplement to their weekly wages, but not a large sum. For the better players, coaching was a way of getting more money out of the game, so playing coaches were popular – in 1959, seven of the eight clubs had them, paying £300 or more for a top-line captain-coach. Still, John has no doubt that *"virtually all players would have played for nothing in these times, as the attitudes of the era stressed the importance of being the best you could be".*

The money, while nice, was mostly incidental. And South was the best team in the country, as they played and beat all comers from every State in end-of-season and tour games. In the post-war period until the end of 1954, South had an unbeaten record against VFL clubs such as Collingwood, Carlton and Footscray, as well as against teams from South Australia, Tasmania, New South Wales and the ACT, both in WA and in the Eastern States. There was fierce State pride in football (and sport in general) and the South teams certainly set themselves to win these interstate club matches, especially against the Victorians who dominated State football. This attitude was fostered from the top as Pat Rodriguez, the WANFL president in the 1950s, was a passionate West Australian, implacable in his opposition to the Vics, as shown by the league's reluctance to clear WA players to VFL teams.

The importance of State football is amply demonstrated by the two week interstate tours the No. 1 WA side would regularly tackle, playing Victoria, Tasmania and South Australia on the one trip. There were no restrictions on the number of players from any club, so it was not uncommon for some sides to lose five or more of their best players for one or two league fixtures while the State team was away. In 1958, despite not being one of the top sides, South lost eight players to the carnival squad and promptly dropped its next two games, severely denting its finals chances. However, State football was the pinnacle of the game and club considerations were secondary; a far cry from how State and club football would be viewed in the 1990s when premierships were valued well above State honours. In a striking contrast of different eras, Sheedy, the East Perth captain-coach, stood down from a match in 1957 to ensure his fitness for a State game the next week. In the 1990s, with the advent of the AFL, many players would do the reverse, as club priorities in the national competition took precedence over State football.

It was also the norm in this era to select a No. 2 State team, who would play a VFL side in Perth when the No.1 side was away. These games on a Saturday, with a return match on the Tuesday, were always well attended and provided more WA players with a taste of higher-level competition. Many of the 1956, '58 and '61 ANFC championship squads had graduated from the No. 2 State side, although this did not apply to John, who was only ever selected in the No. 1 team. It was also usual for two clubs to tour the Eastern States in August, where three or four games against local league and/or combined district teams would be played over a two week period. The WANFL fixtures were arranged so the teams on tour started the season a week earlier so they could be absent for a weekend in August without disrupting the fixtures. In 1959, East Fremantle toured the Eastern States, combining football with sightseeing, with the cost of the trip coming to £3600. Thoughts of injury risk, staleness or overload were never considered and, indeed, the clubs spent a lot of time fund-raising for them. The players relished the chance to see other parts of the country and to play against Victorian, Tasmanian and South Australian sides despite the WANFL finals only being a month away. In the 1950s winning a flag was important, but there was still room for plenty of social life.

The football clubs were the hub of the district in the 1950s and much community socialising had a football link, particularly after the War when many commodities remained in short supply. There were club picnics – usually advertised with the incentive of hot water being supplied – annual reunions, weekend country trips and lots of Saturday night cabaret dances to keep club supporters entertained. Perhaps best of all and most fondly remembered were the pleasant Sunday mornings, which all clubs indulged in. The players would usually meet at the club around 9am on the Sunday after a match, perhaps jog a few laps of the oval and have a rub down and shower before retiring to the social premises for a sing-along and the traditional drinking of the 18 gallon keg, which was part and parcel of the proceedings.

John has great memories of these mornings (even as a teetotaler), as the club spirit engendered was enormous. Every club had its wags and at South, Don Wares and Jack Murray, who gave great service as players in the '40s and '50s, were often the catalysts for 'extending' the drinking hours beyond those permitted by the Licensing Court. For football clubs, liquor licensing laws were restrictive and John recalls kegs often being loaded onto the back of a truck and driven to a bush location, where the revelry would continue. On the rare occasions when the keg remained unfinished, it would simply be buried in the bush for consumption at a later date!

In the early 1950s, before Old Easts left Fremantle Oval and moved to East Fremantle Oval (in 1953), it was not uncommon for the players of both clubs to join up for Sunday morning drinks, especially if one had finished their keg earlier than the other! While matches were littered with physical clashes and no quarter was expected or given during a game, there was great mutual respect for your opponents and any on-field disputes or differences of opinion were quickly settled over a post-match beer. Sadly, this is no longer the case today, as teams rarely mix with their opponents after a match – an unfortunate and probably unnecessary side-effect of the evolution of the game into the full professionalism of the AFL.

Indeed, playing the game in the 1950s was very much part-time and if football couldn't be fitted around work, then players usually retired, missed games, or stepped down from league ranks to lower competitions. Players such as 1957 Sandover medallist Jack Clarke, East Fremantle great ruckman of the 1950s, and Don Langdon, East Perth classy centre-half-forward of the late 1950s and '60s, were farmers travelling from the country each week to play and perhaps train on a Thursday night. However, when seeding or harvesting had to be done, they would miss games, as their work and livelihood came first. In 1959 Clarke was named WA captain for an interstate tour, but missed the trip because it was seeding time and he was needed on the family farm. In the field of butchering, as John discovered early in the '50s when he started his apprenticeship, the work was hard and you were on your feet all day, usually from 7am to 6pm. For some, the work demands and pressures of running their own shops became too much, as was the case with Tony Bellos and Jim Washbourne, both East Perth premiership players in the 1950s, who retired young because of their business demands. Virtually all players worked on a Saturday morning before playing in the afternoon, a stark contrast to the match day preparation of players in the current era, where playing in the AFL now equates to going to work!

For John, his match preparation began the night before by going to bed around 7.30pm after starting work at 5am, which meant a 4am rise for breakfast. After a full day's work in the butcher's shop, Doris would serve up a hearty dinner and it was off to bed early. This was just another sacrifice that had to be made and, while his mates often tried to cajole him into going out on a Friday night, John never went; he did, however, lend them his car, which was often seen parked near the Fremantle Monument late of an evening. The club and his parents were often informed of this, but they knew he was fast asleep at home.

Saturday mornings were no different, with a 5am start. Despite his South allegiances, Wally Doust would offer John a few extra shillings to start early on a Saturday, not for one moment ever considering he might 'wear out' South's star player for the afternoon game. After a busy seven hours in the shop, John would have a light lunch which Doris had on the table waiting for him – generally salad and bread and butter as he could never stomach the traditional steak and eggs. His boots were polished and his bag packed, as this was the match-day contribution of brother Bill and sister Diane. There wasn't much time to spare as league games started at 2.45pm, coming back to 2.30pm in 1958.

~

The 1950s saw many great players put their mark on the game. Four ruckmen won Sandover Medals – Merv McIntosh, Graham Farmer, Brian Foley and Clarke – with McIntosh (1953-54) and Farmer (1956-57) winning two each. Of the other medallists, three were rovers (Jim Conway 1950, Steve Marsh 1952 and John in 1955) with centre-half-back Fred Buttsworth (1951) and ruck-rover Ted Kilmurray (1958) winning the others. Wingman Frank Allen (1950) joined them in 1997 when retrospective medals were awarded to players who had missed out on a countback. The grand finals were also close, hard-fought tussles, apart from 1953 and '54 when South easily beat West Perth (59 points) and East Fremantle (78 points). The next highest winning margin was 23 points (East Perth defeating Subiaco in 1959) and four grand finals were decided by a goal or less (1950, '51, '55, '58), with Perth's great fight-back in 1955 to triumph over Old Easts by two points perhaps the best of the decade.

For John, three players stood out – Marsh, Farmer and Ted Whitten – and, for various reasons, he regards these players as the best of this era. Marsh, his boyhood idol, is not surprisingly regarded as the best he played with, although, because of different circumstances, they only played together in 18 games[6]. According to John – *"Steve had it all; fearless courage, hardness and great skill and was always at his best in big matches when the game was in the balance. He was a fine leader, both at South as captain in 1956 and as East Fremantle captain-coach in 1957-58"*. Polly Farmer is John's choice as the best WA player of the 1950s, partly because of *"the great influence he wielded over the game with his handball"*. While he was an outstanding player in his own right, he revolutionised the game with his innovative use of this skill *"to put players 10-20 metres in the clear, establishing handball as an attacking weapon, rather than a disposal of last resort. His skill and expertise in ruck play was instrumental in forging the careers of players who benefited from the possessions he gave them"*. East Perth small men such as Kevin McGill and Paul Seal, to name but two, enjoyed feeding off Farmer's ruck dominance as the Royals reigned supreme in the last half of the decade.

The player John regards as the best of the era – and the best he has seen – was Victoria's Mr Football, the late Whitten. John first saw him when South played (and beat) Footscray in 1953 in an end of season match at Subiaco Oval and then in State games in '57 and '59. Playing at centre-half-forward, Whitten won the Simpson Medal against WA in '57, with John not

---

6. Steve Marsh stood out of football in the first half of 1955 in order to receive his Provident Fund money and in 1956 John's knee injury restricted him to just nine games. In 1957 Marsh left South to coach East Fremantle and never played for the Bulldogs again.

playing, but making his debut as a newspaper columnist and commenting that *"... Whitten is the finest footballer I have seen. He could play any of the key positions, but was just as good when playing on the ball as a ruck-rover, such was his versatility"*. His skills were second to none, both as an aerialist and for gathering and disposing of loose balls on the ground but, above all, what John has as his lasting impression of Whitten was his toughness – *"He shirked nothing and thrived on physical confrontation as a method of intimidating his opponents"*.

Mixed with his physical approach was a generous dash of arrogance and a deep passion for the game that would later translate to his unabashed love for State football and the 'Big V'. He was also 'a rascal', with a fine sense of humour and a flair for practical jokes. In the 1959 game in Melbourne when WA were annihilated by almost 30 goals, John remembers that Whitten was at his passionate, arrogant and cheeky best as he made sure his rivals were kept up to date with the score and their own shortcomings. Umpires were not immune from being informed about their mistakes, which probably cost Whitten a Brownlow Medal, a tie for third in 1959 being his best result over 20 seasons (1951-70). It was Whitten's attitude that John (grudgingly) respected, as well as his talent as a player – they would later become good friends and work together in 1984 when John coached an Australian side which toured Ireland for a series of Gaelic football (hybrid rules) games against the Irish national team.

The 1960s

Chapter 8
Battling on

John, remembering when he discarded his (new) knee brace early in 1960:

> "... it's going to take me six months to break this in, so either I'm going to go under or get through...".

After being named South's new coach, one of the first things Marty McDonnell did was visit John at the Maypole butcher shop in High Street. Being aware that John had not been contacted by any club officials about the coaching position, he expected a hostile reception. But John, while a little cool, shook hands and offered his congratulations and pulled up a chair to sit down and listen to what the new coach had to say. While disappointed at not being re-appointed coach, John had no axe to grind with McDonnell, but the way the decision was handled saw him lose respect for the men running the club, which was never regained – *"Once again, it reinforced my belief that, whatever the cost, being open and honest is vitally important, especially when the news is bad. Otherwise bridges are burnt too easily and friendships put at risk, leaving people walking away bitter"*.

In reality, John was not surprised South made a change (although he was keen to carry on), because he appreciated his current limitations as a coach. If South had come to him and expressed the view that a change was needed, he probably would have agreed. But the lack of communication from the committee was poor club politics and shabby treatment of their best player. McDonnell badly wanted John to play with South in 1960. He was well aware of his ability and reasoned that the developing team could ill-afford to lose a player of John's calibre. While he expected John might want to leave after being overlooked as coach, he emphasised that he was a priority player. He wanted him as a leader on the ground, setting an example for the rest to follow and told John he had plenty of time to pursue coaching in the future, as he was still only 21 years of age. He outlined his plans for improving the side, which included increasing training from two to three nights a week, as well as more man-on-man drills and impressed John sufficiently with his football knowledge that, when the meeting broke up, he committed himself to play with the Bulldogs.

~

For pre-season training, fitness was again strongly emphasised as a key ingredient by the new coach, who introduced a regime of long distance running, the likes of which not even John had attempted before. McDonnell recruited former armed forces PT instructor Colin Junner, who used to run several miles from home to Fremantle Oval for training and run up to an hour with the players, before running home again! After one particularly arduous run, John quipped to McDonnell that he felt more like a racehorse being set for the Perth Cup than a footballer, adding that he thought he could run a place! For once, John reined in his own personal programme, such were the demands of club training.

South was buoyed by the return of rover Barry White after a season's absence and saw promise in some new recruits, notably local brothers Tom and George Grljusich. On the debit side, they lost Tony Parentich and Eric Grose, who had retired. Veteran John Colgan was elected captain by the players, with John his deputy. South's practice match form was indifferent and, while they were expected to improve on the previous year's standing, they weren't seen as likely premiership contenders. East Perth was again well fancied, while West Perth, who had also recruited a former Footscray player in Arthur Olliver as coach, was tipped as the big improvers. South was due to tour later in the year, along with East Perth, so the two clubs opened the season on April 9 at Perth Oval, a week before the other six clubs.

John began the game wearing a new knee brace recently received from America but, because he didn't have a chance to break it in, it proved stiff and badly irritated the skin around his knee to the extent that it restricted his movements. At half-time he ripped the brace off, throwing it to South head trainer Tommy Bottrell, saying *"... it's going to take me six months to break this in, so either I'm going to go under or get through..."*. He got Bottrell to wrap tape around the knee and went out for the second half – the first time in four years he had played without a brace. His second half was better than his first, getting on top of Tony Bellos in the centre as South powered to a comfortable (and surprising) 29 point victory. It was the last time he wore the brace [7] in a game, deciding there and then (at the scene of the 1956 'crime') that he would ride his luck; he enjoyed the feeling of 'freedom' in his left leg, which had been missing since 1956.

Two further wins followed, with John in good form in the centre to put the club in a buoyant mood. Their new social premises, the Griff John Pavilion, was also nearly complete. They stretched their winning streak by accounting for Perth at Lathlain Park to remain the only unbeaten side, but the win was soured by John being reported on charges of kicking, abusive language and disputing the umpire's decision. This was only the second time (and the last) that John had been reported and he suffered suspension for the first (and only) time in his career, something he is not proud about as *"I was always a ball player"*. He received three weeks after being found guilty of kicking Perth's Roy Harper, which he strenuously denied, although he did admit to thinking about it. He remembers accidentally collecting big Perth ruckman Reg Zeuner in the windpipe with an elbow just before the incident with Harper, who probably attempted to 'square up', which provoked the confrontation. With respect to the kicking charge, the evidence of central umpire Ray Montgomery was corroborated by a boundary and

---

7. The brace was kept by Tommy Bottrell in his kit for some time, before passing it to the boot studder for safe keeping. It remained as a club 'heirloom' until the late 1980s when it disappeared from the boot of Eileen Bond's car during a clean up at the clubrooms. In 2003, former East Fremantle player Michael Regan contacted John, telling him he had the brace, but when John viewed it, it was clearly not the one he had used, despite it bearing his signature!

reserve umpire, so he was resigned to 'getting time' as the hearing went on. He was cautioned for disputing umpire Montgomery's decision, while the abusive language charge was dropped.

To make matters worse, the team's No. 1 ruckman Jack Sumich was also suspended for two weeks on a kicking charge, so the side was without two stars. Their absence was noticeable and South was lucky to scramble a draw against East Perth, before losing their first game, to Swans at Bassendean. However, a two point victory over West Perth gave them five wins and a draw from the first seven matches, putting them on top of the ladder. McDonnell (and the South committee) was well satisfied and a return to the golden era was being enthusiastically mooted as they settled into the newly-opened social premises.

In the Foundation Day derby (his second game back), John was forced off the ground in the third quarter with a strained hamstring; an injury that kept him out of football for five weeks, including the State game in Perth against Victoria. Although he was named in the State squad, he broke down at training and was forced out, as had been the case in 1956. This was particularly frustrating for John, as it was the first opportunity for WA to have a crack at the Vics since the Melbourne debacle. However, despite a spirited opening, WA was again outclassed, losing by 34 points in a game where, probably for the first time, both teams were captained by players having the same name [8]!

John returned for South's clash with West Perth after a searching fitness test at Thursday's training where McDonnell had him competing man-on-man for over half an hour. However, his form was patchy, which matched that of the team as South hit a slump, losing four from five games. The season's third derby had Fremantle buzzing, not least because rumours swept town on Friday that John had severed a finger at work and had been rushed to hospital! The club happily denied the rumours, but he had a poor game anyway – made worse by a recurrence of his hamstring injury which sidelined him for another four matches, while South at least regained some form and cemented a top four position by winning three of those fixtures. John was back for the round 20 encounter with West Perth at Fremantle, a game that would probably decide which of the two teams would grab the double chance. This was John Gerovich's 100th league match, with John coming up for his 77th despite getting a slight head start on his team-mate back in 1955.

It was a crackerjack game as both sides swapped the ascendancy early, but South clawed to a 19 point lead at three-quarter-time before a pulsating last quarter. In the final minute, Gerovich, who had kicked 9.4, had a shot for goal from deep in a pocket, but failed to register, leaving the scores tied. Unfortunately for South, a draw was good enough for West Perth to score a top two finish, leaving South third, regardless of the results of the final round of matches. The only interest then centred on whether Gerovich could kick another nine goals against Claremont to reach the century for the first time. He achieved this feat with comparative ease, bagging 10.3 to finish the qualifying rounds with 101 goals and 77 points, giving him a conversion rate of only 57%. However, this was typical of the enigmatic Gerovich throughout his career. John bagged six goals as he regained some form in South's 113 point demolition of Claremont as the Bulldogs warmed up for their first finals game in four years.

---

8. East Fremantle ruckman Jack Clarke captained WA and Essendon centreman Jack Clarke captained the Victorians.

Their opponents were Old Easts, who had been easily beaten in the last qualifying fixture by East Perth and were likely to be missing a few regulars through injury. However, South had Gerovich in doubt with a thigh strain but, after beating Old Easts in five of their past six encounters, were warm favourites. South led by 14 points at quarter-time, but it was obvious Gerovich was unfit and unable to run at any speed. He played through to half-time, but South was virtually playing with 17 men and finished the half 25 points down. South bridged the gap to 12 points, but eventually went down by 17 points as Old Easts coach Steve Marsh had ruckman Jack Clarke defending stoutly a kick behind the play. John kicked two goals, but didn't have anywhere near his usual influence on the match. On McDonnell's advice, he had taken the morning off work to be well-rested for the game, but the change in routine backfired. Being accustomed to waking at 4am, John found that he couldn't sleep in and tossed and turned before rising about 7 o'clock. Then, without work to distract him, he burnt up nervous energy thinking about the game and he has no doubt this contributed to his poor display. This was the first and last time he would break his match day routine and it's a point he has emphasised to players regularly over many years as a coach – *"Maintain your regular routine wherever possible, as it's easy to play the game in your head before it starts, when you have time on your hands"*.

It was a disappointing finish to what had been a good season – 13 wins and two draws for a team still in the rebuilding mode – and the results vindicated the appointment of McDonnell as coach. For John though, it was a disappointing, frustrating year as he managed only 12 matches, losing seven to hamstring strains (which also cost him a State guernsey) and three to suspension. He finished well down in the Walker Medal count (won by Sumich) and polled the lowest total of Sandover Medal votes in his career – two, although, once suspended, the umpires may have decided against awarding him votes. The medal was won for the third time by Graham Farmer, continuing the success of ruckmen.

In the remaining finals, West Perth had the better of East Perth in the second semi and repeated the dose two weeks later to win its first flag since 1951, with Foley having the better of Farmer and winning the Simpson Medal. In late October, South left for its Eastern States trip, which included a visit to Flemington for the Melbourne Cup. John has vivid memories of being one of the 102,000 people there to see the mighty *Tulloch*, the 3/1 favourite, beaten into seventh place by the 50/1 long shot *Hi Jinx* in the centenary running of Australia's most famous horse race.

~

John threw himself into summer training for 1961, determined to have a better season. When club training began in the new year, it was again a spartan endurance programme of long distance running, but he relished the hard work and his legs adapted well. In February he was named captain, the first South skipper to be appointed by the committee, rather than elected by the players. The committee felt the time was right for a change, amending the club's constitution to give the board of management this power, rather than leaving it with the players. The change was perhaps prompted by the increasing professionalism of the game; player payments were escalating and it's likely the committee reasoned that if the club had to pay the players more to play, then it should have the power to appoint its on-field leaders. Colgan, in his last season, was appointed John's deputy, meaning the pair had swapped positions.

Chapter 8 – Battling on

While making the 1960 finals had left the club optimistic about '61, South had lost some good players, especially Sumich, who had gone to London to study engineering on a university scholarship. Finding a replacement proved difficult, with rival clubs boasting big ruckmen of the calibre of Farmer (East Perth), Clarke (East Fremantle), Foley (West Perth) and Keith Slater (Swan Districts). The season opened on April 15 with a derby at East Fremantle Oval, but Clarke gave the Old Easts small men an armchair ride and South trailed all game to lose by 48 points. The opening round was notable for a qualifying round attendance record of 36,396 people watching the four games. Against Subiaco the next week, John scored five goals and Gerovich nine to account for 14 of the team's 19 goals. In *The Sunday Times* the next day, Subiaco's new coach, former Fitzroy player Dan Murray, lamented that *"... we couldn't do anything about Todd and Gerovich..."*.

The following Tuesday was Anzac Day and the WANFL had organised a State trial game – this was an ANFC championship year, to be played in Brisbane in July. John captained one side and played in Subiaco colours against a team in Perth colours, skippered by Laurie Kettlewell. Selection in the carnival side provided a strong incentive for good early season form; certainly John was keen to play in Brisbane and did his chances no harm by being named his side's best player. Two months later, despite missing two recent games with an ankle injury (*"... if it wasn't my knee, then it was something else..."*), he was selected in the WA squad. This carnival ranks as John's greatest playing highlight as WA won a keenly-fought championship, triumphing over the Vics to win the national title for the first time in 40 years and breaking a run of 10 consecutive Victorian carnival victories, stretching back to 1924.

~

In the carnival lead up, WANFL president Pat Rodriguez stoked the WA fires by suggesting a loss in Brisbane might see the State relegated to the second division with the minor football States of New South Wales, Queensland and the ACT, as well as the VFA. He backed coach Jack Sheedy's request for the early naming of a squad, with a group of 30 named a month before the carnival. John and team-mates Colgan, Gerovich and Tom Grljusich were in the squad and Sheedy declared that no 'crocks' would be taken to Brisbane. This point was reinforced by chairman of selectors Frank Fuhrmann, who bluntly told the group – *"I have to emphasise the need for physical fitness. These are obligations to your mates and coach"*. Sheedy also advised the players to take two pairs of boots to Brisbane in case it was wet!

On the Wednesday before the team's departure, Colgan, who had been named captain, reluctantly stood down because of injury but, after an appeal by South, the veteran was able to accompany the team as the official runner. Haydn Bunton (Jnr) was elevated to the captaincy, with John vice-captain. The side contained names such as Farmer, Clarke, Gerovich, Slater, Mal Atwell, Ray Gabelich, Denis Marshall, Les Mumme, Con Regan, Norm Rogers and Ray Sorrell and was regarded as a well-balanced combination. The surprise selections were John Turnbull, at 19 the 'baby' of the side and in only his first season of league football with Swans, and Don Williams, the former Melbourne player who had represented Victoria at the 1958 carnival and was now playing strongly for West Perth at centre-half-forward. He had not been named in the initial squad, but clinched his place with a brilliant game on the previous Saturday. With an open selection policy, East Fremantle and Claremont had five players in the team, Swans and East Perth four, West Perth three, South two and Subiaco one, with Perth not having a representative as Neville Beard withdrew with injury. The Victorians continued their restricted selection policy of no more than three players from any one team, but still appeared a formidable side, captained by Ron Barassi, with Ted Whitten his deputy.

The opening game was a brutal encounter between Victoria and South Australia, which John believes played an important part in WA's victory. In 1960, South Australia had inflicted Victoria's worst defeat in interstate football, beating them by 69 points at the Adelaide Oval, so the Vics were keen to square the ledger, while the Croweaters wanted to repeat the dose – the feeling between the sides was apparent early in the game. SA captain Neil Kerley weighed in with some ferocious tackles and bumps, particularly on the smaller Victorian players, so the Vics responded in kind, principally through Barassi and Whitten and, for three quarters, the two sides pounded each other relentlessly. The small 'Gabba ground contributed to the carnage, as there were few open spaces to be found. After leading by three points at the last change, the Vics wore down the Croweaters to win by 58 points. However, Victoria had been 'softened up' by Kerley and his gallant team and John has no doubt this fiery encounter took its toll when WA played them to decide the championship.

WA opened its campaign by overwhelming Tasmania by 111 points, with Farmer dominating the ruck, giving Bunton a free ride at ground level. John played on a wing, as Sorrell was preferred in the centre, and both were in great form as Tassie struggled to match the speed and skill of the Sandgropers.

The WA-SA game was regarded as one of the finest interstate matches ever played. The Croweaters, with Kerley again throwing his weight around, led by 21 points after a seven goal first quarter, but while WA controlled the second term, they kicked a wasteful 3.12, to be nine points in arrears at half-time. However, in the third term, with Mumme dangerous around the goals, John on top of John Cahill on a wing and big Gabelich playing with great vigour in the ruck, WA held SA to just one goal while adding six themselves to lead by 21 points. All the momentum was with the Sandgropers, but Kerley was not finished and he inspired his team to a two point victory. In the WA rooms SA coach Fos Williams remarked – *"... it was a tragedy this match was played in Brisbane and not in Adelaide or Perth where it would have drawn a record crowd. It's one of the greatest games I've seen and I must pay tribute to the manner in which it was played"*. Victorian coach Len Smith also described it as one of the best games he had been privileged to see. The narrow loss left WA with the task of beating Victoria to win the championship. The Vics had accounted for Tasmania by 61 points, which meant that if SA beat Tasmania, the three major States would finish with two wins each if WA downed Victoria, leaving percentages to decide the winner.

WA loosened up with some swimming and jogging at Surfer's Paradise as they prepared to tackle the Vics, who they had not beaten since 1948. Early estimates suggested a margin of two goals or more would be necessary for WA to wrest the title. WA's massive win over Tassie gave it a healthy percentage, almost matching Victoria's, who had recorded victories by about 60 points in each game. SA, after torrid encounters with Victoria and WA, was a weary team and only fell over the line against Tasmania by seven points, leaving them with a percentage of only 86.2. WA's percentage was 162.2 and Victoria's 166.5, so the scene was set for a battle royal to decide the carnival.

On a wintry Brisbane afternoon only 7500 people saw the game, which proved to be one of the finest interstate matches ever played. The 'needle' began before the first bounce as Bunton pulled off a master-stroke of gamesmanship over Barassi as he 'conned' him with the coin toss, which left the Vics fuming. There was a strong breeze blowing and as the WA team prepared to run onto the ground, John remembers Bunton asking Sheedy *"... Jack, do you want to kick with the wind first up?"*. Sheedy had no hesitation in answering in the affirmative, to which Bunton replied *"... righto, I'll fix it"*. Sheedy guessed what Bunton was going to do and attempted a mild protest, but the team was out of the rooms. John had a fair idea of what Bunton was planning and watched approvingly as he dashed away from the coin toss indicating that WA would kick with the wind while the coin was still in the air! A dumbfounded Barassi was left to pick up the coin before protesting vigorously to the umpire[9], but it was to no avail as players from both sides were already moving to their positions. However, WA failed to take full advantage of their captain's skulduggery as they kicked 4.6, with the Vics on target with four straight goals. At half-time, the game and the championship appeared lost as Victoria then kicked seven goals to one to lead by 31 points.

Sheedy exhorted his players to lift and give the Vics no easy kicks, as their small brigade led by Allen Aylett had wreaked havoc. WA had plenty of rugged individuals who rose to Sheedy's demand and, in a tough, hard-hitting third quarter, the likes of Atwell, Rogers, Gabelich, Williams and Dennis Barron wrested the initiative back. With well-applied vigour they created openings on the small ground for John, Bunton, Mumme, Sorrell and Derek Chadwick as WA posted six goals to one to finish just three points down. The Vics had the breeze in the last quarter and looked well placed to win their 11th straight championship but, buoyed by the fight-back, Sheedy went for broke and put Gabelich into the ruck. His vigorous attacks on the ball (and the man) wore down the tiring Vics, and WA capitalised with three goals to take an early lead, which they tenaciously clung to.

With five minutes remaining, WA led by three points, but with percentages set to decide the carnival victors, the margin didn't appear sufficient. With just two minutes left, rover Joe Fanchi[10] immortalised himself into the annals of WA football when he calmly put through a goal to take the margin to nine points. After a frenetic final minute, the game finished with Williams taking a spectacular mark in the centre. WA's percentage was calculated at 143.7, while the Vics was 138.9. It was Fanchi's score that gave WA the championship, as a three point margin would have seen Victoria ahead by 0.4%, although a point on his kick would have been enough; a four point win would have given WA the title by 0.5%.

There were joyous scenes in the WA rooms and no-one was more delighted than Rodriguez, who was also the ANFC president. For John, it was his playing career highlight – it was one that brought special memories and forged strong bonds between the WA players despite their club allegiances. The victory celebration dinner that night also feted Gabelich who won the Simpson Medal for his great display and was selected in the All Australian team, along with John, Clarke, Farmer and Sorrell. The next morning saw the weary team start a 14 hour trip

---

9. In this era, umpires did not witness the coin toss, as the sportsmanship of the captains was relied upon. However, this incident probably triggered a change as the umpires soon became involved in the toss, perhaps because Ted Whitten reportedly tried this ploy back in Melbourne in Footscray matches.
10. He earned the epithet 'Golden boot' for his carnival-winning goal.

back to Perth, stopping at Adelaide, then Cook on the Nullarbor and a further unplanned stop at Kalgoorlie to refuel as 110mph headwinds slowed their journey.

More than 600 people greeted the plane as it touched down on the Goldfields, giving the players a taste of what was to come at Perth Airport. When the plane finally landed at 8.15pm, an estimated 6000 people mobbed the team in a reception that John remembers as *"simply awesome"*. Barriers set up to keep the well-wishers away from the arrival gates were trampled as the players were showered with confetti, with parents thrusting their children at them as they strived to get the first autographs from the championship-winning team. The sheer delight of the crowd left an indelible mark on John; he knew this was what it was like to win a premiership and he thoroughly enjoyed the moment.

Later in the week, the Perth Lord Mayor, Sir Harry Howard, hosted a civic reception for the national champions after a victory motorcade through the city, when thousands of people lined the streets. The players were presented with a commemorative medal to honour their achievement in recording only WA's second carnival victory. It was a marvellous two weeks for John, who was thrilled to make the All Australian team and beat the Vics, having been on the receiving end of the 178 point drubbing in 1959. It was sweet revenge and perfectly matched one of his favourite maxims in football – *"Don't get angry, get even"*. Wresting the title of national champions from the Vics went a long way towards balancing the ledger.

With Jack Sheedy (driving) and Haydn Bunton in the victory parade in Perth following the 1961 Australian Championship win.

Returning to work and South after the carnival was not easy; John was carrying a bruised chest and a badly corked leg and he failed to recover in time to play in the derby the next weekend. Before the carnival, South had struggled and dropped out of finals contention. Going down to Old Easts by 29 points then put them on the bottom of the ladder as Perth drew with Swans to move up to seventh. With six games remaining, it was a battle with the Demons to see who would claim the wooden spoon. Apart from the under-age competition during the War years, South had not finished last since 1936 and the club was desperate to avoid a poor finish. However, it was not to be, as the Bulldogs managed just one more win.

John recovered to play in all games, and displayed consistently good form to eventually win his third Walker Medal, polling 70 votes to win from Tom Grljusich on 42 and Gerovich on 34. In the Sandover Medal he polled 12 votes, 10 behind the winners, Perth's Beard and Old Easts Sorrell, who lost on a countback, but received his medal 36 years later[11]. John was not fancied for the medal as most pundits regarded his season as consistent rather than spectacular, which he probably agreed with. Winning the Walker Medal rewarded him with a holiday, courtesy of long-time Bulldogs supporter George Bukevich, who had promised the winner a week's stay at any WA hotel. On learning that John was to be married early in 1962, he promptly doubled the prize to make it accommodation for two!

John was also given a presentation from the club to mark his 100th game, which was acknowledged on July 8, in round 13 against Perth. However, in actual fact this was his 90th game, as an error had been made in 1960 when he played 12 games taking his tally to 79, but in the annual report this was incorrectly recorded as 89. This misprint was carried over to future years and the mistake never corrected, which helps explain the discrepancy in John's total games of league football, which has been reported as high as 146 by some club and newspaper sources.

In the 1961 finals, Subiaco beat East Fremantle (now coached by Clarke[12]) and East Perth, who had only lost two games, easily accounted for Swans by eight goals. John has little doubt that Bunton and his Swans team 'closed up shop' on East Perth in this match, saving their best tactics for the grand final, as they probably couldn't have beaten the Royals twice. Swans beat Subiaco in the preliminary final, coming from 21 points down at the last change to win by 16 points, with a young Bill Walker kicking four goals. They went into their first open competition grand final since entering the league in 1934 as rank outsiders, given the ease of East Perth's second semi win and their dominance over the year. However, in what *The Sunday Times* referred to as *"the greatest upset in WA football history"*, the 1960 wooden spooners held an early lead all game, winning their first premiership by 24 points. The sheer joy of victory for the long-suffering Swans supporters reminded John of the Brisbane triumph and he was more than a little envious of Bunton, who experienced both. This was the first of

---

11. In 1997 the countback system was dropped and medals were awarded retrospectively to seven players who had lost in previous years by polling less 'first' votes.
12. Steve Marsh resigned as coach after round 20 when the club failed to back him in a dispute over the umpiring of Ray Montgomery against Swans. Marsh felt Montgomery was being vindictive towards him and asked the club to lodge a complaint with the WANFL, but when this was refused he stepped down from the coaching position two weeks before the finals.

a hat trick of premierships for Swans, but after that it would be 19 long years before John was the coach to again provide their supporters with that special feeling.

~

The end of 1961 proved a busy and eventful time for John, with an approaching marriage in January after becoming engaged to Meryl Booth towards the end of the season. The couple had known each other for several years as Meryl worked in Fremantle and lived nearby in Hampton Road. For their honeymoon they holidayed at Yallingup, in the South West, to take advantage of John's Walker Medal prize. He was also asked by representatives of the Perth Football Club to apply for the position of playing-coach for 1962; the job had become vacant after the sacking of Bob Miller midway through the 1961 season, with Dick Walker filling in as playing coach. After giving the idea some consideration, he decided against it and declared that he would play for South, saying – *"I have been well treated by South Fremantle and hope the side will rise next year. Every side has its lean period and I feel ours is at an end"*. More than 20 years later he would again be sought by Perth to coach, but would also decline, amid some controversy.

In this period, John was spending some time with East Fremantle backman Don Ainsworth, who had suffered a knee injury early in 1961, forcing him out for the year. With his successful return to playing after his own knee problems, John was the acknowledged expert on these injuries and many players in this era who suffered similar injuries sought his advice, which he was only too pleased to give. The now-unused American knee brace was offered to Ainsworth while he attempted to build up his leg muscles with plenty of beach work and cycling.

In the midst of all this, John had been offered the chance to manage the butcher's shop at Rottnest Island, a small holiday resort 20km off the coast from Fremantle. The opportunity excited him and Meryl, but they would need to live on the island and how this could fit in with training and playing league football he didn't know. Returning by boat from Rottnest was a one or two hour trip, depending on ocean conditions, and by air it was 20 minutes, but there was no airport close to Fremantle, so getting to training regularly looked difficult. He was captain of the side and therefore a member of the match committee, so attending Thursday night selection meetings loomed as a further problem. After discussions with McDonnell, he decided to take the job until Easter, which would give him time to assess the impact on his football and see how he liked it. McDonnell and the club gave their blessing by re-appointing John as captain despite his impending absence from most training sessions.

~

Stung by their last-place finish in 1961, South embarked on an Australia-wide recruiting campaign, with an experienced ruckman high on their list. They turned up Glen Bow, who had played 25 games for Geelong, as their No. 1 recruit and welcomed to league ranks Ross Bowe, a brother of Ron. In addition, Murray MacDonald, Archie McDonald and John McCormack had all returned after absences due to work and/or injury. These players, along with John, Gary Scott, Ron Doig, John Brindley, Don Byfield, Tom Grljusich, Colin Beard, Ashley August, Stan Badham, Frank Johnson, Fred Seinor and Keith Smith, would all have consistent seasons. They offset the loss of Don Stewart, Barry White, Charlie Tyson, Parentich and Colgan, who had all retired after long and distinguished careers. Swans were early favourites for the flag, retaining virtually all their premiership players, but after contesting the last six grand finals (winning three), East Perth were considered to be on the slide, particularly as Farmer had finally been lured to Victoria to play with Geelong.

After losing first-up to Perth, South won its next three games, with John in good form in the centre, being voted best-afield against Claremont [13] and winning a hard-fought contest with Sorrell in the derby, but was a little quiet against Subiaco. In an early sign of the times, he was forced to take medication to play in this game as he suffered sea-sickness crossing from Rottnest to Fremantle on the Saturday morning. Normally he would fly back to the mainland, but on this day he was forced to take the ferry. John freely admits to being a poor traveller and passionately dislikes boats and planes, often breaking out in a cold sweat, but particularly when conditions are a little rough. Despite being a keen fisherman, he has never owned a boat and to this day avoids travelling by sea or air whenever possible!

The next week South played the reigning premiers at Bassendean and were completely outclassed, losing by 78 points. It was in this game that Bunton, playing as a loose man a kick behind the play, was reported to have had 80 kicks, although this cannot be verified as statistics were not recorded as they are in current times. John remembers him getting *"a lot of it"*, but whether it was 80 kicks or not, remains a part of WA football folklore. South bounced back against West Perth to record a comfortable 38 point win, which set up a top of the table clash with East Perth to finish off the first round. In a game remembered as one of the finest played at Perth Oval, the sides traded goals in the first half; at one stage, 24 consecutive goals were scored without a point being registered. John was in scintillating touch in the centre, providing Gerovich with sufficient opportunities for him to return to form with eight goals. With their two stars firing, South wore the Royals down to win by 39 points and claim top spot on the ladder. In a remarkable turn-around, South had gone from bottom in 1961 to top in seven games, with five victories in the first round matching their total wins for the previous season. The club was in a buoyant mood, particularly as the side was getting consistent contributions from more of its players. There was no longer an unhealthy reliance on the form of John and Gerovich, as had been evident in past few seasons. The ruck brigade, the Achilles heel of the 1961 season, was in good shape with Bow, Seinor and Scott playing well. The only downside for South was that their captain was still stationed at Rottnest and, while his form had been good (he was running second in *The Daily News* Footballer of the Year Award), his appearances at training had been infrequent.

John was torn about whether to stay at Rottnest or return to live in Fremantle. As captain, he felt he wasn't meeting his obligations to the club by living and working on the island, which bothered him. Vice-captain Scott was deputising for him at selection meetings and acted as the link between the coach and committee and the players. On the other hand, he enjoyed running the shop and it represented a great business opportunity for the newlyweds. Keeping in shape wasn't a problem, as he had plenty of beach to run on and he had always been content to train alone. Most lunch times he could be found kicking the footy on the small, sandy oval or running on the beach at Thompson Bay. He enjoyed being removed from the hurly-burly life

---

13. This was his 100th league game, almost exactly seven years to the day since his league debut.

in Fremantle as a star footballer, especially one who had injury problems, as literally *"every man and his dog"* enquired about his knee. Although his left knee had not cost him any games in the past few seasons, it was always the first thing people asked about and he grew tired of this. He still felt he was on borrowed time, but didn't need to be reminded of this by everyone he met. Mentally, he felt refreshed by the change of routine and decided to stay on the island for the rest of the season, although the prospect of boat trips back and forth almost caused a change of heart!

In May John caused a minor sensation by withdrawing from the State squad selected for Eastern States' games against Victoria and South Australia. In *The West Australian* he explained – *"... it would have been difficult to find someone to take charge of the business; I haven't been able to train regularly with South Fremantle because of my work and I would have missed State training for the same reason"*. He continued – *"... I'm married and this means responsibilities that didn't exist before. I have to take the long range view of things"*. However, chairman of selectors Frank Fuhrmann was not having any of it. John had been a fixture in the State team since his 1955 debut, missing only two games when unfit, and Fuhrmann wasn't about to let him withdraw when he was fully fit and in good form. He phoned John at Rottnest to discuss the situation and later announced that the selectors would name an additional player, but emphasised that John would not be dropped from the squad and they hoped he could overcome his work difficulties.

South Fremantle's two stars of the late 1950s and early 1960s – John at training with John Gerovich (right).

In the opening game of the second round, John increased the pressure on himself to reconsider his decision by turning in a best on ground performance at centre against Perth, leading South to a 62 point win and McDonnell to remark it was the best individual performance he had seen in WA. Col Wilkinson, reporting in *The Sunday Times*, commented that his game *"... underlined the tragedy it will be if he doesn't play in Melbourne..."*. The next week John announced he had overcome his business problems and was available for selection. He was duly named vice-captain, with Bunton retaining the captaincy. Keen to beat the Vics for the first time in Melbourne, the side left Perth on Sunday, June 10 to allow time to train in Melbourne conditions for a week before the game. John was employed by *The West Australian* to file daily reports on the team's training and on the Thursday he commented that *"the WA players should not be afraid to use the drop kick on the MCG cricket pitches (it had been wet for a few days), but must concentrate as the mud makes the ball sticky"*.

After WA's surprise win in the national championships, there was a great deal of interest in the game and 64,000 fans turned out. The first quarter was a fast flowing affair and WA scored five goals to four to lead by five points before an eight goal second term by the Vics blew the game apart. The match then resembled the debacle of two years earlier as Victoria kicked 26 goals to nine to win by 102 points. John wasn't prominent and finished with a strained groin muscle in what was his 13th (and last) WA game; he was unfit for the SA match a week later, in which a tired, 'flu-ridden and depleted WA lost by 32 points at the Adelaide Oval.

At home, South faced second-placed Swans at Fremantle and, although John was in doubt, he declared himself fit; however, he was in obvious discomfort and kicked only with his right foot until forced from the field in the last term as the Bulldogs went down by 13 points. The next Wednesday, South head trainer Tommy Bottrell was dispatched to Rottnest (the first of many such trips) to treat John's leg with hot poultices and massage before putting him through some beach sprints. His intensive treatment did the trick and, although he told McDonnell he was fit to play, the coach insisted on his own fitness test; he had John go through a 20 minute full pace workout.

John was best-afield in South's 18 point win over West Perth and Ron Davidson's headline in *The Sunday Times* said it all – *"West had no counter for dynamic Todd"*, who again showed his penchant for wet weather football with a first class display in the centre. A six point win over East Perth saw South finish the second round on top and John shared a £35 jackpot provided by *The Daily News* for the player of the round, with Slater and Dick Walker.

The third round began poorly for South, with losses to Perth and East Fremantle causing a drop to third place. Many players, including John, were strangely out of form and the team was in a mini-slump, but the return State game against South Australia provided a chance to regroup. For the first time in eight seasons the State team ran out without John, who had missed selection (along with many others) after the earlier mauling by the Vics. His omission was a surprise and created plenty of press debate, but he had little to say, preferring to concentrate on his own form and South's prospects. Desperate to arrest the slide, McDonnell wanted every player at training – there were no exceptions as the team endured some searching sessions to shake them from their slump.

On the Thursday morning before the game, John was expecting to be picked up at Rottnest by committeemen Ron Warren and Noel Conigrave, who had volunteered to fetch John by boat for training. John remembers waking to a stormy day and, on surveying the seas from the island, remarked to Meryl that *"they won't get here"* as the white caps and wind were prominent to say the least. About 11am however, the duo turned up at the butcher's shop, much to John's surprise (and horror!), and announced that while the water was *"a bit rough"*, they had had no problems getting over from the mainland. The usual cold sweat John got before each boat trip was magnified about 10-fold as he followed them to the wharf, where their 16-foot runabout, with no canopy or cover, was tied up. He remembers scanning the waters for other boats, but there were none to be seen; even the fishing boats were taking a lay day. Realising that any protests would be futile, he positioned himself at the front where at least there were some hand rails to hold onto. A teenage boy asked for a ride back to Perth and the intrepid seamen were happy to oblige, so he climbed aboard and lay down in the back underneath a tarpaulin.

The next two hours were, in John's words, *"the worst of my life"* as the small boat was tossed like a rag doll by the heavy seas – *"I can vividly recall the boat pitching through the air as it hit the oncoming swell and then belly flopping into the trough between waves, while I was hanging on for grim life, absolutely saturated and with a heaving stomach. I was absolutely petrified and there were no lifejackets"*. Mid-way through the return crossing, Warren and Conigrave realised the trip was an *"unwise decision"*. Their lives, as well as the team's star player and a passenger were at risk, but there was nothing to do but carry on. Many times it was necessary to throttle down and float with the swell for fears they would somersault backwards as the rough seas pushed the little boat well north of Fremantle. They eventually put ashore near Scarborough, with the boat somehow still in one piece, but John was *"absolutely finished"* – *"My legs were like jelly and my knuckles white from the tension of gripping the hand rails"*. At training he had nothing left to give and trained poorly, a fact which didn't escape the eye of the coach, who kept him out for extra work (*"a real good flogging"*).

On the Saturday, South met Claremont in a game the Bulldogs needed to win; otherwise, they would drop to fourth spot. John was named in the centre and his clash with Denis Marshall was one of the pivotal contests. The 1962 annual report records that John *"seemed lethargic"* and Marshall had his measure. John puts it more bluntly – *"I felt terrible, it was one of my worst games and Denis gave me a real hiding"*. South managed a 30 point victory to break their run of outs and McDonnell later said that, unless John could travel by air, he would not be asked to train again with the team!

Losses to Swans and West Perth left South with the task of beating East Perth in the last round to guarantee a finals berth. Faced with a virtual fifth final, John paid for a friend to mind the butcher's shop and stayed in Fremantle to train with the team. On the Tuesday, McDonnell took the squad to the Fremantle golf course, where they played mini-golf and ran some fairways, but did little football training. John was impressed by the novel approach in the lead up to such an important game and made a mental note about not being afraid to gamble, especially when the stakes are high – an attitude that would later become prevalent in his coaching. Back at the club, the players enjoyed a feast of fish and chips – a far cry from the pasta dishes of the modern era – as McDonnell reminded them of the importance of Saturday's match.

The game started in sensational fashion, as Sheedy, who had retired as a player earlier in the season, led the Royals onto the ground for his 338th (and last) game. He stationed himself in a forward pocket and soon wielded an influence, helping East Perth skip away to a four goal lead. However, South rallied and by the change scores were tied, only to see the Royals 20 points clear at half-time before the game tightened up again. In the last quarter, South slowly got on top and a long drop-kick goal by John clinched a seven point win. From wooden spooners the previous year, South had made it into third spot and were to play West Perth in the semi-finals.

John again stayed on the mainland to prepare and the match was considered an even money bet; even though South had lost to the Cardinals by 31 points three weeks earlier, their win over East Perth was their best display for a month and West Perth had struggled in its last game. South opened with a flurry and, despite John, Badham and Bowe all receiving heavy knocks, they ended the first quarter 29 points up. The early physical approach paid dividends for West Perth in the second term as the Souths small men struggled, with John and Badham labouring with back injuries, and the Cardinals drew level. The second half was fairly tame and, despite leading by nine points at three-quarter-time, South failed to goal in the last term, eventually losing by 13 points. As in 1960, the game was a disappointing finish for the Bulldogs after playing some great footy, beating all sides except Swans and heading the table for much of the season. It was a game where John was again hampered by injury and, although he played it out, he exerted little influence. Swans proved too good for Old Easts in the second semi and again in the grand final, to win their second flag in a row.

~

The 1962 season equalled John's most complete season of his playing career; he had 21 games and missed just one match while on State duties in Melbourne, mirroring his debut season of 1955. In previous seasons, such a high tally of games would have guaranteed him the Walker Medal, some media awards and, at least, a high finish in the Sandover Medal. However, he finished only third in South's fairest and best, 13 votes behind the winner Bow and he polled only 12 votes in the Sandover, 10 behind Bunton. This was as many votes as he received in 1961 from 17 games; in 1959 he polled 11 votes from 12 games. The media awards were scooped by Bunton, who had enjoyed an outstanding season. John also missed State selection (when fit) for the first time in eight seasons, all of which confirmed that, by his own lofty standards, he'd had a relatively quiet season. While his best games were probably as good as they had been in the past, he had more 'average' games as he couldn't find the same consistency, both quarter to quarter and week to week. There is little doubt that his decision to live at Rottnest contributed to his season and, while missing training may have freshened him up each week, the lack of 'real' football training with the team took its toll and his ball handling skills suffered. Kicking the ball around by himself or with a mate on the small Rottnest oval simply wasn't enough to compensate for the group training he missed.

In addition, John felt that he and his left knee, had *"just about run their race"* and his absences from training made him feel like a stranger at the club when he stayed on the mainland in the weeks leading up to the finals. As captain, he knew this was unsatisfactory for both the club and himself and shouldn't continue and, despite not missing any games in recent seasons, *"I felt my time was almost up. My knee was getting worse with each season and took longer to come up after a game"*. Without an intact ACL, the instability in the knee joint often leads to articular cartilage damage, which generally causes arthritis, and the increasing wear and tear on the joint had probably caused such damage. His knee made a horrible grinding noise (it still does) when he moved it and this seemed to be getting louder each year. He sought some specialists' opinion and they all strongly recommended that he stop playing football.

For the first time in his life he contemplated a year without football, a thought previously unthinkable. He didn't want to leave Rottnest, as the business was going well and he enjoyed the island lifestyle. The thought of not having to travel back to the mainland on a weekly basis was appealing to both he and Meryl, particularly as their first daughter Debbie had been born in October 1962. The prospect of early morning flights to and from the island (or worse still, boat trips!) with a young child wasn't relished. In the end, this probably firmed up John's thinking as he put family, lifestyle and business before football and announced that he would not play in 1963.

Chapter 9
Time to retire

John, remembering his playing days:

> "Playing is so much easier than coaching. If I wasn't injured I would never have contemplated retirement, I would have just kept on going"!

The summer of 1962-63 was the first the 24-year-old John could remember where he hadn't been sweating it out on an oval or a beach preparing for another football season – and he enjoyed the change. He had no second thoughts about his decision to (at least temporarily) retire from football, but at Fremantle Oval they were just starting to realise he might be serious. Initially South had not taken his 'threat' to heart. After all, their most dedicated player lived and breathed the game and left no stone unturned to remain in the top bracket of players. The club was fixed on one issue – they did not want John to commute from Rottnest to the mainland, as he had done in 1962. They rallied a group of supporters to find suitable work to entice John back from the island and through various business contacts they came up with a manager's position in a Fremantle wholesale butcher's shop. No doubt their disappointment was acute when John declined the offer and reiterated his decision not to play by officially notifying club secretary Joe Maffina that he was unavailable.

The club was now galvanised into action. They had already lost the reigning Walker medallist ruckman Glen Bow back to Victoria and were loathe to lose John as well, particularly as he had completed a full season in 1962. After their first semi-final loss, they were keen to go a step better in '63. They tried desperately to change his mind, sending a steady stream of committeemen to Rottnest to speak with him; coach Marty McDonnell also endeavoured to persuade him to reconsider. However, he remained steadfast and refused to alter his decision, which eventually forced South to raise the prospect of legal action, as they considered he would be in breach of contract if he didn't play. While reluctant to take this step, the club obviously felt this would force John's hand, but they underestimated his resolve; it simply made him more determined to stay out for the year.

South felt it had a solid hold over John, as in May 1962 he had signed a five year contract to play until the end of 1966. This was the first (and only) playing contract he signed and was instigated at his request in response to South's decision to recruit and pay Bow to play. Bow was obtained from Geelong and John felt aggrieved that as a loyal, 'local' servant, he was not afforded the same privileges. After some lively meetings with the committee, he and John Gerovich were offered five year contracts at £100 per season. The complication for John was that South advanced him the bulk of the £500 in 1962 so he could buy a block of land. South considered itself to be £400 out of pocket and in May 1963 their solicitors served him a writ demanding repayment, or to start training within 14 days. John was absolutely livid and declared himself unfit to play because of his old knee injury, adding – *"I know I have obligations to the club and, if I were fit, I would be keen to play. However, a specialist has advised me not to play football again and I would be foolish not to be guided by him"*.

A week later, his own solicitors issued a defence and added a counter-claim for damages to really raise the stakes. John admitted he had been advanced the money and a term of the indenture was that he would play for five years and repay the money (or part thereof) if he refused or neglected to play for South in this time. However, he claimed it was agreed that any repayment would be waived if he wasn't capable of playing because of injury suffered while playing for the club. He submitted this was now the case, citing the 1956 incident when he first hurt his knee, which had since been made worse by continuing to play. In his counter-claim, he vented his spleen on the committee, claiming the club displayed negligence in employing him as a footballer in 1962 when it knew he was suffering from a knee injury and demonstrated further negligence to his health and well-being by insisting he continue to play. This was more than South had bargained for and they beat a hasty retreat, with the only dialogue occurring between the respective solicitors. John was happy to let the matter rest there, convinced he owed South nothing, having given them great service and loyalty over eight seasons, although he was disappointed they had resorted to legal action. The issue remained unresolved for the rest of the year, but was not raised in court hearings as South was perhaps more pre-occupied with their on-field performances.

~

Apart from John and Bow, South had retained the team that made the previous year's finals, so the club was optimistic of at least holding its ground in 1963. However, the season was disastrous – a 66 point defeat by Perth in the opening game (in which Gary Greer made his league debut in John's No. 10 jumper) was only a sign of worse to come. South lost their first five matches and won only two of 11 in their worst start since a wooden spoon finish in 1936. There was marginal improvement in the second half, as four wins from 10 matches doubled their start, and they avoided the wooden spoon, finishing seventh, two games clear of Claremont. Apart from captain Gary Scott, Ross Bowe (who won the Walker Medal), Ron Doig and Fred Seinor, the side had few consistent performers. Gerovich had a bad run with illness and injury, playing only 10 games and robbing the side of much firepower, with rover Stan Badham the side's leading goal-kicker on 28.

At season-end, the club was not only looking for reasons why it had slipped back to near bottom, but was also looking for a coach as McDonnell had unexpectedly resigned. In fact, McDonnell caused a sensation by informing the players of his intention to quit at three-quarter-time of the last qualifying game, against East Perth at Perth Oval. Although he urged the players to *"fight the game out"*, they appeared stunned by his surprise announcement and the margin blew out from 47 points to 117 as East Perth added 13 goals to two. McDonnell wanted the players to know of his decision before anyone else and he felt the committee had not fully supported him throughout a difficult year. In the finals, Swans came from fourth position to defeat East Perth, Perth and East Fremantle on their way to a hat trick of premierships. Ray Sorrell, with 20 votes, won the Sandover Medal by one vote from Perth's

Frank Pyke, although East Perth centreman Syd Jackson also polled 20 votes in his first season, but a two match suspension ruled him ineligible.

~

For John, the 1963 season effectively didn't exist. Making the most of his football 'sabbatical', he took little interest in the game; he didn't watch a match, read few newspaper reports and didn't feel any urge to kick a ball. He immersed himself in the free and easy Rottnest lifestyle and basically divorced himself from the game. He virtually became a teenager again and did all the things you do at age 16-20, which he had previously willingly sacrificed for football. However, he admits that if he had not been based at Rottnest and removed from Fremantle and the football scene, he would have found it impossible to step away from the game which had been such a dominant force in his life.

For many West Australians, Rottnest is their 'island paradise' and a regular holiday destination where one can escape the pressures of work and city living. Located 20km off the coast, it's possible to sit on the beach or in the hotel on a clear day and view the skyline of Perth and Fremantle and feel like you are a million miles away from your troubles. This was exactly how John felt; it was a break from everything, especially the grind of rehabilitating himself from injury. There are many tranquil bays and beaches at Rottnest and he fished and swam in them all, as they are only a short bike ride from the settlement area, with no private cars permitted on the island. Crayfish are plentiful in the reefs surrounding the island and he found great pleasure in diving for them, as well as laying pots. He also discovered beer (previously taboo!) as he found new friends among the Rottnest workers who lived on the island. The daily routine for most employees involved heading to the pub for a few beers after work and John soon found himself visiting the hotel regularly, although not always with Meryl's blessing – *"The pub scene was not something I'd ever really experienced, as alcohol was something I never wanted (or missed!) in my teenage years as it wasn't going to help my football"*. Now he enjoyed the camaraderie produced by a few drinks and happily spent time at the *Quokka Arms* after work.

He also took up golf, finding the game very challenging and regularly playing nine holes on the island's sandy course. The house that went with the butcher's shop was situated on a small hill overlooking the golf course and was a short walk to the first tee, so John often played early before work. His golfing exploits were good enough to make *The Sporting Review* newspaper, although not for any holes-in-one or birdie putts! In a social competition, he hooked a tee shot high into a tree between the fourth and fifth holes and, to his surprise and the amusement of his playing partners, the ball lodged in a fork 25 feet above the ground. Displaying his usual competitive spirit and not wanting to drop a shot, he climbed the tree and hit the ball out, landing it about 10 yards closer to the hole, much to the amazement of his fellow players!

There was plenty of time for things like golf with the shop busy in the warm months, but a drop-off in visitors during winter saw the shop open from 10am-noon and 4pm-6pm. By the summer of 1963-64, John was feeling thoroughly refreshed and rejuvenated, mentally and physically, and without the strain of training and playing, his knee felt fine and his body in general felt good, as he had limited his weight gain to only a few pounds. However, he admitted that – *"I was almost out of touch with reality, becoming too familiar with the laid-*

back Rotto lifestyle". This view was shared by Meryl, who hadn't particularly enjoyed the year on the island given the limitations imposed on the lifestyle by a young baby and a husband hell-bent on reliving his teenage years. Therefore, despite the attraction of managing the shop, they decided it was time to move on in case he became a Rottnest 'native' and slipped further into the easy, undisciplined existence which might also get him divorced! He announced his intention to return to the mainland in January and attempt a comeback to league football with South, which signalled the end of the legal wranglings.

~

In its search for a new coach, South signed East Fremantle star centreman Sorrell, the reigning Sandover medallist who was untried as a coach. The appointment caused surprise in football circles. Perhaps South felt that after losing players as coaches to Claremont (Ray Richards), Subiaco (Charlie Tyson) and East Fremantle (Steve Marsh), it was time to square the ledger. It was rumoured that John had applied for the job, but this was not true. At the time of Sorrell's appointment, John hadn't announced his intention to leave Rottnest and, given the legal situation, it's unlikely he was even considered. The appointment of Sorrell was not all plain sailing as East Fremantle, beaten grand finalists for the second year in a row, were loathe to clear their champion to their arch rivals, especially after winning a Sandover. Perhaps recalling the hard bargain South had driven in 1957 with Marsh, Old Easts placed a £1500 transfer fee on Sorrell. South were outraged; the fee was three times the usual for the era and they rejected the demand [14] and, with Old Easts refusing to budge, a stalemate resulted. A group of East Fremantle supporters suggested Sorrell be swapped for John, but there was little enthusiasm for the idea by either John or South. If John was going to play football again, then, despite his disappointments over the club's legal action, he still only saw himself in a South jumper. East Fremantle eventually modified their demand to £1250, which South paid after a special fund-raising drive, and they now had two of the best centremen the State had seen; players who had comprised two-thirds of the 1961 All Australian team's centreline. Jack Sumich had completed his studies in England and there was great hope the trio could turn the side around after the disappointment of 1963.

On leaving Rottnest, John abandoned butchering, at least for the time being, and, with the club's help, he took over as manager of a squash centre in High Street, Fremantle. He relished the chance to work at something different, which was also an ideal way of regaining peak fitness. Running a squash centre in that era included playing with anyone who asked and there were plenty of people who fancied a match against John Todd! It was not uncommon for him to play up to 10 games a day five days a week, which served as an arduous, but enjoyable, supplement to pre-season football training. He soon picked up the finer points of the game and got pretty good at controlling the 'T', making his opponents do most of the running.

John also returned to coaching, taking on the South thirds team, which gave him extra training sessions as he couldn't help but join in the drills he set for the young players, not expecting them to perform anything he couldn't do himself. All of this equated to an enormous

---

14. Later in the season, Claremont would stun the football fraternity, both in Perth and Melbourne, by placing a £4000 transfer fee on Dennis Marshall, who was seeking a clearance to Geelong.

Chapter 9 – Time to retire

workload, even for a player as dedicated as John, and concerns that he was burning himself out were soon raised. In *The Daily News* on March 20, Cyril Casellas reported under the heading *"He is a tired Todd"* and questioned the wisdom of playing so much squash, adding that *"... the dynamo has run down"*. South officials expressed concern that the hard wooden floors and sharp movements would affect his legs, especially his knee, but, by and large, these comments fell on deaf ears. John's mind was once again firmly focused on football and he was determined to come back and play at his best – indulgences like a beer at the Rottnest Hotel were a thing of the past.

~

South's practice match form was impeccable, not losing a game, with the only sour note coming when Sorrell broke some ribs and was forced out of the season-opener, which removed one selection dilemma as John was the automatic selection at centre. It was a derby at East Fremantle Oval and the protracted clearance wrangle over Sorrell added spice to the game, which attracted 12,000 fans, many no doubt enticed by John's return to league football. He didn't disappoint and was a popular choice as best-afield as South upset the more fancied Old Easts to win by 26 points. His low, raking drop-kicks continually found their targets and, after an even first half, South gained the ascendancy. It was an impressive return after 12 months out of the game and John went on to be South's best player over the first four matches, slotting easily back into football as if he had never been away. His form was a tribute to his mental toughness. Few people knew he had been close to withdrawing from the side before a best-on-ground effort against East Perth after resorting to sleeping pills to get some rest the night before, such was the pain in his left knee. On the Saturday morning he stood in the water at Leighton Beach for over an hour to loosen the stiffness in the joint, as, even at this early stage, the pounding of the squash court was taking its toll.

However, his knee was not the only thing under strain. Part of the squash court arrangement was that the cleaning would be done by Meryl, who was not exactly privy to this deal and hated it, making her resent the situation even more. Making it worse was the fact that John was busy every night at the club as the thirds trained on alternate nights to the league and playing squash during the day left little time for her and Debbie. Meryl was desperately unhappy, but John was wrapped up with his own problems and failed to recognise her feelings. The pain in his knee was worse, but he stuck with the job and, although his early season form was good, he doubted how long he could keep going for. After a year's break he was enthusiastic about playing again, but the knee soreness was worse than before. Mentally he found it hard to cope with the pressures of the job, football and family and he became, in his own words, *"pretty difficult to live with"*. As is typical of these situations, he almost unwittingly turned on those closest to him and Meryl bore the brunt of it. Eventually she left, taking Debbie with her to Deniliquin, in NSW, where she stayed with relatives – a decision that caught John by surprise. He wanted them back, but Meryl stayed put and it was 1965 before John could entice her home.

~

Despite an aching left knee, he held his form, polling three votes in *The Daily News* Footballer of the Year Award in round seven to share the first round jackpot of £35 with Bill Walker. His form was so good that Sorrell had been forced to leave John in the centre and play himself at half-forward and even at centre-half-back. John's form was such that he was an automatic choice for the WA side, preparing for a three-State tour in June and, in a sign of the times, triple premiers Swan Districts had 10 players in the squad, reminiscent of South in their golden era.

In the derby to open the second round, John strained a groin muscle after suffering soreness for several weeks; obviously the legacy of too much squash and the injury could not have come at a worse time. He withdrew from the State squad as the injury refused to respond to intensive treatment, although John doubted he could play three games in seven days anyway as his knee was now very sore after matches. Eventually South were left without a representative when Sorrell, Scott and Seinor were all overlooked as the selectors chose eight Swans players to make the trip [15]. The groin injury kept John out for three weeks, even though he prematurely returned against Subiaco, only to have the injury flare again, forcing him to miss the next month. At the same time, Sorrell missed matches due to hamstring and knee injuries and would manage just nine games for the season, with South notching just four wins to the end of the second round to slip out of finals contention.

The groin was slow to respond, but by August John was keen to play again, having missed eight of South's past nine games. However, with South firmly out of the finals race, John mischievously suggested he play in the reserves side to try and help them win the premiership. In *The West Australian* of August 13, Geoff Christian quoted John as saying – *"I don't think I will be of much use to the league team for the remainder of the season. The reserves team seems certain to play in the finals and I'm ready to play there if needed"*. To qualify for the finals, John needed to play at least three reserves matches, but South quickly scotched this, as chairman of selectors Jim Mills replied in *The Football Budget* – *"The principal objective of every player at this football club is to assist the league side to win matches, regardless of what position that side holds on the premiership table"*. This laid the matter to rest and John's one and only reserve grade game for South remains the 1954 grand final, where he kicked seven goals on debut.

He returned to the league side the next week against East Perth and Col Wilkinson reported in *The Sunday Times* that John *"showed all his old artistry at centre"* as South had their seventh win for the season. Despite missing eight matches, John was poised to make a late challenge for *The Daily News* Footballer of the Year Award as he was only three points behind the leader, West Perth's Mel Whinnen. The next week against Subiaco he continued his good form until his left knee twisted awkwardly in a tackle and he was forced from the ground, having again strained the medial ligament. The injury ended his comeback season, which petered out badly after the first eight games which had been probably as good as any in his career. He managed just three appearances in the second half of the season due to groin and knee problems and, in two of those, he was forced to the bench early. It was a disappointing return for the considerable effort he had put into preparing for the season and it weighed heavily on his mind. His left knee had been sore for the whole season, restricting his ability to train. This was no doubt due to the

---

15. Despite having a good side (on paper at least), WA were yet again thrashed at the MCG by the Vics, losing by 112 points. In 1962 the margin was 102 points, in 1959, a massive 178 points. The tour then saw WA trounce Tasmania, before suffering a narrow loss to South Australia. The tour also marked the end of Swans dominance of the local competition; with their State players injured and/or tired from the gruelling trip, they slumped from league leaders to sixth position, winning only two of their last 11 matches.

onset of arthritis in the joint, caused by the grinding of bone on bone which happens when the cartilage is absent. As South lost its final three games, he seriously considered that his *"time was up"*. He was weary of being injured and, more specifically, the mental grind of getting through the rehabilitation process again; he could feel his resolve slipping away. Making things harder was the continued absence of Meryl and daughter Debbie.

Before any decisions could be made on his future, he had South's thirds team to guide through the finals. They had finished second after winning 12 of the last 14 games, but suffered a loss of form in the finals, losing in 'straight sets'. Although disappointed, John enjoyed coaching the team and knew this was where his football future lay. He took great pleasure in seeing some of his players graduate to the league side, notably Kevin Frazer and Franz Tomka, while others who would later make their mark were Frank Legena and Graeme Reilly.

~

John's injury-plagued season probably cost him his fourth Walker Medal, as from 11 games (but only eight completed) he polled 37 votes to finish third behind Scott and Tom Grljusich. He polled a creditable 12 votes in the Sandover Medal to finish equal sixth as a young Perth rover named Barry Cable won the first of his three medals. In the finals, Claremont just headed West Perth (now coached by Clive Lewington) for fourth spot and surprised the pundits by scoring hard-fought wins over Subiaco and Perth before winning an epic grand final against East Fremantle. Tigers centre-half-forward Ian Brewer kicked two late goals after East Fremantle defender Norm Rogers, the eventual Simpson medallist, went down with cramp, allowing Claremont to snatch a four point win and their first flag since 1940.

John was inundated with press enquiries about his future and while he harboured doubts about playing on, he didn't let on in public, preferring to simply say he would play on if his knee allowed him to do so. In *The Sports Review* he said – *"If my knee will stand up to it, then I'll be back next season. Besides, I've still got one unfulfilled football ambition – to be a successful league coach. I'd like to do that before I bow out of football"*. He rested his knee and forgot about football for several weeks and, with Meryl still away, he fell in with his mates and discovered the nightclub scene. He recalls it as *"a crazy time and I soon realised it wasn't for me and I needed to get my act together"*. He returned to the squash court and Leighton Beach and resumed training, trying again to entice Meryl home, promising a fresh start. His mind had now swung back to playing again (if possible) as he had received an attractive offer to be playing-coach at Burnie, in Tasmania. The soft muddy grounds appealed to John and he was keen to make the move, believing the time was right to coach at league level again. He kept South informed of developments and hoped the club would look favourably on a clearance, but was dismayed when the Bulldogs put a £1500 transfer fee on his head! This was way out of reach for the small Burnie club, who played in the North West Football Union; they couldn't afford both a coaching fee and a transfer fee and negotiations soon broke down. For the second time in his career, John had been denied a transfer to a Tasmanian team to take up a coaching offer, yet he remained loyal to South and started pre-season training under Sorrell.

By February 1965, he felt he was *"going up and down in the one spot"*. On the sand, his knee didn't feel too bad, but on the oval and doing football drills, the soreness returned. The regular squash workouts didn't help and he knew the job had to go, something he was happy to do if it would entice Meryl and Debbie home. He left the squash courts and applied for membership of the Waterside Workers' Federation, where jobs on the Fremantle wharf were keenly sought. Because Bill Todd (Snr) was a union member, John had some preference, although not guaranteed automatic acceptance. There were about 70 new places available, but several hundred applicants, such was the popularity of the wharf. He was duly selected, but the system required the chosen applicants to be named one by one before a full meeting of the members, who could voice an objection if they desired. He managed this step and only had to pass a medical examination to be admitted as a full union member. On the day of the assessment, he was in line behind Norm Rogers, who was surprisingly rejected because of a knee injury. Rogers had had a cartilage removed from his knee and it troubled him on occasions, but five months earlier he had played well enough in the grand final loss to Claremont to win the Simpson Medal! John was devastated – if Rogers had been knocked back, then what hope did he have, given his well-known history of knee problems. He was duly (and quickly!) passed over and it was back to the butcher's shop.

In the early intraclub matches of 1965, John really struggled. His knee was stiff and sore and plainly restricting his movements and, while he put on a brave front and spent many hours in the ocean working on the joint, it had little effect. While he knew this was probably the end, *"... mentally I couldn't bring myself to admit defeat after so many years of overcoming the frustrations and blocking out the negative thoughts"*. Eventually, John Colgan's brother Bill, who had helped John back in 1956 when he went to Kalgoorlie to visit Kris Martinovich, took him aside and simply told him it was *"time"*. In a strange way, this virtually removed the burden of making the decision from him; he respected Colgan and knew he was right and it was *"acceptable"* to agree with him. On March 4, 1965 John announced it was over, saying that in other seasons he had been able to overcome the knee trouble, but this year *"there was no strength left in it"*. Soon after announcing his retirement, he was cheered to find that Meryl was prepared to come home, which helped his mood and put to rest a tough phase of his life. In his usual manner of finding a positive from a negative, he remembers this period as *"a great learning curve for life"*.

~

In coming to grips with the fact he wasn't playing any longer, John stepped back from any formal involvement with South, taking on a role of schools' coach for the district, which involved organising coaching sessions at primary schools, usually with the help of the league players. He became a regular football columnist with *The West Australian* and, with respected sports journalist Geoff Christian acting as his ghost writer, John reported on a game each week. He found that, without any emotional involvement, there was much he hadn't discovered about the game. He used this opportunity to analyse the playing styles and tactics of other teams, which he had paid scant attention to while playing with South. Working out where games had been won and lost was a fascinating exercise and one that he recommends for any budding coaches. This experience helped greatly in his later coaching, as he became aware of how a match could change and what measures you could adopt to alter the flow of a game. He also noticed the game's better players such as Walker and Cable, who monopolised the Sandover Medals from 1964 to '68. Again, in his own playing career, he simply hadn't paid much attention to the opposition – *"the opposition had to worry about me, not the reverse"*.

Chapter 9 – Time to retire

The newspaper job sometimes had him reporting on South's matches and, usually, from their point of view, it didn't make for great copy. South had a terrible season, losing their first seven games and finishing last, with only five wins and a draw. Injuries and poor form saw the club use 49 league players and Sorrell was forced into retirement mid-season with injury problems, although he did return for the last few games. Walker won the first of his four Sandovers, pipping Cable by one vote and, for the third year in succession, the team finishing fourth took the flag. East Fremantle, who scraped into fourth spot with only 11 wins, accounted for West Perth, Claremont and Swans to win the premiership, thereby avoiding becoming beaten grand finalists for the fourth year in a row.

~

There is no doubt John was one of the playing greats of WA football despite his relatively brief and injury-riddled career. In reflecting on John's time as a player, it's appropriate to mention his 'stolen games', which sadly comprised the bulk of his career. At the end of his last season in 1964, John had taken the field in 128 league games for South (although the annual report for this year lists his tally as 138). In 1956, when he first injured his knee at Perth Oval, he was only two quarters into his 28th game. Therefore, after refusing to yield to the torn ACL and shredded cartilage in his left knee, which doctors told him should have finished his career, he 'stole' another 100 games in seven seasons over the next eight years. Certainly, in about 12 matches he left the ground with injury (knee, hamstrings, groins or shoulders) but, for most of the others, his play was almost the equal of what he displayed in winning the Sandover Medal in his debut season in 1955. While he perhaps never quite reached those heights again, from 1957-64 John won two Walker Medals, played another 10 State matches and made an All Australian side at the 1961 Brisbane carnival – not bad for a footballer who played within the restrictions imposed by his knee injury. While virtually all other players of this era who suffered a similar injury were forced out of the game; he simply refused to concede defeat – "It's hard to get through football (and life) without some sort of setback, but what typifies the champion is being able to absorb the knocks and overcome setbacks".

In recent times, John has been honoured in several ways for his playing deeds [16], such was the impact of his play in his short, but brilliant career. Almost all of WA's post-war footballing legends such as Jack Sheedy, Steve Marsh, Graham Farmer, Bill Walker, Barry Cable, Brian Peake, Stephen Michael, Graham Moss and Ross Glendinning played well over 200, if not 300 games. John is the only one to have achieved similar status with less than 150 games. In Australian football, perhaps the only similar story is that of John Coleman, the great Essendon and Victorian full-forward of the late 1940s and early '50s, who played only 98 games before his career was tragically cut short in 1954 by a serious knee injury. He has been honoured by the naming of the Coleman Medal for the leading goal-kicker in the AFL each season.

---

16. In 1997 he was inducted into the Western Australian Hall of Champions and the Fremantle Dockers Hall of Legends. In the Subiaco Oval redevelopment of 1999-2000, Gate 7 was named the 'John Todd Entrance', and in December 1999 he was named at centre in *The West Australian* newspaper's 'Team of the Century'. In the 1970s he was named in the South Fremantle champion team 1946-76 and in the WA champion team 1945-75, commissioned by the Subiaco Club.

What then made John such a great player, that, whenever he declared himself fit, South had no hesitation in picking him? For one, he was a terrific 'first up' player. Despite his many and sometimes lengthy absences, he invariably played well in his first game back, as though he had been playing regularly for weeks. It never took him a few games to 'find his feet again' – he simply slotted back into the team and did what he did best, gather plenty of possessions and use the ball with great effect. There is no doubt he was a player who could turn a game, such was his ball-getting ability and disposal skills.

John Colgan, who played on a wing alongside John for much of their careers, remembers him as *"... efficient like a Bradman. I can't remember him ever fumbling a ball. I would often find myself just standing there clapping his outstanding feats"*. Gerovich, who arrived at South with John in 1954 and who was the lucky recipient of many perfectly executed stab passes, regards him as *"... pound for pound, the best player I have seen"* and. in the current era, sees similarities with Collingwood's Nathan Buckley in the way he effortlessly gathers possessions. Tony Parentich, who took over at centre when John was first injured, says he *"... never saw a better mover. His timing to take the ball off hands was immaculate"*.

Their memories of John are of regular, sustained brilliance in all sorts of weather and against good sides and bad. All three agree that he was a ball player and an attacking player who was not very defensive in his play. John himself agrees with this description; he saw himself as an attacking player, with plenty of flair and eyes only for the ball, but admits to not being a great tackler or spoiler, as *"the opposition had to worry about stopping me"*. His lesser attention to the defensive skills of the game, however, didn't cause any resentment among his team-mates. While Colgan and Parentich both say he wasn't the greatest 'team' player in the side, he more than compensated for this with his brilliant ball-getting ability. He wasn't a great team talker or organiser on the ground, which probably reflected two things – his shyness, which made coaching South at age 21 difficult, and the fact that he was more than good enough to win the ball in most situations by himself. He usually didn't need the help of his team-mates.

His competitive instincts were intense, to say the least, and in the heat of a game he was often prone to vitriolic outbursts against opponents or umpires. In current times he would be charged with racial vilification for some of the things he said then, as would probably most players of that era. However, these barbs were merely short-term insults designed to break an opponent's concentration, not a seriously intended slur on their race, character, religion or upbringing. After the game they were quickly forgotten as players from both sides shared a drink. That this opportunity no longer exists he sees as a failing of the modern AFL era. In his view, the game is now tampered with so much that good-natured banter and gamesmanship on the ground is almost impossible, lest it be misinterpreted as a slur on an opponent – *"In the '50s and '60s it was part of the game and created much of the folklore which stimulated interest in footy"*. While he does not condone racially-inspired taunts or 'sledges', he does lament the lack of characters in football now – *"The game is so sanitised that players have little opportunity to express themselves without incurring the wrath of the coach or the controlling body"*.

To sum up John's playing career, it is appropriate to mention two things – how he mentally prepared himself each week and who he regarded as his toughest opponents in his nine seasons of league football. The secret to the first point is simple – he had a burning desire to be the *"the greatest player the game had ever seen"* and this was pretty much the sum total of his mental preparation. In contrast to players like Farmer, who would 'psyche' himself into a mental zone to prepare for a game [17], John hardly gave the match a second thought on Saturday mornings. He was busy at work in the butcher's shop and, when he finished, it was often a rush to get home, eat lunch and get to the game.

There were no set plays and, compared to today's modernised football, few specific strategies and as he thought little about his likely opponent, his mind concentrated on his own game and he didn't expend any nervous energy leading up to the match. While this approach worked for him, it wouldn't suit everyone as different individuals require different preparations to bring them to their peak. In today's fully professional game, it would be even more difficult to achieve, given the emphasis on tactics and strategies now prevalent. However, he believes many players burn up too much nervous energy before games – *"With no other work to distract them, they can easily play the game before it starts. The tactical concentration on zones and set plays and the like rob players of their instinct for the game, leaving them with less chance to express themselves and put themselves on display"*. Again, in part at least, the game is the poorer for these developments in his view.

When asked to recall his toughest opponents, John named two centremen and two half-back flankers, all from different clubs. In the centre Kevin Clune (Claremont) and Peter Amaranti (Subiaco, although he started at South) were always hard to beat. Clune was *"like a dog at a bone, always at you"* who played it hard and physical, while Amaranti was also physical in his approach and a stay-at-home centreman who played the position well. He was one of the few players who forced John, to some degree, to worry about his direct opponent. The half-backs were Ray Marinko (West Perth) and Tom Guthrie (East Fremantle) who are remembered as hard, tough defenders who *"gave you no room... against these two players, I always earned my kicks"*.

---

17. Steve Hawke, in his book about Polly Farmer, records that he would regularly prepare for games by deliberately concentrating on things that he hated, in order to work up a degree of hatred for the opposition. These things ranged from the dentist, to other players, to historical episodes, such as the oppression of minority groups by more powerful opponents. A favourite was the treatment of the Red Indians by the US army and government in the 1800s and 1900s.

Chapter 10
A coach again

John Gerovich, recalling John's return to coaching in 1966:

> "He expected a hell of a lot and was absolutely intolerant of anyone not putting in a wholehearted effort".

John, reflecting on his coaching at South Fremantle in this period:

> "I was probably too hard for the times, I pushed too hard".

After two poor seasons under Ray Sorrell, the South Fremantle committee was becoming impatient and threw open the league coaching position, encouraging Sorrell to re-apply. The job attracted 16 applicants, including John, and on October 26, 1965 he was surprisingly (according to most pundits) named as the new coach. He promised to inject discipline into the club and rekindle team spirit, which he felt had dropped away. He wasted little time. Training started on November 8 – unheard of in this era – with a heavy concentration on specialised skill work, with the tough conditioning work left for the New Year. He made it clear Sorrell was welcome to stay and play and that he had no plans to play himself. The centre position was Sorrell's if he wanted it and could regain his fitness after playing just 22 games for South in two seasons. However, Sorrell was undecided about his future and didn't join the pre-Christmas training squad. Rumours of a rift between the two men again surfaced, having first been aired in 1964 when Sorrell placed himself in the centre, pushing John to a wing despite his good form in the pivot. John was – and still is – quick to dispel these rumours. In 1957 he had helped Sorrell when he was suffering with a knee injury during the finals and they often roomed together on interstate trips. He had also made the 1961 All Australian side as a wingman and had no problems playing there when coached by Sorrell [18].

After Christmas, as in 1959, John put his charges through a tortuous programme. Utilising the services of Colin Junner, he had the players running many miles on the Fremantle golf course and up sandhills at the beach, demanding that South be the fittest team in the league. It would also be 'his' team, as he convinced the club to make him the sole selector, following the trend adopted by Jim Conway at Claremont. He also worked hard on club and team spirit and in March at the traditional guernsey presentation, he gave each player two jumpers – one for matches and one for training. He expected all players to train in club colours and received a rousing reception

---

18. Sorrell asked for a clearance back to East Fremantle, saying he had never been fully accepted at South, which rankled the Bulldogs, who had gone to considerable lengths to secure his clearance from Old Easts on appointing him coach. Remembering the hard bargain driven by Old Easts in 1964, South held up Sorrell's clearance until the June 30 deadline and then only on the payment of $2500, the equivalent of the £1250 Sorrell had cost South two years before. However, injury continued to dog him and he only played four more league games spread over 1966 and 1967, before retiring after 178 games.

when he said that any player who chose to do otherwise would be dropped from the list and barred from the club! It was an early taste of the iron discipline he would impose in an attempt to improve South's standing. There would soon be more of the same to come.

~

The club had no experienced or interstate recruits to boast about in the build up to the season, but had high hopes for many talented juniors from the thirds and fourths, the latter grade being introduced in 1965. Much was also expected of defender Franz Tomka, wingman Frank Legena, rover Charlie Osmetti, full-back Graeme Reilly and ruckman Ivan Glucina, all of whom had been blooded in the past year or two. Forward Graham Scott, brother of captain Gary, also shaped as a likely prospect. On the debit side, ruckman Fred Seinor had moved to the country, leaving a hole in the following division. South's practice match form was reasonable and John was optimistic of a good season, declaring that he was happy to be paid on results only. He told Bob Cribb, in *The Sports Review*, that "... *if we don't go somewhere this year I could be a few hundred dollars out of pocket. But mark my words, we are going places*".

Much pre-season talk concerned how teams and players would handle the change in the handball rule. The 'flick pass' had been outlawed, with the rule amended to read that the ball had to be held with one hand and struck with the clenched fist of the other hand. The change was favourably received by all of the WANFL coaches except East Fremantle's Bob Johnson, who considered it would slow up the game. John was all for he change, believing it would bring back the art of handball by forcing players to handball with both hands. He himself had never used the flick pass because it left a player open to being penalised for throwing.

On Easter Saturday South travelled to Lathlain Park to tackle Perth in the opening game in a match that pitted together the league's only two new coaches, with Mal Atwell moving from East Perth as playing coach in place of veteran Ern Henfry. Perth had just missed the 1965 finals and were a popular pick to beat South first-up. They did more than that. In a nightmare return to coaching, John watched Perth absolutely destroy his side with a powerhouse display of tough and slick football. At quarter-time the scoreboard read Perth 6.8 to 0.2; at half-time it was 13.12 to 1.7; at the last change it was 19.18 to 4.8; and the final score was 27.25 (187) to 6.8 (44). As a result of the massive win, Perth headed the table with a huge percentage of 425 and Frank Pyke, Graham Jenzen and Max Jancey took the first three places on the league goal-kicking tally.

The South players were quick to feel the wrath of their coach, copping a fearful tongue-lashing after the game. A ferry trip to Garden Island had been planned for Sunday, but the day was stormy and wet and the players assumed it would be cancelled as they arrived at the wharf, expecting to be sent on a long run by the still furious coach. However, John surprised them all and ignored his personal trepidation about boat trips and bad weather by announcing they would train on Garden Island, saying he didn't care if they all got seasick. The ocean was rough and many players were queasy on the crossing, not the least John, who relived the nightmare of the Rottnest-Perth trip four years earlier. The weather was so bad the ferry couldn't berth at the designated jetty and the players had to take small rowboats through the shore break to reach the island.

The players tackled a beach run and trained for two hours before breaking for some fishing and lunch. The fish were biting (no doubt aided by the berley added to the water!) and there

Chapter 10 – A coach again

was plenty to barbecue for lunch before they reluctantly re-boarded the ferry for the return trip. The weather conditions had worsened and most stomachs (including John's) were quickly heaving. He felt absolutely terrible and parked himself next to Glucina, tightly gripping one of his legs with both hands to grimly hang on as the boat lurched from wave to wave. By the end of the trip, which the skipper nearly aborted at one stage as visibility fell dramatically, his thumb and fingerprints were imprinted into the flesh of Glucina's leg, but the big ruckman was either too sick or too polite to complain.

After docking at Fremantle, John told the players that the league list would be reviewed before the next session. True to his word and to make a strong point that he would not accept any player, senior or junior, not putting in a 100% effort, he dropped Keith Smith, Osmetti and John Gerovich from the list, adding that he would *"... drop the lot if necessary"*. This caused a sensation in the press as John had close ties with all three players, especially Gerovich, having started his career at South with him. Gerovich was acknowledged as one of the champions of the era, with his spectacular high marking thrilling fans for a decade and it's likely John dumped him to make an example to the rest of the team, indicating that reputations and seniority did not cut any favours. However, Gerovich took the demotion badly and announced his retirement, saying *"... I don't feel inclined to be made a scapegoat at this stage of my career"*. In *The West Australian* on Saturday April 16, sports editor Ted Collingwood wrote of the *"Dark days at South"* as Gerovich stuck to his decision and John reiterated his call that he intended to instill discipline and dedication into the club, adding that *"... I am far from finished with this type of disciplinary action"*. Such blunt and uncompromising statements would characterise his coaching for the next four decades.

After a full week of tough man-on-man training, South faced arch-enemies East Fremantle, keen to put the previous week behind them. With derbies often bringing out the best in the underdog, club hopes were high but, despite a plucky showing, South tired – perhaps because of the heavy week on the training track – and went down by 14 points. Losses to Swans and Claremont saw South win-less after four rounds and firmly anchored on the bottom of the ladder, with the only bright spot being that Gerovich had returned to the fold. Then, almost unexpectedly, the team clicked and successive wins against Subiaco and West Perth eased the pressure, but losses in the next two games made this only temporary.

On a personal note, the only respite for John (and Meryl) was the birth in May of their second daughter, Kylie, which provided a terrific diversion (albeit temporarily) from the pressures of coaching a struggling team. With only two wins from eight games, John was desperate for more consistency and, in most games, South experienced bad patches where the opposition had capitalised and scored freely. The younger players seemed lost, as South lacked a hard core of experienced personnel who could show the way. Watching from the bench was frustrating for John, so he decided to get closer to the action and try to pinpoint and offset the cause of the fade-outs.

~

On the Monday Foundation Day holiday of June 6, rumours swept Fremantle that John was going to play in the derby that afternoon. Anecdotally, there are reports of people who were busy in their gardens, throwing down their tools and hurrying to Fremantle Oval without changing their clothes as the 'grapevine' worked overtime. Certainly, the crowd swelled considerably in the 30 minutes before bounce-down and eventually a crowd of 14,000 witnessed the match. It's reasonable to assume several thousand had turned up on the chance that John might play.

In the South change rooms there was a bubbly atmosphere, fuelled by an air of nervous excitement and anticipation which had emanated from John's announcement an hour beforehand that he would lead the side out. The decision to play had been warmly received by the players, although it had caught them by surprise. John had only confided in Gary Scott, Barry White (the league runner) and president Bill Collins, with no other players or committee people knowing about his late inclusion. In fact, it was only on the Monday morning that he decided to play and he deliberately wanted to avoid distracting the team [19] or alert the opposition. To quell any suspicion, he had South head trainer Tommy Bottrell take his bag to the ground and he certainly wasn't named in *The Football Budget*, forcing him to run out in the unfamiliar No. 4 guernsey as Graham Scott had taken over No. 10. When he led South onto the ground, the Fremantle faithful gave him a rousing ovation as they welcomed their prodigal son back after an absence of 22 months. He lined up on a half-forward flank, having told the team that he didn't plan to chase kicks, but wanted to help 'direct traffic' when things got tough.

After an even first quarter in a tight scrappy affair so typical of derbies, South was woefully inaccurate in the second term, managing just seven points to go in at half-time nine points in arrears. John had picked up several possessions, while his opposite number, big Bob Johnson, had kicked three goals at full-forward and was proving a handful for Colin Beard. South clawed their way back into the game and at the final change the margin had closed to a point. John pleaded for an all-out effort and they responded magnificently, scoring seven goals to two and winning by 33 points. John saved his best for last. In the final 10 minutes he showed all his old class to kick a goal and then, twice in succession, swooped on the ball as it spilt from marking contests and delivered perfect stab passes to Gerovich and Don Gardiner, who both goaled to seal the victory. The ecstatic South supporters invaded the oval and chaired John from the ground as the members gave the team a standing ovation. It was a perfect finish to a day John rates as one of his best moments in football. With 19 kicks, five marks and two goals he certainly justified his decision to play again after a two year absence and, more importantly, there is little doubt that his presence on the ground gave the team inspiration and guidance.

In the press reports John said – "*... I decided to play because our form has been patchy and if I was on the spot these bad patches could be eliminated*". He answered the inevitable questions about whether he would continue playing by simply saying he would try to play regularly, but reiterated that he would just "*potter around on a half-forward flank*" and wouldn't be doing any roving – "*My idea is simply to guide the youngsters; to be an urger*". While this may have been his intention, to the thousands of fans privileged to witness his comeback, he had done considerably more than 'potter around'. It was an inspiring cameo performance, made all the more remarkable by his total lack of match play since August, 1964. One of his trademarks as a player was that he invariably played well first-up, even after an absence of 22 months.

---

19. During the week, Jack Sheedy said on television that John would play in the derby, which John quickly denied to quell any publicity. He was aware that if the gamble of playing failed and he broke down again and the team lost, then he would look pretty silly and he had no wish for any extra pressure to be placed on him by the press.

South half-back cum centreman Gary Greer, who would go on to play more than 200 league games for South and East Perth, has strong memories of the game, particularly the fans still streaming into the ground during the first quarter, no doubt in response to radio reports confirming that John was playing[20]. Another is simply John's skill and fearless play, where in one passage he beat two opponents, spun quickly out of trouble and speared a stab pass onto Gerovich's chest, as he had done so many times before. That night a newspaper cartoon depicted Gerovich on a fast lead, with hands poised to mark, but the ball was already 'through' him, leaving a neat football-sized hole in his chest. The caption simply said *"Toddy's back!"*. The front page of *The West Australian* the next day carried pictures and story of his comeback, such was the interest generated by his return.

However, John remembers that his comeback could easily have come to an early and abrupt end. After starting against Trevor Sprigg, who was injured early in the second quarter, John played on Lenny Fode, who was a good friend at the time. John recalls a passage of play when Fode had a great opportunity to shirtfront him, but let it go, prompting John, in his usual arrogant way on the field, to tell Fode that he wouldn't get another chance and *"wouldn't play another game"* for letting him off the hook. Fode was best-described as a battler, playing only 14 league games over 1965-66, but he and John remain friends and both still remember the incident. When John later asked why he hadn't collected him, his response was a blunt – *"I just couldn't do it"*. Perhaps because of his friendship, or maybe because of not wanting to spoil the spectacle for the fans who had flocked to the oval to see a football legend play again, he let the chance pass by... to his eternal credit.

Many people remember this derby as John's last game; that he only came back for the one outing and inspired the struggling South to a great win over their arch-rivals. This may be a product of the passing years, or a subconscious desire to create a perfect ending, but in reality he played three more games over the next four weeks before a strained thigh muscle saw him abandon plans to play out the season. His last game was against West Perth at Leederville Oval on July 9 and there was no fairytale ending[21] as South kicked just two goals, losing by 63 points with John forced off early with the thigh injury. It was his 132nd game for South and, despite press speculation in 1967 and '68 that he would again pull on the boots, he never did, although he did turn out in some pre-season practice matches. The match was South's fourth loss in a row since the derby and, with only three wins from 13 games, they were two games adrift in last position.

John continued to turn the team over, rewarding good form in the reserves with quick promotion as he blooded young players for the league side's future. He used 43 players in the league side and, at various stages of the year, 20 players with senior experience found themselves dropped off the list as he refused to tolerate poor form or slack attitudes. Certainly by season's end he had achieved the goals he set on his appointment and, despite being young and inexperienced, South generally played with great spirit and discipline as he had promised.

---

20. Joe Merillo, who had grown up marvelling at John's play in the '50s and '60s and who was now in his first season of league football with West Perth (he played 67 games from 1966-71), remembers he was driving through Perth when radio reports of John's return were aired. He immediately did a U-turn and headed straight to Fremantle Oval to see John play one more time.
21. Joe Merillo was in the West Perth side on this day, so played (briefly!) against John for the first and only time.

In the last eight games, South won three, with the highlight being a stirring one point victory over Old Easts in the third derby. Their worst losses were by 41 and 35 points to Perth and East Perth respectively, the eventual grand finalists, leaving many scribes suggesting that South was primed for a return to the top four in 1967. On Channel 7's *Sunday World of Football* show late in the season, John echoed these sentiments and declared that South could be a premiership contender next season with the addition of a top class rover and some key forwards. The team's defence was reasonably sound, with Beard finding his niche at full-back to comfortably win the Walker Medal and Murray MacDonald solid at centre-half-back, with good support on the flanks from the likes of Greer, Tomka, Kevin Miller and Don Grljusich. Glucina, Bob Bucat and Bob Carson had done a serviceable job in the ruck and country recruit Gardiner had blossomed in his second season to hold down the centre position. However, the team had struggled to kick goals. From 12 games, Gerovich had managed 31 goals; next best was Peter Dougan with 24 and Graham Scott, who won the Caris Brothers' best first year player award, with 21.

At John's behest, the club embarked on a nationwide recruiting drive for some experienced players as they announced his re-appointment for 1967. In the 1966 annual report, John's enthusiasm and dedication were amply recognised – *"Never before in the history of the club has a coach dedicated himself to the job at hand as in this season. John made the coaching position an almost full-time job, being available every day of the week and almost for the full 12 months of his appointment"*. In the part-time era of the 1960s, the long hours he spent at the club were not the norm, but he knew no other way. He put as much time into coaching the side as he had into his own game when he played, which simply reflected his passion for the game and the challenge of coaching again. At age 28, John was a more assured coach than in 1959 and he was far more confident when addressing the team and never shirked an issue with a player. If he saw a problem or felt someone wasn't giving 100%, then he dealt with it immediately, regardless of the circumstances. Gerovich played under John in both of his coaching stints and remembers him in 1966 as *"a harsh disciplinarian"*. In 1959, because of his youth, he wasn't able to put such intense demands on the players, especially as he was coaching men several years senior to him. In 1966 he was older than every player apart from Gerovich, so *"putting the acid"* on them was naturally easier. Alongside his discipline was John's infectious enthusiasm for the game and this balanced nicely against his iron will, providing a good mix for the players, who greeted the committee's unanimous re-appointment with alacrity. Despite finishing last for the second year in a row, there was an air of cautious optimism about the coming season at Fremantle Oval.

~

Perth headed the table at the end of 1966, followed by East Perth, West Perth and East Fremantle, who finished four games clear of Claremont; therefore the top four was safe weeks before the finals, with the only interest being the finishing order. Bill Walker won his second successive Sandover Medal, again by a vote over Barry Cable and Johnson, in his final year as captain-coach of Old Easts, won the goal-kicking with 89, ahead of Swans Eric Gorman on 68. In the finals, West Perth accounted for East Fremantle in the first semi; Perth won their first-ever second semi-final beating the Royals by five points; and East Perth then won through to the grand final by downing the Cardinals by seven goals. In the grand final, first year coach

Atwell triumphed over his old side, coached by Kevin Murray, and led the Demons to their first flag for 11 years, with a 16 point win. These sides would contest the next two grand finals, with the same result to give Perth a hat trick of premierships.

~

John decided on a change of tack with the 1967 pre-season training. Many players had been in training for 10 months by the time the '66 season ended, due to the November start in '65, so he adopted a later start and concentrated on short, sharp skill workouts, rather than gruelling endurance runs. He thought the spartan pre-season he had put the players through for 1966, when the summer was at its hottest, had made them stale as the season wore on, *"... and I was keen to avoid a possible repeat"*.

Helping this decision was the club's latest Eastern States tour, scheduled in January for a change. Two years in the planning and after extensive fund-raising, a party of 74 players and officials left Perth by train on January 11. After brief stops at Kalgoorlie, Port Augusta and Adelaide, they arrived in Melbourne on the 14th and the players were promptly dispatched on a run around Albert Park before heading to Moonee Valley for the races. Canberra and Sydney were the next stops, with receptions from the local clubs and the use of their grounds for training on most days before the group joined the *TV Galileo* at Circular Quay (much to John's dismay!) for the return sea journey to Perth. To the players' horror, John called daily PT workouts on the sports deck, usually in front of a crowd of interested passengers. Fortunately, the weather was kind on the return trip, with sea-sickness not an issue. John remembers this trip clearly, not only for the sights that were seen and the people met, but because of the strong bond forged among the players. Living in *"each other's pockets"* for 17 days and nights provided a perfect opportunity for the players to 'gel' together. He believes this trip played an important part in the improved showing South was to produce.

The club's Australia-wide recruiting campaign threw up many likely prospects and they were given every chance in the early practice games. The best would prove to be long-serving player and administrator Brian Ciccotosto, Max Richardson (brother of Wayne), who would later play 211 games with Collingwood, and Kellerberrin rover Norm Cox, a star in the 1966 Mobil Country Football championships. Wingman Rowley Daw, who had played one game the previous season, was expected to step up and John had high hopes for giant ruckman Glucina,

1967 – Leaving for the Eastern States on South's pre-season trip. Saying goodbye to Meryl, Debbie (left) and Kylie.

who had been steadily improving for the past three seasons. The team had a small core of experience with Beard, Gerovich, MacDonald, captain Gary Scott and Seinor, who was still domiciled in the country, but keen to play again. John knew that his 'middle tier' of players such as Dougan, Greer, Grljusich, Miller and Graeme Smith, with two or three seasons behind them, would have to accept more responsibility to get the side up the ladder. He particularly rode this group hard at training to get the 10% improvement he expected in players from one season to the next. He had recruited old friends Ray Richards and Bill Colgan as selectors and re-formed the match committee after dispensing with it the previous season.

In the week leading up to the season-opener, John squashed persistent rumours that he would play again, fuelled by his appearance in most of South's practice matches, but a nagging leg injury had dispelled any fleeting thoughts about playing. He broke with tradition and summoned the league side to a team meeting on the Friday night before the match and talked tactics so the players could *"sleep on it"* as he found many of them too tense to absorb this information pre-match. These Friday night team meetings would become part of the routine for the season.

South's first game was against Subiaco, who had replaced Keith Slater as coach with former St Kilda player and coach Alan Killigrew, who was renowned for his passionate and fiery addresses. Subiaco had also recruited Bob Johnson, who had left East Fremantle, and their team now possessed the league's two leading goal-kickers from recent seasons, with Austin Robertson (Jnr) returning after a season with South Melbourne. These two were thought likely to pose problems for the South defence and most scribes favoured the Maroons to notch a first-up win.

However, after an even first half – and in a pleasant change from the first game of 1966 – South kicked 10 goals to two in the second half, to win by 39 points; this was backed up by a hard-fought win over West Perth at Leederville Oval the next week. However, the bubble burst as Swans inflicted their usual early-season victory over South seven days later. The 39 point loss gave John plenty to coach on, as he prepared for the first derby. Old Easts, under new playing-coach Bert Thornley, had been hard hit by injury and were without a win and South was always on top, winning by 14 points. Better was to come and, with Gerovich back in the side, South downed reigning premiers Perth. A win over Claremont set up a top-of-the-table clash with the unbeaten East Perth. This was South's biggest game since the 1962 finals and John worked overtime on the younger players to prepare them for the occasion, which was also Scott's 200th league match. A big crowd of 17,200 fans flocked to Fremantle Oval and the South fans went home happy – the Bulldogs jumped the Royals early and won by 40 points. The win left South second on percentage behind East Perth, which was a welcome contrast for the club and the coach after the previous four seasons, when the Bulldogs were virtually out of finals contention after the first seven games.

The team's good form continued over the next month with comfortable victories over Subiaco, Swans and East Fremantle and, with nine wins from 11 games, South was three games clear in second spot. However, losses to Perth, East Perth and East Fremantle (in Gerovich's 200th game) caused concern as the team ran 'hot and cold', with some experienced players struggling. John showed his ruthless coaching style by replacing captain Scott at half-time in one game after a poor display. Such moves were rare in this era, as coaches kept their reserves for the last quarter in case an injury left them with less than 18 fit players on the field. One of John's obvious traits as a coach was a preparedness to take risks, with Seinor also sent to the bench early in one game and Ciccotosto, despite some impressive performances in his first season, back in the reserves after a poor match. This was another of John's coaching ploys – he would often *"test the mettle"* of younger players by unexpectedly dropping them *"to see how they would handle it, to see how they coped with setbacks and disappointments"*.

The centre position was a difficult spot to fill, but there were no thoughts of a comeback as John tried several players there including Greer, Scott, Max Richardson and a young Tony Micale, who would later marry John's sister, Diane. With four qualifying rounds left, South was two games clear in second place ahead of Perth, but their recent form was far from convincing. John varied training by moving to the Fremantle golf course (as Marty McDonnell had done in 1962) to freshen up the players and attempt to sew up second spot. Top position was out of reach, as East Perth was three games clear after dropping just two matches.

The last four games were disastrous. Initial losses to West Perth and Perth left the Bulldogs clinging precariously to second spot. The press was speculating about player unrest at South, based on John's benching of experienced people like Scott and Seinor, and in *The Sporting Review* of August 18, John replied – *"There's no dissension – we are 100% happy. I feel the criticisms are stirred up by people trying to create news"*. The next week saw South suffer an agonising three point loss to Claremont, who were making a late charge for the top four, and Perth upset the Royals, giving them second place on percentage. This set up an intriguing set of fixtures for the last round, with Claremont playing sixth-placed Swans and holding a better percentage than South and West Perth, currently third and fourth. A Claremont win and a loss by either of those sides would see them tumble from the four. With South up against the Royals at Perth Oval and West Perth away to seventh-placed East Fremantle, South appeared most vulnerable.

John rallied his experienced players, calling for a do-or-die effort and insisting they *"steady the ship"* when the pressure went on. He also got a full muster of players at training for virtually the first time in the season, as Cox, Seinor and the four other country-based players made special trips to Fremantle to train. At half-time, in appalling weather with torrential rain lashing the city, it looked as though South would miss the finals as they trailed by 35 points. Despite a second half rally, kicking six goals to two, South lost by 13 points and all attention was focused on radio reports from Bassendean and East Fremantle ovals, where high drama was being played out. Old Easts finished all over a tiring West Perth to win easily and Swans, four goals behind Claremont at three-quarter-time, stormed home with seven goals to send retiring captain-coach Fred Castledine and veteran ruckman Keith Slater off on a winning note. Their upset win confirmed South and West Perth as the first semi-finalists but, despite not being out of the top four for the whole season, John faced a big task to turn the slump around in his first (of over 30) finals games as a coach.

In the week leading up to the first semi, history was made when Walker became the first (and only) player to win three successive Sandover Medals, as he tied with Claremont rover John (Buzz) Parkinson on 19 votes. It was the first time in WANFL history that two players could not be separated by a countback and in probably the tightest count on record, four players – Cable (for the third year in a row), Claremont's Lorne Cook, West Perth's Brian France (who only played 12 games) and South's Cox – were runners-up on 18 votes. Cox's first year effort was all the more meritorious considering he had lived and trained in Kellerberrin as he worked on the family farm and it gave the club a boost in the finals build-up.

Against the Cardinals, South started quickly with the wind and had 11 scoring shots to four, but could only register 2.9. However, with a dominant ruck division led by Seinor, they played better into the breeze, led by 21 points at half-time and were never seriously threatened, winning by 39 points. The performance was solid and unspectacular, but John was happy with the commitment of the players, particularly his senior brigade who all weighed in with good contributions after indifferent recent form.

In the second semi, Perth produced a repeat of the previous year by downing East Perth by five points after just one point separated the teams at the previous two changes. This set up a preliminary final re-match of the last qualifying round, where East Perth had triumphed by 13 points. It was also the first preliminary final between the two teams and their first finals clash since the 1956 grand final. Although East Perth had only lost four home-and-away games for the season, John was optimistic about South's prospects.

The team met for their now-customary Friday night briefing, with John declaring a 9pm curfew, emphasising the importance of good rest and relaxation before the match. Not one to rest on his words alone, John visited the homes of all the players from about 8.30pm onwards to check on their whereabouts. Greer remembers that John was forced to visit his house twice after finding no-one at home on his first visit just before 9pm. Greer and his wife had dinner at his parents home and when John returned a few minutes after 9 o'clock and Greer greeted him at the front door, he was challenged as to where he had been 15 minutes earlier!

The preliminary final was played before a crowd of 27,000, with the Royals favoured to win. John was concerned that the 'hype' of the finals might over-excite his younger players, so he had soft orchestra music floating across the change rooms as he urged them to focus on the task at hand and not get distracted by any physical or verbal jousting from the experienced Royals. South led by 10 points at the first change, as Seinor and Glucina won the ruck duels to give Osmetti and Cox plenty of opportunities, and by half-time the break was 23 points. However, almost right on the siren, Mal Brown (as he would do so often in his playing career), 'decked' Keith Smith and an all-in brawl developed as the players left the arena. Gerovich and Greer remember that the players were livid at what Brown had done and were keen to square the ledger. John saw trouble in the emotion-charged atmosphere and had the players sit quietly or lie down as the orchestra music played, telling them to focus on the task and play the ball, not the man. He also reminded Miller, who was playing on Royals star Syd Jackson, of his opponent's match-winning ability. John knew that of all the East Perth players, he was the one who could swing the game if given any leeway.

For whatever reason, South was flat after half-time and Jackson turned on one of the best halves of finals football seen in WA. With Miller playing loose and chasing kicks, Jackson notched up the goals as East Perth stormed back to take the lead. John sent the runner out to Miller to tell him to tighten up on Jackson and *"sacrifice your game for the team"*, but he received a caustic reply from Miller via the runner and Jackson continued to find space in the Royals forward line. John knew the side was in trouble, as the Royals ruck brigade of Eddie Pitter and Terry Freemantle were on top of Seinor and Glucina, giving rovers Keith Doncon and Hans Verstegen an armchair ride. While he was seething with Miller's attitude, he left him on Jackson, keeping his reserves for the last quarter. Greer, who had played on Jackson before with some success, was on top of Mark O'Donoghue in the centre and John was loathe to move him. East Perth led by a goal at the last change, but South was coming home with the breeze. However, Jackson put paid to any Bulldogs comeback, finishing with seven goals for the half as East Perth kicked nine goals for the quarter to win by 40 points.

In the aftermath, John was duly taken to task for not moving Greer onto Jackson, but shrugged off the criticism, explaining that Greer was winning his position and he had expected Miller to rise to the challenge. Privately, he was ropable about Miller's virtual refusal to play tight, but he resisted the temptation to publicly castigate one of his players, although Miller soon learned of his coach's displeasure at what John regarded as putting himself above the team. John was full of praise for his side, saying that to rise from last to third was a great achievement and, although he was disappointed at fading out so badly, he conceded East Perth and Perth had the edge over the season. Having led by 23 points at half-time, John felt a grand final appearance was there for the taking, but the club had little hesitation in re-appointing him as coach for 1968. To conclude the 1967 season, Perth powered home to beat East Perth by 18 points to notch their second successive flag, while Swans beat East Fremantle in a knock-out night series contested by the bottom four clubs at the Claremont Showgrounds.

~

For the new season John followed a similar pre-season programme with short, sharp workouts rather than long, slogging fitness sessions but, unfortunately for the players, there was no Eastern States trip to break the routine. Spirits were high at the club and there was an expectation that the side would again make the finals, but the pre-season form wasn't exactly what John desired and he conceded he was unhappy with the team's form, with many seasoned campaigners playing poorly. In *The Daily News* of April 5 he said "... *many players who are resting on their laurels will have to improve considerably or play with the reserves*". Much of his concern centred around the key defensive positions, as South faced the new season with no established full-back or centre-half-back. Beard had been recruited by Richmond (the first South player of note to be lost to the VFL) and MacDonald was back on the farm and unlikely to play. Newly-appointed captain Seinor had been injured in a car accident and would miss the start of the season, and wingman Daw was still overcoming a knee cartilage operation. Gerovich, now in the twilight of his career, was also an uncertain starter because of work commitments. The only potential plus was the return of Tom Grljusich, who had been playing with Central Districts, in South Australia, for three seasons. However, the two clubs were locked in a bitter clearance dispute which would see him on the sidelines for the early part of the season. In the probable absence of MacDonald, Grljusich loomed as a likely replacement at centre-half-back, so the club was desperate to secure his clearance.

With the lack of key defenders, most scribes rated South as a potential finalist, but not likely to trouble Perth, who were clear favourites to record a hat trick of flags. Much interest centred on the likely fortunes of West Perth and Subiaco. The Cardinals, much to the chagrin of East Perth, had lured Graham Farmer back from Geelong as captain-coach to replace Bob Spargo. Although now 31 years of age, Farmer was still an imposing figure in the game and was expected to lift the Cardinals closer to a grand final after their third and fourth placings in the past two seasons. Subiaco, the 1967 wooden spooners, had signed Haydn Bunton (Jnr) as captain-coach, hoping he might repeat his magic of 1961 when he took Swans from last to first. The WANFL also trialled a pre-season night series between all eight teams, after the success of the 1967 end of season night competition. This was eventually won by East

Fremantle, but most clubs did not field their best sides and public interest soon waned, despite the excellent facilities at the Claremont Showgrounds.

In the season-opener, John's comments about players resting on their laurels proved right on the mark. After leading Claremont by 26 points at the last change, South wilted to lose by eight points. As in the previous two years, John reacted savagely, re-assessing the league list and working the players over on the training track. Once again, senior players Gerovich and Dougan felt John's wrath and were dropped to the reserves and, for the second time under John's coaching tenure, Gerovich retired in protest at his axing. Again though, this would prove to be short-lived. The team responded with solid wins against Swans and Old Easts, but a 10 goal effort by Subiaco's Austin Robertson (Jnr) stopped their momentum. When further losses to West Perth and Perth left South with two wins from six games, John rallied the players for a huge effort against East Perth, knowing the club could well have been out of the finals race by the end of the first round. Over 12,000 people flocked to Fremantle Oval, lifting the total attendance for the first round to a record 303,112, to see a committed Bulldogs lead the Royals throughout and record a 31 point win. Grljusich under-scored his importance to the side with a best-on-ground performance, as well as being South's top individual scorer. The win lifted South to fourth place on percentage, but already Perth and West Perth had cleared out at the top of the table, so the remaining sides were vying for third and fourth spots only.

After 10 rounds, South was third with six wins, which was a good recovery after their poor start, but the State side was in Adelaide for round 11 and missing Grljusich and Graham Scott left the South forward line severely undermanned. Up against Subiaco, the only bright spot for South was that the Maroons would miss Robertson, who had posted 77 goals from 10 matches and was an automatic selection for the State side. However, his absence was not enough to tip the scales in South's favour and a loss sent them tumbling to fifth place. Defeats by top teams West Perth and Perth in the next two weeks just about removed South from final four calculations as the league fixtures went into recess for a week, with WA playing Victoria at home.

On the weekend of the State match, South (minus only Grljusich) went to Northam for a social game and, desperate to resurrect South's season, John invited both Gerovich, who had been playing with Sunday league club Cockburn-East Fremantle, and MacDonald, who had been playing in the country, to have a game. He also played himself (just for fun!) and, despite a typically good first-up performance, he quickly ruled out any return to league football. Gerovich got plenty of the ball and though he kicked 1.11, John was sufficiently impressed to ask him to return to the club. He also wanted MacDonald back, but farming commitments prevented that. The next game against East Perth, as in the first round, assumed great importance for South's prospects and, despite the social nature of the weekend, John started to gee up the players, emphasising that it was virtually a grand final, requiring a do-or-die effort.

Over 13,000 people attended Perth Oval for the game, some perhaps attracted by the prospect of seeing Gerovich soaring for a mark again as John decided to take a punt and play him, even though he was underdone. South had the best of the first term, but after quarter-time were completely outplayed as East Perth recorded a resounding 73 point win. With so much at stake, John was bitterly disappointed and didn't hide his feelings from the players. He accused several of being *"soft"* and *"not wanting it badly enough"*, which made it *"impossible for the rest of the team"*. In his three recent seasons as coach, this game was the most frustrating and disappointing one. The defeat left South two games and percentage out of fourth spot, with bleak prospects for the rest of the season. South beat the bottom three sides over the next three weeks, with Gerovich vindicating his recall with 19 goals, and this set up the clash with Subiaco as the match to determine South's fate. They had to beat the Maroons, or fall two games plus percentage behind them with only three matches to play. John again rallied his senior players for a special effort, but was left profoundly disappointed by the result. Robertson kicked 10 goals for the second week in a row and Bunton roved tirelessly to set up a 46 point win as South trailed all day. This loss confirmed that, for the first time since the Page final four system was introduced in 1931, no Fremantle side would contest the finals, as Old Easts were floundering in seventh spot.

John took the defeat hard. Again, with so much at stake, the side had hardly fired a shot and he felt some of the players lacked the heart for the big games and were too content to remain in their *"comfort zones"*. They couldn't (or wouldn't) meet the challenges required to be successful and he couldn't fathom why this was so. Given his own dedication to the game, he found it hard to understand lesser degrees of commitment by players, especially after tasting finals football the previous year. Why their hunger to succeed wasn't the same as his played heavily on his mind and he eventually concluded that his message wasn't getting through to the players. While he knew the absence of key defenders Beard and MacDonald left the side weaker than in 1967, he nevertheless felt the team was still under-achieving and not playing to its potential. As a result, after a 26 point loss to West Perth the next week, he announced he would not seek re-appointment as coach for 1969. In *The West Australian* of August 19 he explained his position – *"It may be thought that my decision not to re-apply was because South has not had a good season. This is not the case. Rather, I believe a coach should not hold the position for more than three years"*[22]. He further added – *"South has plenty of talent available, but I think an experienced captain-coach is needed on the ground to bring the best out of them"*; this was a view accepted by the South committee, who said they would seek a playing-coach for the new year.

There is a perception in football circles that sides often rise to the occasion in the aftermath of a coach stepping down – or being sacked – but, in reality, this is often not the case and it certainly wasn't for John. Up against league leaders Perth at Lathlain Park, South fell apart in the second half, losing by 110 points in an inglorious display. However, after a tough week on the training track, the players responded to their retiring coach in the last game, upsetting third placed East Perth by 31 points at Fremantle Oval. On the same day at Subiaco Oval, Robertson kicked 15 goals (and 11 points) of Subiaco's 19 for the match to give him a qualifying round record total of 157 goals, one more than Bernie Naylor's 1953 figure. With Subiaco taking fourth spot, all four city teams were in the finals, with Old Easts having their worst season on record, winning only four games.

East Perth just got over a fast-finishing Subiaco in the first semi, with a goal from Vic Evans 16 seconds before the siren producing a three point win. In the second semi, Perth, who had lost only two games and West Perth, with only three losses, met in a hard, slogging contest, with a final quarter burst by the Demons enabling them to qualify for their third successive grand

---

22. Luckily, particularly for Swan Districts, John didn't hold himself to this view in future years, as all of his coaching appointments in the '70s, '80s and '90s, apart from two years with West Coast, were for four seasons or more. In 2002 he coached Swans for the 19th season.

final. In the preliminary final, East Perth surprised by dominating the first three quarters, but then, as in the first semi, needed a late goal to win by three points. However, they couldn't prevent Perth from notching their third straight premiership (by 24 points) as Sandover medallist Cable finally beat Walker into second place and also made it a hat trick of Simpson Medals. Perth follower Noel Wilson set an enviable record by being a member of two premiership teams on the same day. After playing in the victorious Perth reserves side, Wilson was called into the league team as Bob Page pulled a muscle running onto the ground and had to withdraw.

~

The end of 1968 saw John frustrated and disappointed at South's failure – there is little doubt the team was a couple of players short of being a good side, particularly in the key defensive positions. Graeme Reilly did a reasonable job at full-back, but centre-half-back remained a trouble spot and the side conceded the second highest points against tally. Injuries and poor form forced South to use 40 players in the league side, with Grljusich, despite his late start, the team's best, winning the Walker Medal although he only played 15 games. The Scott brothers, Greer, Richardson, Glucina and Tomka had consistent years, but the side lacked some brilliance.

John reflects on these years as ones where *"I probably pushed too hard for the times"*. While the players were paid to play football in a more structured fashion than in the 1950s, their employment was still the priority and John feels his training demands and Friday night meetings were probably a little excessive for the era. However, it was consistent with his attitude to football – he had always adopted a *"whatever it takes"* approach and naturally expected his players to do the same. This style didn't endear him to some of the players, but a coach can never please all the people all the time and some certainly resented his harsh discipline. Miller was one player far from being a fan of John's coaching methods and style, especially after the 1967 preliminary final, but he still played regularly in the league side during 1966-68. Gerovich, with his short-lived retirements in 1966 and 1968, was another who *"had his moments"* with John's uncompromising approach and remembers him as *"expecting a hell of a lot and being absolutely intolerant of anyone not putting in a wholehearted effort"*. Greer agrees with these sentiments, but adds *"If you tried hard to do what he asked, then he would give plenty of encouragement"* as he was all for the team and the players and was always enthusiastic and dedicated. When necessary, he was also brutally frank about a player's form and attitude and Greer remembers that *"... you knew he wasn't kidding. You always knew exactly where you stood"*.

While John remained content that it was time to step down as coach at the end of 1968, his football desires and ambitions nevertheless still burnt brightly. He knew he wasn't done yet with coaching. The elusive premiership, which he had failed to experience as a league player, loomed as a goal that just had to be achieved as a coach. However, he was happy to bide his time and take a break from league football, although he wouldn't sever his ties with the game completely. He told South he was available to help coach their junior sides and was one of the first to welcome the incoming coach in former Melbourne half-forward Hassa Mann when he arrived in WA. In December, he was named playing coach of Sunday league side South Perth. Ever the opportunist, he took the job primarily to improve himself as a coach, keeping an eye to the future.

Chapter 11
Football in the 1960s

Ken Miller, the WANFL president, in 1967, confirming that the league would refuse clearances to Eastern States clubs that were influenced by monetary offers:

> "WA has no intention of becoming the nursery of Victorian football as Tasmania has been in the past".

The 1960s was a time of growth for WA football, with attendance records for qualifying rounds and finals regularly broken. In 1960, the season's total attendance, including finals, was a little over 700,000, while, by 1969, more than 930,000 fans went to the football. Records for a single match (26,760 watched East Perth play West Perth at Perth Oval on June 7, 1969) and grand final (51,385 for West Perth versus East Perth) were set. To accommodate the increasing spectators, the clubs and the league sought to expand seating facilities at their ovals. In 1967 Old Easts opened a new $70,000 pavilion at East Fremantle Oval and patrons were charged an extra $1 to take advantage of the under-cover seating. Most clubs had improved their covered seating during the decade and, in 1969, the three-tier stand built at Subiaco Oval for $500,000 was opened to provide seating for 7800 fans.

The increase in spectators raised the revenue base of the league and the clubs, which were further swelled by a growing bar trade. All club premises were now fully licensed and most had amalgamated their football and social clubs into a single entity, requiring a full-time club secretary or manager. In 1960, the WANFL paid a $6000 dividend to each club; by 1969 this had swelled to almost $30,000 and the combined turnover of the eight clubs totalled $1,136,000. In tandem with these increases came higher player payments, from about £10-12 a winning game per player in 1960, to $50-100 for a win and a smaller amount for a loss by the end of the decade for regular league players. In some cases, clubs signed their star players to contracts for fixed sums, as South did with John Todd and John Gerovich in 1962. There were also incentive payments and long service funds and, at South, Gary Scott and Gerovich each had $1200 paid into their Provident Fund on playing their 200th league games in 1967. By the end of the decade, clubs were spending $10,000 or more on player and coaching payments each season and most were also paying their reserve players a small amount per match.

The 1960s were also a time for innovation on and off the field. The media profile of the sport boomed as television became more established in Western Australian households. In 1964, the Sandover Medal count was televised live for the first time by Channel 7 and their Sunday morning football review, *World of Football* was hosted for much of the decade by Frank Sparrow, with panellists Steve Marsh, Mick Cronin, Marty McDonnell, Stan 'Pops' Heal and former umpire Fred Woods, and rated well. Likewise, the ABC's Channel 2 *Football replay* (hosted by Jim Fitzmaurice) went to air at 7.15pm on Saturdays and kept many people home until at least 8 o'clock. Their Sunday night replays of VFL match highlights, which started late in the decade, raised awareness of Victorian teams and players in WA. The replay rights for showing games became an additional source of income for the WANFL and in 1963 the league received £500 for TV rights, a fee which attracted criticism from some quarters as being excessive! In the same year the VFL received £3000 from TV stations, although this covered live telecasts as well as replays. These figures pale into insignificance and reflect the growth in football as an industry in the past 40 years, when compared to the $100 million per year paid for the AFL TV rights in 2002-2006.

Radio also traded heavily on football's increasing profile. All four games were broadcast by different stations (6WF, 6PR, 6IX and 6KY) and most had football preview and review shows, which included league team announcements on Thursday nights. Many clubs also held their own radio shows on Friday nights or Saturday mornings to keep members informed of club events. South started its own show in 1960 and the inaugural compere was the venerable George Grljusich, in what was his first stint in a long career in radio broadcasting. The print media also used star players such as John for weekly game reports and columns, providing many with useful additional part-time income.

Perhaps conscious of the possibilities raised by television coverage, the league introduced time clocks, firstly at Subiaco Oval in 1966, then at other grounds in 1967, courtesy of a sponsorship from Caltex Australia. The scoreboards also began displaying the progress scores of other games and padded goal and point posts for player protection were now the norm. In 1964, the first cheer squad appeared as about 10 young girls urged Claremont on during the finals and in 1965 the league expanded club teams to four by introducing a fourths competition, to be played on Sunday afternoons along with the thirds[23]. The move met with general agreement from the clubs as it seemed an appropriate way to foster junior talent from their districts, but it would only survive for 10 years before being disbanded after the 1974 season. The WANFL also experimented with night football in 1967 (end of season) and 1968 (pre-season), but poor crowds and a lukewarm attitude by the clubs in the latter year saw the concept abandoned. There were two significant rule changes in the decade which became permanent fixtures. In 1966 the flick pass was finally outlawed and in 1969 the oft-mooted out of bounds on the full law, providing for a free kick to the other team, was eventually introduced.

The use of walkie-talkies, initially to speak with team runners when they were on the ground away from the bench, came about in 1964 when Claremont's Jim Conway and West Perth's Clive Lewington trialled their use. As the decade wore on, coaches experimented with sitting in an elevated position and using them to relay messages to the team bench, as became the norm from the 1970s. However, their use was not widespread in the '60s, partly because playing coaches were still more common than non-playing coaches. All clubs had playing coaches for at least part of the decade, with South (Marty McDonnell 1960-63 and John 1967-68), Claremont (Jim Conway 1964-68), West Perth (Arthur Olliver 1960-63 and Clive

---

23. In 1960 the thirds competition was switched to Sundays so home and away fixtures were the same as the league and reserves. However, this caused initial problems for South, as the Fremantle Council refused to allow Fremantle Oval to be used on the Sabbath.

Lewington 1964) and Perth (Bob Miller 1960-61 and Ern Henfry 1962-65) having the longest periods of non-playing coaches.

While there was increased emphasis on fitness, little changed in tactics in the '60s and, for John, the game was still one where *"you played your position and played man-on-man and either had a personal win for the day, or you lowered your colours"*. There was no interchange rule, so players were mostly left in their positions and, if having a poor game, coaches appealed to their competitive instincts to lift, rather than move them elsewhere. The individual clashes of star players did much to promote the game, providing a talking point for the media and the public in the build-up to the weekend. In the early '60s John Todd versus Ray Sorrell, Graham Farmer versus Keith Slater or Brian Foley and Austin Robertson versus Mal Atwell were eagerly-anticipated match-ups. Later in the decade it was Bill Walker versus Barry Cable, Farmer and Bill Dempsey versus Fred Seinor and Gary Scott, Mal Brown versus Bob Shields, and Robertson versus Trevor Sprigg. One certainty for the fans was that these individual clashes were guaranteed to eventuate, as there was no 'cloak and dagger' deception attached to team placings, as is the unfortunate habit these days. This is another aspect of the modern game that John laments, especially as the good players *"rack up plenty of possessions, but don't have the personal challenges of yesteryear"*. For example, to watch James Hird and Nathan Buckley or Ben Cousins and Michael Voss regularly play on each other head-to-head would provide a terrific talking point for the media and a great spectacle for the fans.

~

The most controversial issue of the '60s, both for the WANFL administrators and the clubs, were interstate clearances. The trickle of players in the late '50s going to play in the VFL had grown into a steady stream as many great names of WA footy were lured to Melbourne. However, it was not without a fight, as the WANFL, led by Pat Rodriguez initially and after his 1964 death by Ken Miller, remained steadfast in their opposition to clearing WA players to Eastern States clubs, particularly the Melbourne VFL sides where the requested transfer was simply about *"more money to play football"*. Unless the transfer was for work or family reasons and/or had the blessing of the club, the WANFL attitude was that WA football had to be protected and standards maintained by keeping the best players in the State. In part, this was to ensure the State side remained as strong as possible, as interstate rivalries were intense. The annual State games and the ANFC championships every few years were important events on the football calendar. In the years before State of Origin came into vogue, neither Rodriguez nor Miller wanted to see any home-grown WA players representing another State (especially Victoria) against Western Australia. As far as the clubs were concerned, they were only going to lose their champion players if compensated by substantial transfer fees.

As a consequence, protracted clearance wrangles became the norm as the VFL talent scouts increasingly turned their attention West. The first big name to head to Victoria was Farmer, who left East Perth at the end of 1961 to join Geelong. Although he had earlier stated his intention to play in the VFL in 1962 to both East Perth and the WANFL, a clearance wrangle nevertheless ensued, as Royals president Fred Book stood firm (unofficially) on a demand for a £2000 transfer fee. Geelong was outraged, but couldn't officially pay a fee as this was illegal under the Coulter Law, which applied to all VFL clubs, but not those in WA. Under the table payments for clearances, or club members or supporters paying the fee on behalf of the club, were regular (unofficial) occurrences to sidestep the rule. Eventually East Perth accepted a cash offer of £1500 for Farmer's clearance, but they held out until the week before the first match of the 1962 season.

In late 1963 East Fremantle broke new ground with a £1500 transfer fee on Sorrell after South named him as their new coach and early the next year Claremont rocked the football world by asking for £4000 for Denis Marshall, who wanted to join Geelong. Such large clearance fees stretched club finances, both in the WANFL and the VFL, and South eventually parted with £1250 to get Sorrell, with the money coming from members; it was subsequently recouped in 1966 when Sorrell was cleared back to Old Easts [24]. South was so incensed by the issue, it took a motion to the WANFL seeking to ban transfer fees, but the clubs were split on the issue and the vote was lost. The Marshall clearance saga dragged on for weeks as Claremont refused three applications from Geelong, but mid-season he was cleared when the clubs came to (unofficial) terms. In the same season, Graeme John won a clearance from East Perth to South Melbourne despite emphatic assertions from Book that he would not be cleared under any circumstances.

However, it was not all one-way traffic – the Victorian clubs also made it difficult for their players to move West. When Kevin Murray was appointed captain-coach of East Perth in 1965, he had to submit four clearance applications before Fitzroy finally relented on the eve of the season. In 1966 (as in '61), State players selected for the ANFC carnival had to sign a WANFL contract declaring they would play in WA until the end of 1968 or be dropped from the side. The WANFL played hard-ball in extracting this loyalty pledge, but with the carnival being a career highlight, selection was eagerly anticipated. The only escape clause for a player seeking to move interstate within the contract period was for their WA club to sponsor a waiver request, but there were no guarantees the league would agree to this. East Fremantle centreman Bert Thornley signed the contract and went to Hobart for the carnival, but the next year was embroiled in a clearance controversy.

In 1967 the VFL clubs embarked on several public recruiting raids into WA, partly because at the time they were banned from recruiting Victorian country players. Thornley, in his first season as captain-coach of East Fremantle, signed a form four with Carlton mid-season to play in 1968 and therefore felt obliged to step down as coach, although he continued as a player. Norm Rogers took over as coach as the press sought clarification from the WANFL about Thornley's chances of obtaining a clearance. While he made no specific comment about his circumstances, WANFL president Miller left no doubt about the league's attitude – *"The intense interest Victorian clubs are showing in West Australian players is largely brought about by the present embargo placed on country recruiting in Victoria. WA has no intention of becoming the nursery of Victorian football as Tasmania has been in the past"*. He confirmed the WANFL would refuse clearance applications when it was convinced the movement of a player had been influenced by monetary offers.

---

24. Of the $2500 eventually paid, Sorrell actually contributed $500 from his own Provident Fund.

Such statements did not deter the Victorian clubs and they approached players such as Walker, Cable, Fred Lewis, Peter Eakins, John McIntosh, Syd Jackson, Colin Beard and Greg Brehaut. Of this group only East Perth's Jackson (to Carlton), South's Beard (to Richmond) and Thornley would move to Melbourne for 1968 [25]. Carlton, mindful of the WANFL's hard line on clearances, reportedly offered Thornley $2000 if forced to stand out of football. In 1968 this proved the case as South, East Perth and East Fremantle, no doubt with the tacit approval of the WANFL, refused to accept Carlton and Richmond offers for their players, who all sat out of the game for a year. The tough stance softened the next year and they were finally cleared, with Beard the last, mid-way through the season, and all three went on to play in VFL premiership teams [26].

Perhaps mindful of the messy saga, the WANFL delegates unanimously voted in 1969 to amend the clearance regulations to allow players 23 years or older and with 120 games or more to be released, providing their clearance was approved by their club. Much to Beard's chagrin, in this same year the fickle nature of the clearance issue was demonstrated when South cleared Max Richardson to Collingwood (to join his brother Wayne) without any protracted wrangling, even though Richardson had only played 40 games and two seasons for South, compared to Beard's 161 games and eight seasons.

~

The '60s saw five of the eight clubs win premierships, although eight were shared between three teams. West Perth started and finished the decade with flags and Swans (1961, '62 and '63) and Perth (1966, '67 and '68) each notched a hat trick of premierships. Claremont (1964) and East Fremantle (1965) won one flag apiece, while East Perth played in six grand finals (1960, '61, '66, '67, '68, '69), but lost them all. Only South and Subiaco failed to make a grand final, with the Bulldogs third place in 1967 under John their best for the decade, but they also collected four wooden spoons (1961, '65, '66, '69), making the decade their worst on record. Subiaco fared a little better, making the finals four times (1961, '64, '68, '69), with their third place finish in 1961 their best.

In interstate football, the glow of being Australian champions in 1961 faded as WA struggled for much of the decade. The Victorians were beaten once (at Subiaco in 1965) but, on most other occasions, WA was thrashed, particularly at the MCG. Against South Australia, honours were even, with WA usually winning at home and losing in Adelaide. In 1963 WA suffered a rare loss to Tasmania at Subiaco Oval. The 1966 ANFC championships were held in Hobart and WA, with Murray as captain-coach, had high hopes they could retain their title; after wins against the VFA, SA and Tasmania, they played Victoria to decide the championship. A gallant WA led narrowly at each change, but faded as the fresher Victorians, who had enjoyed an extra two days' rest, won by

---

25. Eakins joined Collingwood in 1970 and McIntosh went to St Kilda the same year.
26. Beard played in the Richmond premiership team of 1969, Thornley with Carlton in 1970 and Jackson with the Blues in 1970 and '72. In the 1970 grand final, Thornley was the player Ron Barassi took off at half-time, replacing him with Ted Hopkins, who kicked four second-half goals as Carlton fought back from a 44 point deficit to beat Collingwood by 10 points.

15 points. The turning point was possibly an injury to centre-half-back Brian France, who limped off in the third quarter after completely outclassing Darrell Baldock, with the star forward then dominating the last term. The 1969 carnival in Adelaide saw WA out of contention with a loss to SA in the first match and Victoria took the crown for the 14th time in 17 attempts.

Two great players stood out by virtue of their achievements over the decade – Walker and Cable. They won all the Sandover Medals from 1964-68 [27], five Simpson Medals (Walker in 1967; Cable in 1966, '67, '68 and '69), gained All Australian selection (Walker 1969; Cable 1966 and '69) and each played in a hat trick of premierships. Cable also won the Tassie Medal at the 1966 carnival. John has no hesitation in naming them as the outstanding players of the 1960s, but will not be drawn on who was better. He remembers Walker as a brilliant ball-getter with great foot skills on both sides of his body and a player who, particularly in his early years, was an outstanding goal-kicking rover – *"No-one read the ball off hands better"*. Cable was a different type of player, not a big goal-kicker, but one who could set up play from defence as he could dropkick the ball 60 metres with great precision *"... and his handball skills, even early on, were very good"*. John was only opposed to the pair a few times as a player but, when coaching against Swans and Perth in 1966-68, he never tagged them, as it wasn't part of the game in those days. He hoped for the best by throwing the challenge to the South rovers to match it with them, but usually they *"weren't quite good enough"*. He believes Steve Marsh was just as good as Walker and Cable and, but for his *"quick tongue with the umpires"*, might also have won multiple Sandover Medals.

Closer to home, John has special admiration for two South players – Gary Scott and big Ivan Glucina. Scott played almost every position on the ground at South and proved virtually indestructible. In 1969 he set the then Australian record for consecutive games played when he racked up his 205th match, beating Jack (Skinny) Titus, the great Richmond player of the 1930s and '40s. Scott was an extremely honest player who gave his all for the team; he made an excellent captain because of these qualities. John recalls a story about Scott that perhaps typified the era, when players had superstitions about their preparation. In the mid-1960s Scott played *"an absolute blinder"* in a match when John was coach, *"probably the best game he ever played"*. John remembers the next week *"he couldn't get near the ball and had a terrible game"*. Absolutely crestfallen, Scott apologised for his performance, adding that he *"just couldn't understand it"* as he had done everything the same as the previous week. He had eaten exactly the same meals on the Friday and Saturday, worn the same clothes to the ground, played in the same shorts and socks, warmed up in the same way, even shaved on the Saturday morning at exactly the same time! John's response was simple – *"There are only six days between bad games and good games"* and to forget the other stuff! *"If you get caught up with superstitions and routines, then you're in big trouble"*, was his blunt advice.

Glucina was a giant of a man and remembered by WA supporters in the '60s for his massive hands, which would swallow the ball. He was the classic late developer, as many ruckmen are. In his first year with South in 1962, he won the Burley Medal for the fairest and best player

---

27. In 1967 Claremont's John Parkinson received a medal when he couldn't be separated on a countback from Walker. In 1970 Walker was beaten on a countback by Pat Dalton, but received his fourth medal 27 years later when the system was retrospectively abandoned, while Cable won his third Sandover in 1973.

in the WANFL thirds competition, but over the next three seasons he managed only 17 senior games. It wasn't until John took over as coach that he blossomed, partly due to maturity, but also because John gave him plenty of time and encouragement. In the early 1960s John recalls watching Glucina actually miss the ball with his foot when trying to kick it in one game, such was his rawness. However, he had a heart that matched the size of his hands and a fierce determination, spending countless hours practising the basics of marking, kicking and handball. At John's urging, he joined an athletics club to improve his coordination and, although he always ran last in the competitions, whether it was sprint or middle distance events, he gradually improved. In 1967 he played a full season in the league side and was an important member of South's resurgence to make the finals. Along the way he had plenty of knockers, but John kept faith with him as he saw the time and energy that Glucina was prepared to put into improving himself. He capped a remarkable development by playing for WA against Victoria in Melbourne which John says *"was a great example of what can be achieved with desire and determination"*.

The best teams of the decade were Swans, coached by Haydn Bunton (Jnr) and Perth, coached by Atwell. John has a great admiration for Bunton, who overcame significant adversity to play football; he had suffered polio as a child and having to wear leg calipers. In 1959, a serious car accident shattered one of his kneecaps and put him out of the game for a year, but throughout the 1960s he rarely missed a game, making light of any injuries[28]. In one match he played the second half with a wad of cotton wool stuffed into a deep gash in his scrotum, refusing to leave the ground to have it stitched until the match was over. John was impressed by both his hardness as a player and his coaching prowess, taking Swans to their first premiership in 1961 and repeating the triumph in the next two years. He remembers Bunton the player as *"being so hard you could hit him with everything and he wouldn't flinch, or even bother to look over his shoulder to see who it was"*. John cannot recall Bunton ever retaliating after *"wearing one"* from an opponent, despite the amount of illegal attention he regularly received. In 1961, John looked on with envy as Bunton put together a premiership side from nowhere, after Swans had finished last in 1960 – *"He put some steel into them and made them refuse to accept defeat"*. Although Swans weren't the best team in 1961 (East Perth had lost only two qualifying round matches), he coached them to win on the day that counted most; holding back some strategies to nullify Farmer's influence until the grand final, taking the risk that his side would get there. What John took from Bunton's handling of Swans were two important points – *"in any game, but especially finals, the best team doesn't always win and you are always a 'chance' and sometimes you have to risk losing in order to ultimately win, by perhaps keeping your best card for when it counts the most"*.

In a similar fashion to Bunton, John feels Atwell gave Perth a physical presence in 1966, '67 and '68 that they had perhaps lacked earlier in the decade. The side had lost preliminary finals in 1963 and '64 and finished fifth in 1965, but were immediate trendsetters in '66 under Atwell, who led by example as captain-coach, with inspirational use of vigour. As a result, their smaller skilful players, led by Cable, stood taller and got harder as they enjoyed plenty of protection in the packs from players such as Max Jancey and Bob Page, who followed Atwell's

---

28. Bunton went on to play 301 games of league football (excluding State matches) in three states – WA, SA and Tasmania.

lead. In 1967 they probably weren't the best side, as East Perth finished four games clear on top, but Perth had their measure in the finals, with Atwell proving an astute coach as well as an inspirational captain. In 1968 the Demons were a stand out according to John, as they lost only two games and had strength all over the ground. By now Atwell's influence as a player was waning, but his presence on the field remained important, as he was still capable of inspiration and calculated aggression when the team needed a lift. In Perth's premiership years, when John coached South, the Demons proved to be their bogey side. South could only beat them once in the three seasons, losing the other eight games by an average of 58 points.

The 1970s

Chapter 12
Coaching the enemy

Merv Cowan, the East Fremantle president, announcing John's appointment as coach in December, 1972:

> "Todd's natural enthusiasm to assist youth, his vast football experience and his local knowledge were factors that led to the unanimous decision to name him coach".

The years of 1969-72 represent the longest continuous period in which John was not involved in league football, either as a player or senior coach in a career spanning 1955-2002 [29]. However, he was not lost to the game in those four years; he first threw himself into the coaching position at South Perth and contemplated a return to playing. Despite the coaching frustrations at South, his life still revolved around the game and he needed some involvement in the transition period. *"I enjoy football and it would be hard to break away without being associated with the sport in some way"* was his simple explanation when asked why he had taken the South Perth job. The club played in the South Suburban-Murray league competition and had tasted little success since being formed in 1931, a fact that further attracted John to the position. He replaced former Claremont player Ian Aitken, who had taken the team to fourth place in the previous two seasons, and immediately set about bolstering their strength by recruiting several South reserves players.

He started training in early January, several weeks earlier than was normal for Sunday league clubs. The training was harder than usual for this level of competition, but he did it all himself to set an example; also he knew of no other way. His knee stood up well to the pre-season programme and regular running; gym work over the previous two years had kept his legs in good shape and he was eager to don the boots again. When the season began he resisted the urge to rove and played mostly off a half-forward flank, with the occasional run in the centre. Despite only playing 14 of the 20 qualifying rounds, his form was sufficient to add one more club fairest and best trophy to his collection. Although the side won a respectable 14 games, they missed the finals on percentages and had to be content with fifth spot.

---

29. The only other years where he was not formally involved were 1963, when he spent the year at Rottnest; 1965, when he retired as a player; and 1999, when he (first) retired as a coach.

While John enjoyed playing again, the failure to win a finals spot left him disappointed and determined to improve the team's position the next year. In 1970 he recruited more South reserves and border-line league players, the most notable being Tony Micale, and they topped off the side nicely. John only played eight games as knee soreness and niggling muscle injuries curtailed his games, but the team swept all before them. They went through the qualifying rounds unbeaten, with just two narrow wins (two and 13 points) and all other margins 27 points or more. Ten games, including the last four, were won by more than 100 points and the side looked to have a mortgage on the flag. However, a premiership remained elusive. He was forced to coach from the sidelines as South Perth bowed out by 50 and 36 points in the second semi and preliminary final. Once again, *"the best side for the year doesn't always win"* and *"take nothing for granted"* became prominent thoughts as he grappled to find reasons for the fade out.

With hindsight, he has little doubt the big margins in the last four games left the team with a *"soft underbelly"* which was exposed in the finals. In early October, when Hassa Mann led South Fremantle to the WANFL premiership, he was both pleased and envious in equal proportions. In 1971, after losing several players who weren't replaced and with John not playing, South Perth struggled to win nine games and finish seventh. At the AGM a disillusioned John *"paid out"* on the committee and the players, expressing disappointment at their failure to retain the playing strength of the previous year and their *"indifferent"* attitude to training and winning. His brief flirtation with a lower tier of competition was over.

In reality, it's surprising John lasted for so long in the Sunday league. Probably, it was only the lure of playing again that kept him going in the first two seasons, but by 1971 his playing days were over and coaching at this level was never going to satisfy his desire for success. Clearly, he was out of place in the Sunday league, as the level of commitment by the players often left him frustrated and bewildered – *"While there were many former WANFL players scattered among the teams, which meant a good standard, there was frequently a poor roll-up at training, as much for social reasons as work commitments; many players didn't let playing on a Sunday interfere with their Saturday night social activities, which I found hard to take"*. While he appreciated the difference in commitment between the WANFL and the Sunday league, he still found it difficult to coach, especially when players would miss training without explanation and arrive for games in a hung-over state. This was totally foreign to him and he often delivered a fearful *"spray"* when his temper got the better of him. Micale recalls one occasion where John 'sacked' former Perth player Bill Mitchell at half-time, telling him to concentrate on selling real estate and stop wasting everyone's time as he would never amount to anything as a footballer [30]. John told Mitchell to collect two clearance applications from the club secretary in case he lost one on his way out of the ground! George Daly, who later became a successful horse trainer, was another player who regularly copped a serve from the coach, being told many times to stand on the boundary line and *not move* because he was crowding the forward line. This instruction happened so often that it became a standard piece of repartee in conversations involving Daly in the bar after a game.

---

30. Bill Mitchell never played for South Perth again, but did become successful in financial circles and in the late 1980s was a member of the West Coast Eagles inaugural board that both appointed and then dismissed John as coach. He admits John summed him up correctly as his heart wasn't in playing, so is happy to credit John with launching his commercial career.

John's penchant for adopting the unusual to get a better performance from the team is also well remembered at South Perth. For the second semi-final of 1970, he told the players to bring their toothbrushes to the match. Always trying for an edge, he had the players clean their teeth before running out so they felt *"fresh and relaxed"*. He used this ploy as a simple distraction to help relieve the tension of being red-hot favourites. The expectations of success at the club were enormous and he was concerned the players would *"get flattened"* by it. His concerns were borne out as the team played well below par and lost by 50 points. The next week he gave each player a pill just before running out, telling them it would *"help get them through"*. The pill was just an Aspro, but he didn't tell the players what it was as he sought to contrive *"a lift"* for them, concerned that the size of the previous defeat had knocked their confidence. This also had little effect as they slumped to a 36 point loss, but his flair for something different to gain an edge would remain with him for all his career. Some 30 years on John reflects on his time in the Sunday league as *"not great"*, because the players and the club were more social than serious, which conflicted too much with his own attitudes. For his family though it was a pleasant time as Meryl and the kids enjoyed the relaxed atmosphere at the games. The smaller crowds and grassy banks at most grounds were a nice change from the WANFL venues and playing on Sundays instead of Saturdays meant there was no rush to get to the game after working at the butcher's shop or doing deliveries for six to seven hours on Saturday mornings.

~

In 1971 John was nominated by South Fremantle to be a State selector, replacing Kevin Merifield, who had stepped down. He joined long-time Swan Districts administrator Tom Moiler and former West Perth player Ron Bewick, with Graham Farmer the coach. He expressed the strong view that open selection was vital to maintain the prestige of State football, with some clubs lobbying to follow the Victorian method of restricted selection to prevent sides losing too many players to the State team while still playing regular season matches, as had often happened in the 1950s and '60s. The WANFL eventually took this view for the game against South Australia in Adelaide in July and adopted a selection policy which stipulated a maximum of three and a minimum of two players from each club, much to John's disgust. The side was further complicated by injuries to several leading contenders and the selectors were forced to 'pinch hit' with Perth key defender Bob Shields at centre-half-forward as they juggled the selection quota.

Keen to play a useful role, John sat in the grandstand to get an elevated view and different perspective of the game, relaying any thoughts by radio back to the bench, where Farmer was sitting. He recalls – *"Polly thought this was a good idea, so I found a spot at the back of the grandstand, surrounded by South Australian supporters. Midway through the first quarter I saw a potential move and called down to the bench, but Polly never uttered a word, he just turned the radio off!"*. Such was the difference between being the coach and a member of the selection panel. John had little to say for the rest of the game as WA struggled on the heavy ground, eventually going down by 27 points. The loss was the 10th consecutive defeat for WA in Adelaide since 1938 but, for John, the silver lining to a dismal day came soon after when the WANFL delegates in the travelling party announced that the selection quota system would be abandoned for the game against Victoria in Perth in two weeks' time.

For this game Farmer returned to the side in what would be his last State match and John volunteered to be the runner, rather than sit on the bench or in the grandstand. While Farmer was at least forced to listen to what John had to say as he relayed information from the bench, he didn't really enjoy the role or the game. The 38 point loss by WA was the eighth in their last 10 State matches, as the Victorians led throughout after a four goal first quarter burst by full-forward Peter McKenna. The game is best remembered for the shirt-front of Barry Cable by Leigh Matthews, forcing Cable from the field, but by that stage the Vics were well on top and the incident did little more than briefly liven up a fairly predictable contest. This game marked the end of John's involvement as a State selector, as he found the job frustrating and unfulfilling. Not being the coach and therefore not in charge of the team, was not something he enjoyed and he knew he would never make an assistant coach or selector.

When he announced that he would not seek re-appointment, he fired some broadsides at the WANFL administrators, claiming that no progress was being made in State football. In an interview with Robert Bennett in *The Daily News* he criticised the system, saying *"... you can't pick a State side a week before an interstate match, give it a couple of training sessions and expect it to perform well. South Australia showed what kind of attitude needs to be adopted. They trained for weeks in advance and groomed a side"*. He advocated a neutral State coach and the selection of younger players rather than the big names such as Farmer and Cable. He also reiterated his dislike of the quota system, saying it demeaned the honour of State selection. Never one to leave quietly, he finished by saying that – *"recommendations for the betterment of WA football were submitted three or four years ago and every year the State selectors have been putting in a report, but WA football is still in the same groove"*.

~

Stepping down from the South Perth coaching job and the State selection panel, John was snapped up by South Fremantle to be their junior and schools coaching supervisor, to develop young talent in their area. The job appealed to him, as he enjoyed nurturing youngsters in the skills of the game and it provided an excellent avenue to move on from the coaching frustrations of recent years. In 1972 he also did some media work, in newspapers and radio, which again provided some useful extra income for the family. Towards the end of the year he and Meryl set up their own butchering business, buying a shop from Barry White, John's old roving partner at South. Meryl generally did the deliveries in the family's Mini Minor, which meant several trips back to the shop to complete all the orders, especially when daughters Debbie and Kylie went along to help!

John's name certainly helped things get started and business was slowly increasing when he was visited by Merv Cowan, the East Fremantle president. Old Easts were in the market for a coach, as Alan Joyce, who would later coach Hawthorn to premierships in 1988 and 1991, was returning to Melbourne after two years. The club had a good batch of promising young players, but they needed to be taught how to play and Cowan felt John had no peer as a teacher of skills and the finer points of the game. The club had just experienced its worst period in a long and successful history. Since their come-from-behind win over Swans in the 1965 grand final, Old Easts had only made the finals twice, losing to West Perth in the first semi of 1966 and again to the Cardinals (by three points) in the 1971 preliminary final, when Garry Fenner's last-gasp shot at goal registered a point. Before 1966 the club had only missed the finals three times since their inception in 1898, winning 23 premierships and being runners-up the same number of times. But they had now missed the finals in five of the past seven seasons. Cowan felt the rot had to stop and he believed a contributing factor to the decline was a lack of stability at the top, with six senior coaches between 1966 and '72[31]. It was time to develop a team by encouraging young players, as well as instilling some discipline in the side and he believed John had the credentials to do both.

The job appealed immensely to John. He was curious why East Fremantle, with such a long and proud history, were regularly missing the finals and he wondered what was lacking. Their recent circumstances fitted perfectly with his coaching style, as he always preferred to take on the underdog role and pick up a team with little recent success; he wanted to go in and develop from below, accepting that it might take time. The challenge of lifting teams from the bottom has always attracted him and, with all his appointments over 43 years, he never stepped in to coach a team that had made the finals the previous year.

On December 6, 1972 Cowan told the East Fremantle members that John would be coach in 1973 on a one year contract. He said that *"Todd's natural enthusiasm to assist youth, his vast football experience and his local knowledge were factors that led to the unanimous decision to name him coach"*. Graham Melrose, with whom John would form a long and successful relationship at East Fremantle and later Swans, was re-appointed captain to assist with the transition. John said he was *"looking forward to the challenge of coaching a league side again"*, adding that *"I have learnt a lot in the last five years. I have a new perspective on football and added confidence in myself"*.

Down the road at Fremantle Oval the announcement was not well received. Apart from losing his services as the junior coaching supervisor, the South committee had just recommended John for life membership, to be confirmed at a meeting on the coming Monday. As had occurred with Steve Marsh 15 years earlier, some South committeemen were outraged that John had defected to the enemy and wanted to scrap his life membership. Doris received a terse letter from one committeeman accusing John of 'treachery' and making it clear he would not vote in favour of the honour when the nomination came up. However, cooler heads prevailed and his 18 years of loyal service to South as a player and coach were duly rewarded with life membership.

The great rivalry between the two Port clubs was enhanced by John's appointment and was further stimulated by the release of the 1973 fixtures, which had a Fremantle derby listed for round one. The battle lines were clearly drawn as he embarked on the next stage of his coaching career.

When John first met the East Fremantle players in mid-December, they were no doubt pleasantly surprised to learn that training wouldn't start until January 30, 1973. He warned the players to have plenty of miles in their legs, but deliberately chose a late start because he knew that, under Joyce, the team had endured two Spartan pre-seasons. Joyce had followed the lead of his Hawthorn coach, the great John Kennedy (Snr) and introduced commando-style

---

31. Bob Johnson (1966), Bert Thornley and Norm Rogers (1967), Norm Rogers (1968), Eric Sarich (1969), Eric Sarich and Harry Neesham (1970) and Alan Joyce (1971-72).

training, so John was mindful they had *"done it tough"* for two years and needed some respite. The late start also gave him and Meryl more time to get established in the butcher's shop. The family only had one car and the deliveries and errands Meryl and the girls did had to be finished by 4.30pm, so John could be at the club by 5 o'clock. He also had to find a reserves coach and was pleased when Steve Marsh accepted the job, giving East Fremantle two of WA's best post-war footballers and two Sandover medallists on its coaching panel. With former captain-coach and 200 game player Norm Rogers coaching the colts, the club had a wealth of talent and experience for the development of its young players.

On the first night of training, John surprised the players by bringing out the footballs and taking a number of handball drills, rather than checking whether they had miles in their legs. He stressed the need for dedication and sacrifice to be successful, reminding the players of the club's poor record since 1966. He emphasised that the team must come first and individuals who wanted to buck the system would not be tolerated.

There was little experience in the team, so the young players were given every opportunity to press for league selection. In 1972 the East Fremantle fourths had won the flag and the under-18 side were champions in the inter-district competition, so there was a good crop of young talent coming through. However, there was little experience to blend with this. Full-back Eddie Donnes, with 110 games, was the most experienced player ahead of Alan Prosser (100) and captain Melrose on 98. The next best was Rex Townsend on 57 and then the likes of 1971 Sandover medallist David Hollins, Doug Green, Gary Gibellini, Clinton Farmer and Bob Becu with around 40-50 games each. The only recruit of note was South Melbourne rover Russell McHenry, while Brian Peake, who had notched 12 games in his debut season, was expected to consolidate his place. However, there were still many gaps in the side. Pundits predicted a bleak year, with some suggesting Old Easts might sink to the bottom of the ladder, but John was confident the enthusiasm of his young brigade would see them build healthy reputations.

The 1973 season saw the introduction of the centre square (although it first appeared as a diamond shape), a long-mooted change to the rules to reduce crowding at centre bounces. The WANFL changed to a board of directors comprising one from each club plus the WANFL president and vice-president, moving away from the cumbersome committee system of two delegates from each club and a board of management that sat above them. Another innovation was sponsorship of $2000 each from Woolworths, Motorama and Claridge for the best-performed club in each of the three qualifying rounds.

Two Victorians joined John as new coaches – St Kilda rover and 1967 Brownlow medallist Ross Smith joined Subiaco, replacing Haydn Bunton after five seasons at the helm, and former Melbourne player Dennis Jones had taken over from Peter Steward at West Perth. On the eve of the opening round, John raised the stakes for the derby by heading his 'Todd Talk' *Daily News* column with a blunt *"I hate red and white"* as he responded to verbal jousts from South coach Mal Atwell, who had earlier written about his (and John's) first clash as coaches in 1966 when Perth trounced South by 143 points. South had triumphed in seven of the previous nine derbies and were favoured to win again.

Chapter 12 – Coaching the enemy

The game turned out to be a 'blinder'. After a stirring pre-match address from their new coach, Old Easts turned on a nine goal burst in the first term to lead by 50 points. However, some astute positional changes by Atwell sparked a revival and at half-time Old Easts only led by two points in an amazing turn-around. The press and radio commentators had Old Easts 'dead and buried' at this stage, as it was generally felt their late start to training would leave them underdone. John exhorted his young players for a third quarter effort with the breeze and they finished 23 points ahead. In a desperate last quarter, with Melrose and McHenry both roving in the backline, Old Easts bottled up the play to win by one point. While South's inaccuracy of 11 points for the term cost them dearly, many were due to the pressure applied by Old Easts as they displayed admirable fighting qualities, much to the coach's delight.

However, these qualities were sadly missing at Leederville Oval a week later when West Perth led by 48 points at the half and 44 points on the final siren. A loss to Swans the next week served as a further reality check, as there was little to enthuse about in either game for Old Easts. John promoted more youth, and narrow, but unconvincing, wins over Claremont and Perth at least stemmed the tide and reinforced his decision to blood new players. The team was still coming to terms with John's style of coaching and his demands and the blending of experienced players with youth. The side finished the first round of fixtures with heavy losses to Subiaco and East Perth, but John continued to express confidence that his players would *"get better week by week"* and that a finals spot was not beyond them. It's unlikely that many of the East Fremantle faithful enjoyed the same optimism, given their record over the past seven seasons.

As the second round unfolded, John rode the players hard, demanding a greater effort and more discipline and worked on their self-belief, telling them they were good enough to make the finals. A strong self-belief has always been one of his main characteristics, both as a player and coach, and he strove to impart this into the team, despite their relative inexperience, which can often breed doubt in young players. The side downed West Perth, but were then thoroughly outclassed by 63 points by South in the derby; this resulted in a torrid week of training, ending with the players summoned to a Friday night team meeting at East Fremantle Oval. Still smarting over their insipid derby display and concerned about their attitude, John made them listen to a full replay of the radio description of the match (video recorders were not yet in vogue), which contained many less-than-complimentary comments about the team and certain individuals. The meeting lasted almost three hours and dented many plans for dinner, but it got the desired result. The next day, in atrocious weather, Old Easts started fast, kicking three goals in eight minutes and Swans never got back into the match, with the 23 point win equivalent to more like eight goals given the conditions. The players had responded to the radio 'barbs' in emphatic fashion, but two more wins were soon followed by two losses, as the side remained frustratingly inconsistent.

After 14 rounds, Subiaco, East Perth and West Perth seemed certain finalists, with East Fremantle and South Fremantle battling it out for fourth. However, Old Easts were becoming injury-riddled; in particular, followers Becu and Fenner looked likely to be out for the season, so John threw the gauntlet down to Neil Ferguson and Richard (Buster) Browne to carry the ruck and urged his experienced players to lift the younger ones as they chased the finals berth. Cowan and the committee publicly backed John and gave some impetus to the finals push by re-appointing him coach for 1974-75.

Old Easts opened the third round with a derby, but were again outclassed by South, leaving them almost 20% behind the Bulldogs in fourth spot, but level on points; that was the week John was presented with his life membership at South. A nine goal loss to West Perth appeared to end their finals hopes, particularly as South upset East Perth to go a game and percentage ahead. Despite these setbacks, John continued to talk up his team's chances, declaring his young players still capable of improving. He overhauled the side and gave league opportunities to players such as rover Tony Buhagiar, who had started the season in the under-19s and thereby joined a rare group of footballers to play in all four grades in the one season.

John's by-now brother-in-law Tony Micale had also joined the club from South Perth, where he won the fairest and best in 1972. John offered Micale the chance to play league football again, but made it clear there would be no favours, emphasising that he would make it tough for him. In fact, John went out of his way to ensure this was the case pre-season, trading on the bitter rivalry between East and South, and goading players such as Gibellini and Mal Dobson to *"sort out"* the former Bulldog and test his resolve. Micale weathered the storm and eventually earned respect in the club by playing well, although it was the second round before John finally selected him in the league side. While he became a league regular, his mistakes incurred a little more of the coach's wrath than was the case with other players, but Micale understood the situation and had no problem with it – *"It probably helped me be accepted by the other players"*, suggests Micale. One player who suffered from a lack of opportunities was Farmer, who played 21 league games for the year, but started 11 matches on the bench.

After beating the three bottom sides, Old Easts reclaimed fourth spot as South stumbled but, with two rounds to play, the Bulldogs were still favoured to make the finals as they faced Perth (7th) and West Perth (3rd), while Old Easts had the top two teams in Subiaco and East Perth. John's view was blunt – *"We face a tough programme in our final two games, but if we cannot beat top sides at this stage, then we don't deserve to play in the finals"*.

The Subiaco clash attracted plenty of interest as Austin Robertson (Jnr) seemed set to break the WA aggregate career goals record of 1203, held by Ted Tyson, the great West Perth full-forward of the 1930s and '40s. Robertson needed three goals to better Tyson's tally and, with 64 goals for the year, was averaging slightly better than this per game. Subiaco was one game clear on top, but not yet safe in the top two and, with so much at stake, the game began with plenty of needle. The backlines put enormous pressure on the forwards and at half-time Old Easts led by two points, extending the lead to seven points at the final change. Robertson had kicked two goals, but 15 minutes into the last quarter he notched his third to take the record – this also spelt the end for Old Easts. As John remarked later in *The Daily News*, *"... that record-breaking goal by Robertson lifted Subiaco and with the crowd behind them, they shot away from us"* as the Maroons rattled on eight goals to win by 24 points. He added ruefully *"... I would have preferred Robertson to kick the three goals early, but instead he achieved the milestone at a critical stage of the game"*.

John remained upbeat about their finals chances, although they were now not complete masters of their own destiny. South held fourth spot by almost 18% leading into the last set of fixtures, so Old Easts had to beat East Perth and hope the Bulldogs would lose to West Perth. East Perth and West Perth were level on points and separated by just over 1% and a loss by either side would probably cost them second spot and the double chance.

Chapter 12 – Coaching the enemy

During the week John again demanded that senior players such as Melrose, Prosser, Donnes, Green and Hollins show the way, given the side's inexperience. Melrose, in particular, was at his best as Old Easts led by 17 points at half-time. In the third term against the wind they again outscored the Royals to extend their lead to 29 points. With the lure of the finals so close, Old Easts ran away with the game to win by 55 points, and radio reports of the South-West Perth score were going their way. It was a tense 10 minutes, but West Perth held South off to win by eight points to give them the double chance and confirm Old Easts in fourth place.

While John was pleased to make the finals, some warning bells were already sounding in his head. They would play East Perth again the next week and the ease of their win bothered him. Despite playing for the double chance, East Perth were strangely below par and John knew that in a sudden-death final they would be a vastly different proposition. That night in the East Fremantle social club he heard many players declare they had East Perth's measure and would have little trouble beating them again. He tried to nip this in the bud, but knew they were in trouble; misplaced confidence is so easy to get, but so hard to shift without suffering a beating. At training John repeated himself ad-nauseum about not taking East Perth lightly, about the need to be hard and desperate and about respecting the opposition and the side trained well enough, but he wasn't convinced their *"heads were right"*. East Fremantle was favourite, a surprising situation given that East Perth had won 14 games for the season and beaten Old Easts twice.

The semi-final represented the first of six final round clashes between John and Mal Brown as rival coaches, although they would later all be between Swans and South – starting again in 1980. On a wet and windy day, the first quarter was an even affair, but a seven goal second quarter by the Royals realised John's worst fears, as Old Easts fell away to trail by 36 points at half-time. The rejuvenated Royals rammed home the advantage in the second half, winning by 49 points – a turn-around of 104 points in seven days. John was far from pleased – the side had capitulated far too easily despite his repeated warnings. The next day in *The Sunday Times* he launched a stinging attack on the attitudes of many players at the club, saying – *"They want their booze and women – all the good times in life and they want to be champion footballers at the same time. They certainly aren't professional enough in their approach"*. The manner of the loss rankled him more so than the loss itself, as it reflected a superficial attitude to the game – a mixture of complacency and insufficient desire and commitment. He vowed to put it right, threatening that anyone who couldn't, or wouldn't, commit themselves to the cause would be moved on.

His strong stance was backed by the club and in the 1973 annual report president Cowan pulled no punches, highlighting five areas of weakness where the team needed to improve:

- The disturbing manner in which the team fell apart if they got four goals or more behind.
- The fact that too many players were reported, hence the club was not at top strength for all games.
- The inability of the top six to eight players to combine for the team.
- The insipid performances against South Fremantle.
- The lack of anticipated development in four to five of the team's better players, regularly failing to produce four quarters of consistent football.

The committee decreed that no player whose services were required for 1974 would be cleared *"in any circumstances"*, as the club was mindful of its slip in 1972 after being a kick away from the '71 grand final. In the remaining finals West Perth led throughout to beat Subiaco in the second semi, downing them for the fourth time in the season. However, they lost Phil Smith, who headed the goal-kicking for the qualifying rounds with 81; he would miss the grand final. Subiaco outlasted East Perth by 10 points in the preliminary final, a game which marked the end of Brown's playing and coaching career with the Royals. Subiaco was the sentimental favourite in the grand final as the club chased its first flag in 48 years. On a wintry day, they eventually found a way to beat the Cardinals. After being a point behind at half-time, Subiaco kicked seven goals to two in the second half to end the longest premiership drought in WA football history, with half back Dennis Blair winning the Simpson Medal.

~

The 1973 season, in which John returned to league coaching after a four year break, marked his fifth year as a senior coach, with 108 games, including three finals. He has no doubt he was a better coach in 1973 than he was in '68, simply by virtue of his extra experience. His three years at South Perth and time in the media and as a State selector was all valuable as *"you can always take something out of new experiences"*. While he had matured somewhat as a coach, his basic philosophies and principles had not changed – *"train hard to get very fit, be disciplined and tough, both mentally and physically, and play for the team, always"*. It didn't matter who kicked the goals as all team members shared the glory of success by playing their part, as small and as unglamorous as it might be.

At East Fremantle there was a general lack of individual and team discipline and, while these characteristics improved across the season, more was required for success. John rode the players hard in 1973 to instil greater discipline and commitment and many recall being on the receiving end of a Todd tongue-lashing, which pulled no punches and had no areas 'off-limits'. Micale was a regular recipient and recalls two incidents. In the last game of the 1973 season he gave away a free kick in the final term by 'decking' an East Perth player, an undisciplined act which cost Old Easts a certain goal. Although the game was safe at that stage, Micale knew he would incur John's wrath and, as he looked across the ground, he could already see the coach on his feet. He was playing on the wing on the outer side of East Fremantle Oval, but eventually the ball moved to the members' wing and Micale could hear the 'serve' he was copping from John. Summoned to the boundary line, Micale was dressed down by John in front of the members for a good minute as he vented his anger on the lack of discipline and respect for the team – but was then told to get back to the game! Micale concedes he deserved the serve, but believes that copping it in front of the members helped him become accepted at East Fremantle, after starting his career at South. That night many players and members offered their sympathy to him!

In another game at Claremont Oval, Micale was taken off in the third quarter after a poor match and was walking back to the bench around the boundary when he noticed John striding towards him at a fast clip. From about 15 metres away he delivered a stinging attack on him, the central theme of which was *"... how did a gutless bastard like you ever marry into my family..."*. In the heat of a game there was never any time for worrying about players' feelings! However, while John had no compunction about letting players know exactly what he thought of them and their actions at a particular time (which sometimes became personal), there was a large dose of brutal honesty mixed in and it was all done to get the best out of the player, either short-term or long-term. While in current times it's more accepted (even by John) that some players and personality types don't respond positively to verbal attacks, in the 1960s and '70s it was the usual method of attempting to get more out of a player. It was certainly the view that if you didn't respond to a serve, then you were mentally weak.

If most WA football followers of the 1970s were asked for their opinion of John as a coach, they would probably respond with something like *"tough"*, *"ruthless"*, *"hard taskmaster"* and, his most common trait, *"a savage tongue"*. He would not take exception to any of these descriptions, which accurately characterised his coaching at this time. But it's also true that he would do anything for his players, such was his enthusiasm for the game. Despite his frustrations with the East Fremantle players after the semi-final loss, at a night out for the team some weeks later, John picked up the bill out of his own pocket, effectively wiping out his coaching payment for the season. This came as an unwelcome surprise to Meryl when she found out, as the family wasn't that well off and she had budgeted on his coaching money. The family business was going along steadily, but John was at the club virtually every night of the week, plus he still did schools coaching during the day, so the opportunity to work the shop to its maximum was affected. This was of little concern to John; like school many years before, he was not inclined to let work unduly interfere with his coaching. By November of 1973 his planning for the 1974 season was almost complete.

Chapter 13
A premiership at last!

Laurie Elliott, John Todd's fitness adviser at East Fremantle in 1974, talking about the physical conditioning of the players:

> *"The main thing to teach footballers is that they can keep going even when they think they have had it. This can be done only by a lot of strenuous running and by building up dedication and purpose. They have to reach a mental condition when they know they can overcome their fatigue and their team-mates will too".*

The first semi-final fadeout in 1973 really became the making of season 1974. The heavy defeat sorted out in John's mind players who weren't going to measure up and the soft mental approach of several team members galvanised his thinking. In contrast to the previous year, he planned a tough pre-season programme, enlisting the help of Laurie Elliott (brother of champion Australian athlete Herb) as his fitness advisor. Elliott was a fine distance runner with a strong mental approach to training, a trait John rated highly and which matched the team's requirements. Pre-Christmas training was physically demanding, but in January they really challenged the mental toughness of the players.

At a Sunday morning session the players were told to eat breakfast before an 8am meeting at the club. Expecting a flogging, most players elected not to eat and, when a bus took them to Yanchep, a beach area 80 minutes' drive north of Perth, the concern was heightened as they pondered what was in store for them. Elliott's instructions were brief – stay on the beach, start running south (towards Perth, some 60 miles away), but take it steady. John's parting message was simple – *"Hang in with someone who runs better than you for as long as you can and challenge yourself to improve"*. With no mention of a finishing point, the players took off, noting with some alarm how soft the sand was, how strong the breeze was – and that John and Elliott were joining in.

Tony Micale started running with Graham Melrose and remembers that Franz Tomka, the South Fremantle back-pocket player who was seeking to switch to Old Easts, took off at a cracking pace and was soon out of sight. An hour later after a slogging eight miles or so, they found Tomka lying face down on the beach asking that he be *"left to drown"* rather than keep on running. Micale called him a *"weak bastard"* and told him to get up, which he eventually did, struggling on at the rear of the pack. The strong breeze was in their faces and the soft sand was calf-deep in places, causing many to stumble and fall, which made progress extremely difficult. There were no such luxuries as drink stops and still no mention of a finish point by Elliott, who traversed up and down the group from back to front to back again, cajoling the players to keep going and to help each other. John, at 35 years of age, was running mid-pack and berating those behind him to catch up, especially those 10 to 15 years his junior, for not keeping up with *"an old bloke"*.

After three hours, the players were well spread out along the beach, forming small groups and working together to pick each other up when they fell as they continued south. The wet shorts were causing bad chafe and bleeding around the groin (John included), but still Elliott kept them going. In parts the beach was blown away and they had to pick their way carefully over sharp and slippery rocks. Eventually, after 20-odd miles and about four hours, the leading players were called to a halt at Mullaloo Beach. Barry Wilson missed the call (he was delirious, according to the others!) and kept running for a few more miles before he was stopped. In contrast, Kerry Coates and Ron Bentley quit after a few hours on the sand and headed inland to the main road, where they flagged down a taxi and got a ride to Mullaloo, borrowing money from a trainer to pay the fare when they got there.

At Mullaloo, the exhausted players who hadn't had any food or drink for the morning invaded the beach side delicatessen, emptying the fridge of drinks and telling the alarmed shopkeeper to book it up to the club – about $500 worth [32]! On the bus home the players slept or sat quietly, simply not having the energy to talk about what they had been through. Most spent the rest of the day in bed. While John and Elliott were privately pleased with the efforts of the players, they gave them little respite as they added to their mental conditioning. In particular, they exploited the displeasure of the group with Coates and Bentley, whose taxi ride was common knowledge. Many were scathing about the incident, feeling the pair had 'baled out' on them and taken a soft option while they slogged it out. Two days later at the Ascot racecourse, the players ran four laps of the track (about six miles) before Coates and Bentley paid the price for their taxi ride and had to run two extra laps, finishing down the home straight through a gauntlet of their less-than-impressed team-mates.

Two weeks later John organised a weekend camp at Lancelin and the players were again put through the wringer by Elliott. A 10-mile beach jog and countless runs up and down the sandhills again stretched the players physically and mentally [33]; John extended the discipline by telling several (including Bentley) to get their hair cut or not bother coming to training the next week. The players were left in no doubt about their requirements for the season – be disciplined, be prepared to make sacrifices to achieve success, and be willing to persevere and stick together, through thick and thin.

~

The searching pre-season the players endured, in particular the Yanchep to Mullaloo run, became a pivotal experience for the team. The bonding and unity created by the run (and the taxi ride) was enormous and served as a terrific rallying point throughout the season. John feels it gave the players *"great belief in their ability to push through when things got tough and I reminded them of this regularly throughout the year"*. Melrose agrees, remembering that *"the players were surprised they got through it, gaining great belief and confidence"*. Micale believes *"the premiership was won that day because of the tremendous bonding effect it had on the*

---

32. On receiving the bill, president Merv Cowan called a meeting of the players to explain, in no uncertain terms, that the club was not paying and they were responsible for it, to which John took exception. Who eventually paid the bill is unclear.
33. In one session, Eddie Donnes became separated from the group and got lost in the sandhills. A few hours later, badly sunburnt and dehydrated, he stumbled back into camp, much to the relief of club officials.

players". By season-end, the run had gained considerable publicity and, with Old Easts winning the flag, other coaches tackled tough and challenging training workouts for their players; pre-season training almost became a survival of the fittest in the late '70s.

John sensed a new resolve among the players and he confidently predicted success for the side in 1974 [34]. The club had recruited Tasmanian ruckman Kerry Williams and tyro wingman Chris Hicks from Geraldton and both would prove important, along with forward Paul Nicholls, who had been overseas for two years playing English county cricket. The only significant loss from 1973 was Alan Prosser, who had returned to Bunbury.

The club was lucky to recruit the unknown Hicks, who had walked into the office in January seeking a clearance to East Perth. Not lacking self-confidence, he told general manager Bob Uittenbroek that he was a great footballer and probably fitter than the East Fremantle players. Bob immediately called John down to the club and, after Hicks repeated claims about his ability and fitness, John invited him to train with the squad that night. Hicks was warned to prepare to be challenged at training, being told that the squad had been training hard under Elliott since November. Hicks completed the full session and, as the players left the ground, John called him over and for the next hour pushed him through extra laps, sit-ups, push-ups and sprints. Uittenbroek saw this from the bar and remembers several members imploring him to stop the torture but, knowing what was happening, he watched with admiration as Hicks refused to give in. After the session, Uittenbroek found Hicks prostrate on the floor of the change rooms unable to speak. He gave him a jug of lemon squash and saw him home, telling him to return in the morning. When John rang the next day to tell Uittenbroek to sign Hicks, the forms were already prepared. Having survived and passed his first 'character test', Hicks would go on to be an important player in the 1974 side.

~

The season opener was at home to the Cardinals, the beaten grand finalists of the previous season, and more than 10,000 people saw East Fremantle kick themselves out of the game, dominating the first quarter with 12 shots on goal to West Perth's two; however, the scoreboard read 1.11 to 2.0. West Perth eventually won by four points, despite having 20 scoring shots to Old Easts 31. However, the next three weeks saw a win over South, a draw with Swans, and a 12 goal thumping of Claremont, with tyro rover Tony Buhagiar kicking seven goals. The diminutive Budgie had first come to John's attention early in 1973 when he watched a colts game when Buhagiar was late after his arranged lift failed to turn up, so he ran several kilometres to the ground. He made light of this setback and still played strongly, impressing John greatly with his attitude. He saw *"something special"* in Buhagiar and pushed him through the ranks so quickly that he played in the league side in the first semi-final of 1973.

The next game against Perth at Lathlain Park was the first of five meetings for the season. Old Easts put in a strong last quarter to win by 13 points and followed up with a solid victory over Subiaco. They were on top of the table after six games, followed closely by South and an improved Swan Districts. To finish the first round, Old Easts were away to East Perth, but went into the game without Melrose, Doug Green, David Hollins and Brian Peake, who were

---

34. The club had adopted the slogan of *"24 in '74"* as it sought to record its 24th league premiership.

in Adelaide with the State side. The star quartet proved difficult to replace and the side went down by four points in a tight finish; a defeat that cost them top spot, but Old Easts still secured the $2000 Winterbottom Cup for the best-performed side.

The second round began poorly as Old Easts suffered a drubbing from arch-enemies South Fremantle, with John berating the players at the long break, demanding a harder attack on the ball, but the side failed to respond and South increased their lead to six goals by three-quarter-time. An incensed John stormed onto the oval at the final break, but walked away from the group less than one minute later. He bluntly told the players he was extremely disappointed in their lack of response to his half-time address and left them to organise themselves. Not surprisingly, South went away to win by 49 points. Five weeks later, Old Easts were back on top after four strong wins, with Melrose leading the side with distinction and forwards Nicholls and Noel Avery finding the goals. They finished the second round at home to fifth-placed East Perth, but the Royals again proved too good and inflicted an upset 22 point defeat. The loss put Old Easts back to third spot, half a game behind South and Perth, but every side bar West Perth were still in the running for the finals.

After comfortably beating West Perth in the lead-up to the derby, president Cowan threw the gauntlet down by declaring that no player would be cleared to the Eastern States next season unless the club won the 1974 flag. This strong stance threatened the planned move of Melrose, who had signed with North Melbourne. If the statement was designed to provide motivation for the clash with their arch rivals, then it was a resounding failure as South again had Old Easts measure, winning by 35 points. Remarkably, South would win only one more game and miss the finals, perhaps to the relief of Old Easts. South had recently been rocked by the forced retirement of full-back Graeme Reilly, who had been diagnosed with a brain tumour.

The third derby defeat of the season provoked a strong reaction from John and he put the players through a torrid week, starting on Sunday morning. The heavy training looked to have taken its toll when Swans, fighting hard to secure a finals spot for the first time in nine years, led by five goals to one at quarter-time. In characteristic fashion, John exhorted the team to greater efforts, bluntly stating that leg weariness was *"all in the head"* and would not be tolerated as an excuse. The side pulled together and went on to win by 35 points. A narrow four point win over Claremont the next week returned Old Easts to top spot amid controversy as Claremont appealed to the WANFL to have the match result reversed, claiming that umpire Ron Powell erred in awarding a free kick to produce a double goal without the ball being bounced in the centre. The protest was dismissed as the East Fremantle players were taken for training by Ron Barassi, with the North Melbourne coach invited to WA as part of East Fremantle's finals build up. Barassi and John were on good terms, having a mutual respect from their State battles, in particular the ANFC carnival of 1961. While in Perth, Barassi warned of the threat to Australian football of the growing popularity of soccer and suggested that a national competition be seriously looked at – which became a reality 13 years later. He also questioned the role of the drop-kick in the faster modern game, saying he doubted it would survive for much longer. Old Easts got home by four points against Perth, keeping their unbeaten record against the Demons intact. The victory set them up for a top place finish, leaving them six points clear of South, Perth and Subiaco and eight points ahead of Swans, with just two games to play. The next fixture loomed as a crunch match, against Subiaco, where a

Chapter 13 – A premiership at last!

win would secure top spot, and a loss could leave them needing to win the final match to make the finals. Almost 12,000 fans flocked into East Fremantle Oval to see Old Easts win by 18 points and guarantee top spot.

With a second semi-final berth secured, John worked the side hard, virtually ensuring *"they couldn't win the last match"*. He trained them for an extra hour on the Thursday night before the game, after Tuesday's session which had involved plenty of competitive man-on-man drills. The final round of qualifying matches was a promoter's dream, with the three spots underneath East Fremantle up for grabs between South, Perth, Subiaco and Swans. The topsy-turvy season carried through to the last qualifying game as Perth thrashed Swans by 10 goals and bottom side West Perth were comfortable winners over South, at Fremantle Oval. Subiaco had an easy win over Claremont and, at Perth Oval, a tired East Fremantle not surprisingly lost to East Perth by nine points. The result was privately pleasing to John, as he did not expect to win, but the effort and attitude of the players in being the better side for much of the match boosted his confidence for the finals as he knew he had left them without the legs to finish off the game. Perth snatched second spot, Subiaco third and Swans hung onto fourth place, two points clear of South, who slipped from the four after having been on top for much of the season.

~

Melrose soon added to the club's success by winning the Sandover Medal with 20 votes, two ahead of Swans half-back Stan Nowotny. Third was East Fremantle centre-half-back Green and the club easily topped the team totals (81 votes, with East Perth on 69); this reflected the spread of talent in the side, with Melrose's win not unexpected as he had claimed most of the media awards. The count saw Swans four time medallist (1965, '66, '67 and '70) Bill Walker fail to poll a Sandover vote for the first time in his career, which began in 1961.

The next day Melrose was forced home from training with influenza, being confined to bed, and missing the lap of honour at the first semi-final in recognition of his medal win. By the Monday, after Swans had upset Subiaco by 23 points to advance to the preliminary final, Melrose's illness and absence from training was causing some alarm, but it also became a germ of an idea for John. He was concerned about Old Easts being favourites for the second semi, given they had beaten Perth in all three qualifying matches, and he was keen to avoid complacency. Feeling that Perth had a potential advantage as underdogs, he embellished Melrose's illness by turning it into a 'flu epidemic and on the Tuesday, five players – Melrose, half-backs Coates and Bentley, ruckman Williams and rover McHenry – were reported to be ill and forward Glen Durnthaler in doubt with an ankle injury. The next day half-forward Avery was added to the list of 'flu victims but, in reality, only Melrose was ill – the others were fit and healthy, but were let off training early to add substance to the story. John had no doubts about their condition, as he had put plenty of work into them leading up to the last home-and-away game and a short training session was all they needed.

Only his assistant coaches Steve Marsh and Norm Rogers, president Cowan and the players concerned were privy to the deception as the story spread through the city and dominated the sports pages of the newspapers. The club was inundated with 'flu remedies from worried supporters and boxes of Vitamin C and other supplements were delivered to East Fremantle Oval by former champion player, coach and now pharmacist Charlie Doig. On the Thursday night John kept up the ruse by delaying naming the side for 24 hours to give his 'flu-riddled players every chance to pick up, emphasising that *"... we are not pulling the wool over anyone's eyes"*. The club released a hoax line up, with names such as Peake, Coates, Avery, Durnthaler and Williams declared unfit and left out. In the Saturday edition of *The West Australian*, the page 6 cartoon depicted a group of East Fremantle players with runny noses drinking cough syrup at one end of the oval, with the caption *"Oh no! The ball is coming back again"*. The back page headline by Geoff Christian, the newspaper's chief football writer, was very direct – *"Is the East Fremantle team a big bluff?"*.

When the team took the field on Saturday there were 13 positional changes from the placings released the previous day and all players (supposedly) affected by influenza were in the side. The first three quarters were tight, with Old Easts five points ahead at the last change after little more than a goal had separated the teams at any stage. John opted for fresh legs and brought on both reserves, Williams and rover Mario Turco, who added great drive as the team kicked eight goals to clinch victory by 23 points and a place in the grand final.

On the Monday, Christian's lead story said *"Drop kicks pave way for Old Easts"* and then took issue with John's hoax, declaring in his second headline that *"Todd does football a disservice"*. He viewed the 'flu epidemic, designed to mislead the opposition, the public and the media, as an *"immature concept"* and that the game *"deserved a more responsible approach than that provided by Todd"*. Christian suggested the ruse had probably kept many people away from the game, as they felt Old Easts were fielding a patched up side, given the number of players likely to be missing. However, the crowd of 26,079 was slightly bigger than in the past two seasons for the second semi and larger than the first semi a week earlier, suggesting the publicity regarding the supposed 'flu epidemic had little effect.

The hoax remained something of a sore point with Christian for many years, although he and John later had an amicable relationship. When the two men discussed the incident some time later, John was quite brazen (and correct) in remarking to Christian that *"... history will remember East Fremantle won the flag in 1974, with no mention of any 'flu epidemic"*. Whether the hoax had any influence on the game is difficult to gauge, but it certainly had people talking about the final, which John rated as a good thing. The negative sentiments of Christian about the deception did not faze John, Cowan or the East Fremantle committee and the WANFL had no rules in place at the time about the naming of teams.

In the grand final build-up, all East Fremantle players were fit and healthy as they prepared to play Perth for the fifth time in the season, with the Demons beating Swans by 15 points in the preliminary final. Old Easts were obviously favourites, but John again sought an angle to help reduce the pressure on his players, but also perhaps given them an edge. The only change was the inclusion of the more experienced McHenry for Turco, who was in his first season of league football. John ran out the 27 players who had been the core of the team over the season, as only 32 players had been used in total, with the other five playing one or two games each. There was no rule preventing more than 20 players running out and he wanted to reward those players who had missed the team, but had still made an important contribution. In addition, this would obviously confuse Perth, who at least initially couldn't be sure who was going to actually make up the chosen 20. In addition, he voluntarily gagged himself from making any comments to the media and also sought out Sir Ross Hutchinson, who hailed from John's home town of Deanmill and who had coached premiership teams at East Fremantle (1937), West Perth (1941)

Chapter 13 – A premiership at last!

and South Fremantle (1947-48), to speak to the players before the game. The players were also instructed to bring their toothbrushes along, as he had done at South Perth four years earlier.

On the morning of the game Melrose suffered the distraction of seeing his car roll backwards across a road and through a neighbour's fence, but fortunately he wasn't in the vehicle at the time! Hutchinson spoke about what it means to win a grand final, suggesting that, after the initial euphoria, there was sometimes an emptiness as you come down *"off the high"* and that the real appreciation of a flag win may not sink in until some years later; however, it can never be taken away, it's always a wonderful reminder of the virtues of hard work, self-sacrifice and perseverance. When John made his final address, he urged the chosen 20 to relish the opportunity and not let their less fortunate team-mates down. He instructed the 27 strong group to run at their opponents as they entered the arena, hoping to intimidate them by the increased size of the squad. Most of the 40,748 spectators only became aware of the extra players when seven players (instead of two) ran to the reserves bench.

East Fremantle kicked into a slight breeze and, after the usual frenetic first 10 minutes of a grand final, they had two early goals on the board. However, at quarter-time Perth led by 10 points even though Old Easts had registered an equal number of scoring shots. In the second quarter, with Peake and Gibellini controlling the midfield, Old Easts asserted their dominance, but kicked a wasteful 5.6 to 3.1 to lead by seven points at half-time. Against the breeze, John instructed his team to handball more and retain possession by running harder and, though Perth skipped out to a 12 point lead, Old Easts rallied to finish only two points down as Buhagiar kicked a brilliant goal on the siren.

At the final break John again used his 'shock trooper' tactic of the second semi as he brought on the high-leaping Williams in place of wingman Micale. He also reminded the players of the pre-season 20 mile beach run, telling them that what they faced now to win the flag was insignificant compared to what they went through that day. The belief engendered in the team by that epic run carried them through the last quarter, kicking six goals, and it was only in the closing minutes that Perth salvaged some late goals to leave the final margin at 22 points.

Late in the last quarter of the 1974 grand final, despatching runner Laurie Elliott with another message. Laurie Watson (left) and Steve Marsh watch anxiously from the bench.

Photo courtesy of
The West Australian.

So, exactly 20 years on from starring in the 1954 reserves grand final for South Fremantle, John finally tasted premiership success again, this time as senior coach of their bitter enemy. The victory gave East Fremantle its 24th premiership, which set an Australian club record, eclipsing the 23 flags (to that time) of Port Adelaide in the SANFL. The popular picks as best players were wingman Peake and ruck-rover Gibellini, who tied for the Simpson Medal with Perth wingman David Pretty. Others to play well were ruckmen Becu and Ferguson and defenders John Grljusich (younger brother of George and Tom) and Bentley, who restricted Perth forward Murray Couper[35] to just two kicks for the match. The premiership was a great personal reward for Grljusich, who had not missed a game for the year, after playing reserves for the whole of the 1973 season. For the Demons, wingman Pretty and first year rover Robert Wiley (six goals) were their best players.

Almost 10,000 fans jammed the East Fremantle social hall and flowed onto the oval that night to celebrate the victory, which ended the longest premiership drought in the club's history.

~

For John, the long-awaited premiership was *"my greatest moment in football"* and fully vindicated his tough and disciplined approach to the season. In *The West Australian* he said *"... the premiership belongs to the players because they buckled down to the hard work, accepted the discipline and brickbats and emerged triumphant"*. Christian wrote that East Fremantle were *"... swept to success on an irresistible wave of self-discipline and team spirit. There is one repeating theme – how men mastered their temperaments and accepted the rigid rules of discipline"*. There was no better example than Melrose who, after winning the Sandover Medal, attributed his success to a critical change in attitude, saying *"... I decided it was time to stop bucking the system and adopt a more mature attitude towards the game, my opponents and officialdom"*. His new-found self-discipline rubbed off onto many team-mates and they largely fell into line with the demands John made of them. However, when tested, his response was tough and uncompromising and he didn't shy away from measures he thought were necessary to enforce the discipline he required from the players. At least once in the 1974 season, Coates was stood down from the league side for drinking the night before a game. On several occasions John (sometimes with a reluctant Marsh tagging along), visited local watering holes on a Friday night to see if any players were present. Cowan often said the players were *"a mad bunch"* and played hard off the ground as well as on, so John's discipline was the only way to get them to fully realise their potential.

Probably, the side was not super-talented; the standout players were Melrose, Hollins and Green, with Peake and Gibellini emerging as quality players. The remainder were a mix of young players like Buhagiar, Hicks and Alan Reid, along with solid, reliable types like big men Donnes[36], Becu and Ferguson, half-backs Coates and Bentley and forwards Avery, Durnthaler

---

35. Couper later explained his poor performance on the after effects of taking a dose of sleeping pills the night before the match, which left him lethargic.

36. John has great admiration for Donnes; his kicking skills weren't great, but he was reliable as a defender, rarely attempting to mark, preferring to spoil vigorously. John later found out that Donnes was short sighted and couldn't see the ball clearly until it got close! John learnt this after a tight derby when he heard that Donnes had asked his South opponent who had won because he couldn't read the scoreboard! He then organised some contact lenses for him. Reid was also another player who couldn't see well. When John asked him why he hadn't done something about it, he thought what he was seeing was normal, not knowing any different.

Chapter 13 – A premiership at last!

and Nicholls. Together, they all had good years and, with no serious injuries, only 32 players were used in the league side; a statistic generally associated with successful teams.

The physical and mental conditioning by Elliott was an important factor in the team's success. The players knew they were fit and gained great confidence in their capacity to fight back from difficult situations. After the grand final win, Elliott was recognised as one of the important contributors to the victory. When asked by Colin Hopkins, of *The West Australian* for his theories on the conditioning of footballers he responded with *"... the main thing to teach footballers is that they can keep on going even when they think they have had it. This can be done only by strenuous running and building up dedication and purpose. They have to reach a mental condition when they know they can overcome their fatigue and their team-mates will too"*. He went on to add *"... when you get players pushing themselves you build up tremendous comradeship between them"*, before relating the story of the Yanchep to Mullaloo run and how Coates and Bentley had failed to complete it – *"The rest of the squad were quite critical of them; they believed they had been let down. The players responded to the criticism and worked harder to redeem themselves in the eyes of their team-mates"*.

Melrose remembers that Elliott *"... set a fine example and got them to do the work without any revolt"* as he established a fine rapport with the players. For this reason, John drafted Elliott

The first flag. Raising the cup with captain Graham Melrose and Eddie Donnes (left), Chris Hicks (middle, partly obscured), Glen Durnthaler and John Grljusich. Photo courtesy of The Sunday Times.

into the job as league team runner mid-season, but after a career in athletics rather then football, Elliott admits that on more than one occasion he messed up a move ordered by John. In the grand final, Elliott vividly remembers forgetting which players he was supposed to move in a three-way switch! *"It was early in the last quarter when the scores were close and, as I ran out, I told myself that I better not mess this one up, but I did! In the end I had to ask Bob Becu who he thought John would have wanted to switch, but he just gave me a wide eyed look and said nothing! I figured the players worked it out OK, as I avoided going back to the bench for a few minutes, but when I did there was nothing said".*

~

Two weeks after the grand final, the side flew to Adelaide for the Australian club championships between the premiers of the WANFL, SANFL and VFL, plus a composite Tasmanian team. East Fremantle were drawn against the SA premiers Sturt in their first game and John was keen to win because he wanted to pit his team against VFL premiers Richmond as a yardstick as to how good the side really was. However, after two weeks of celebrating the premiership victory, the players saw no reason to stop and most sampled the Adelaide nightlife on the Friday before the Sturt game. The side put in a lethargic, indifferent performance, but still only lost by nine points. John was ropable, as the chance to play Richmond was gone; he attributed this to the poor preparation of several players. He ordered a 6am training session the next day, which he hoped would curtail their Saturday night, but several players were late or did not turn up at all, which absolutely infuriated him. He prevailed on Cowan to fine the offending players, but the president was cool on the idea as the players were not being paid for these fixtures, therefore he was not sure the club had the authority to fine them. The players got wind of John's desires to sanction them and some openly challenged Cowan's right to fine them when they weren't receiving match payments – nothing eventuated. The lack of support from Cowan left John livid, as the players knew they had challenged his authority. With many years of hindsight, both John and Melrose see this incident as a key factor in the side's inability to be successful in the next two seasons, as the tough, disciplined approach of 1974 was compromised. John felt that *"... some of the players thought they were untouchable...".* Despite easily beating the Tasmanian side and finishing second to earn $4000 in prize money, the Adelaide trip, in John's mind, was a very costly one.

~

For season 1975, the only loss from the premiership team was Melrose, who went to North Melbourne. In January, John took the players to Busselton for a weekend camp where the first sign of a change (for the worse) in attitude became evident. Urged on by several players, Micale put it to John that they go into town for a few beers, to which he agreed, but declared an 11pm curfew, to be back on the team bus to return to camp. John went with the group, but at 11 o'clock only he and Donnes were on the bus! The players paid a heavy price the next morning with 100x100 metre stride-throughs in the middle of the Busselton trotting track, but the disregard for his curfew did not bode well for the season. In 1974, to ignore one of the coach's orders, particularly a curfew, would have been unthinkable and it was the first tangible evidence of the fall-out from the Adelaide incident.

Chapter 13 – A premiership at last!

In February, John was appointed State coach, the day after South Fremantle full-back Graeme Reilly lost his battle with cancer. In the practice match period, the major news item concerned Mal Brown, who had returned from Richmond and, much to the chagrin of East Perth, had joined Claremont as captain-coach. In their first intraclub match, Brown was reported and subsequently suspended for 15 weeks for interfering with and abusing an umpire. Early signs of a premiership hangover were appearing as East Fremantle struggled, losing by big margins to West Perth and Perth in practice matches. Ferguson became the first of what would become a long list of injuries with a knee operation for a torn cartilage before the season began. Compounding their ruck problems further was a car accident that left Williams with a broken leg.

The poor pre-season form was played down by John, who said practice matches *"didn't worry him greatly"* as he had used them to experiment with the side, playing State centre-half-back and new captain Green up forward and trying a number of players on the ball to cover the absence of Melrose. He had also scheduled a later start to pre-season training, as the Australian club championship meant the players were still in action in mid-October when some clubs had already started training for 1975. He was confident the players would respond when the season began, as he challenged them to become the first team, since Perth in 1967, to successfully defend the premiership. The pundits agreed, making Old Easts flag favourites, with Perth and Swans the likely challengers.

In addition to Brown at Claremont, Subiaco and West Perth had new coaches with Hawthorn stalwart (and later long-time Carlton coach) David Parkin replacing Ross Smith and former Fitzroy reserves coach Graham Campbell taking over the Cardinals. On the playing arena, the centre diamond was altered to a square, which all league coaches thought was a positive move as it allowed the centre-half-forward and centre-half-back, plus the wingmen, to start in a better (more natural) position at centre bounce-downs.

~

The season opener was a derby at East Fremantle Oval and 13,000 fans were there; eight players were missing from the premiership 20. The most notable new face was Gerard Neesham, who would go on to play in premierships with Swans and Claremont (as captain-coach) and who would become the inaugural coach of the Fremantle Dockers in 1995. Old Easts got home by eight points, but the next two games saw losses to the improving West Perth and Swans, the latter by 76 points as injuries and an indifferent attitude started to hurt. Wins against Claremont and Subiaco rekindled East Fremantle hopes that '25 in '75' remained a possibility, but three consecutive losses left the side seventh, with three wins from the first eight games.

To compound the situation, Gibellini walked out on the club, declaring he would not play with East Fremantle again while John remained coach. He had missed a compulsory 6am Sunday training session and told club officials that *"... I can no longer put up with the constant criticism handed out by Todd"*. John said little other than declaring he wanted Gibellini to resume, while Cowan and Uittenbroek bluntly said his services were required and he would not be cleared under any circumstances. After further discussions with Cowan, Gibellini returned to the fold a few days later and made himself available for the next match. The walkout did nothing to alter John's approach as, above all, the team is always more important than any individual. He was riding the East Fremantle players hard to arrest their form slump and the fallout with Gibellini [37] didn't change his stance. However, the controversy sparked the side, as they scored a 33 point win over South in the Foundation Day derby, then followed up with victories over West Perth and Claremont on the weekend the State side went to Melbourne to tackle Victoria, with Ferguson appointed captain-coach for the game.

~

Coaching the State side created more controversy. After the June split round, John and the selectors Hassa Mann, Bob Graham and Sonny Maffina announced a 21 player squad, with the East Fremantle representatives being Green, who was appointed captain, Peake, Hollins and newcomer Mick Jez. At the first training session John wasted no time in putting his stamp on the team. Generally, most State training sessions are short, sharp skill workouts with an emphasis on allowing the players to get to know each other. He dispensed with this approach and put the players through a vigorous session of tackling and bumping, much to the dismay of the respective club officials watching. He told the players to be prepared to commit their bodies in Melbourne, particularly if the ground was wet and slippery – *"I don't think there is enough physical contact in the WA game and our players lack confidence. They must be prepared to meet more physical opposition than they encounter in local club games"*. The players responded well to the session and received a standing ovation from the crowd when they left the oval. The next week he kept the theme alive with a practice match against East Perth on the Tuesday before the team left for Melbourne on Thursday. However, on the Tuesday the selectors dropped a bombshell by relegating Brian Adamson from the squad, replacing him with Swans full-forward Max George. It was the first time a player had been omitted (when fit) from a State squad of 21 so close to the game, and the WANFL were so embarrassed they offered Adamson a free trip to Melbourne to watch the match, which he politely declined.

West Perth seethed over the decision and suggestions emerged of a personality clash dating back to 1971 when Adamson joined Sunday league club South Perth when John was coach. John bore the brunt of the criticism over Adamson's axing, but said it was all a matter of *"team balance"*. There was no personality clash; John believed Adamson's slight frame would be too easily pushed aside by the Vics and that was why they brought in the burly George, who had kicked five goals against Victoria in 1974. Years later John would explain the decision as simply a case of *"horses for courses"*, but at the time it caused a furore, with Adamson receiving plenty of sympathy for what was seen as an unjustified sacking [38]. The issue guaranteed the team plenty of press coverage, with cartoonists in *The West Australian* and *The Daily News* satirising the controversy, with John's nose bearing the brunt of the satire!

The side was treated with virtual contempt by the Victorians, with representatives from three VFL clubs at the airport to meet the team, but only to be first in line to speak to the WA players about their prospects of playing in Melbourne next season. This absolutely infuriated John

---

37. Gibellini remained a regular member of the league side that season, but joined Perth in 1976.
38. Adamson would later represent both WA and SA in State football.

and he implemented a ban on officials speaking to the players before the game was over. He bluntly told the press that *"... we are not here to sell players, but to win a football match..."* and he called for a three year ban on interstate clearances to halt the player drain from WA[39].

The game represented the first round of a new look Australian championships. Instead of a week-long carnival, the winners of round one (Victoria versus WA) and round two (SA-Tasmania) matches would play off for the championship. Despite plenty of incentive, WA failed to match it with Victoria, being outscored in every quarter to lose by 81 points. Stan Magro won the Simpson Medal for WA's best with a gutsy display as he relished the physical confrontation, while George had a poor game, kicking only one point. John gave credit to the WA players, saying *"... they tried hard, but Victoria was too professional. The players will reap a lot of benefit from the game and I hope they take this knowledge with them and implement it through club football"*. On a personal note, the heavy defeat stung him, similar to the debacles of his playing days in the 1950s and '60s, when WA was regularly humiliated in Melbourne.

~

On the weekend of the State game, Old Easts scampered to a nine point win over bottom side Claremont, who had only won one match for the season. The win left Old Easts just percentage out of the four and hopes were high the side would finish strongly. However, the next week, as would be characteristic of the season, they were upset by seventh-placed Subiaco and failed to take the opportunity to sneak into the four. Losses in the next four matches, including a four point defeat by East Perth who played the last quarter with only 17 fit men, spelt the end for Old Easts, causing much frustration for the coach. He threw the side around, varied training, vented his spleen (again!) on the players and generally tried everything to break the slump. However, as is often the case, things got worse before they got better. A 16 goal loss to Swans at Bassendean represented the lowest point of the season as the home side kicked 11 goals to one in the final quarter. The huge defeat sparked the side and, after a gruelling week of training, Old Easts found some form to easily beat Claremont, who were again missing captain-coach Brown, out with his third suspension for the season. East Fremantle finished off the season beating Subiaco, Perth and fourth-placed East Perth to take fifth place with 10 wins.

The strong finish buoyed the club and left many reflecting on the long injury list as the major cause of the slide. Buhagiar missed most of the second half of the season, Durnthaler played two games, Hicks seven, Green 10, Grljusich missed the last half of the year, Williams played four games, Ferguson missed the first five matches, Nicholls and Peake missed seven matches each and McHenry retired on medical advice after two games. All these players were in the premiership 20 of 1974 and their extended absences, coupled with the loss of Melrose, left the team lacking its previous quality. John used 41 players in the league side, as opposed to only 32 the previous season. However, while he knew the injuries had taken their toll, John was more concerned about the poor attitude and lack of discipline which he felt stemmed back to Adelaide at the end of 1974, when the club failed to back him over his desire to fine players for not attending a training session during the Australian club championships. For much of

---

39. In 1975, eight players from the WA teams of the previous year were playing in the VFL or the SANFL.

The 'Adamson affair', June 1975. Cartoon courtesy of *The West Australian.*

Chapter 13 – A premiership at last!

1975 the prevailing attitude among some players was that *"we will switch on when we have to"* which John recalls Ron 'Bozo' Bentley telling him on a number of occasions. However, it never happened, despite John making it clear that football and good form didn't operate like a tap that you could just turn on and off. At their best, Old Easts were certainly still a good side, but an indifferent, over-confident and slack attitude saw the finals well out of reach.

The final round saw an irresistible West Perth complete a rags-to-riches story, accounting for Swans in the second semi and then South by a record 104 points[40] to win the flag after finishing last in 1974. Forward Barry Day set an individual grand final record by kicking seven goals in the last quarter, with evergreen centreman Mel Whinnen collecting the Simpson Medal. A record 52,322 people attended the game, with the gates closed at 2.45pm. The 1975 Sandover Medal went to East Perth's Alan Quartermaine in a surprise result, beating team-mates (and favourites) Peter Spencer and Ross Glendinning, with Swans half-back Stan Nowotny also finishing equal second, as he had the previous year.

~

In November John called the players in for a meeting to start pre-season training for 1976 and left some of them uncertain about their future, expressing the view that *"... there was a lack of dedication, application and desire to be the best"*. He bluntly added that *"... we know who are the bludgers and who are the workers. We will be releasing four or five players who fall into the first category"*. He delved into his bag of tricks and came up with karate sessions for pre-season conditioning, hoping the discipline required would rub off on their football and help with a general lift in attitude. He utilised Merv White (brother of Barry, his roving partner at South), who held a black belt and was a strict disciplinarian – he was given licence to ride the players hard. In January John followed through with his vow to get rid of 'the bludgers' and, in a bombshell decision, the club announced that Gibellini[41] was no longer required, along with Coates and Williams. Cowan told the other players that they either threw their weight fully behind John or look elsewhere, as solidarity became a key word at East Fremantle.

The pre-season period was low-key as John refused any media interviews; he also declined to have East Fremantle players compete in an athletics event for the clubs organised by Claremont, saying it would be *"an unnecessary diversion from our training programme"*. Their practice match form was encouraging, with new country recruits in full-forward Jim Sewell and wingman/rover John Simms playing well and former full-back Trevor Sprigg, returning after four seasons' coaching in Tasmania, slotting in well at centre-half-forward. Losses from 1975 were full-back Donnes, who had retired, and ruckman Ferguson, which left the club short of back-up followers to assist Becu. This was made worse by the departure of giant schoolboy ruckman Graeme Carter, who had been plucked from the colts by North Melbourne on a $27,000 three year contract deal. The 'poaching' of Carter rocked WA football circles, as the exodus of senior (and now junior) players to the VFL was of serious concern. Despite this, there

---

40. This result expunged East Fremantle from the record books, as the club against whom the greatest grand final winning margin was recorded, which previously was their 78 point loss to South in 1954.
41. In March Gibellini was cleared to Perth for a then record WA transfer fee of $20,000.

was a heady feeling of expectation at the club, which was only partially shared by John, who still harboured some lingering doubts about the attitude and mental toughness of some players.

The season started well enough, with solid wins in three of the first four games, with the only blemish being a one point loss to Claremont at East Fremantle Oval after the home side had led by 51 points midway through the second quarter. However, three losses to finish the first round of fixtures saw Old Easts in sixth place. A 12 goal victory over the win-less Subiaco (on the day two field umpires were first used in WA), with future Australian Test batsman Graeme Wood kicking five goals, restored some faith at East Fremantle. However, a 14 goal loss to Perth was followed by a 15 goal defeat by Claremont, leaving the finals a forlorn hope. Two consecutive wins, then two losses saw the fickle form continue... John's frustrations bubbled over when he was fined $100 by the WANFL for publicly criticising the performance of umpire Graham Ashworth after a narrow loss to West Perth. Still, worse was to come. After a nine goal defeat by bottom side Subiaco, the character and desire of the players were openly questioned by both John and Cowan. On the Tuesday night, John called all the players in for a no-holds-barred meeting at which he launched a blistering attack on their attitude.

Later, he broke his self-imposed media gag and told Ross Nicholas of *The Daily News* that the players "... *accepted defeat far too easily...*" and too many were simply social footballers, as he had heard them discussing plans for the Saturday night minutes after being beaten by 10 goals, an attitude he simply found impossible to understand – "*It's not a matter of winning each week, but simply being a competitor. We have fallen short in this area and readily accepted the humiliation, which is uncharacteristic of East Fremantle. They lack character*". It was his last roll of the dice to try and salvage something from the wreck of the season. Stung by the harsh criticism, the players upset third-placed Perth by nine points and followed up with a 12 goal trouncing of Claremont, which left them one game out of fourth spot with four rounds to play. A third consecutive victory, this time by 55 points over Swans at Bassendean, had the spirits soaring at East Fremantle Oval, but this was their last win as heavy defeats by East Perth, South and West Perth followed and the late season charge spluttered to a halt. Old Easts eventually finished fifth again, but this time with one less win (nine) for the year.

The finish to the qualifying rounds saw Perth lose second spot to South by a mere 0.9%, with East Perth two games clear on top and West Perth fourth with a three game break. The lead up to the last round was overshadowed by the exploits of the controversial Brown, who immortalised Claremont player John Colreavy by sending him back onto the ground late in the round 20 clash with West Perth, after he had been replaced at three-quarter-time. At this time no interchange was permitted, thereby contravening the rules and Claremont's total (losing) score of 13.18 (96) was later annulled by the WANFL directors [42]. Five days later Brown resigned as Claremont coach and was granted an open clearance.

During the finals East Perth's Peter Spencer won the first of his two Sandover Medals and Claremont's Graham Moss became the first West Australian to win a Brownlow Medal in the

---

42. Brown appeared before the WANFL Tribunal to explain his actions, saying it was done to highlight the need for an interchange system so teams were not forced to leave injured players on the ground. He was banned for a year from acting as a club official, but this did not include playing.

VFL, playing for Essendon. Perth stormed into the preliminary final with an 11 goal last quarter against West Perth and then East Perth, with only 16 fit players for the last half, beat South by 33 points in the second semi. Perth won its way into the grand final where it again proved the masters of East Perth (as in 1966 and '68), with a hard-fought 23 point victory.

~

At East Fremantle Oval the post-mortems were brief. Both John and Cowan knew his time as coach was up, with the players simply not responding to his message. Certainly his harsh disciplinary approach was not enjoyed by some players; rumours of a players' strike had surfaced during the 1976 season, but nothing materialised. On September 6 John resigned as coach despite being contracted for another year, saying *"... it was in the best interests of the club"*. He said there was no ill-feeling between the committee and himself, but added *"... the players did not show the club the respect it deserved, treating their football far too casually"*. Again, as he had at South in 1968, he spoke of his coaching style having a limited time span, as he freely admitted to *"being ruthless in many ways, but there are no short cuts to success, though many footballers think otherwise. We had the players, but not the application"*.

Cowan agreed, saying they had let Todd down as he praised his dedication and application to the job. Cowan's view of John's time at East Fremantle is noteworthy – *"... the players were a wild bunch, therefore they needed the discipline that Todd imposed to get the best out of them. At the end of 1976 he simply had no tricks left in his bag; he had done so many unusual, crazy and unexpected things that in the end the players stopped listening and weren't responding to his message"*. Both he and John agreed that the side under-achieved during his four years at the helm. While the loss of Melrose after the 1974 premiership was a severe blow, there was still sufficient talent within the side to make the finals, but the players had lost their edge. They weren't hungry enough for further success, and lost games against likely finals opponents. They could not, as Bentley told John, simply *"switch on when we have to"*.

There is no doubt some players breathed a sigh of relief when John resigned – his abrasive tongue and physically (and mentally) demanding style wasn't always popular and many were hoping for a change with a new coach. But their hopes were dashed when Alan Joyce, who had played under John Kennedy (Snr) in the Hawthorn sides of the 1960s, was re-appointed after an earlier stint in 1971-72, when he had introduced commando style training and placed a heavy accent on discipline. John had often told the players, particularly those feeling hard done by, that *"... don't think the bloke who follows me will be any easier"* as all coaches are tough and uncompromising in general, demanding great commitment by their players. Styles may differ somewhat, but in this case they didn't – one wonders how aggrieved the East Fremantle players felt on the news of Joyce's appointment.

While John had no definite plans, he told Meryl he still hadn't fully proved himself as a coach and something *"still burned inside him"* that was yet to be quenched. East Fremantle wanted him to be the director of their junior coaching, but he wanted another league job. There were vacancies at four clubs – South, Claremont, Swans and Subiaco – and the one that appealed most was Swans. They were the 'ugly duckling' of the competition, being the youngest club, having entered in 1934, and also the least successful, with only three premierships (1961, '62 and '63). The club had endured a horror 1976 season after making the preliminary final in '74 and '75 under Jack Ensor. Former Footscray ruck-rover Stuart Magee took over as playing coach for '76, but the side crashed to seventh, winning only seven games, and Magee resigned before the end of the season. Swans had advertised for a coach in August but, with only three applications, chairman John Cooper said the appointment would be delayed. When the position was re-advertised, John was quick to apply.

Chapter 14
Off to Bassendean

Swan Districts president John Cooper remembering the 1978 'player crisis':

> "... some players indicated to me that either Todd had to go or they would leave. Well, you can't have players running the footy club, so I bluntly told them to do as they were told or else to move on, which they did".

At Bassendean Oval, a boardroom brawl was in progress over the coaching appointment. President John Cooper wanted John, as he believed the club needed an experienced and successful coach rather than a rookie, as had been the case with all the appointments made since the departure of Haydn Bunton (Jnr) in 1964[43]. However, a majority of the board (4-2) favoured triple 1960s premiership player Colin Maynard, who had coached the Swans colts and under-19 sides with some success in the early '70s, but hadn't coached at league level. Swans general manager Stan Moses had virtually guaranteed Maynard the job as he was privy to the board's mood, but Cooper argued fiercely for an outsider to give the club a fresh outlook and a shake-up. He sought Merv Cowan's opinion of John and received a glowing endorsement, as Cowan indicated that *"... we would be getting a very good coach and virtually implied the club would be mugs not to give him the job"*. Cooper steadfastly refused to endorse Maynard and eventually won over another board member and then used his casting vote to give John the job.

On October 6, 1976 he was announced as the new Swans coach (ironically, the same day Alan Joyce was appointed East Fremantle coach) and Cooper explained the choice by saying *"... we need a seasoned league coach and I'm delighted Todd has the job. We have a lot of talent and Todd is the man who can get the best out of our players. I hope he is with us for many years"*. In response, John said he was looking forward to the challenge at Swans and that *"... discipline and hard work will be my two main points next season and I'm sure the players will respond"*. The Swans players, according to 246 game and dual premiership full-back Tom Mullooly, greeted the appointment with a sense of both trepidation and challenge, knowing they were in for a tough programme with a volatile coach, but appreciated that this was probably needed to be successful.

However, one senior player less than enthusiastic about the appointment was Stan Nowotny, whose first thought on learning John was the new coach was *"I'm not playing!"*. This stemmed from an incident when John was coaching at East Fremantle in 1976, when Nowotny was playing on Brian Peake and getting 'towelled up'. At three-quarter-time, John walked past Nowotny and gave him a pretty explicit description of his shortcomings as a player, to which

---

43. Since Bunton's time, the club had been led by 'first time' league coaches Fred Castledine (1965-67), Tony Nesbit (1968), Bill Walker (1969-71), Jack Ensor (1972-75) and Stuart Magee (1976).

Nowotny responded with some expletives of his own and therefore he had little inclination to be coached by the man. However, one of John's first actions was to meet with Nowotny and tell him it was in the past and the vitriolic attack was only designed to (further) break his concentration so Peake could stay on top. He told Nowotny he wanted him to captain the side in 1977, which suitably buried the hatchet!

Sadly, Maynard could not accept the decision, immediately severing his ties with Swans and has not returned to the club since. In 2002, he refused a nomination for the Swans Team of the Century, which was disappointing as the club was unable to honour him as a triple premiership, 160 game player and life member. John felt this was a tragedy for the player and the club, similar to the celebrated fall-out of Kevin Bartlett with Richmond "... *it's a crying shame when people walk away bitter*".

~

The Swans job loomed as a tantalising challenge. Apart from the Bunton 1960s era, Swans had been extremely unsuccessful and represented the classical underdog. Based on third place finishes in 1974 and '75, John felt there was a reasonable amount of talent to work with, as did Cooper and the administration. However, to add depth to the ranks and evaluate the club's playing stocks [44], John issued an open invitation to players who had left Swans in recent years to return and try out again for league selection. Players who took up the offer included Roy Arbon, Stroud Dale, Paul Mountain and Barry Stockden, who had all drifted back to country or Sunday football after playing in the early '70s. They soon realised they were back in the big league and a greater commitment would be required to survive under John's new regime.

To run the pre-season programme, he pulled off a major coup by getting Herb Elliott, the great Australian runner, to take the job (as brother Laurie was unavailable). He opened up by putting the players through some fitness testing at a health club, seeking to identify those who had high levels of endurance and could play regularly on the ball. Elliott was blunt in his assessment of the player group, suggesting there were a few who could run on the ball continuously; some who could *"pinch hit"* if needed and many players who simply *"should be dead"*, such was their poor fitness level. John wasted no time in raising the tempo of training, telling Elliott to find out who was mentally strong enough to stand up to a spartan running programme. The player group was split in two; the half shaping as likely midfielders ran with Elliott, working on hilly 10-mile or longer runs, while the new faces and position players were taken by John, who put them through a searching interval running programme, complete with hundreds of sit-ups and push-ups per session. Elliott's group wore T-shirts which listed his 10 commandments of running; the first aptly reflecting the programme – *"Don't ever stop uphill!"*. Four times a week the players went hard at it, with Elliott running alongside cajoling and berating them to greater efforts, much as Percy Cerutty had done to him on the Portsea Beach sandhills some 20 years earlier.

On one hot Sunday morning, running on gravel tracks through the John Forrest National Park east of Perth, ruckman Greg Frost, who had good endurance for a tall player, tried to take on Elliott in the run home. Despite his 40-odd years, Elliott was still in good shape and mere

---

44. Spending money on recruiting was not a strong option as the club had recorded a $48,000 loss in 1976, the biggest in its history.

Chapter 14 – Off to Bassendean

footballers were no match for his distance running prowess; Frost soon conceded the point as Elliott sped to the finish of the 12-mile course. John had just finished dressing down the position players, who had run a shorter course, for taking to the drinks before everyone had finished [45]. As the endurance group struggled in, an old man walked past and asked whether one of the players was missing, as he had seen a runner keel over a few hundred metres away. A quick check showed that Frost was missing and he had, in fact, succumbed to dehydration and overheating and collapsed. The semi-conscious Frost was taken to hospital, where he remained for a few days as he recovered, much to everyone's relief.

After this incident, the players were content to take each other on, but left Elliott to his own devices. Certainly, some simply could not keep up, either physically or mentally, as the searching programme took its toll. In keeping with the mental toughness theme, soreness and minor injuries were largely ignored by the two men driving the campaign and Elliott's philosophy was *"... if you have a sore spot, keep on running until it goes away"*. While it was some 17 years since his gold medal mile run at the Rome Olympic Games, Elliott's influence on many of the players was profound and the values and attitudes he imparted, while not immediately bearing fruit in terms of team success, would stay with them.

Elliott told many stories about his own training and the one John remembers best (and has related many times) concerned Elliott and his Australian rival Merv Lincoln. Elliott had arrived at Melbourne's Olympic Park to train and noticed Lincoln on the track, so he sat in the stand and watched the workout. Lincoln was doing 200 metre surges, followed by a 200 metre jog and did lap after lap, covering 20 or more while Elliott watched. The session impressed Elliott, who resolved to tackle it himself as he ventured onto the track but, as he limbered up, he realised Lincoln had been doing his surges with the breeze and his jog recoveries into the wind. Elliott tackled the session in reverse, thereby doing it harder than Lincoln, which he reasoned would give him a mental edge on his rival. Lincoln never managed to beat him in a race and Elliott maintains he always had Lincoln's measure, as he was mentally prepared to do it tougher and not take any easy options.

~

One night in February, after training had returned to Bassendean Oval, John was standing in the middle directing a drill when approached by a tall, strongly-built man wearing shorts, T-shirt and thongs. John saw him coming and got in first by asking *"who are you and what do you want?"*, although he knew full well who the man was. *"I'm Ron Boucher and what do you want me to do?"* was the short and curt reply. After a brief discussion about where Boucher had been and why he hadn't fronted for training so far, John said if he wanted to play for Swans then he better start training immediately, so he sent him off to run 30 laps of the oval. Boucher kicked off his thongs and quietly set out on the 15 kilometre run. More than an hour later he finished the 30th lap and walked back to the middle of the oval and asked John *"is there anything else?"*. As he had done with Chris Hicks at East Fremantle three years earlier, John decided to test Boucher's character and resolve and had him hold a heavy punching bag while the players crashed into it, one after the other, until all 50 of them had taken a turn. He

---

45. As was typical of the era, there were no drink stops on the run as it was thought that greater mental toughness would result from abstaining from fluids.

then set Boucher some shuttle runs, starting with 10 times out and back over 20 metres and then nine repeats, eight repeats and so on down to one. Again Boucher quietly tackled the task and was then ordered to complete 200 sit-ups and press-ups. By this stage it was dark and the rest of the players had finished, so John called it quits; he was quite impressed with Boucher as he had simply *"got on with it"* without a word of protest. On being told that he'd done enough for the night, Boucher simply replied by telling John that he could *"go and get stuffed"* and he would play in the country rather than at Swans!

So ended the first meeting of the two men who would become such an integral part of the club's future success in the early 1980s. Boucher was true to his word and played country football in 1977 [46], but at the end of the year John, who saw real strength of character in him, sought him out and enticed him back to the club for the next season.

~

After the hard pre-season, the practice matches provided only little respite for the players as the side performed indifferently, losing to East Perth by 77 points in the final outing. Subsequently, the training remained tougher than what the players were accustomed to. There was only a small core of experienced players at the club, with captain Nowotny (149) heading the list, ahead of Steve Gillespie, former Footscray and Carlton player Gordon Casey (recruited in 1976) and Mullooly as the only players with more than 100 games. Eight others had 50 or more games, so the club was relatively inexperienced, but John had seen this before as the level of experience at East Fremantle in 1973 was quite similar. They seemed a good bunch of young, developing players, but although he felt the side wasn't premiership material, he believed there was sufficient talent to be competitive. No-one at the club, including John and Cooper, expected the disaster that season 1977 became for Swans.

In the opening game, Swans were at home to South Fremantle, now being coached by Percy Johnson who had won the race to replace Colin Beard. Neither side had been impressive pre-season, so Swans were marginal favourites only because of the home ground advantage. Mal Brown was making his debut for South after parting company from Claremont, but Swans went into the match with only one new player – ruckman Alan Sidebottom, younger brother of Garry. The side was also notable because it was the first time since 1961 that champion rover Bill Walker was missing from a season-opener, having retired in 1976 after 305 games. After an even first half, Swans gradually wore South down and finished with a flurry, kicking 11 goals in the last quarter to win by 37 points. It was a bright opening, but the excitement was quickly tempered by John, who was annoyed by a lack of discipline in the last 10 minutes which allowed South some easy goals – he fined all the players $25 each! To be 'rewarded' in this fashion after scoring 25 goals and winning by six was foreign territory to these players, but it reminded them again that John was not like any coach they had experienced before.

The next three games were a taste of things to come – Swans were never really in touch and slumped to sizeable defeats against West Perth, East Perth and East Fremantle. However, a resounding win against Claremont raised team spirits, but this would be short-lived as their second victory would be the last for 15 weeks, with a shocking run of injuries compounding

---

46. From his debut in 1971 to 1976, Boucher played 76 games, but never really consolidated a place in the league side. From 1978 to 1984 when he retired, he added another 117 games, almost all as the side's no. 1 ruckman.

the shortcomings of the team. The next week, a 'flu epidemic conspired to further erode the playing stocks and an inexperienced line up lost by 88 points to reigning premiers Perth, who had 18 goals by half-time. A 47 point loss to Subiaco, who only had one previous win, put the team back on their heels and set John on the warpath. He put the players on notice they would all be re-assessed over the next month and inevitably some would be given their marching orders. Swans were missing State players Mark Olsen and Keith Narkle as they suffered their worst defeat of the season, a 122 point loss to the Bulldogs at Fremantle, while WA recorded its first win (by seven points) against South Australia in Adelaide since 1938. Although he knew the side was under-manned, John reacted savagely and told several players, particularly those who had returned to the club at his invitation, that their services were no longer required as he announced that younger players would be given more opportunities. He called for the WANFL to establish a transfer list where clubs could nominate players they no longer required, but no action was taken at league level.

After losing by 45 points to West Perth, several more players were told to go as the youth policy was cemented into place. After nine rounds, the club had used 39 players in the league side, mostly because of injuries, especially to centre-half-forward Garry Sidebottom, who sat out the first half of the season with a groin complaint [47] and Nowotny, who had a similar problem. Other players had injuries which forced them out for between one and three games, which made it impossible to build a stable team and underpinned the side's poor form. The player merry-go-round continued for several weeks, with the smallest losing margin being 13 points as the younger players swapped places regularly in the league side. For the last few games of the season, Sidebottom returned and provided a focal point in attack and finally, in the last game against Subiaco, the 15 game losing streak was stopped, with Sidebottom kicking eight goals and Swans winning by 10. In the week leading up to the game, John had been re-appointed coach for 1978 and, after the game, which ended his worst season of coaching or playing, he retained his sense of humour by quipping that *"I stressed to the players the importance of winning the first and last game of the season, I just neglected to tell them to win some in the middle as well"*.

The horror year was a great disappointment to John, but he refused to dwell on the negatives, preferring to highlight positives such as the opportunities provided to the younger players, the chance for the players and himself to learn from the great Herb Elliott and the strong resolve that should be built in the players by enduring such a poor year. *"You learn a lot when you reach rock bottom, you learn a lot about yourself, which generally holds you in good stead for the future. You certainly learn that you don't want to return there very quickly"*, was his positive spin on the season and it only added to his personal challenge to improve the team and find some success. He and Cooper went to the Eastern States on a recruiting mission looking for possible player swaps for Garry Sidebottom, who was poised to join St Kilda.

However, the biggest part of planning for the new season was a self-imposed 're-structure'. The five times a week grind of travelling the 40km from the butcher's shop in Fremantle to Bassendean had taken its toll, mostly on the family and the business. John would leave the shop at 4pm to get to training by 5 o'clock, leaving his staff to close up and he would often return

---

47. Although the term was not in common use then, there is little doubt the injury was osteitis pubis, which would become more common in the AFL in the late 1980s.

after training to prepare orders for the next day. This punishing schedule, coupled with 5am starts on Fridays and Saturdays, left little spare time for Meryl and the girls. One night late in the year he informed Meryl that he was going to sell the butcher's shop and coach Swans full-time for the princely sum of $200 a week! Meryl, realising the futility of arguing with John on matters of football, told him he was mad and started to think of where she could get a job! As a yearly salary, this was less than some players were getting, but that made no difference.

On December 16, 1977 Cooper announced that John had taken on the coaching role full-time, explaining that the club had stabilised its financial position and that *"... the days of Swan Districts standing still were past"*. John added that *"... last year there were a lot of ideas for promoting football that I just could not implement because of a lack of time. My love is football and now I can put all my ideas to work"* [48]. As well as coaching the league side, John had responsibility for fostering and developing the club's country and metropolitan zones, a vast undertaking as the country zone comprised the regional centres of Bunbury, Harvey and Collie, a two hour drive south from Perth, and Esperance, a mere nine hours away on the south coast. He also set out to get members and supporters more involved in the club by inviting them to join in two early-morning fitness workouts each week, which he conducted himself at the oval. He had to leave home at 5am for a 6am start, but that was of no consequence to a former butcher who had been accustomed to early morning starts for virtually all of his life. Plus, it was a small way of rewarding the supporters for their loyalty during the dark days of 1977.

~

The scale of the side's inability to compete over the season was reflected in the Sandover Medal as Casey topped the poll for Swans with only five votes; Old Easts centreman Brian Peake won with 24 votes, heading off Claremont captain-coach Graham Moss and Perth rover Robert Wiley. Perth won back-to-back flags, beating East Fremantle in the second semi-final (by 54 points) [49] and in the grand final (by 79 points), kicking a record score of 26.13 (169). The preliminary final saw veteran West Perth centreman Mel Whinnen bow out after 371 games and the first semi was noteworthy as Graham Farmer's last game as East Perth coach. He was sacked a week later to make way for Barry Cable, who would return to WA after being in North Melbourne's premiership side, beating Collingwood in the VFL grand final after the famous draw. While Farmer would not coach a WA club side again, he added one last personal entry to the record books a few weeks later when he coached WA to a resounding 94 point win over Victoria in the first State of Origin match, held at Subiaco Oval on October 8. It was WA's first win over the Big V since 1965 and it firmly established the State of Origin concept for interstate clashes from that day on.

~

In keeping with trends displayed in his earlier coaching appointments, John moved away from spartan endurance runs in the 1978 pre-season. Instead, he put the players through skill drills,

---

48. The impetus for the coaching job to be full-time came from John, not the club, but once the issue was raised, Swans were happy to meet the request.
49. Perth 'paid back' East Fremantle for John's 1974 'flu epidemic ruse in this game, by leaving forward Murray Couper, who hadn't played for several weeks, out of their announced side. Couper played, kicked eight goals, and the Australian Journalists Association decried the lack of ethics shown by the Perth club.

with a heavy emphasis on working in small groups to develop greater team spirit. However, groin injuries dogged the squad and four players, including Nowotny, had operations to rectify the problem; this tested the club's depth as these players struggled to be fit for the opening round. With John working full-time to recruit and develop the best players from the country and the city, little emphasis was placed on interstate recruiting and a player-swap deal for Garry Sidebottom, who left to join St Kilda, did not materialise. Key forward Simon Beasley was recruited from amateur ranks and later kicked more than 100 goals[50] in a season for Swans (1981), before joining VFL club Footscray, where he became that club's highest goal-kicker. University educated and a well-to-do stockbroker, Beasley provided a stark contrast to the majority of Swans players, arriving for training in a suit and looking very much like a member of the English gentry. Consequently, he was often on the receiving end of change room pranks, but he slowly added something to the team's spirit by giving as good as he got and was always in good humour.

Another 'new' face was Boucher, who had been enticed back to Bassendean in a move which president Cooper felt was a waste of time, as he believed the big man hadn't improved *"one iota"* over his previous six seasons at Swans. However, John had seen something special in Boucher at that 1977 training session and, when contacted, the big man indicated he wanted to return to league football and *"become a player"*. Although not tall for a ruckman (6ft 2in or 188cm), Boucher had a massive frame and great body strength and used his weight to good effect in a side that certainly lacked a physical presence. Perhaps fortuitously, Boucher was studying at night school to become a health inspector and couldn't make training at the normal times, so John trained one-on-one with him. Boucher's skills were poor, so John zeroed in on this weakness, both to improve his kicking, marking and handball, but also to test his resolve to make himself a better player. John returned to his childhood games where a dropped mark or a poor kick cost you a lap of the oval as penance; Boucher ran many laps as his hard taskmaster tormented his 'recruit' with unerring stab passes and dropkicks, plus torpedo punts ('Bob Hank's')[51] and floaters that threatened to break fingers if the hands weren't well-positioned. John pushed the big ruckman through his penalties, telling him to hurry up and get back quickly so he could beat him again, which made Boucher even more infuriated with each lap he completed. Little by little his skills improved, but his mental desire to *"not be ordinary"* was developed in spades and over the next two seasons he turned into one of the State's leading ruckmen – to the pleasant surprise of Cooper in particular.

After the disaster of 1977, expectations were fairly low, both in John's mind and in the club administration. The youth policy was still in force, but John knew many were *"tomorrow's players rather than today's"*. The season began with a 39 point loss to East Fremantle at Bassendean and quickly went from bad to worse. The side lost the first 11 games by an average of 58 points, the 'best' result being a 22 point defeat by East Perth in round nine, with the losing streak finally broken against second-bottom side Subiaco, with a 10 goal victory in round 12. At this point, since John's arrival as coach, Swans had managed just four wins in 33

---

50. The only other Swans player to kick over 100 goals in a season is Ted Holdsworth, who managed the feat in 1937 and '38.
51. Bob Hank was a leading South Australian player in the 1940s and '50s, playing over 200 games with West Torrens and winning back to back Margarey Medals in 1946-47; he was particularly adept at kicking torpedo punts. No-one at Swans had ever heard of him, but John soon had all the players referring to these kicks as 'Bob Hank's'.

matches and from round five of 1977, had only beaten one other side twice – Subiaco. It was his worst run in 10 seasons as a coach, but he wasn't about to opt out or lie down.

~

After losing the fifth game of the season to Subiaco by 88 points, John indicated to Cooper that it was time to change direction – he felt some of the experienced players were undisciplined and not giving enough to the team. He told Cooper that *"... we can continue to win five or six games a year with these blokes, or we can clean them out and start again and build a team over a couple of years that might have some hope"*. Cooper agreed with his general assessment of the senior players and gave him the go-ahead to restructure the team. John said *"... this is going to get rough"*, but Cooper told him to do what he had to do and he would handle the boardroom. Newspaper reports of a 'player crisis' at Swans emerged as John challenged many players to lift the bar and do more for the team – or get out.

Early casualties were former State full-forward Max George, who had struggled to find form after a season with Fitzroy in the VFL in 1976 and 80 game rover Brian Close, who had been tried in a back pocket before being dropped; both decided to play in South Australia. More were to follow as 86 game defender Rod Brown and State centreman and vice-captain Gary McDonald fell out with John and quit. Cooper recalls the time well – *"... some players indicated to me that either Todd went or they would leave. Well, you can't have players running the footy club, so I very bluntly told them to do as they were told or else to move on, which they did"*. In the press, Cooper stood firm, saying *"John Todd is on the right track by promoting youth when the experienced players are not doing the work. Too often players blame the coach when their game is not up to scratch. It's time some of them had a long hard look at themselves"*. With the backing of Cooper, John weighed into the press debate, saying he was determined to instil new determination, dedication, character and enthusiasm into Swans – *"Football clubs are built on character and if we lose players because of my beliefs, then that's part of the business"*. He acknowledged that some good players had left the club, but emphasised he had not sacked them; they had chosen to leave as they could not, or would not, conform to the disciplines and standards he required. Other senior players, in particular Nowotny, Casey, Gillespie and Mullooly, kept a lid on their feelings as close mates left the club and just 'got on with it'. There was no suggestion of a player revolt, which Nowotny says he *"would have squashed quickly"* and he remembers the period as a difficult time, but *"... you just had to have faith that the right decisions were being made"*. He felt that the character Cooper displayed in publicly supporting John and not giving the players any comeback engendered a belief that Swans *"... were going in a certain direction and you could get on board or get off, but it was the way we all had to go"*.

Over the next nine games, Swans recorded three wins to make it four for the season, beating eventual grand finalists Perth by 58 points, Subiaco by 25 points and South (at Fremantle) in the final game by 19 points. Coupled with two narrow losses, the last half of the season had been encouraging and there was light at the end of the tunnel. Young players introduced were Don Holmes and Don Langsford, who would become four time premiership players, and Phil Narkle, Mike Smith and Mike Richardson who, after winning flags with Swans, would all play in the VFL/AFL. John believed that *"Humpty Dumpty was slowly being put back together"* but there were plenty around the club who weren't so sure. The mid-season walkout of senior players and a second successive wooden spoon left people questioning whether Cooper had appointed the right man as coach.

Chapter 14 – Off to Bassendean

Board elections at the end of 1978 saw Bill Walker, Swans greatest player, nominate and rumours abounded that his first action would be to sack John as coach. Walker duly topped the poll and soon after Cooper was invited out to his Middle Swan property. Along the way, Walker suggested they visit former coach and club stalwart Fred Castledine, now a successful horse trainer, who had a nearby property. Castledine and Cooper had a long association stemming back to the 1950s and were considered good friends, but when Castledine quickly moved the conversation to getting rid of John, Cooper realised he had been set up. He brusquely said *"Never"* and walked away, refusing to discuss the issue any further. This was the first of several approaches on the coaching issue; there was pressure from all sides, but Cooper stood firm and brushed aside calls for not only John's head, but also his own. He was convinced that the hard decisions would soon bear fruit. He told John to worry about the football side while he handled the board and the bond between the two men grew even stronger, as they saw off the challenges. It would not be the last time they mounted a concerted rearguard action to hold their jobs.

The two men had little to do with each other before John joined Swans, but they established a good working relationship as chairman and coach and remain lifelong friends. Each has great admiration for the other, both believing that, in the dark days of 1977 and '78, their own job was the easier one. Cooper played against John in the '50s, but only saw him two or three times a season, as Swans failed to make the finals. That Cooper played at all was a credit to his perseverance; he suffered from osteomyelitis at age 14 and was told by doctors that he would never play football, but he cobbled together 122 games for Swans, mostly as a no-frills back pocket specialist from 1951-58. John often jokingly introduced Cooper to the players as *"... one of the best players ever to stand on the mark..."* while Cooper's view of John was *"... his knee injury reduced him from being a super champion to just mere champion"*. He remembers watching a South-Swans game in 1961 when Castledine and Max Kelleher, two of the real 'enforcers' in the game, lined up John from opposite sides of the pack, only to see the skilled Bulldog pirouette out of the pack with the ball in hand and send a 60 metre dropkick downfield as the two big men collided, knocking each other senseless. Castledine later said this was the hardest clash of his career and all for a nil result!

While Cooper thought highly of John's coaching philosophy and felt it suited Swans perfectly, his admiration also grew out of a recognition of what he was prepared to do (and sacrifice) for the club as part of the job. Juggling work at his butcher's shop and coaching in 1977 was difficult, although he never complained, but Cooper knew it made heavy inroads into his family life. Going full-time as coach in 1978 helped to some degree, but created new pressures, particularly financial. Cooper knew his coaching salary wasn't great, but the club couldn't afford any more as it recovered from a record financial loss in 1976. To make ends meet, Meryl took a part-time job; the money from the sale of the butcher's shop was soon swallowed up on school and college fees for the girls. In early 1978, when John started recruiting, with coaching and development trips to the club's South-West zones, he was dismayed at the lack of 'black and white' in centres like Bunbury. He implored Cooper to provide jumpers and footballs to give away at junior coaching clinics to raise the club's profile but, with money so tight, he often slept in his van to save on motel expenses. These things mattered little to John, who was content with his decision to go full-time, but Cooper was mindful of the sacrifices and appreciative of his willingness to *"put it all on the line"* to bring success to the club.

Amidst the turmoil of 1978, John somehow afforded to become a part owner of his first racehorse, joining chairman of selectors Bob Manning to buy a galloper from former Swans premiership (1961-62-63) wingman Brian Gray. They called it *Nowotny*, confident that no previous owners would have had the foresight to call a horse by that name. At its first barrier trial, ridden by the great JJ Miller, who John knew well, it won by six lengths! However, when they asked JJ about its prospects, he was blunt – *"Sell him, he's no good"*. However, like kids with a new toy, they ignored the advice of the Melbourne Cup winning jockey and *Nowotny* managed a few wins on country tracks.

More importantly though, the horse helped John keep his sanity intact as he grappled with the many problems at Bassendean. It was his toughest time as a coach. Even when South finished last in 1966 on his return to coaching, the side had been competitive and suffered several close defeats, so he had never experienced the depths of frustration that now confronted him. Coaching is a lonely existence, especially when things aren't going well and *Nowotny*[52] proved to be a good sounding board and a perfect listener. John regularly took the horse for walks or to the river for a swim, speaking to him all the way and releasing his anger and frustration as he went, which *"got my head sorted out again"* so when he got to training he was his normal positive (and passionate) self.

The coach invariably sets the mood of a club – if he is in a despairing frame of mind then the players read it quickly and train and play accordingly so, despite the heavy losses, John always remained positive. While he certainly *"served it up to the players"* to get a greater effort, he could sense when a change in atmosphere was needed and would lighten the mood with some humour. In part, this was also a little bit about self-preservation. The grind of losing regularly weighed heavily as the acceptance of defeat and negative attitudes, which he saw in some players, was totally foreign to him. He had always set himself to be the best and losing, especially without an almighty battle, was not something to which he was accustomed. At one

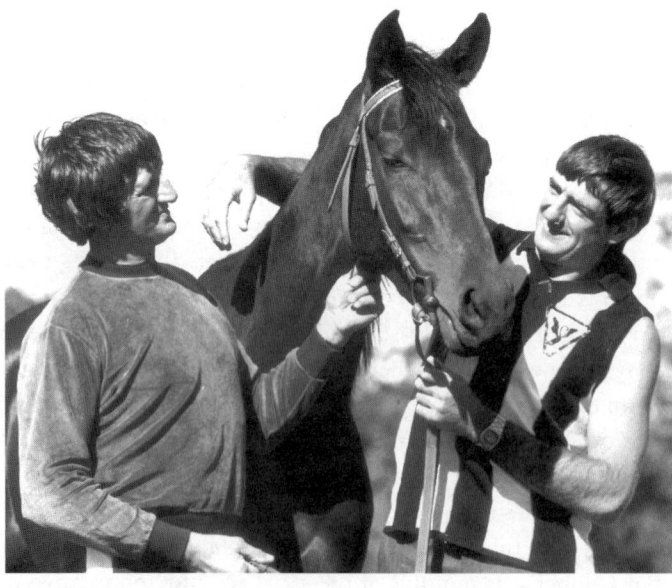

1978 – with Swans captain Stan Nowotny and Nowotny *the horse.*

52. In keeping with the theme of naming his horses after his players, John later called another one *Mullooly*.

Chapter 14 – Off to Bassendean

point late in 1978 he told the players that if they didn't believe they were on the right path, then he would go, but the group, led by Nowotny and Casey, quickly offered reassurance and the issue was not raised again.

~

With Swans upsetting South at Fremantle in the last round, East Perth were catapulted from fifth to second after they beat West Perth in their seventh straight victory, while Claremont, gallant losers to top side Perth, missed the finals by a mere 0.09% despite their 12 wins. East Perth wingman Phil Kelly won the Sandover Medal and the $20,000 prize that Channel 7, amidst some controversy, provided in a sponsorship deal. Perth fell tantalisingly short of their second hat trick of flags as East Perth, led by former Demons premiership players and Sandover medallists Barry Cable and Ian Miller (who won the Simpson Medal), withstood a last-ditch fightback to win by two points. The game is best-remembered for the atrocious weather conditions, with heavy rain and puddles covering most of the arena, particularly in the last 15 minutes as Perth mounted their final charge. A week later the Swans players watched Hawthorn beat North Melbourne in the VFL grand final at the MCG, the culmination of a fund-raising initiative instigated by John, who was keen to extend the football education and expand the football horizons of his young squad. It was another piece in the jigsaw of getting them to strive to be the best that they could be.

~

For pre-season 1979 John got Laurie Elliott back and a tough summer greeted the players, much as East Fremantle had endured in 1974. In one session the players started in Fremantle and were told to run as far as possible up the coast towards Perth in two hours; there were also many sessions at Allen Park, in Swanbourne, where a giant sandhill lay in prey. The hill track was almost 100 metres from bottom to top, with the last 10 metres so steep that it was virtually impossible to do anything other than crawl on all fours to complete the climb, with John and/or Elliott watching and waiting at the summit. With the great player exodus over – 26 players with senior experience had left or retired from the start of 1977 to the end of 1978 – John was keen to reinforce the character and hardness of the young group. He and Cooper both knew that another season like the previous two would spell the end for them. A big plus was the unexpected recruiting of Gerard Neesham, who could not come to terms with East Fremantle after a year overseas playing water polo. With a high regard for Neesham's ability, John was quick to pounce when he heard he was available. To add more experience to the squad, South ruck-rover and State player Eddie Bauskis was recruited, as John declared that *"... you can't go to Woolworths and buy a bagful of experience"*. He recast the side, turning skipper Nowotny into a ruck-rover to further bolster the midfield with Neesham and Bauskis. Hopes were high at Bassendean, but John hosed down early speculation of a finals berth, emphasising that the side had to develop further and become more consistent.

The opening game proved a big disappointment. Away to East Fremantle, Swans showed all of the traits of previous seasons to be 10 goals in arrears at half-time. After a stinging address at the break, the side kicked eight goals in the third term to trail by only 11 points, with Boucher leading the way with a ferocious display of controlled aggression. However, the effort told and the side slumped to a 39 point loss. A 17 point defeat by East Perth had people around Bassendean fearing a long losing streak might again be in the offing, but a heart-in-the-mouth four point win over Perth at Lathlain Park significantly reduced the tension. There was palpable relief in John's face on the final siren, with Swans kicking only six points in the last term as Perth fought back from a three goal deficit. Two more victories in the next three games, including a club record 31 goals against Subiaco, saw the scorecard at 3-3, although a nine goal drubbing by South to end the round took some gloss off. John warned the players that some faced the axe for their poor display against the Bulldogs, but reminded them that the fourth spot was within reach providing they appreciated the need for hard work.

An eight point loss to top side East Fremantle to open the second round represented a game that 'got away', but the effort showed that Swans could not be dismissed lightly. More of Humpty Dumpty's pieces were falling into place and the self-belief of the players, which had been knocked so severely over two years, was being restored. With the hard decisions on the player group now behind him, John constantly cultivated this, telling them to *"display their wares"* and to get people *"talking about you"*. One of his favourite slants was to recount conversations he had with businessmen who sponsored the club – *"Many of these guys had developed successful businesses and were millionaires, but they would gladly swap it all for a chance to appear on a sporting stage and the opportunity to put themselves on the line, as they had run out of challenges"*. He told the players that these men were envious of their talents and the opportunities they had to really achieve something through football. Nowotny remembers that these stories created an attitude that *"you really had something to offer"* and to never be ashamed of your ability, which was important to the team's development. Some of the fire and brimstone of past years had been replaced by positive reinforcement in challenging the players to get better.

Swans scored three wins in four games, beating top-four sides East Perth and Perth by 26 and 27 points respectively and Subiaco again by over 100 points, losing only to third-placed Claremont. However, two losses to finish the second round – the first a disappointing one point defeat by lowly West Perth after squandering a five goal three-quarter-time lead and then an 11 point loss to top side South Fremantle – left the side two clear games adrift of fourth spot. Three close defeats by a combined 20 points had cost Swans dearly, but their performances against the top sides had been full of merit and no rival could take them easily. However, the team fell apart the next week with their worst performance of the season, losing to East Fremantle by 82 points, which virtually ended any finals hopes.

Against Perth, round 3 1979, the elation of winning a close one (4 points). Sharing the experience is selector Bob Manning.

Livid at their poor display, John (not for the first time) drove around all night as he searched for reasons for the inglorious performance. After bad losses he was often better in his own company, as he found it impossible to be civil and engage in polite conversation. He would replay the game in his head over and over, trying to fathom why players had made certain mistakes and not done things he expected of them. During these 'night drives' he would select next week's team and decide on what tack to take for training, often not returning home until near dawn. While he told Meryl he was *"going out to think"*, it did little to ease her worries that he might have an accident, driving tired and with a mind occupied with football and therefore not focused on the road. She remembers these nights as *"like waiting for your teenage children to get home safely after a night out"*. Rarely could she sleep until she heard John's car in the driveway.

After this particular game he decided to make or break the team for the rest of the season. Sunday morning training was at Perry Lakes Stadium, the venue for the 19th Empire Games in 1962, but using the grass warm-up athletics track rather than the tartan. John told Elliott it was time to prove how much reserve capacity the players actually had; to see if they were mentally strong enough, so he instructed him to *"run them until they break"*. Elliott told the players to *"stride the straights and jog the bends"*, but gave no indication of how many laps were ahead. After an hour Nowotny remembers thinking *"he must tell us to stop soon, this is crazy"*. But after another hour they were still at it. By now, the senior players had twigged as to the purpose of the session and pulled the group together, refusing to be broken. The sore and sorry stragglers were supported and helped along by the rest, who resolved not to let them quit. The battle of wills continued for another 15 minutes before John, gladdened by what he had just seen, called a halt. He told the players if they could run like that for over two hours on a Sunday morning, then they had so much more to give on a Saturday afternoon! He credits this training session as a catalyst for the future success, not only for the rest of 1979, but in seasons to follow – the senior players resolved to work even harder to achieve success and demanded that the rest follow suit.

As an exercise in testing and developing mental toughness, it certainly had the desired effect – Swans won their last five games by an average of 70 points, the smallest margin being 47 points, with their lowest score being 20.22. They beat Perth, Claremont (who would finish top), Subiaco, West Perth and South (who finished second), but it was too late to secure a finals berth and they finished two games shy of East Perth in fourth spot. Remarkably, for a team finishing fifth, they had the highest tally of points scored (2673), as in 16 of the 21 games they kicked 15 goals or more and over 20 goals in nine games. Their points for tally was boosted by an amazing win against Subiaco in round 19 at Bassendean. Earlier in the year Swans had kicked a club record of 31.16 against Subiaco, but this day they eclipsed that total by three-quarter-time. In a goal-scoring feast, Swans led 8.4 to 7.1 at the first change and 20.5 to 11.5 at half-time. They went one better in the third term, adding 13 goals to lead 33.9 to 15.5 and a seven goal finish left Swans with a record 40.11 (151) to Subiaco's 20.7 (127), which remains the only match in WA football history where the two teams tallied 60 goals or more. Subiaco's score is the highest recorded by a side that has lost by over 100 points. Swans full-forward Mark Olsen kicked 13 goals, while for Subiaco, a young Gary Buckenara bagged nine. Apart from grand finals, this game remains one of John's best memories.

In 1979 Swans beat the Lions by over 100 points each time they met. That was particularly sweet for John, who reminded the players they had a point to prove, as it was Subiaco president and former umpire Lance Perkins who had labelled the team a disgrace the previous season and questioned whether Swans should remain in the competition after Subiaco had beaten them by 88 points. This really infuriated John and he was not remiss in returning the favour.

The 1979 finalists no doubt breathed a sign of relief that Swans missed the four, as they had finished the season in irresistible form. How far they might have gone is one of football's great intangibles, but John refused to peer into the crystal ball, saying *"… we only have ourselves to blame and it should make us all the more determined for the future. We took a long time to learn the art of winning this season, but that isn't surprising when you consider we won only four games last year. The turning point came when we beat Claremont in the last round; the players realised they could go a long way"*. The side had a strong engine, with ruck-rovers Nowotny and Casey, Boucher leading the ruck, the Narkle brothers on the wings and Neesham or Craig Holden in the centre. The goals came from Olsen[53], with 85, while Beasley added 49 and newcomer Ian Williams 41, with the two wingmen providing 45 goals as well. The defence was led by Mullooly and Gillespie, but the side lacked a class rover and a tall defender and centre-half-forward was a 'floating' spot, as both Olsen and Beasley were best suited to full-forward. Nevertheless, most of Humpty Dumpty had been put back together. John was re-appointed as coach for 1980 without any debate on the issue.

After Kelly won his second successive Sandover Medal (and another $20,000), East Fremantle outlasted East Perth in the first semi-final by two points in one of the best finals games for many years. The match proved to be Cable's last as a player, as later in the year he would almost lose his leg (and his life) in a tractor accident on his outer-suburban hobby farm. In the second semi South regained their composure after being thrashed by Swans in the final qualifying round and beat Claremont by 20 points. The first derby grand final since 1954, when South completed a hat trick of flags (and John burst onto the scene with seven goals in the reserves), was now in the offing. Old Easts were favoured to down the Tigers, who were playing in their first finals series since 1972 and, after just two points separated the teams at the last change, Claremont failed to kick a goal and East Fremantle won by 27 points. A record 52,781 fans turned out for the grand final, with Subiaco Oval bursting at the seams as Old Easts gave former East Perth player Bradley Smith a premiership in his maiden season of coaching, storming home with an eight goal last quarter to win by 33 points. Earlier in the day, Swans won the reserves premiership, the first repayment of the youth policy and development that John had started two years before.

---

53. He was pipped for the league goalkicking total by East Fremantle rover, Kevin Taylor, who scored 86. Taylor was the first rover to top the list, and, with the addition of his goals in the finals, finished with 102 for the season.

Chapter 15
Football in the 1970s

WANFL president Jim Davies welcoming the start of the NFL Wills Cup involving teams from Western Australia, Victoria and South Australia, in 1976:

> "I hope that this 12 team competition will be the forerunner of a fully national competition that will embrace teams from all States of Australia".

The 1970s saw great changes in football, on and off the field. The game evolved from a part-time pursuit fitted around work commitments and run largely by volunteers, to an industry providing full-time employment for coaches and administrators and generous financial rewards and incentives for teams and players. The impetus was television – the game rode on the back of changes in the TV industry and benefited directly from commercial opportunities presented by the electronic medium. In 1971, the WANFL and TVW Channel 7 were at loggerheads over perimeter advertising at league grounds, with the commercial station objecting to the free advertising given to club and WANFL sponsors via their vision. Consequently, they refused to show matches live or on replay, leaving the ABC as the only station televising games, although all three stations in Perth, including STW Channel 9, ran football preview and/or review shows. Channel 7 continued to televise the Sandover Medal count, presented for the first time in colour in 1975.

In 1977 they again started televising games as advertising emerged as a source of income and by the end of the decade the WANFL had negotiated a three year TV rights deal with Channels 2 and 7 that was worth $112,500. This sum was far in excess of amounts received in the '60s [54] and reflected the tremendous growth in football revenue and turnover of the '70s. Sponsorship, marketing and advertising opportunities became plentiful for the league and the clubs, as football continued to be the premier winter sport and businesses sought an affiliation with the game. The league's first real sponsorship arrangement was in 1973 when the Woolworths, Motorama and Claridge Cups were introduced, with $2000 prizemoney for the best-performed team in each qualifying round. In 1974 Rothmans provided cash bonuses for the finalists as a forerunner to a $22,000 sponsorship by Phillip Morris in 1975. The Sandover Medal, amidst much criticism, also attracted sponsorship, with Channel 7 putting up $25,000 prizemoney in 1978 for the three top vote-getters; the year after the count had been opened to the public for the first time, at $20 a ticket.

In 1976 former Channel 7 producer Harry Kelly became the first WANFL marketing manager and, by the end of the decade, annual sponsorship of the competition was over $200,000, split

---

54. In 1963 the fee was £500 for the season.

between major sponsors Marlboro[55] and Town and Country Building Society, plus a number of associate sponsors. Annual league dividends to the clubs followed the same upward spiral, increasing from $25,000 in 1970 to over $100,000 per club in 1979. The clubs also developed new sources of revenue, including team sponsorship, media-driven entertainment opportunities and transfer fees. In 1975, East Perth put sponsor names on their league team's tracksuits for $100 each. A year earlier West Perth and East Perth started their own Sunday football panel shows, complete with a replay of the previous day's game, as both clubs had hired closed circuit TV systems; an innovation soon copied by all the clubs. In the second half of the decade, radio stations ran regular Friday lunch-time panel shows at suburban hotels or club premises, usually with hundreds of people in attendance. As a result of these initiatives, bar and dining room profit for many clubs topped $100,000 a year by 1979, as the clubs became a favourite watering hole and used their amenities to host a variety of functions. By the end of the decade, the game also had its own weekly paper, with respected football writers Alan East and Peter Poat (who also published *The Football Register*) starting *Westside Football* in 1979.

Further adding to club coffers were transfer fees – although clearing players to Eastern States clubs remained a sore point for both the WANFL and the clubs. The 1970s saw fees escalate and in the early part of the decade the asking price for a top WA player had soared past $20,000. In 1974 East Perth demanded $35,000 to clear Mal Brown to Richmond, while in 1975 Subiaco wanted $50,000 to clear centreman Peter Featherby to Footscray and South Fremantle placed a $75,000 price tag on Bruce Monteath, who had left to join Richmond. While the actual clearance fee paid may have been less than these figures, by the end of the decade, clubs were asking around $100,000 for their best players, as this, albeit reluctantly, became a lucrative source of income. In 1979 most clubs turned over more than $500,000, whereas in 1970 a figure of $60,000-$100,000 was the norm; player payments rose as club income swelled. In 1979, Swans, by no means the richest of the WA clubs, spent $105,000 on 'player allowances', which included $20 a game for the reserves; some clubs also paid their colts players, with West Perth the first to do so in 1975. Leading players were now on contract and receiving up to $500 a game, with injury and incentive payments built into the deal. In a full season, with a high finish in the club fairest and best and/or the Sandover Medal, a leading player could earn $8000-$12,000 a season, which matched the full-time wage of some occupations. In 1974 East Fremantle spent $21,364 on player payments and a good season for an established league player might have earned them up to $3000.

There was also expansion in the range of player awards on offer, many of which were orchestrated by the WANFL via their marketing division to provide incentives for players to stay in WA rather than move to Victoria and South Australia. The WANFL was always under pressure from the clubs to make it more attractive for players to stay in WA and it was regularly called on to subsidise player payments, much as the SANFL did in the late 1980s to prevent a player exodus when the expanded VFL/AFL competition began. However, it rebuffed these requests[56], preferring to use marketing opportunities to increase the financial awards on offer, such as Channel 7's sponsorship of the Sandover Medal and the introduction of the Swan

---

55. The WANFL regularly had to respond to negative comments about accepting sponsorship money from cigarette companies, but explained its position as *"exercising freedom of choice"*.
56. In 1975 Swan Districts announced that $20,000 would be split between their top six vote getters in the fairest and best award, as an incentive to keep them in WA.

Brewery/6PM radio station champion footballer awards, which were telecast by Channel 9 and offered $15,000 in prizes in various categories. Radio 6PR and Solar King hot water systems put up $20,000 for their footballer of the year, best first year player, leading goal-kicker and the respective club fairest and best winners.

In 1977 Claremont captain-coach Graham Moss finished second to Brian Peake in the Sandover Medal (with no prizemoney), but won over $9000 worth of awards, while in 1978 and '79 Phil Kelly collected $40,000 for his Sandover Medal wins, but didn't claim any other media awards, which were shared between Moss, Featherby and Perth rover Robert Wiley. Whether the extra awards had any influence on players staying in WA or not is doubtful, because the challenge of proving yourself in the VFL was as important a factor as money in deciding to go. In the cases of Kelly, Featherby and Wiley, it wasn't enough as all three soon went to the VFL, while Moss had already been there and returned home to coach. However, the right of clubs refusing to clear a player and making them stand out of football, as had occurred in the '60s and early '70s, was gone by the end of the decade, as the legal issue of 'restraint of trade' was tested in the courts in several celebrated disputes.

In 1977 Stan Magro's attempt to play with Collingwood was blocked by South Fremantle, who refused to consider a clearance until 1978, providing he came back to WA and completed the season. In May, Magro went to the Federal Court in Melbourne claiming restraint of trade under the *Trade Practices Act* and the judge agreed, ordering South and the WANFL to show just cause as to why he should not be cleared to Collingwood. Six days later the league and South joined in a High Court action seeking an order prohibiting further proceedings under the *Trade Practices Act*, fearing that players could be declared 'free agents' and cross to another club without a clearance. This bought some time for the system, but as legal opinion advised that Magro would win the case, he was leased to Collingwood for the remainder of the season and withdrew his Federal Court action, leaving each club to pay their own costs. In 1978 the death knell for clubs having the power to refuse a clearance was sounded when Brian Adamson won a court-ordered clearance from West Perth to SANFL side Norwood, claiming restraint of trade. Clubs now knew they could not hold a player against his will and negotiating a suitable transfer fee or player swap were the only options left. A part of the game had changed forever.

On-field, much changed as the game continued to evolve. Apart from the introduction of the two-umpire system in 1976, there were two significant rule changes that became entrenched as part of the game. The centre square (first introduced as a diamond shape in 1973), had remained since 1975 to reduce overcrowding at centre bounces. John thought this was a good innovation, although he is less convinced about the line across the centre circle to keep the opposing ruckmen in their own half. In 1978 the interchange rule was introduced at the start of the second round of qualifying fixtures and has become an accepted part of the game. While originally designed to avoid teams completing games with less than 18 fit players, the rule has since enabled coaches to employ regular player rotations, particularly through the midfield. This has driven the speed of the game ever upward, with a consequent increase in the number of injuries, at least in the AFL [57]. While John sees the rule giving coaches plenty of flexibility

---

57. University of South Australia Professor Kevin Norton in researching the game (using videotape replays) from the 1960s to the 1990s, has nicely demonstrated an increase in the speed of the game and the number of collisions that players are likely to encounter.

with the bench players, he dislikes the almost obligatory set rotations of players off and on the ground – *"Players in good touch don't need to have their flow interrupted by a spell on the bench"*. While he accepts that rotations might help players see out the game better, he laments this current trend as the last quarters are often a question of survival of *"the freshest"* rather than *"the fittest"*.

The game also lost one of its fundamental skills, as the drop kick faded into oblivion. In 1974, Geoff Christian wrote in *The West Australian* about East Fremantle's second semi-final win over Perth under the headline *"Drop kicks pave way for Old Easts"*, but by 1977 they were pretty much gone, with the drop punt the preferred kick due to its smaller margin for error. John believes the stance taken by Ron Barassi against the use of the drop kick when coaching North Melbourne in the early 1970s began its demise. With their success in making five consecutive VFL grand finals between 1974-78, most other clubs followed their lead. After playing in an era where the drop kick reigned supreme, John feels there is still a place for the kick in certain circumstances in today's game, but most players don't have the necessary skills (or the perseverance to develop it!) to execute it correctly. He maintains that a drop kick (compared to a drop punt) is easier to mark and travels with greater stability. While there is no scientific evidence to support or refute this, a coach brave enough to re-introduce the drop kick would no doubt please the purists and certainly get people talking!

The style of the game also started changing in this decade. In the 1960s the convention was to play virtually four ruckmen, as the ruck-rovers were tall or high-leaping players who could contest bounce downs and throw-ins. In the 1970s, the ruck-rovers became more like rovers as the running game came into vogue. John was instrumental in this development at East Fremantle when he used the likes of David Hollins, Gary Gibellini, Kerry Coates and Peake as ruck-rovers, changing them off half-forward or half-back flanks, which in itself was an innovation. His following division in the 1974 East Fremantle premiership side was Neil Ferguson (ruckman), Hollins and Graham Melrose, which was the first time in a grand final of the decade that a smaller player had started as a ruck-rover. Previously, genuine ruckmen had started off as ruck and ruck rover [58], but after 1974 the rest of the decade's premiership sides all had smaller, more mobile ruck-rovers in their first ruck. This was the first structural change he made at Swans in 1977, with the side previously playing four tall ruckmen, and it involved the move of Stan Nowotny from a half-back flank to a ruck-rover in 1979. Since the mid 1970s a fleet of mobile midfielders have been an essential ingredient of modern football teams, following John's trend.

Another small innovation in the late '70s was the coaches' box, at least for the home-ground coach. Earlier in the decade coaches often sought an elevated position in the grandstand to view the game and relay messages to the bench via walkie-talkie radios. However, several coaches complained that the opposition could either jam the frequency or tap into it and know team moves before they happened, so radios soon went out of favour as a means of communication. In 1978 John prevailed upon Swans president John Cooper to erect a coaches' box at Bassendean and the resulting structure on top of the clubrooms was like *"something out of Gilligan's Island"* as John recalls. It was nothing more than some scaffolding

---

58. In 1971, Graham Farmer and Bill Dempsey started for West Perth; in 1972 Mal Brown and Brad Smith for East Perth; and in 1973 Mike Fitzpatrick and Peter Burton for Subiaco.

with a large canvas tarpaulin stretched around it housing some plastic chairs, and was far from windproof or waterproof! The tarpaulin often came adrift and rain would come in from all sides, absolutely saturating John and chairman of selectors Bob Manning. The club used an old telephone with a hand crank and a line down to the dugout to communicate – on one occasion John remembers losing his cool and throwing the 'phone out of the box. A couple of minutes later a small boy (with the phone in hand) appeared at the top of the ladder leading to the box and in a polite voice said *"Excuse me Mr Todd, you dropped your 'phone"*.

However, perhaps the greatest change in the '70s was the advent of the national football league (NFL) club competition, which involved sides from all States and would set football on the path to a national competition a decade later. The NFL games followed on from the club championship that saw the premier teams of WA, Victoria and South Australia joined by either the Tasmanian premiers or a composite State side, with the games played over a weekend in Adelaide in early October. This series began in 1972[59] and continued through to '75. In 1976 the NFL instituted the Wills Cup as a 12 team competition comprising sides from the three major football States. WANFL president Jim Davies enthusiastically welcomed the start of the competition, saying *"I hope this 12 team competition will be the forerunner of a fully national competition embracing teams from all States of Australia"*. WA was represented by the three top sides from 1975 – premiers West Perth, runners-up South Fremantle and third-placed Swan Districts. The games were mostly played in Adelaide, at Norwood Oval under lights on a Monday or Tuesday, giving WA players their first taste of night football, mid-week games and travelling interstate to play all wrapped up in one! Although West Perth and Swans had home day games at Subiaco Oval, the WA sides performed dismally, failing to win a single match. In 1977, the VFL opted out of the competition as they were unhappy about the matches being televised live back to Melbourne and considered that the NFL was intruding on their sponsorship, merchandising and marketing activities. The NFL called their bluff and invited teams from the VFA, Tasmania, the ACT, Queensland and NSW to fill the breech and came up with a 22-team Ardath Cup competition, with $150,000 prizemoney.

In Perth, Channel 7 returned to the fold to provide replays of the NFL matches, with East Perth and East Fremantle reaching the semi finals and the Royals finishing runners-up, earning $24,000 as they went down by eight points in the grand final to Norwood, who were playing on their home ground. In 1978 the competition went into recess as the VFL and the NFL continued to bicker. The next year the VFL took the series over, with club sides from WA and Victoria competing in the $375,000 Escort Cup as South Australia opted out in protest at Victoria's actions. The series started pre-season on a knockout basis, with most games in Melbourne at VFL Park, with this format remaining in place for several seasons, as the national club competition consolidated itself alongside the regular State league fixtures. In the main, coaches and players were enthusiastic about the competition and eagerly awaited the fixtures as the opportunity to play in Melbourne against VFL sides was keenly sought. This was certainly John's view, as he challenged the Swans players to *"take them on"* and *"do the State proud"* when the chance presented itself. These games were a good experience for the young Swans and played a useful part in getting them to *"aspire to greater things in their football"*, which was important in their development as players.

---

59. This series is best remembered for the clash between Mal Brown and Carlton, when the East Perth captain-coach took on virtually the whole Blues team in a no-holds-barred brawl.

Despite more exposure to the Victorian and South Australian football scene being provided to clubs and supporters by these new competitions [60], State football, particularly in the last half of the decade, remained the pinnacle of the game and enjoyed great public support in WA. Until the mid-1980s when John would coach WA to successive Australian championships, the 'golden era' for WA was triggered by successes against both South Australia and Victoria in 1977. For much of the 1960s and '70s there was a degree of 'sameness' about State football and since the epic carnival win in Brisbane in 1961, WA had only beaten the Vics once (in Perth in 1965) and never in Melbourne [61] and also had failed to beat South Australia in Adelaide since 1938. State football suffered a little from the expectation that Victoria would win wherever the game was played and that South Australia would beat WA in Adelaide [62] with the reverse applying in Perth.

All this changed in 1977. First, a WA side, coached by Ken Armstrong, broke the Adelaide drought with a stirring seven point win on the centenary day of South Australian football and later confirmed their current superiority with a 40 point win in Perth. In 1978, WA repeated the dose, but with interest, winning in Adelaide by 69 points as Moss kicked seven goals. However, in 1979, with Neil Kerley back at the coaching helm, South Australia won for the first time in Perth since 1962 [63], spoiling WA's 150th year celebrations. In June 1977, Victoria beat WA (as usual) by 63 points in Perth but, at the end of the season, State of Origin football arrived to completely change the outlook on interstate contests. The brainchild of Subiaco marketing director Leon Larkin, the game had been planned for two years, but failed to gain the endorsement of firstly the WANFL and then the VFL. However, on October 8, 1977 – after an agonising week's delay due to the drawn VFL grand final between Collingwood and North Melbourne – it all came to fruition as over 25,000 fans saw a WA side, bolstered by some almost-forgotten champions, whip the Vics by 94 points, their worst defeat in interstate football. The State of Origin concept could not have wished for a better beginning, as the humbled Victorians immediately set about planning their revenge. It came the next year as Victoria thrashed WA by 100 points in Melbourne under State of Origin rules, but WA again proved too good at the Australian championships in Perth at the end of the 1979 season when they won a tight deciding game by 15 points to win their third Australian title. The championships were the first played under State of Origin rules and helped rectify the earlier disappointment as part of the State's 150th anniversary year. The new method of selecting State teams was here to stay.

~

During the '70s most clubs won at least one premiership, with only Claremont and Swan Districts missing out and Swans the only team not to contest a grand final. Four clubs won two flags each; West Perth (1971 and '75); East Perth (1972 and '78); East Fremantle (1974 and '79) and Perth (1976 and '77), with the other flags going to South Fremantle (1970) and

---

60. The VFL also had great exposure in WA from the ABC replay of *The Winners*, which began in 1977 and soon became required viewing at 6pm on Sundays.
61. The closest loss came in 1970, when WA, led by Graham Farmer, went down by six points.
62. Such was the degree of frustration that, in 1974, after losing again to South Australia in Adelaide, WANFL general manager Peter Bowler mooted that WA should give serous consideration to using red (instead of yellow) balls as the WA players had not handled the red South Australian football with the same confidence as the local ball!
63. In this game, East Perth half-forward Grant Campbell set an enviable record representing WA in both junior (Teal Cup) and senior ranks in the same season.

Subiaco (1973), which ended a 49 year drought for the Lions. Interestingly, six premierships were won by sides that missed the finals the previous year – South in 1970, West Perth in 1971 and '75, Subiaco in 1973, Perth in 1976 and East Fremantle in 1979. In the case of South and West Perth (1975), they went from wooden spooners to premiers in one season and three coaches (Ross Smith in '73, Graham Campbell in '75 and Bradley Smith in '79) tasted premiership success in their first year of league coaching. The title of the best team of the decade belonged to East Perth, who only missed the finals once (1974) and contested four grand finals. In fact, since the arrival of Jack Sheedy as captain-coach in 1956, the Royals only missed the finals four times (1962, '64, '65 and '74) in the 24 years to 1979, contesting 14 grand finals, but only claiming five flags.

The Sandover Medals in the '70s were again shared mostly between rovers, ruck-rovers and centreline players, with two exceptions – in 1972 Perth's Ian Miller became the first centre-half-forward to win the medal and in 1975 East Perth's Alan Quartermaine was victorious, having played mostly off a half-forward flank. In 1971 East Fremantle centreman Hollins scored a runaway win, polling 26 votes to beat perennial place-getter Mel Whinnen by 10 votes, amid persistent rumours before the count that he was the winner, prompting heavy late betting on him. The WANFL reacted swiftly, firstly confirming the legitimacy of the votes cast and then launching an inquiry into the alleged leak, but nothing of any substance was discovered. East Perth dominated the Sandover Medals with four winners, while East Fremantle and Perth each had three winners, with an 11th medal for the decade awarded in 1997, when Swans Bill Walker was presented with a record fourth medal retrospectively, after losing on a countback to Perth centreman Pat Dalton in 1970.

The game lost many champions from the 1960s and '70s in this decade, with Haydn Bunton and Graham Farmer playing their last games, but both continued their coaching careers. In 1974 Subiaco goal-kicker Austin Robertson (Jnr) retired after 251 games and a WA record of 1274 goals. In 1976 Walker, Bill Dempsey and Tom Grljusich all retired after more than 300 games each, followed the next year by Whinnen. After starting his career in 1960, Whinnen had the dubious distinction of kicking off the 1977 season as the 'grandfather' of the league, with almost 170 games more than the next most experienced player. In the same year Brown called it quits as a player after 10 games with South and a career total of 218, but he was back the next year as South coach. And then, at the end of 1979, Cable was forced from the game with 405 senior matches, but he continued to coach East Perth. Collectively, these players tallied more than 3000 league games in Perth, Adelaide and Melbourne and shared in 20 premierships from 1956 to 1978.

Among the players John saw most of in the 1970s, the East Fremantle quartet of Doug Green, Melrose, Peake and Hollins were rated most highly and, in his early years at Swans, Nowotny, Mullooly, Boucher and Keith Narkle stood out. Melrose had *"great skills on both sides of his body, was hard at it and had outstanding leadership qualities"* which would also come to the fore when recruited by John to Swans in 1980. Green was a consummate defender *"rarely beaten, although not hard-hitting and set a great example to the rest of the team"*. Peake was *"tough, hard, fearless and skilful all in one and his versatility made him an extremely valuable player"*, while Hollins was *"an exceptional player with great speed and skill, but didn't fully realise his potential as the opposition were able to physically intimidate him and disrupt his concentration"*.

Of the Swans players, Nowotny was *"a great leader by example and had no peer for sheer hardness and competitiveness"*. John also admired his ability to improve his somewhat awkward kicking style and adapt his game to convert himself from a half-back flanker to firstly a ruck-rover and then, in the 1980s, a key forward. Mullooly is similarly recognised for his ability to turn himself from a wingman/forward into a *"reliable and dependable full-back, not unlike Doug Green, when thrown the challenge in the late 1970s"*, making the position his own until his retirement in 1986. Boucher became *"a feared player who made his team-mates stand taller"* and eventually improved his marking and kicking to become a goal-kicking ruckman when resting in the forward line. Before 1978, these elements of his game were certainly lacking. Narkle was a *"wonderfully consistent player who could be counted on to at least break even on his wing and rarely had a bad game. His speed and brilliance always made him a threat to the opposition"*.

The 1980s

Chapter 16
Close, but not quite

John, reflecting on the need for finals experience:

> "... is often hard-earned and can't be bought at Woolworths".

John Cooper, remembering the push to get rid of John (and himself) at the end of 1981:

> "... some of my best and lifelong mates at Swans thought if I was that close to Todd then we both should go".

The finish to 1979 buoyed the club immeasurably after the dark days of 1977 and '78. Expectations for 1980 were lofty and breaking the 17 year premiership drought looked within reach. Pre-season, the optimism grew with the acquisition of Graham Melrose, back from North Melbourne, and the signing of Canberra rover Ed Blackaby. John and Melrose had formed a close bond as coach and captain at East Fremantle in 1973-74 and, as a tough and skilful midfielder, in addition to his leadership qualities, he was the type of player the side needed to complement the young tyros. Blackaby had represented the ACT in the national carnival in Perth at the end of 1979, so John had seen him in action after he had been recommended by former Swans captain-coach Don Scott (1956-57). Blackaby was a leading player in Canberra and had resisted many overtures to play in Melbourne, but he liked what he saw of Perth, so, despite being 27 years of age, Swans punted and recruited him.

The other notable addition was former South Fremantle defender Tony Solin, recommended by Gerard Neesham after playing with him in Darwin over the summer. On the debit side, full-forward Mark Olsen was let go by John, who simply ran out of patience with him. Despite kicking 85 goals the previous season and with an impressive record [64], Olsen was not the most reliable of kicks for goal and did not embrace repeated efforts by John to instil a more dedicated approach. He wouldn't willingly put in extra goal-kicking practice, even though John regularly reminded him of former South great Bernie Naylor's philosophy and practice ethic. With Simon Beasley now established and more suited to full-forward than centre-half-forward, John reasoned he could afford the 'hard call' on Olsen without losing too much.

---

64. He had been the club's leading goal-kicker for four seasons, with tallies of 50, 46, 79 and 85. Swans cleared him to East Fremantle for 1980, but he broke down with a knee injury in his first game and never played league football again.

With Swans on the threshold of success, he wasn't going to stick with any player regardless of their record if he didn't fit the team structure or wasn't disciplined enough to work at their game to be *"the best they could be"*.

The pre-season matches produced an early disappointment, with an 82 point thumping by VFL side Melbourne in the Escort Cup but, in typical fashion, John was quick to move on, saying the disappointing loss left the club free to concentrate on the premiership season. In a practice match against Perth, John faced press criticism for leaving a young Murray Rance (in his first game) on mercurial Demons forward Peter Bosustow, who finished with 11 goals. Early in the match he sent a message to Rance saying he would not be shifted, whatever the circumstances, and to *"push through it"*. It was a typical Todd tactic with young players; apart from unexpectedly dropping them to see how they dealt with disappointment, he liked to test their mettle by throwing out a challenge to play first-up on a good player to see how they coped with potential adversity. Rance, who had to wait until 1981 for his first senior game, but would go on to play 238 games of WAFL/VFL football for Swans, Footscray and West Coast, remembers the match well. Despite getting a personal hiding from Bosustow, he feels it was a useful experience and appreciated knowing he wasn't going to be shifted as it allowed him to concentrate better during his baptism of fire.

John was happy with what he saw that day and said *"I was pleased with Rance's attitude and I believe he will make it as a league player. It's no good a player having tons of natural skill if he doesn't have the attitude and character to overcome adversity"*. A significant aspect of the pre-season period was the move of Nowotny to centre-half-forward. John and Manning spent hours debating the various players for this role, particularly with Beasley now at full-forward. With no obvious key forward in the ranks, they put Nowotny there because *"he would compete and not let the ball rebound easily"*. Nowotny relished the challenge of a new role and found it easier than expected, as he basically continued to play like a backman. In his view, *"forward line players needed to be robust, so I really tackled as hard as I could"*. The move proved a great success over the next four seasons as the Swans forward line became noted for its hardness. Nowotny again achieved State selection in 1980, giving him the enviable record of being picked when playing three different positions – half-back, ruck-rover and centre-half-forward.

~

The opening game was at Bassendean against the reigning premiers East Fremantle. Swans led by 10 goals at three-quarter-time and added 10 more in the last term to win by a resounding 111 points. It was a taste of things to come as they won the first 13 games and, after five victories to wind up 1979, this made 18 in a row, the best winning streak in the club's history. WAFL[65] major sponsors Marlboro parted with a $20,000 incentive much sooner than expected for the first team to win 12 games in a row. Swans did it in a canter, as they produced irresistible football, kicking more than 20 goals in each of the first eight matches. In round five Swans had 59 scoring shots to beat the win-less Subiaco by 131 points and round six saw

---

65. In 1980 it was decided to dispense with the 'N' (for national) and the WANFL officially became the WAFL.

a record 22,350 people cram Bassendean Oval for the clash with second-top side West Perth, who had lost only one game. Swans turned the contest into a rout and, after leading by 22 points at half-time, they kicked 10 goals and nine goals in the third and fourth quarters, restricting the Cardinals to three. Such was the midfield dominance that eight players (Mike Richardson, Melrose, Neesham, Keith and Phil Narkle, Don Holmes, Mike Smith and Ian Williams) had 20 kicks or more.

The 126 point win was sweet satisfaction for John, who had little time for West Perth. The ill-feeling stemming from John's 1975 decision to drop Brian Adamson from the State team was definitely mutual. The simmering discontent of Cardinals supporters followed John from Old Easts to Swans and was further fuelled by a 1979 match when West Perth beat Swans by one point, after which coach Graham Campbell termed it the greatest comeback win in the club's history! John thought this was *"a bit rich"* considering the game didn't push West Perth into the top four or a finals spot and he said as much, also suggesting that Campbell's positive reinforcement (pump them up!) style of coaching had West Perth *"running on bullshit"* and when you scratched the surface there was little substance underneath! The feud was always publicly denied, but continued into the 1980s and all Swans-West Perth games were well-attended with many fiery incidents, off and on the field.

The sheer brilliance of the team's play certainly drew the fans in and, to finish the first round of qualifying fixtures, almost 20,000 people flocked to Fremantle Oval to see South take on Swans, but the result was never in doubt, with Swans winning by 39 points. Few things in sport capture the public's imagination more than the underdog getting out of the cellar to win regularly and Swans were perennial underdogs. As John regularly reminded the players, Swans had a negative win/loss record against every team in the league, the closest to 50% being Subiaco who, at that time, they needed to beat in every match for the next four seasons to square the ledger [66]. Swans consistency and excellence in performance was probably matched only by the club's efforts in 1962, when they led the competition all season. In 1980, home crowds at Bassendean were higher than ever and even at away games the fans attended in great numbers. Swans crowds were less than 8000 only three times – when playing bottom side Subiaco – and on 12 occasions topped 10,000. The average attendance for home games was 12,788 and 260,477 people watched Swans in the qualifying rounds, 30,000 more than in any other year in the club's history.

In the second round, the side maintained the momentum, even when missing five players on State duties in round 11 when Melrose provided an early return for Swans recruiting investment by kicking five goals in the third term to spark victory over Claremont. He had been in good form over the year and, in tandem with Neesham, Blackaby, Holmes, Richardson and Williams, formed a potent midfield which rival sides couldn't cover. The centreline of the Narkle brothers with Smith in the middle was superb, giving the forwards a steady supply of opportunities, enabling Beasley to lead the goal-kicking, with Blackaby, Williams, Richardson and resting ruckman Craig Hoyer also regular contributors. John likened coaching the side at

---

66. At the end of 2003, of the traditional eight WAFL clubs, Subiaco was the side that Swans had their best win/loss record against; however, it is only 47%.

this time to being the captain of a large ship – *"A steady hand on the wheel was all they needed. I just let them play, such was their desire and touch. While I knew it couldn't last the whole season, I had great pleasure in watching them play at this time"*. It was the best patch of form produced by any of the teams he coached, but after the 12th win was achieved against Subiaco by 11 points on a bleak and miserable day at Bassendean, most pundits felt the side was overdue for a loss. With the pressure of winning the $20,000 prizemoney removed, many thought West Perth could end their streak and, after the first round humiliation, the Cardinals were keen for revenge.

The game was a crackerjack affair and saw John embroiled in further controversy at the end. Swans scored the first goal, but West Perth took charge and kicked the next seven to lead by 39 points. A seven goal third term restored the initiative to Swans on the back of Boucher's ruck ascendency and, in a grandstand finish, Swans got home for their 13th win by two points, as the parochial Cardinals crowd urged their team on in the hectic finish. On the final siren, with plenty of feeling in the air, John gave the West Perth members a very public two-fingered salute, prompting complaints to Swans president John Cooper and also the WAFL. At West Perth's trophy presentations after the game, acting president Ron Bewick expressed his disgust at the incident and called on the WAFL to take disciplinary action against John. The next day John offered no apology and said his actions were in response to the *"torrent of abuse"* directed at the Swans coaches' box and bench from the West Perth members – *"I was sickened by the boos and abuse that greeted two injured players (Melrose and Alan Sidebottom) as they were helped from the field. Those West Perth supporters did not let up for the entire game, so perhaps they deserved a gesture of my contempt"*. That was his simple explanation, although there was no doubt the gesture contained a small element of contented gloating, given that it was West Perth on the other end of the result.

The wins over Subiaco and West Perth were by the smallest margins of the season, with the previous average winning margin being 63 points, so perhaps the side's form was tapering off. Two weeks later the bubble burst when second-placed South Fremantle won a tight, torrid affair by 19 points. In many ways, that brought some relief to the club. The players certainly felt added pressure as the streak continued and, for John, with the side winning each week, it was difficult to get the players to appreciate where they needed to improve so the team could get even better. After losing to South, he had something to coach on and a more receptive audience, particularly after East Perth inflicted a 76 point defeat two weeks later. Blackaby was unfortunately hospitalised with glandular fever and hepatitis after playing only 11 games. Illness and injury would dog him over the next four seasons, preventing WA fans from seeing the best of him. His absence was vital as John felt he *"was the nearest thing to a true rover like Bill Walker, his goal-kicking talents and reading the ball off the packs were just terrific"*.

A few weeks later, Williams went down with a knee injury, further limiting the side's goal-scoring and roving options. Boucher was suffering from strained stomach muscles which would restrict him for the rest of the season and he missed games in the build-up to the finals. Nevertheless, after the East Perth debacle, the team bounced back to win the next four games by comfortable margins before again going down to South (by 46 points) in the final home-and-away fixture. It was South's 12th straight win, but wasn't enough to dislodge Swans from top spot and a further $10,000 in prize money. With 18 wins, including 13 in a row, the side won over $40,000 for the year, the best qualifying season in the club's history. However, the real business was about to start, with South looming as formidable opponents.

~

For the second semi-final, Swans welcomed back Nowotny, Richardson and Jon Fogarty, who had all missed the clash with South. The day was wet and the game physical as Boucher threw his weight around, giving away several 15 metre penalties and getting reported in the process. Beasley gave Swans the initiative with five first-half goals to provide a 16 point lead and John implored the players to push on and win *"because Boucher needs a week's rest"* before the grand final, such was the delicate state of his strained stomach muscles as he lay in pain in the change rooms. However, South lifted and kept Swans goal-less in the third term to lead by 11 points at the last change, heralding a final term that was a torrid affair as both sides slugged it out in greasy conditions. With a few minutes left, South led by five points when a late shot on goal by Langsford hit the post for Swans. The Bulldogs then posted a goal to win by 10 points, inflicting a third consecutive defeat on Swans for the season. Boucher rucked strongly to take the honours from Sandover medallist Stephen Michael[67] on the day and was a popular pick as Swans best, along with Melrose, Neesham and Beasley, who kicked six goals. After the tribunal decision went Boucher's way, John set about getting the side up to tackle East Perth, who had beaten Claremont in the first semi. Despite missing Nowotny with injury, Swans kicked seven goals to two in the first quarter, extended the lead in the second and returned to their early season form in the third, kicking 13 goals to three to finish 76 points clear and into the club's first grand final since 1965. Melrose kicked nine goals and Beasley seven and, while he was happy to reach the grand final, John was concerned at the ease of the victory and reminded the players that South had been their masters in their past three encounters.

After such a long time in the wilderness, grand final week at Swans was full of hype, with media and supporters swarming over the place. When Nowotny failed to recover from a thigh injury and with Blackaby and Williams sidelined, Swans went in without three of their first choice players. South were missing former Subiaco half-forward Neil Randall and one-time Swans rover Paul Mountain, who joined the Bulldogs in 1977 after starting the year at Swans. Only eight Swans players had tasted finals football before 1980 and just Melrose and Neesham had played in a grand final. South certainly had the edge in finals experience, with most of their side playing in finals over recent seasons, including the previous year's grand final loss to East Fremantle, and this factor worried John the most – but there was little to be done about it – *"Experience, particularly in finals, is often hard-earned and can't be bought at Woolworths"*.

On the bus to the game, John became more concerned about his players' mental preparedness. A prize for the winners was a charter flight over Perth and, as a passenger jet flew overhead, a few players remarked *"that will be us on Monday"*. While he quickly reminded them they

---

67. Michael was South's first Sandover medallist since John's win in 1955.

"had it all still to do", the comment left him concerned to say the least. In the rooms he kept things simple and low-key, mindful of the lack of finals experience. He told the players to keep three things in mind – *"Keep your eye on the ball, go for your shots and don't panic"*. As the players prepared to enter the arena, cannons were fired and smoke and noise filled the tunnel and he sensed the focus was disrupted by the commotion.

Although Swans scored the first two goals, the signs weren't good as some players looked flustered and unsure and only South's inaccuracy (nine shots on goal to four) saved them from being further behind than the 10 point quarter-time deficit. Swans had no answer as the Bulldogs posted eight goals to one in the second term and the half-time margin of nine goals indicated that the game and the premiership was gone. The players were shell-shocked and had little left as South extended their lead to 63 points at the last change, as Maurice Rioli (the Simpson medallist), Noel Carter, Joe McKay and Michael put the game beyond doubt. With the intensity gone from the game, both teams scored freely in the last quarter to leave the final margin at 58 points, giving Souths their 19th win for the season, equalling that of Swans. But, more emphatically, it was their 14th victory in succession and the fourth straight win over Swans, leaving no doubt who was the best team for the year.

Managing a smile in defeat. Congratulating Mal Brown in the South Fremantle rooms after the 1980 grand final. Clive Lewington is in the background.

Chapter 16 – Close but not quite

John paid tribute to South saying *"they were just too good on the day"*. Of his beaten team he added *"Plenty of sides have performed badly in grand finals; South were beaten by more than 100 points once [1975]. We lacked maturity as it was the club's first grand final for 15 years and it was an entirely new ball game; we didn't measure up to the pressure. However, we have a strong core of players with plenty of character and that will help us redeem ourselves"*.

~

Never a good loser, John took the defeat badly and had no doubt the lack of hardened finals campaigners clearly provided an edge for South. They also had the hunger that sometimes only losing finals can bring. With Swans, the finals were new and exciting for most of the players and the pain of recent defeat wasn't there, despite the frustrations of 1977-79. In addition, the preliminary final thrashing of East Perth was not the preparation John preferred, with the ease of the win giving some players the belief that the second semi-final loss was an aberration and that the team had rediscovered the magic of their early season form. The side was still not settled at centre-half-back or centre-half-forward and the absence of Nowotny in the grand final highlighted these problem areas even more. A key position player was on top of the recruiting list for 1981.

All these factors saw the side fall short of the ultimate goal, as John's old side (and Brown) proved to be his nemesis. However, the dark days of 1977-78 seemed an age ago and this grand final loss would prove to be the only one he would experience. Looking back over his coaching career he has no hesitation in naming the 1980 side as the best he has coached, but without a flag to show for it – *"they are not given the recognition they deserved for the quality of football they produced"*.

~

For season 1981 the expectations at Swans were enormous. The old football adage that *"you must lose one to understand what is needed to win one"* was given plenty of voice around the club. The only losses were Casey, who had returned to Victoria, and young ruckman Craig Hoyer, who had joined Hawthorn, but the team gained a ready-made midfield replacement in Leon Baker, who had finally been enticed up from Bunbury. Although he only had three seasons at Swans before joining Essendon, Baker is regarded as one of the best players to represent Swans and made their Team of the Century in 2002.

The club also pulled off a recruiting coup by signing North Melbourne's Daryl Sutton, who appealed as the key position player Swans lacked, but he came at a hefty price as a carefully hatched plan to recruit him came unstuck at the finish. Swans vice-president Bill Walker and finance director Rod Sergeant wanted to avoid a huge transfer fee by first getting Sutton cleared from North back to Glenorchy, his Tasmanian club, and then Swans would deal with them for a lower clearance fee. Sutton had made the 1979 All Australian team playing with Tasmania, so his asking price from North was upwards of $100,000. After weeks of clandestine negotiations, Walker left for an overseas trip believing the deal was done for only a moderate transfer fee and he was aghast when he returned to find that the club had spent close to $150,000, banking on future transfer fees to fund the deal. John was excited at the prospect of having Sutton in the team, but Walker told him to get the best out of the star recruit for one year, because he would sell him to the highest bidder at the end of the season as the club simply could not afford the agreed price.

Pre-season, Swans were touted as certain grand finalists and many players no doubt agreed with this sentiment. A coach's job is always more difficult when the players are lauded in the press, as it's only human nature to feel good about positive remarks and it's easy to expect it all to happen without the required effort. In March, the side received an early wake-up call as East Fremantle won the opening round of the Escort Cup by 71 points [68]. John was livid at the insipid display and questioned the attitude and commitment of the players. It gave the side the spark it probably needed and they started the season much as they did in 1980, by winning the first four games by an average margin of 95 points. This included a 162 point drubbing of Perth, when Swans kicked 38.21 (249) to finish only two points short of the club record score set in 1979 against Subiaco. South Fremantle maintained their winning streak when they won a high-class game at Fremantle by nine points before Swans returned to the winning list with a 10 goal win over East Perth, now coached by Grant Dorrington, who had taken over from Barry Cable. The win set up a top-of-the-table clash with Claremont to finish the first round of fixtures, with both sides winning five games. However, Swans trailed throughout, conceding nine goals in the first term to eventually lose by 46 points. Again, John questioned the attitude of several players, annoyed by their inability to accept the challenges posed by playing the better sides. Even at this stage, the competition was a race in three, as Claremont, Swans and South had demonstrated their superiority over the other sides. Beasley was in irresistible form, scoring 54 goals (and only 14 points) from seven games [69], Baker had shown himself to be a player of class and Rance had played some good games in defence. Along with the core of the side in Nowotny, Melrose, Neesham, Richardson, Boucher, the Narkles, Holden and Mullooly, the team was playing well, but John felt they were doing only *"just enough"* and not playing with any great conviction.

The second round saw Swans start with big wins over bottom-placed Perth (127 points) and West Perth (85 points) and four more victories, including a 48 point margin against South to break a run of five consecutive losses against last year's premiers. The win returned Swans to top spot, with Claremont second on percentage as the two sides again prepared for battle.

The game lived up to its billing, with Claremont winning a see-sawing struggle by two points, with Steve Malaxos kicking seven goals for the Tigers and Beasley six for Swans in a game most scribes described as the best for the season. The win gave Claremont its second Marlboro Cup for 1981 as the best team of the round (with Swans again second) and put them back on top of the ladder. It was Swans only loss for the round, a good return in the circumstances as injuries tested the depth of the club, with Solin, Blackaby, Sutton (who was out of form),

---

68. The match was also costly for young centreman Mike Smith, who badly hurt a knee and would miss most of the season, managing only three games.
69. Beasley also kicked six goals against Victoria to be the first full-forward to win the Simpson Medal, as WA won by 29 points.

Chapter 16 – Close but not quite

Williams, Boucher and Smith all missing matches. Beasley was a sure avenue to goal, with 82 after 14 matches, and the midfield drive generated by Melrose, Neesham and co ensured plenty of scoring opportunities.

To start the third round, Swans handed West Perth a 102 point thumping at Subiaco Oval as the WAFL scheduled more games at league headquarters to allow patrons to take advantage of the new grandstand. Comfortable wins against the other three bottom sides, Perth, Subiaco and East Fremantle followed, with Beasley reaching his century after kicking four against Old Easts. The run to the finals was against the other three top sides, starting with South Fremantle, at Fremantle. South were riddled with injuries and had lost to bottom side Perth the previous week, so Swans went in as warm favourites, but again started poorly, with the Bulldogs kicking six goals to one in the first quarter. South held the advantage and won by 35 points, leaving John again puzzled about the attitude of his players, ripping into them and questioning their hunger and desire to be successful.

After a tough week of training, Swans set themselves up for a big win over East Perth but, after leading by eight goals at three-quarter-time, they failed to goal again, eventually winning by 21 points. Before the final qualifying round, all positions were settled in the four, with Claremont on top, having lost only twice and chasing their 12th consecutive win and $20,000 to emulate Swans feat of last year. Swans were three games clear in second spot, with South safe in third place and East Perth fourth, two games clear of Subiaco and West Perth.

As in 1980, the final game was a dress rehearsal for the second semi and 18,000 people turned out, with Claremont at full strength and Swans still missing Blackaby, Smith and Williams. John was keen to exploit the pressure on Claremont seeking their 12th consecutive win (and the financial bonus) and he demanded a fast start, which the team delivered. A 14 point quarter-time lead was extended to 27 points at the half as Sutton and Melrose led the way. With a 21 point lead at the last change, Swans seemed poised to finally beat the Tigers, but Claremont responded with an eight goal finish to win by 15 points and take the $20,000, with Malaxos kicking six goals. With 16 wins, Swans had qualified for the second semi for the second successive year, losing to only two other sides – but they were the first and third placed teams. Swans had only beaten South once in eight attempts over two seasons and Claremont had proved their masters three times in 1981, although one win was by only two points. It was a remarkable season for scoring by the top sides, with Swans scoring a total of 3035 points, 300 more than in 1980, but their total was also 300 less than Claremont's, who kicked a whopping 3352 points. Third-placed South totalled 2941 points for, 500 more than any of the other five sides. Both Swans and Claremont finished with percentages over 150 and South's was 122.6, almost 30% better than any other team. No-one had any doubt that the flag was a race in three.

~

To prepare for the second semi-final, John took the players on camp for the first weekend of the finals, looking to find that little bit extra in team bonding and unity. He was reasonably confident, but knew that any of the three sides could beat each other on the day. Again, his team was the least experienced in finals, as Claremont were playing their third consecutive finals series and South their fourth. Swans were virtually at full strength, with only Richardson and Smith missing, while Claremont's strength was its three-pronged attack of Warren Ralph, Malaxos and Brett Farmer, who had kicked 252 goals for the season, plus the dangerous Krakouer brothers, Jim and Phil.

To counter the Krakouers, John introduced the tagging role, using Bill Skwirowski to run with Jim. 'Skira' was a disciplined player with great stamina and he played the role to perfection, frustrating Krakouer with his close-checking, but still picking up possessions. With their speed and skill, the Krakouers were regular goal-scorers for Claremont, so closing down these options occupied much of John's mind in the lead up to the match. A particular dilemma was who to play on Malaxos, who had kicked 13 goals in their last two encounters – he finally opted for Craig Holden, who did a great job restricting him to a single goal. Ralph (four goals) and Farmer (one) were also kept relatively quiet, but it was to little avail as Claremont won their first second semi-final since 1938 in convincing fashion. After a tight first half, the Tigers beat Swans for the fourth game in succession, 14.24 (108) to 12.9 (81), with only their inaccuracy keeping the final margin at 27 points.

It was a lack-lustre performance by Swans and, after a long night drive to clear his head, John went after the players on the Sunday morning. He paired them off in their likely positions and got them to wrestle each other, making it clear that all positions in the side were up for grabs, so *"your (wrestling) opponent might get your spot"*, as he stressed that much more aggression was needed in their play. Nowotny remembers thinking that this was a strange way of fostering team spirit in a crisis, but it certainly wasn't a good time to argue! Amid some tough physical training, Swans prepared to play South, who had beaten East Perth in the first semi, with the preliminary final being staged on a Sunday for the first time to accommodate the VFL grand final.

It proved to be an amazing game. In a tough and dour contest, South led by a goal at quarter-time and Swans by four points at half-time. Midway through the third term Blackaby goaled to stretch the lead to 16 points. As the flags were waved, South coach Brown is reported to have said *"that's it, we can't win the game"*. While this spur of the moment comment didn't indicate he had conceded the match, he and the other 34,000 people watching could not have predicted what was about to unfold. Sparked by their big three – captain Noel Carter, centreman Rioli and ruckman (and dual Sandover medallist) Michael – South kicked an incredible 10 goals to one to finish the term to put the game out of reach for Swans. Although the deficit was a not-impossible 38 points, the momentum was all with South and John (and the players) knew the game was gone. The shell-shocked Swans conceded another 10 goals in the last quarter as South cruised into the grand final, winning by 73 points, with a final score of 28.10 (178), just three points less than Swans had kicked in 1980 when they demolished East Perth.

John refrained from giving the players a tongue-lashing, but spoke of how the loss should help build more resolve and character for the new season. He said to the press – *"Swans [and Claremont] have struggled for years to get where they are. They are still getting rid of the attitude of underdogs in finals and this match will help these players"*. It was a remarkably composed response from a bitterly disappointed coach, as once again South had proved to be their bogey team, particularly in finals. Claremont completed the best season in their history by outlasting South by 15 points to win their first premiership since 1964, leaving Swans clearly isolated as the club with the longest current premiership drought, a point which was not lost on John.

~

A season that had promised so much therefore ended with bitter defeat for Swans. The side had won only one of five finals matches in 1980-81 and, while clearly one of the best three teams in the competition, had only notched one victory against both Claremont and South out of eight clashes in the season just gone. In addition, the club had spent beyond its means in recruiting Sutton and there was precious little to show for it. Cooper knew what was coming and on the Monday after the preliminary final he declared that it was imperative Swans retain John as coach. Board elections were due and there were many influential members who thought John had run his race. While he had done a great job getting Swans back into the finals, it was thought that he wasn't the coach to deliver premiership success.

Cooper told John to get on with planning for next year while he set about shoring up both their positions. He was challenged for the presidency by Alf Charleson, who had been president in 1972-75 and a rival group also ran for the board with a clear (but not publicised) intention to depose John as coach. Cooper argued strenuously that Swans were now in exactly the same position as Claremont had been at the end of 1980, having been badly beaten in finals in the previous two years. But he pointed to Claremont's 1981 success as proof that John needed to be retained to ensure continuity. It was a tough and bitter election campaign, with many old friendships tested and Cooper remembers that *"... some of my best and lifelong mates at Swans thought that if I was that close to Todd, then we both should go"*. However, in the end he prevailed, and saw off the challenges, retaining the presidency and most of the current board. John's tenure at Swans continued.

However, it did seem that the 'Humpty Dumpty' John had so painstakingly put together would soon be missing some important pieces – the VFL talent scouts invaded WA and Swans looked likely to lose up to four players. Beasley, who finished the year with a club record 119 goals, was set to join Footscray, with his work as a stockbroker taking him to Melbourne. Ruck-rover and dual fairest and best winner Neesham was off to Sydney to play with South Melbourne, who had just relocated to the harbour city, and centreman/defender Holden was set to join North Melbourne.

Also, high-priced recruit Sutton was sold off to Richmond after a poor season when he never really endeared himself to the player group, proving to be a poor trainer despite John's efforts to get the best out of him. According to Nowotny, he *"lived off his reputation"* with no appetite for hard work. Consequently, Sutton never really got into peak shape and suffered several injuries, further limiting his contribution. John remembers him as *"a funny sort"*... *"He had great credentials as a player, but his work ethic was terrible and he never got it together. Perhaps the drier and larger WA grounds exposed him, as he was basically a mark and kick player"*. He may have also suffered a lack of motivation from the smaller crowds and atmosphere of WAFL games, in contrast to the VFL. John saw this in Hassa Mann, who struggled with South in the late '60s and early '70s after coming from Melbourne and admitted missing *"the adrenalin rush"* of playing before noisy and big crowds[70]. Whatever the reasons, Swans were seriously dissatisfied with their prime recruit.

The absence of these players looked daunting, but John encouraged players to pursue the next level of football in Melbourne, something he had been denied. Although there were gaps to fill, he never felt Swans chance for a flag had passed them by, as the finals experience of the past two years was invaluable. He was confident the younger players could step up and take more senior roles and the resolve to succeed would continue to grow – *"When you are close you get hungry and harden up; you go forwards, not backwards"*.

---

70. He now sees the same problem evident in West Coast Eagles and Fremantle Dockers players when they return to play in the WAFL. Peter Sumich, the champion West Coast full-forward, admitted as much when he played with South (with John as coach) in the latter part of his career in 1996-97.

Chapter 17
After 19 years, another hat trick

John, remembering the performance of tagger Bill Skwirowski as an 'unsung hero' in the 1982 grand final:

"... players doing these sorts of roles for the team are fundamental to premiership success".

John's comment after the 1983 grand final:

"Mental toughness won us today's grand final".

John, when asked moments after the 1984 grand final to compare the third premiership to the previous two:

"... almost the best of the three, considering where we came from and what we had to overcome".

To further harden the resolve of the players after two disappointing finals series, John recalled Laurie Elliott for the 1982 pre-season and they endured many tough sessions which tested their mental strength. The Allen Park sandhill in Swanbourne was again a favoured training ground as the two men began the process of getting the younger players to *"raise the bar"* and fill the gaps in the side. By February these were worse than expected as young ruckman Alan Sidebottom and forward Ross Fitzgerald were in dispute with the club and brilliant centreman Leon Baker had decided to travel the country rather than play football. Most scribes felt Swans were about to slip a peg or two and a premiership had probably passed them by. However, John had great confidence that players like Jon Fogarty, Don Langsford, Mike Richardson, Don Holmes, Murray Rance and Brad Shine could improve sufficiently to pick up the slack and the disputes with Sidebottom and Fitzgerald would be resolved.

The absence of Baker was of more concern. In his first season he proved to be a standout and, with the loss of Gerard Neesham and Craig Holden from the midfield, plus uncertainty over the futures of Mike Smith and Ian Williams with knee injuries, Baker was a necessity. The problem was that Baker was determined to go north even though John told him he was crazy as he was good enough to play in the VFL. John organised a job for Baker, but somewhat of a gypsy, he preferred being out of the mainstream. He left on a Saturday after stopping off at Claremont Oval where Swans were playing a practice game and where John took one last shot at getting him to stay. Fate then intervened. A few days later the roads in the north of the State were cut by flash flooding, forcing Baker back to Perth where he decided to take the job and resume playing football. He missed the first few matches before resuming in the centre and, despite his late start, he finished third in the Swan Medal for the league team's fairest and best. Certainly his presence was important to the side, with his skill and toughness in the midfield giving the forwards plenty of scoring opportunities.

Getting Baker back was a significant part of shoring up 'Humpty Dumpty'; John then went after Ron Boucher. Although his recent seasons had seen great improvement on his early years at Swans, John was not content to let the big ruckman rest on his laurels. He challenged Boucher to get into top shape so he could run out games better and reduce the chance of missing games with injury, which had been the case in recent years, and bluntly told him that unless he took marks and kicked goals when resting in the forward line, then he would rest on the bench! He rode him hard at training, again working one-on-one with him, and the big man responded with his best ever season, culminating in winning the Swan Medal.

Boucher was noted for his physical strength, as opponents such as George Michalcyzk (West Perth) and Noel Carter (South Fremantle) would attest, having been picked up by their throats and flung like rag dolls after 'disagreements' with the big man. At training one night Boucher snuck up behind John in the change rooms and applied one of his special headlocks – the sort that make it difficult to breathe! Boucher was legendary for this playful tactic and many players quickly learnt not to pull practical jokes on big Roo. The coach certainly felt the effects as he started to lose consciousness before Boucher sensed the danger and released his hold. A shaken and incensed John told Boucher to *"watch his back"* as he would get even soon enough, by testing out a piece of 4x2 timber on his head! That night, after a particularly tough training session, Boucher was taken to task by several players for not *"finishing the job off properly!"*.

The season opened against East Fremantle, coached for the first time by Ron Alexander, and an inaccurate Swans lost by seven points, 20.28 (148) to 23.17 (155). However, it was their only loss for the first round as they swept through the next six matches, finishing with a 105 point demolition of bogey team South Fremantle. At one stage in the third term Swans led by more than 20 goals as they inflicted a home-ground defeat on South for the first time in two years. South were so bad that coach Mal Brown sent them back onto the oval at half-time to train, but it had little effect as Swans kicked nine goals to two in the third term. The win left Swans on top of the table, but there was no hint of complacency. As Stan Nowotny remembers *"... there was a steely resolve being built up"*.

Midway through the first round of fixtures, Swans had also been drawn to play Collingwood at VFL Park in an Escort Cup game. Having disappointed in the past two seasons in this competition, John challenged the team to take on the Magpies, trading heavily on State rivalries as motivation. Collingwood had started the season poorly[71], but were expected to gain some much-needed confidence by soundly beating Swans, who were regarded as little more than nuisance value by the Melbourne press. The competition was, after all, set up to accommodate the VFL clubs, with all matches after the first round being played on Tuesday nights in Melbourne, so the interstate clubs did all the travelling. There was some added 'needle' with Swans winning the right to wear their own jumpers, forcing Collingwood to play (for the first time ever) without their traditional black and white stripes. The Collingwood side contained players such as Billy Picken, Tony Shaw, Craig Davis, Ray Byrne, former Claremont defender Kevin Worthington, Graeme Allen and Mark Williams, the current coach of Port Power in the AFL. Also playing was a young John Annear, who had joined the Magpies from Claremont two years earlier and would return to WA in 1987 to play with the inaugural West Coast Eagles.

---

71. After playing and losing the previous three VFL grand finals, the club was languishing near the bottom of the ladder, with only one win. Later in the season Tom Hafey was sacked as coach.

On the bus going to the ground Nowotny recalls that *"everyone was quiet; really focused"* as the players prepared to tackle arguably the most famous club in the VFL. Back in Perth, 800 Swans fans had jammed the clubrooms, forcing the doors to be closed, to view a live telecast. Urged by John to be *"excited about playing against players you normally watch on TV"* and to do the State proud, Swans did more than take the game up to the Magpies – they had the audacity to beat them on their home turf! An elated John said of their 10 point win – after scores had been level in the last quarter – *"All the players contributed as a team and we're now looking forward to being back in a few weeks seeking another win"*. However, events would soon change this focus as John became embroiled in a bitter dispute with the VFL, the WAFL and most of the other WA clubs.

The players backed up the next Saturday to beat Subiaco by 69 points, their third win in seven days. *"That's character"* was John's reply when asked about the recent efforts of the players. Swans won five of the seven second-round matches, losing (for the first time since 1979) to West Perth by 61 points and Claremont by 10 points in a top of the table clash. Swans were scheduled to play Richmond in Melbourne on June 1 in the Escort Cup second round, but the date had been altered twice, both times without any consultation with the WA club [72]. The arrogant VFL attitude infuriated John and, when the game was rescheduled the second time, he decided enough was enough. He publicly castigated the VFL for not even discussing the matter with Swans, saying *"... it's time we stood up to the VFL and made it clear we don't want to be pushed around anymore"* and really raised the ante when he declared in his weekly *Daily News* column that Swans would send a reserves side to play Richmond. He wasn't prepared to risk injury to his top players as his first priority was to give Swans the best chance of winning the 1982 premiership, reminding readers that Swans were the only club that hadn't won a flag in the past decade, or indeed, for 19 years. He produced the sting in the tail by pointing out that Carlton had also rested senior players in their Escort Cup match and he declared that the championships were a great opportunity to blood young footballers. He said the total disregard the VFL had shown for Swans in rescheduling the game *"... is a damned insult and it's about time they copped a few insults back! I say treat them with the disdain they show us over the rescheduling of matches"*.

These comments caused a furore on both sides of the country. Firstly, John had *"fired from the hip"* and forgotten to tell president John Cooper of his plans! When the Swans directors met to discuss the issue, most wanted the best possible side picked. Cooper stood firm and said the Board couldn't interfere with a football issue and if it pursued this action they would have to pick the side (and coach it) themselves. It was also possible that John might resign as coach if the board forced his hand, thereby putting the chance of a 1982 flag at risk. Cooper's stout defence of John carried the day and the board backed down – but that was not the end of the matter. The WAFL directors voted 7-1 – with Cooper naturally opposed – to endorse a motion by East Fremantle's Merv Cowan that Swans select their best possible side to *"uphold the image of WA football"*. Cooper argued (correctly) that the WAFL did not have the power to instruct a club about *"... who to select to play where and when"*. He also defended John and the club against criticism from Allen Aylett, the VFL and NFL president who labelled the club unprofessional and ignoring their responsibility to the game.

---

72. The official VFL explanation was that the date was changed because of clashes with State fixtures happening and also because the Sydney Swans were drawn to meet St Kilda, with those two sides playing each other on the preceding weekend as well. John was not impressed by these reasons, feeling that it had much more to do with Swans not being a drawcard, having spoiled the VFL's 'party' by beating Collingwood. Swans vs Richmond was never going to match the TV ratings of Collingwood vs Richmond.

The controversy pleased John who enjoyed making the Victorians *"squeal"* and he remained resolute in his view. He duly named 13 players to make their league debuts, with the only regular seniors being Murray Rance, in his second season, and first year players Peter Sartori and Jeff Davidson; the team in total had only 69 games of league experience. Richmond were close to full strength, with the likes of Mark Lee, Dale Weightman, Geoff Raines, Michael Roach, David Cloke, Barry Rowlings, Mervyn Keane and Brian Taylor[73] all playing, as well as ex-WA players Maurice Rioli and Robert Wiley, along with future long-term West Coast Eagles coach Michael Malthouse. Predictably, the game was a whitewash, with Richmond kicking 33 goals and winning by 186 points. John made no apologies, saying it would be a valuable experience for his young players and then mischievously added that if Richmond had travelled to WA for the game, then they would have met a full strength Swans side! While this cost Swans the chance to advance further in the Escort Cup, it worked to bind the players and the club together even more as they strove for success in 1982.

As the fallout continued, with Cooper cheerfully refusing a demand by two other club delegates that he resign as a WAFL director, Swans were banned from the Escort Cup for two seasons. But this only reinforced the *"Swans versus the rest"* mentality John had fostered and he exploited it for all it was worth. However, he rejects suggestions he orchestrated the incident to produce a rallying point for the team; it was only when the game was postponed a second time that he protested. His only regret about the affair is that he forgot to tell Cooper first, but there was no hidden agenda – it was simply an oversight. As for the Swans players, they fully supported the stand as the WAFL premiership was squarely in their sights. They were content to pass up the opportunity to pit themselves against Richmond, currently the top side in Melbourne, to chase a bigger prize. Nowotny remembers the incident as *"important in helping to gel the players together"* and the resulting furore made it even more vital to win in 1982. In particular, the criticism of both John and Cooper, who was greatly respected by the players, by the other WAFL clubs struck a chord with them and they were determined to make it all worthwhile.

With their regular league players fit and fresh, Swans accounted for South after the Richmond loss – with the reserves also winning – before recording their biggest victory of the season, a 109 point thumping of East Fremantle. After beating East Perth by 20 points, they then recorded their worst performance of the season, losing again to arch rivals West Perth by 66 points, only to bounce back with wins over Perth and Subiaco leading up to Claremont in a game to seal top spot. Almost 15,000 fans turned out at Bassendean Oval and at half-time there was nothing in the match, but then Claremont produced a superb eight goal third term to win by 38 points. It was a costly loss for Swans as it left Claremont only 0.19% behind in second place, with one qualifying game remaining. This match is also well-remembered for the heavy clashes between Boucher and Graham Moss which, to everyone's surprise, saw Boucher come off second-best with a bleeding cut below his eye[74]. Of more concern, however, was the fact that Swans had now only beaten Claremont once in seven games over two seasons and with press speculation over the so-called 'Swanniewobbles', the latest loss did nothing to stem the flow. The last round of fixtures saw Swans needing to beat South to guarantee a top-two finish, while the Bulldogs had to win to take fourth spot from East Perth. Claremont and

---

73. Taylor badly injured his knee in this game, which John later used to further justify his stance.
74. Boucher later explained that he had *"accidentally run into Moss' elbow"*.

West Perth were playing off for the double chance, with the winner a good chance of taking top spot on percentage from Swans.

At Fremantle Oval, Swans were slow to start, but were in control by half-time and eventually ran out 53 point winners, but at Claremont Oval the Tigers were too good for the Falcons [75] by 58 points, taking top spot and $12,000 in prizemoney by a mere 0.31% over Swans. John was philosophical as he said *"... in 1980 we won all the money, something like $48,000, but didn't win any glory"* and set about preparing the side for a third consecutive second semi-final. This was the best run in the club's history, but they had lost the last two and there was no flag to show for it.

~

Swans received a boost when mercurial wingman Phil Narkle won the Sandover Medal, polling 19 votes to beat the favourite, Claremont rover Gary Shaw, by two votes. However, the celebrations were put on hold as the side continued a disciplined and low-key build up. Swans went into the semi as underdogs, a position John always preferred, and the side was virtually at full strength, with only luckless rover Ed Blackaby again out of action. Claremont had a full complement and the only absentees from their 1981 premiership line-up were rovers Jim and Phil Krakouer (North Melbourne) and ruckman Barry Beecroft (South Melbourne). John was confident his team could match Claremont on the ball and close down their key forwards Warren Ralph, Steve Malaxos and Brett Farmer.

All of these elements were to the fore as Swans headed for victory; only inaccuracy in front of goal kept Claremont in with a glimmer of hope. At quarter-time, after 10 shots on goal to five, Swans led by 10 points which became 12 points by half-time, with 17 shots to 10. In the second quarter, John put Phil Narkle into the centre square for bouncedowns, a move he had been saving for the finals since early in the season. Showing no sign of the Sandover Medal 'blues', Narkle continually won the ball from the middle with great support from Boucher, Baker and Fogarty in particular. The lead got out to 33 points before Claremont closed to within nine points before Swans again kicked away to lead by 22 points at the last change. Claremont were unable to make any impression in the final term as Swans broke their run of second semi-final losses by 28 points, 14.26 (110) to 12.10 (82). It was a solid and tough performance, with the desperation and hunger of players keen to end a 19 year premiership drought clearly on show.

John told the players they now had the chance to make their own piece of history by joining the 1961, '62 and '63 grand final players as the only premiership achievers the club had. Several times over the season John had said the time had come for some new names to join club legends like Haydn Bunton, Bill Walker, Keith Slater, John Turnbull, Ken Bagley, Tony Nesbit, Fred Castledine and co. He invited several of those 1960s champions to speak to the players about the premierships they had won and he also had several other sources of ammunition to fire the players up with. He despised the 'Swanniewobbles' tag as it called into question their character and spirit when under pressure and he urged the players to stand tall and show it was a myth. He reminded them of the backlash the club had received over the

---

75. Late in the season, West Perth officially changed their name and emblem from the Cardinals to the Falcons.

Escort Cup saga and emphasised that it was Swans against the rest of the State (and the VFL) and they now had a chance to serve it right up to them all by winning the flag. He reminded the players that the WAFL premiers for 1982 would always be remembered, but the winners of the 1982 Escort Cup had already been forgotten.

Also, his loyal friend Cooper had decided to step down as president at the end of the year, so he prevailed on the players to give him the premiership he so richly deserved for all he had done for the club over 30 years. In addition, Phil Narkle was due to play his 100th league game in the grand final and it was a season where milestones for Graham Melrose (300th game), Nowotny (250), Tom Mullooly and Keith Narkle (200), Boucher (150) and Skwirowski and Alan Cransberg (100) had been rewarded with victories. That was an achievement John and the team were proud about, so he used it as an added spur – they couldn't let their team-mate down on such a big occasion.

Claremont regrouped and beat West Perth in the preliminary final, giving them a chance to defend the crown they had won the previous season. It was the first time the WAFL's two youngest clubs, Swans and Claremont, who had joined in 1934 and 1926 respectively, had met in a grand final – and they were the competition's least successful clubs, with only three and five premierships each. Both sides were injury-free and Swans announced an unchanged line-up.

On the Friday John did an unusual thing – for him. While inwardly very confident, he nevertheless felt an irresistible urge to visit Subiaco Oval – *"something was calling me there, I just had to go"*. He's not a religious man, although he believes there is a God somewhere, but he felt compelled to visit the oval – *"I walked around the empty ground, then laid in the centre and watched the game unfold as I stared up at the sky. I saw Swans well in command, with the flag won long before the end of the match"*. He left the ground with a great conviction that Swans would win the next day and with no nerves about the forthcoming contest. He can't explain what he felt or saw that day, other than it was *"uncanny"*, but he took great confidence from the experience. It's not something he has ever repeated as a coach and has never felt the same compulsion, nor had any similar 'visions'. At the team meeting later that day he told the players that *"tomorrow will be your day of glory if you want it badly enough"* and that *"... you owe it to yourselves to stand up and be counted"*. In the rooms before the game he was calm and confident and the players fed off his mood. In his final speech he compared Swans to a hungry dog, backed into a corner and surrounded by enemies, telling the players there was *"nowhere to run to, nowhere to hide"* and *"the only way out was to stand up and fight as though your life depends upon it"*.

The game unfolded pretty much as he had seen it the day before. Swans had a 20 point lead at quarter-time, 35 at the half and finished the contest in the third quarter by restricting Claremont to a solitary point, while adding 4.7, to lead by 65 points at the last change. The final quarter allowed John, the players and the supporters the luxury of seeing out the game [76] knowing it was won and, although Claremont kicked seven goals to four, Swans coasted home by 49 points. At the final siren the Swans supporters erupted and swarmed onto the oval to greet their heroes as a jubilant John sought out Cooper first and then joined the throng to celebrate with his players.

---

76. President John Cooper left the WAFL director's enclosure and watched the last 15 minutes seated on the grass next to the players' dugout, not wanting to miss the fervour of the occasion.

Chapter 17 – After 19 years, another hat trick

It had been a ruthlessly efficient display by Swans, who simply strangled the life-blood out of Claremont. All the Swans players played their part as they won the midfield battles and clinically reduced the goal-scoring options of the Tigers. Ralph kicked two goals opposed to Mullooly, Malaxos kicked one under guard from Skwirowski, and Farmer, after kicking six in the second semi, failed to register a major opposed by Peter Kenny. Captain Melrose was superb in a back pocket, winning the Simpson Medal, and centreman Baker, ruckman Sidebottom and wingman Phil Narkle were all rated highly for their performances. John and Melrose again stood together on the dais to accept the premiership cup eight years after they had done so for East Fremantle in 1974. In the change rooms, several players threw their runners-up medals from 1980 into the bin, as they savoured their new reward.

It was pandemonium at the club as the celebrations continued through the night. After the initial euphoria, the night brought a sense of relief for John and the players, with all the hard work and disappointments of the past six years finally over. John was touched most by many long-time and elderly Swans supporters who offered thanks for giving them something else to talk about, other than just the 1960s, indicating they could now die *"a little happier"* for having witnessed another Swans premiership. John was full of praise for the players, including the likes of Beasley, Neesham and Holden, who had moved to the VFL, Casey and Gillespie, who had recently retired, and Blackaby, Smith and Williams, who had missed the game due to

1982 – breaking the 19 year premiership drought for Swans. Being chaired off the ground with captain Graham Melrose. Murray Rance has John on his shoulders.

injury. He also had special admiration for Skwirowski, who only had six possessions, but completely blanketed Malaxos. Playing strictly for the team, he had dragged the dangerous Tiger away from the goals at every opportunity. While not widely recognised for his efforts, John rated him as the unsung hero of the game – *"... players doing these sorts of roles for the team are fundamental to premiership success"*.

In *The West Australian* on Monday, Geoff Christian reported that the Swans team *"was totally obsessed by victory"* and Claremont could not match *"... the sheer competitiveness of a Swans line up that did not have one weak link, a faint heart or a man who did not contribute to the victory"*. He also commented on the calm composure of John over the finals period, saying, *"There must have been some inner sense that told him Swans would prevail"* [77]. Swans did prevail on a wave of hunger for success, which John had carefully cultivated over the year. Claremont, even without the Krakouers, probably had more talent, particularly in their forward line, but Swans simply refused to be denied. The side didn't have a recognised centre-half-back, centre-half-forward or full-forward, yet Cransberg, Rance, Nowotny, Fitzgerald and Canberra recruit Kenny did the job over the season as they rotated regularly through these key positions. The centreline of Baker and the Narkle brothers was perhaps the team's great

Enjoying the moment with Swans president John Cooper. Photo courtesy of Alan East and Westside Football.

---

77. John had not mentioned his visit to Subiaco Oval before the game to Christian and, in fact, has told very few people about it.

strength and John often quipped that *"I went home happy on a Friday night because I knew the centreline would get 80 or 90 possessions the next day"* as they were rarely beaten. Coupled with strong efforts from ruckmen Boucher and Sidebottom and 75 goals from rover/forward Mike Richardson, the side had enough scoring opportunities and a defence led by Mullooly and Melrose was tough and resolute. It had taken six years, but John finally had his second premiership as a coach, won in emphatic style by a team he had developed from scratch. But, it had been a near thing – without the unwavering support of Cooper at the end of 1978 and 1981, it could have all been very different.

~

For the 1983 season, John flashed back to 1975 and reflected on East Fremantle missing the four after claiming the 1974 flag. The players had had little time off after the premiership and John found them *"flat"* in January and February of 1975, so he gave the Swans group a long holiday and didn't start training until January 5 of the new year. He punted on the players returning refreshed and enthusiastic, which they did, although the risk was a slow start to the season with rival sides having an edge in fitness after a longer pre-season. Again the side had lost players to the VFL with Richardson going to Collingwood and Sidebottom to St Kilda, but Neesham had returned after one season with Sydney and Smith looked as though he had overcome his knee problems. Swans were favourites for the flag and John felt the side was good enough as long as the desire remained strong. After so long in the wilderness, he sensed that the players were not satisfied with one premiership – *"... they have pride and won't accept being ordinary again"*.

With no Escort Cup fixtures to worry about, John concentrated on the first game, which was against Claremont who were keen to avenge their grand final defeat. They did so in convincing fashion, winning by 40 points on the day Swans unfurled their fourth premiership pennant. Wins against East Perth and East Fremantle were followed by a 65 point defeat by West Perth, who always brought out the worst in John. He fined the whole team their match payments for *"our disgraceful display"*, lamenting the lack of competitiveness. In his *Daily News* column he admitted some players could feel harshly treated as they had tried to lift the side, but *"... Swans won a premiership playing team football and a one-in-all-in policy is the only success formula I know"*. With more money in the game, he could use fines rather than dropping a player for any indiscretion, believing the team shouldn't suffer by being without a player's services when an individual stepped out of line. However, he made sure the team knew about it, announcing the fine to the group and then having the player explain his actions to his team-mates. Over the next month the side continued to struggle, recording wins against bottom sides Subiaco and Perth, but losing badly to South (70 points) and Claremont again (34 points).

After eight games, the possible slow start had certainly materialised and, with only four wins, Swans were in unfamiliar territory in fifth place; they had been on top of the ladder at this stage of the previous three seasons. The side was missing Melrose, who would soon retire because of a persistent knee problem, Neesham and Kenny, but was simply not playing near its true capacity. John knew it was all about attitude, but instead of working the players over, he sensed they were a little uptight and tense and not enjoying their football or each other's company as much as they normally would. The players were expecting a tough session after the Claremont loss, but instead he *"threw the switch"* and delved into his bag of tricks seeking to break the tension. He asked Vicki Sheppard, a staunch club supporter and sponsor who ran a hairdressing salon near Bassendean Oval, to smother a football with as much hair as she could. He produced the ball at training and told the players it was pubic hair and it was the only football to be used for the session. He then sat back and watched the players trying to pick up, kick, handball and read the bounce of the hairy ball, which provoked great mirth and merriment! He remembers the players *"didn't know whether to lick it or kick it"* as they chased the doctored ball around, with plenty of ribald comments – *"In all my time as a coach, it is the funniest training session I've conducted and it certainly loosened up the players, who trained with great spirit and camaraderie"*.

How much impact the session had on the attitude of the players is a matter for conjecture, but the side began a winning streak which stretched to 11 games, starting with a three point win over the Falcons and growing weekly to a 140 point demolition of Subiaco. However, after 19 games and 15 wins, Swans were third with South on top, having lost only twice, and Claremont second on percentage over Swans. East Perth and East Fremantle were fighting for fourth place, but seven games behind Swans and Claremont! The Swans bubble burst against South in round 20, losing by 44 points, but a big win in the final home-and-away match against Perth saw them finish with 16 wins for the third successive season; however, it was only good enough for third place. Still, many scribes thought Swans were the team to beat for the flag despite the slightly better records of South and Claremont.

~

As the reigning premiership coach, John was appointed State coach for 1983, a role he relished, but had only done once before when the result was a drubbing by Victoria in Melbourne in 1975. He was keen to put this right and looked forward to games in Perth against South Australia and Victoria, with the WAFL breaking with convention and appointing a six man selection panel which included two other current coaches, Mal Brown and Graham Moss. The chairman was Bill Walker, who had taken over the Swans presidency from Cooper, with former players Lorne Cook (Claremont) and Ken McAullay (East Perth) making up the panel. The Australian championship was to be decided between the three major States and, with WA's two games in Perth, the side was rated a good chance.

The Victorians were (as usual) content to play away from Melbourne, but suffered an early setback in losing by 52 points to South Australia in Adelaide. This opened the door for WA as a win over the Croweaters would leave the championship to be decided against the Victorians. The SA game was not played under State of Origin rules and the selectors named nine debutants in the WA team [78], with an 11 goal to six second half producing a 24 point win to deny SA the championship. For the Victorian game, WA could select one player from each of the 12 VFL clubs, but in the end only used 10. The game was scheduled for a Tuesday, after the success of the previous year's mid-week fixture when 30,000 fans attended, but this time, with the prospect of a championship win in the offing, more than 44,000 spectators crammed into Subiaco Oval.

---

78. Making their WA debuts were Murray Rance, Don Langsford and Tony Solin (Swans), Mike Aitken, Michael Mitchell and Steve Goulding (Claremont), Paul Harding (East Fremantle), Willie Roe (South Fremantle) and Peter Thorne (East Perth). The SA side contained future Carlton stalwarts Stephen Kernahan and Craig Bradley.

At half-time, facing a 20 point deficit after kicking a wasteful 1.7 in the second quarter, John used the huge crowd to implore the players to fight back, saying later he did not want the side *"... to slide away to a big loss in front of so many West Australians"*. He delivered a stinging attack on Boucher, who had been quiet, and the big man lifted, giving the side a real physical presence around the packs. The last change saw the margin reduced to eight points, but Victoria scored the first two goals to kick 21 points clear. WA mounted a final thrust and when Gary Buckenara (then with Hawthorn) kicked his seventh goal minutes from the end, the home side hit the front. Kevin Taylor crumbed a goal two minutes later to extend the lead and WA looked the victors, but a late Victorian goal saw the home side just hang on for a three point win. It was WA's fourth championship win and left the Vics without an interstate victory in the year for the first time ever.

It was a great day for WA football and John was rapt to hand the Victorians a record they would rather do without. He became the All-Australian coach, 22 years after the 1961 Brisbane carnival when named on a wing as an All-Australian player. He was full of praise for the players, saying that *"... sheer guts won this game for WA. The response to the WA cause from the players was magnificent"* [79].

1983 – after the win over Victoria in Perth to clinch the Australian Championship. With Paul Harding (left) and Stephen Michael, the Tassie medallist. Photo courtesy of *The West Australian*.

In the first semi, Swans were favoured to beat East Fremantle, who had convincingly downed East Perth in the last home-and-away fixture to take fourth spot. A five goal lead to Swans in the first quarter was extended to a 59 point winning margin, with the young East Fremantle side never seriously challenging; this bothered John leading up to the preliminary final, concerned that the side lacked the *"hard edge"* so vital for finals success. He was convinced that, without some sort of spark, the side would struggle as they were playing *"without any real drive or passion"* – this led to the biggest gamble of his coaching career.

---

79. Maurice Rioli won the Simpson Medal (his third in three years) and captain Stephen Michael the Tassie Medal for the best player over the carnival.

The final was against bogey side South Fremantle, who had kicked themselves out of the second semi against Claremont by scoring 3.12 in the second quarter and losing by 21 points. John told chairman of selectors Bob Manning that he didn't think the players could win in their current frame of mind and he needed to give them a spark; something to really play for. He said he was going to drop Nowotny, who had indicated he would retire at the end of the year after captaining the team from 1977-81 and was greatly respected by the players for his tough approach. He was a big part of the heart and soul of the team and Manning's jaw dropped when John told him what he planned, but he knew he wasn't joking. He said *"If you drop Nowotny and we get beat you'll get lynched"*, but John simply replied that *"if I don't, we'll get beat anyway"*. The die was cast. However, with emotions running high, John told Manning he couldn't bring himself to tell Nowotny and asked him to deliver the bad news.

At the final training session Manning called Nowotny aside and told him, explaining that it was felt that South could cover him and some *"unpredictability"* was needed in the side. Nowotny, whose form was solid, had no inkling of his fate and was shattered by the news. He told Manning *"you know I'll always give my best and make a contest"* which added to the emotion. Told to keep the decision to himself, Nowotny attended the team meeting as normal as John went through the general tactics for the next day, then finished by announcing the team, concluding simply by saying *"Nowotny's out"*. An eerie silence settled over the room as the players tried to comprehend this totally unexpected twist. Struggling to control his emotions, John quickly left the room lest the players see that he wasn't in complete charge of his feelings. Nowotny remembers that most of the players wouldn't look at him, as they didn't know what to say, but after a couple of minutes the shock subsided and several players sought out John for an explanation. Still feeling terrible and fighting his emotions, he was in no state for debate, so he simply told them to *"go out and play for him, you might just get him into another grand final"*. The next day, Swans smashed the finals hold South had on them as they atoned for the demoralising 1981 preliminary final defeat, powering to a 74 point win set up by an eight goal third term.

Heading into the grand final, Swans were confident of beating the Tigers, believing they had an edge in mental toughness and that some of the Claremont players would wilt under physical pressure. John, Manning, Nowotny and Mullooly all recall relishing the opportunity to play them because *"we knew we had their measure"*. There was no debate over whether Nowotny would play or not – the players had made sure he would finish his career in a grand final, a point which John exploited to the fullest. The unlucky player to make way for him was Paul Werner, another Canberra recruit who had kicked three goals in the final and was the side's leading goal-kicker for the year. However, he understood the situation and told Nowotny that if he had to lose his place, then he was glad it would be for him. John didn't declare his hand before the game, keeping Claremont guessing and when Werner ran out with the side and went to the bench, the Tigers and the crowd were unsure whether he or Nowotny was in the final 20.

While Nowotny's selection was confirmed early in the week, the quandary for the selectors was whether to bring Boucher back after missing six weeks with a knee injury. Manning and fellow selectors, Kevin Clune, Tom Stannage and Max Kiernan were against including him, but John felt his physical strength could further intimidate the Claremont players. The issue remained alive until the morning of the game. At a park near Subiaco Oval, John had Boucher and Michael Johns, who had joined Swans mid-season from Subiaco, perform some ruck and marking contests. He made Manning and Stannage stand well apart so they couldn't discuss things as they watched the two ruckmen go at it. Manning remembers that *"Boucher could hardly jump and looked very proppy"* and both he and Stannage remained steadfast that he shouldn't play. Still John vacillated and asked Boucher whether he thought he could get through. The big ruckman indicated that he would and finally John went with his gut instinct and gave Boucher the nod, meaning that Johns was out of the side, much to the dismay of Manning and Stannage.

Ten minutes into the game, Boucher's knee buckled underneath him and he limped off. In the coaches' box, amid the pressure of the opening minutes of a grand final, John lost his cool and turned on Manning and Stannage, blaming them for the decision to include him! In reality, he was annoyed at himself for making the wrong call and took out his frustrations on the men sitting beside him. At quarter-time he gave the crestfallen Boucher an almighty serve and told the doctor to *"jab him"* so he could possibly get back on the ground. Swans had edged to a 10 point lead with Peter Sartori doing well in the ruck in Boucher's absence and, early in the second quarter, John shifted Baker from full-forward to the centre and sent Nowotny onto the ground. As Nowotny ran from the dugout, the crowd erupted and the players lifted – John remembers thinking that *"we're certainties"* as the Swans faithful reacted. At half-time, with Baker starring, the lead was 23 points and John played on Boucher's injury, telling the players it was time they carried him, instead of the reverse which had often been the case. He reminded the players that it was Nowotny's last game and *"to not let him down"*, using the crowd's reaction as an indication of the esteem in which he was held by the Swans supporters. It was powerful stuff and the side was primed to claim a second flag; while the Tigers never gave in, Swans took a 28 point lead into the last quarter and eventually won by 21 points.

At the presentation of medallions to his victorious players, John reserved a special comment for Nowotny, saying – *"It gladdens my heart to introduce to you Stan Nowotny"*. On the lap of honour, there was a poignant moment when a limping Boucher fell behind the group, but a couple of team-mates came to his aid and supported him to the finish. In the change rooms amid all the excitement that goes with winning a grand final, there were emotional scenes as Boucher wept, unable to hide his disappointment at not contributing to the effort. Johns, the man he replaced, was also distraught, having never played finals football before joining Swans and John finally persuaded him to accept his own medallion, telling him that he deserved one. With every grand final win there are always desperately unlucky players who have just missed selection and for them it can never have the same feeling.

John commented that *"mental toughness won us today's grand final"* and added that Simpson medallist Brad Shine and Nowotny *"are what Swan Districts is all about. It is a wonderful club filled with my type of people. They are hard workers who rally together and play their football with a wonderful spirit"*. He gained more pleasure from this second flag than he did in 1982, mostly because there was such a sense of relief attached to winning the first one. Both then, and now, he is convinced the players won it for Nowotny and it wouldn't have happened if he hadn't provided the emotional spur by dropping him for the preliminary final – *"Sometimes you do things that aren't in the textbook and pull a rabbit out of the hat. However, while this one worked, in coaching there is a fine line between genius or dunce!"*. Nowotny carried the hurt for a long time despite playing in the grand final and retiring with two premiership medallions; but now says that it's *"well in the past"* and *"something that he (John) thought was best for the team"*. In 2002, when John finally retired from coaching, Nowotny gave an emotion-charged speech at the trophy presentations, having to pause several times to gather himself. The admiration and respect he has for John was obvious.

~

In 1984, the lure of a hat trick of premierships to match the great deeds of the 1961, '62 and '63 sides was strong motivation and John framed much of the planning for the players on *"creating your own piece of history"* and *"getting closer to those guys from the '60s"*. No WA team had won three successive premierships since Mal Atwell's Perth sides of 1966, '67 and '68 and John used this as a rallying point. As was now the norm for the top WA sides, Swans were again losing several key players – heading to the VFL were Phil Narkle (St Kilda), Baker (Essendon)[80] and Smith and Kenny (Carlton), while Nowotny and Cransberg had retired.

Cransberg was a surprise loss, as he was in his early 20s, but after 115 games and two premierships he put his career first by taking a senior position at the Alcoa refinery in the South-West. In his usual style, John dwelt on the positives, saying that *"on one hand I'm disappointed*

1983 – presenting Stan Nowotny with his premiership medallion.

---

80. Baker would soon have the enviable record of playing in four consecutive premiership sides, as Essendon were victorious in 1984 and '85.

by the loss of such a great group of players, but on the other hand their absence can help us win a flag. These players have all tasted success and if they had been here for this season they may have been a little less enthusiastic than some of the others. Those on the way up will grab their chance to play league football and reach the heights of those whose places they have taken". To add depth, John sifted through the other WAFL clubs looking for players with 50-80 league games, believing that they *"should be ready to have an impact, they know what is required and can be concerned about the team, as well as their own performance".* In 1983 he recruited rover Barry Kimberley (Perth), Leigh Brenton (East Fremantle), forward Ken Marshall (Subiaco) in addition to Lions big man Johns, who came over mid-year. While only Kimberley and Brenton made the 1983 grand final side, all four would play important roles in 1984, as John also added midfielder Chris Allen (East Perth), defender Kim Hetherington (East Fremantle) and forward Brett Farmer (Claremont). In part, these players were looking for greater opportunities, and the chance to play at WA's top club under John, now widely regarded as the State's leading coach, was enticing. When approached, the players jumped at the offer to move clubs.

As the season grew near, the WAFL made the major decision to appoint an independent board of directors to run the game, a requirement imposed by the State government in return for financial assistance. John was in favour of the move, as it removed the influence of club interests and loyalties from the decision-making process at league level. After almost 30 years in football, he threw in a few development ideas of his own for the board to consider. In his *Daily News* column he advocated shortening the game to four 20 minute quarters with no time-on and playing all matches at Subiaco Oval, with two on Saturday and two on Sunday to maximise the new facilities. Further, he thought the point posts should be eliminated to improve the skill of goal-scoring. He acknowledged that these radical ideas might take years to come into being and he was certainly correct – 20 years on, none of the proposals have been adopted. However, he still feels the game is too long and *"blow outs"*, which are reasonably common, could be minimised with shorter quarters. Even in 1984, he was the elder statesman of WA football and he would continue to speak his mind on the game, often to the chagrin of the administrators, right up to his retirement in 2002.

In the practice games, John again found more controversy. Swans were playing Footscray in the South-West town of Collie, with former Richmond player Michael Malthouse in his maiden year of coaching. Early in the game Swans realised they had 19 men on the field in what was an honest mistake, but John and the coaching camp let the situation linger, hoping to get through to the end of the quarter without drawing attention to a player being taken off (and not replaced). When the error was discovered after a count by the umpires, the situation became ugly as the Footscray camp accused Swans of blatant cheating. Former East Fremantle ruckman Andrew Purser, who was in the Bulldogs side and the recipient of a few *"sprays"* from John early in the game, was particularly incensed and wanted to fight John then and there[81]. Cooler heads prevailed and the two men were restrained as the insults flew, but the game continued, with Footscray winning easily.

The WAFL board took a dim view of the issue and sought to discipline John, but Swans president Bill Walker argued (correctly) that the game was not an official WAFL fixture and

---

81. Later in the season Purser would lead the WA ruck against Victoria in the State of Origin clash in Perth, with John in charge of the side, and their differences forgotten.

the board had no authority to impose any penalty, adding that the club would handle the matter internally. Christian wrote in *The West Australian* that John would be disciplined by Swans over the incident, at which John exploded! He told Walker, who never planned to impose any penalty, that he would refuse any sanction and the two men traded barbs (some personal and relating back to their playing days) in the boardroom at Bassendean Oval. This was their first and only major argument while they were coach and president at Swans, but the ill-feeling simmered for some days before Cooper insisted they get together and sort out their differences, or forget about a hat trick of premierships. The meeting was a success and John and Walker worked together in leading Swans for another nine seasons.

To open the season, a new WAFL initiative saw the first official fixture played outside the metropolitan area. Bunbury was the venue – it was part of Swans country zone and adjoining regions belonged to East Perth, so the two sides did battle, with the Royals winning by 14 points. As in 1983, the performance was a sign of things to come as Swans went up and down over the first round, winning four games and sitting second behind South, but with every team in contention for the finals. The second round returned three wins and four losses (including three in a row for the first time since 1979) as Swans struggled, searching for the right combination. Sitting fourth, two games behind the Sharks [82] on top, but level with fifth and sixth placed Claremont and East Perth, the team suddenly clicked. New full-forward Brent Hutton kicked 19 goals in two games and Swans won all seven games in the third round, kicking 19 goals or more in each match, with 19 points the smallest winning margin. The seven game streak reclaimed top spot and a double chance at the hat trick.

~

Mid-season there was another challenge to be met. No State other than Victoria had ever won two successive Australian championships and the opportunity was there for WA. The Victorians were loudly talking up their prospects, despite not winning a match the previous year, but it nearly came unstuck in Adelaide when they just beat SA by four points. In June, WA went to Adelaide knowing a win over SA would leave a showdown with Victoria in Perth to decide the championship, but well-aware that the 1982 trip to Adelaide under Mal Brown had resulted in a 116 point thrashing. John called on Haydn Bunton (Jnr), now back in Perth coaching Subiaco after another coaching stint in Adelaide, to take a training session and talk about the conditions at Football Park and the likely composition of the SA side. WA again went with youth and 10 players were named to make their State debuts [83], with the only established State representatives being Perth pair Robert Wiley and Peter Bosustow, both back from the VFL.

After an even first half, SA led by 16 points at the last change. John rallied the team, telling them to *"remember the people back home watching and listening"* and to take strength from their silent support as the parochial SA crowd vigorously urged on their local heroes. Gradually WA edged back and, at the 20 minute mark, were five points down. The last 10 minutes were drama-packed as firstly WA umpire Mike Ball gave a controversial holding the ball decision against SA in the goal square, allowing Brad Hardie to put WA in front. Minutes later SA's

---

82. East Fremantle changed their emblem and nickname from Old Easts to the Sharks at the start of the 1984 season.
83. The debutants were Don Holmes, Peter Ware, Jon Fogarty and Leigh Brenton (Swans), Greg Wilkinson and Laurie Keene (Subiaco), David Hart, Warren Mosconi and Gavin Carter (South) and Rhett Baynes (Perth).

Chapter 17 – After 19 years, another hat trick

Neville Roberts ran into an open goal and missed, leaving the scores tied. Then Wiley had a long snap on goal, with the ball going through for a point as the siren sound and, despite heated protests from the SA players, SANFL umpire Laurie Argent gave the all clear – WA were home by a point. The crowd vented their anger at the umpires and the WA players who, following John's lead, then responded with some exuberant victory salutes of their own, which further enraged the fans, who pelted the visitors with rubbish as they left the arena. In the rooms Wiley admitted he heard the siren a split second before he kicked the ball, but the rules of the game are clear in this situation – the game officially ends when the field umpire in charge of play hears the siren, so the decision was correct as Argent raised his arms to signal the end when the ball was in the air. This was only the sixth time WA had beaten SA in Adelaide and Wiley had the distinction of playing in the previous three victories (1977, '78 and '84). The chance for back-to-back championship wins was alive and John immediately started planning to take on the Vics.

As was the case in 1983, WA were restricted to one expatriate from each of the 12 VFL clubs, but this year the task looked even more difficult as two or more WA players were with each Melbourne side. Baker or Tony Buhagiar from Essendon, Ken Hunter, Wayne Blackwell or Ralph from Carlton and Purser or Beasley from Footscray were among the dilemmas facing the selectors – *"It was sad that many deserving footballers missed these games because of the restrictions imposed by the VFL. State football was at its peak and those fortunate enough to play took some great achievements and memories from these matches"*. In typical fashion, however, the Vics had no restrictions on selection and were able to pick their best side.

After the previous year's cliffhanger, the game captured the imagination of the WA public and nearly 44,000 people flocked to Subiaco Oval for another epic contest. It opened with WA kicking four goals in seven minutes before a young Gary Ablett announced himself to the crowd with two quick majors. A rare insight into coaching was provided by John as he allowed *The Daily News* reporter Robbie Burns to sit in the coaches' box with himself and Manning. On first sighting Ablett, John said he *"looked fat across the backside"*, but by the end of the game such thoughts were long forgotten as Ablett put on a superb display.

WA's five goal lead was maintained until half-time, despite losing players with injury in the second quarter. When Langsford went off with a dislocated shoulder, John quipped to Manning *"I knew we shouldn't have played any of our (Swans) blokes today"*. Phil Cronan had the unenviable job of playing on Ablett and at the break he asked John *"how do I play on this guy?"*. John replied *"how the hell would I know"* as he recognised that Ablett was *"in the zone"* and virtually unstoppable. He later commented that *"coaches don't always have all the answers and often don't have any solutions"* as he recalled the incident.

The game was played at breakneck speed and injuries were limiting WA's flexibility as the Vics mounted a comeback, with Ablett and Gerard Healy providing sure avenues to goal. The lead was cut to 12 points early in the third term, before WA added four goals only to see the irrepressible Ablett kick two late majors to see Victoria trail by 16 points at the last break. John was left with only 17 fit men and lamented that *"it's out of my hands now – there are no moves I can make. It's up to their guts now"*. Both sides traded goals until the Victorians hit the lead with Ablett getting his eighth, at which John said *"Injuries will cost us this game. Whoever said football doesn't need 22 men? When it's played like this it does. These blokes are out on their feet"*. But once again WA found something and two goals to Wiley restored the lead, but only briefly and, with a minute to play, Victoria seemed set to win. Then, with a last-gasp effort, Allen 'Shorty' Daniels gathered a loose ball and goaled to see WA home by four points. An elated John said – *"It was a courage-plus performance. It's great to be associated with these players and they have developed a special feeling for one another. WA can claim, with pride, the tag of top football State and that's a good feeling"*. Ross Glendinning, fresh from his Brownlow Medal triumph in 1983, and Brad Hardie [84] were the side's best players, while Ablett was a standout for the Victorians. The media rated the game a superb spectacle, with the Melbourne papers claiming WA was now *"the Big W"*, an unexpected compliment from a normally apathetic Victorian press so accustomed to singing the praises of *"the Big V"*.

John has great memories of the 1983 and '84 games – *"The Victorians were playing for keeps, especially in '84, but WA had some terrific players and plenty of State pride. They were outstanding games of footy, probably the best I've seen over my career because of the quality of players involved who approached the game as if there were no tomorrows"*. Premierships aside, these two Australian championship wins were a highlight of his coaching career, especially as they were achieved against the old enemy Victoria. That State football is now off the agenda is a tragedy for current day players whose careers are a lot poorer for its absence, according to John.

John was duly appointed All Australian coach for the second year running, with WA skipper Malaxos captain. However, this year selection in the team carried more than just the normal kudos, as the side was to tour Ireland for a three Test series of modified Gaelic rules in October. However, before coaching Australia, John had a third premiership to attempt to win with Swans.

~

After seven straight wins, Swans were hot favourites for the second semi final, which John greatly disliked. But there was no angle he could work to change this perception. On a wet day his worst fears were realised as underdogs East Fremantle launched a brutal physical assault and, for the first time since 1981, Swans buckled. Down by five goals at half-time, Swans were unable to bridge the gap, losing by 26 points. To make matters worse, Hetherington broke a leg, leaving the side desperately short of tall defenders. To prepare for the preliminary final John imposed a media ban on his players as he set about restoring the *"hard edge"* missing against the Sharks. It was not the first time he had used this tactic, having done it back in 1974 with East Fremantle. He feels that by removing the media, a *"siege mentality"* is created, which helps the side to re-focus on the task of winning the next match without any distractions. He didn't want any players being fed *"bullshit"* by the media about their personal performances in the second semi, which would be contrary to his own assessment. He used the fact that captain Keith Narkle was to play his 250th game and Neesham his 150th to motivate the side, reminding the players that similar milestones had always been honoured in recent seasons. Their opponents were old rivals Claremont, who had beaten East Perth in the first semi, with their prime movers being Sandover medallists Malaxos and Michael Mitchell [85], Daniels, Steve Goulding and Darrell Panizza, with coach Graham Moss now retired. Swans were confident they still 'had the wood' on the Tigers and at the finish they did, but it was a close, hard-fought contest. Claremont jumped to a four goal lead

---

84. Hardie won both the Simpson and Tassie Medals this year.
85. In the first three-way tie in the medal's history and, with countbacks now abolished, East Perth's Peter Spencer won his second medal in 1984, along with Mitchell and Malaxos. In 1983 East Perth ruckman John Ironmonger beat Perth rover Bryan Cousins on a countback, prompting the change, with Cousins receiving his medal retrospectively in 1997.

at quarter-time, but Swans hit back in the second term to finish two points behind. An inaccurate third quarter saw Swans score 3.9 to Claremont's 1.1, but it set up the eventual 21 point victory and the chance for a third flag. In qualifying for their third consecutive grand final, Swans had done it every possible way – from the first semi (1983) and after winning and losing the second semis ('82 and '84).

Leading up to the game, John's main concern was again whether to play Boucher, who had been hampered with injury and managed just three games for the year, the last two in the finals where he was sadly out of touch. Johns and Sartori were in good form and could handle the ruck duties, but Sartori had played mostly at centre-half-forward, so the issue was whether Johns could do it alone and what the options were if he was injured. The final decision was taken to the wire. With the weather fine, John punted on exploiting the taller Sharks line-up with pace and 30 minutes before the bounce he told Boucher he was out and Darwin recruit Kevin Caton was in. Boucher, who had been such an integral part of Swans rise to the top, had played his last game [86]. There's no room for sentiment in selecting teams, particularly for grand finals.

The game was one of the most amazing ever played to decide a WAFL premiership. There was a strong wind favouring the Subiaco end of the ground and John instructed Keith Narkle to kick with the breeze if he won the toss, which he did. East Fremantle were relatively inexperienced in finals football, with only four players (compared to 12 at Swans) having played in a grand final, much like Swans had been in 1980. John wanted a fast start to exploit their lack of experience and it was a sound plan, but he couldn't have imagined how well the ambush would work. At quarter-time, Swans led by 64 points after kicking 10.7 to three points; the East Fremantle players were attacking the man and not the ball and were frequently penalised.

The third premiership seemed as good as won, but the second quarter proved to be equally amazing. Told to concentrate on the ball, captain-coach Ron Alexander led the Sharks back into the game, as they kicked nine goals and kept Swans to one, bringing the margin back to 12 points. There was concern in the Swans camp as the Sharks got their goals easily, without burning up too much energy and, after 10 minutes of the third term, had closed to within a point – a remarkable upset seemed possible. Swans scored the last three goals of the term to lead by 22 points, but the wind was worth about five goals, so East Fremantle were close enough if good enough. John stressed the importance of getting the first couple of goals in the last quarter, as he reasoned the Sharks couldn't have too much *"left in the tank"*. Their heroic effort to get back did tell in the last term and, with Neesham and Simpson medallist Kimberley controlling the midfield, Swans clinched the hat trick by 36 points.

When interviewed on the oval after the game, John rated the win as *"almost the best of the three, considering where we had to come from and what we had to overcome"*. On later reflection, he says *"the first in '82 was special because it broke the (19 year) drought, the second was great for the players, especially Nowotny, and the third was terrific, as hat tricks are hard to achieve in anything and it was won on real grit, as the side wasn't as talented as the first two"*.

---

86. Boucher ran out with the side, creating uncertainty as to who was actually playing, but in the first quarter he appeared on the ground in whites as he helped run water to his team-mates.

Apart from emulating the great Swans sides of 1961, '62 and '63, the third premiership capped the most successful era in the club's history. Since 1980, including finals, the team had won 88 games, losing only 30, for three flags, one grand final loss and five consecutive years in the finals, something the club had never before achieved. In the premiership years of 1982, '83 and '84, there were 53 wins and only 18 losses, a better record than in 1961, '62 and '63 when they notched 46 wins, 23 losses and two draws. The most recent hat trick had also been achieved with a less stable team. Only eight players represented Swans in all three premierships, whereas 13 players featured in 1961, '62 and '63. In total, John used 34 players to win the three flags of the 1980s, while Bunton used 29. John had honed his coaching prowess to where he was *"a master of developing sides, both in the long and the short term"*, as Geoff Christian reported in The *West Australian* after the 1984 win over SA.

In terms of on-field success, the five years from 1980-84 represent the pinnacle of John's coaching career, with successive Australian championships topping off his success at Swans. In analysing his coaching methods and tactics, the successful Swans sides were characterised by their mental toughness and persistence. John coached hard on character, then added tactics and strategies to top off the mix. As in his earlier days at South and East Fremantle, he was ruthless and relentless in his pursuit of improvement in his players – a big part of achieving this was to challenge them regularly to *"raise the bar"* which often tested their character in various ways. The searching pre-season training sessions, such as the Allen Park sandhill climbs, were one method of doing this, while the spontaneous and sometimes vicious personal attacks, in front of the rest of the team or private, were another. Both were designed to get the best out

1984 – Celebrating the hat trick of premierships with Swans. Running a victory lap with captain Keith Narkle.
Photo courtesy of Alan East and Westside Football.

of the players, to make them realise they could give more, both individually and for the team. No-one was immune from a 'serve' and often it was the senior players who bore the brunt. According to Boucher and Melrose, this was because *"we had more to give and it showed there were no favourites"*. Certainly some players couldn't handle his volatile nature; they either learned to cope with it or they moved on. The senior players were again to the fore, explaining to the younger players that when a verbal attack got personal, it wasn't meant to be taken too personally! It was just a response to the circumstances, designed to get more out of the individual. The senior players made it clear that by being targeted it meant you had something to offer. Otherwise, they explained, *"he wouldn't play you!"*.

Some players, however, took time to adjust to John's ways and Rance remembers early in his first year being singled out by him at training for not getting to his feet quickly enough after being dumped. John told the group that *"the next time he lies on the ground, I want you to kick him!"*. The 18-year-old Rance didn't know where to look or what to think, but he knew John was serious. With advice from senior players, he gradually understood that his character was being tested and it was up to him as to how he responded. Sometimes tensions boiled over and both Rance and Don Holmes came (briefly!) to blows with John after severe verbal challenges, but these were soon smoothed over and forgotten; all three men now laugh about these incidents. Cooper recalls seeing John *"do some dastardly things to players"*, but he knew it was his way and the reasons for it. In one game when he saw John physically confront Boucher, he saw red and later told the big man that if *"he (John) ever does that again and you want to give him one, then the board wouldn't act"*. A surprised Boucher couldn't believe his good fortune and mischievously exploited the situation for a *"bit of sport"*. He couldn't wait to tell John, knowing how he would react against Cooper and, sure enough, John went for Cooper straight away, saying *"... you mongrel, you are undermining me with the players!"*. Cooper replied – *"If you do that again to any players and they retaliate, you'll get no help from me"*. And that was the end of it – there were plenty of arguments between the two men, but never any grudges or bad blood.

The verbal sprays John delivered were invariably balanced up with plenty of encouragement if he saw a player was prepared to do some hard work to make themselves better. Nowotny, Boucher and Mullooly all say John gave a player *"great belief in yourself and your ability"* and no-one got a bigger buzz out of seeing a player succeed than John – it was all the thanks he wanted. Probably, the football public mostly remembers the side of John that 'ripped' into players and teams, whereas the passionate and positive self-belief he instilled in players is perhaps not well-known.

Another part of the 'character' development of players involved making them appreciate how fortunate they were to be fit and able to play league football. In the 1980s he struck up a relationship with the WA Paraplegic Association and their wheelchair basketball teams, who played several games against the Swans players. The benefits were equally shared – the players appreciated their legs and what they could achieve with them, but also saw in the paraplegics what could be accomplished with tenacity and spirit to overcome personal adversity. On the other side, the wheelchair basketballers greatly enjoyed playing against and associating with their able-bodied football idols. These games were always willing, with no quarter given, and often the Swans players were knocked from their chairs, as the opposition displayed their tough skills. When Blackaby was ill in hospital for several weeks, John visited him (with the team) regularly. He has always had great empathy for people, whether sick or injured, who were worse off than himself and has tried to help them whenever possible. Many a player he coached or was associated with has been pleasantly surprised to receive a visit from John while in hospital or convalescing at home, despite perhaps not seeing him for many years. He wanted this attitude to rub off on his players so they could develop 'good character' for life, not just football. Allan Jeans, the great St Kilda and Hawthorn coach, always maintained that his primary goal was to make his players *"better citizens"*. John never expressed it in this way, but the character lessons he put before his players had the same effect. Boucher, who admits owing John a lot for resurrecting his career in 1978, summed up his influence by saying, *"When the lunatic (John) came along, he raised the bar and demanded much more. Some players couldn't handle it, but those that could were successful in football and have all been successful in business and life as well"*.

Aside from character, the Swans sides of the 1980s were extremely versatile as John either developed or recruited players who could perform a number of roles; this provided more options, especially when things weren't going well in a match. Building on the positional changes he first saw in 1959 in the State game against Victoria and developed at East Fremantle in the 1970s, he not only had rovers and ruck-rovers changing on half-forward or half-back flanks or out of pockets, but key position players swapping between defence and attack and running players who tagged star opposition performers. In the premiership years of 1982, '83 and '84, the Swans goal to goal line was 'fluid', both week to week and also within games as the likes of Rance, Cransberg, Kenny, Nowotny, Sartori, Baker and Fitzgerald shared the key defensive and forward roles. Only full-back Mullooly was a regular in the same spot. In the centre and on the ball it was a 'revolving door', with Melrose, Neesham, Smith, Baker, Mike and Steve Richardson, Holmes, Shine, Langsford, Fogarty, Kimberley and Skwirowski all taking turns to exert pressure on the opposition and keep them guessing about who their direct opponent was at any particular time. When necessary, taggers such as Skwirowski, Fogarty, Langsford, Shine and Kimberley were asked to run with an opponent, changing with them when they went off the ball or moved positions, which was a new tactic in WA football.

The players responded well to a change in roles during a game, which may have been the essential difference between Swans and Claremont, who lost the 1982 and '83 grand finals. John likens the Claremont sides of 1981-83 to the West Perth teams of the early 1950s, when South Fremantle were a little too good, beating them in the grand finals of 1952 and '53. In the early '80s Moss had a good team at Claremont, but not as flexible as Swans – in particular, their key forwards Ralph, Farmer and Malaxos didn't have any other *"strings to their game"*. The greater versatility of the Swans sides, plus an edge in mental toughness, were important factors in denying Claremont premiership success in 1982 and '83, according to John, who felt the Tigers probably had an edge in talent.

Finally, another trait that characterised his coaching – not only at this time, but for virtually his whole career – was how he operated on *"gut instincts"*. Never afraid to experiment, he would often pull a switch at the last moment and tell a player he was lining up somewhere different. Similarly, if a player looked *"a bit off"* in the opening moments of a game, then he could find himself on the bench within 10 minutes despite being in recent good form. He made these decisions on the observation that the player's *"head wasn't right for the contest"* at that point, as their early efforts and body language were always keenly observed. While he planned for a game as all coaches do, he was never afraid to abandon the plan (or part of it) if his instincts told him to do so.

Chapter 18
Coaching the Green and Gold

Peter McDermott, the Irish manager, complaining about the Australian tactics in the first Test of the series:

"It really went beyond the bounds of sportsmanship".

John, in reply:

"It wasn't a terribly physical game by Australian standards".

In the week after the grand final, John took time out from football and headed north to Lancelin to spend several days fishing before leaving for Ireland for the Gaelic Test series. He also had to decide what he was going to do in 1985. For the first time in his career, he had the choice of several clubs who wanted his services, as his success with Swans and WA saw him touted by the media as the best coach in Australia. He felt this could be his last big decision in football and he needed to get it right; pressure of a different type was building and he found it tough going.

He was out of contract at Swans (who were desperate to keep him) and other clubs in WA, SA and Victoria were interested in his services. Since the championship win over Victoria he'd received enquiries from all over Australia about his plans for 1985. He made no secret of his desire to coach in the VFL, but only at a club he had *"some feeling for"*. One of these was Collingwood, who he had always supported on the Melbourne scene and who had that 'working class' culture he felt comfortable with. He could never see himself as coach of a 'blue blood' club such as Carlton or Melbourne, or Claremont in the WAFL. The other was Richmond, where the link dated back to 1951 when he played for the WA Schoolboys side in Melbourne when they were hosted by the Tigers. Both clubs were chasing coaches for 1985, as were St Kilda, North Melbourne and the Sydney Swans, who all made approaches to him, but there were no firm offers.

On the local scene, Perth had put a strong offer to him after Alan Joyce and Ian Miller had done no better than sixth in recent years while, down at South Fremantle, Mal Brown had stepped down after seven years and there was a concerted push to get South's prodigal son to return as coach. He also had a surprise approach from Harry Morgan, the East Fremantle president, as they were considering replacing Ron Alexander, if not with John, then with Murray Ward. John quickly declared that he wasn't interested and Alexander survived, after Robbie Burns broke the story in *The Daily News*, forcing Morgan to publicly deny the claim, amidst a strong member backlash. Ironically, Alexander, after coaching the Sharks to the 1985 flag, would beat John for the inaugural West Coast Eagles coaching job in 1987. It might have been much different had John been interested in a return to East Fremantle Oval.

The thought of coaching in the VFL was enticing, but complicating the prospect of moving to Melbourne was the likelihood that a national club competition wasn't far away, with one or maybe two WA sides – possibly as soon as 1986. As the premier WA coach, he was perfectly placed to get the job (or one of them) and, as a passionate Western Australian, this was his first preference, providing the chance to coach in the VFL, but still based in WA. He declined the VFL approaches, which left the choice between Swans, Perth or South. The Bulldogs were the outsiders as, by the time South officials spoke to him, he felt he had a moral obligation to either Swans or Perth, but not to a third club.

As he fished, he wrestled with the decision – *"I felt I had just about run out of challenges at Swans and my time there might have been up. Perth represented an enormous challenge, given their poor record and this certainly appealed as I liked to take on the 'underdog' and build a side"*. He was also keen to try and emulate Sir Ross Hutchinson, the only WA coach to take three different clubs to premierships. To have two coaches from the same small timber town of Deanmill achieve this feat had great appeal to John. Money-wise, there was little difference between the two offers, as Perth president George Spalding had forced Bill Walker into a bidding war to match their offer, and either deal would see John making much more than ever before as a coach. Walker worked overtime trying to convince him that being a successful long-term coach at one club was the greatest challenge of all, as you had to move with the times and continually re-invent yourself, which John felt was true. However, he finally opted for the Perth job because of the challenge it represented and the lingering doubts he had about what was left to achieve at Swans. He telephoned Spalding with his decision, but asked that no announcement be made by Perth until later in the week after he had informed the Swans players.

The next day the team attended a premiership celebration dinner hosted by the Midland Shire Council and, when he told several players that he was going to Perth, a highly charged and emotional discussion ensued. With Jon Fogarty leading the charge, the players wanted to know why he was leaving them for another WAFL club when he had always encouraged them to first prove themselves in WA, then take the next challenge of playing in the VFL. When they asked why coaching was any different, John was stuck for an answer. The depth of feeling they expressed and the disappointment they displayed struck at his heart and, although he had made a commitment to Perth, he knew he had to do an about face and reject their offer. He spoke that night to an incredulous Spalding, who threatened legal action, but that never transpired. The news broke the next day and John explained his change of heart by saying he would not have been *"broadening my horizons by taking over Perth"* and added *"there is a special bond at Swan Districts, a bond that has linked us together in recent years and it was never more evident to me than after talking with the players. It's hard to turn your back on that"*. For the third time in his career he had nearly become the coach of Perth but, for once, sentiment crept in and his heart ruled his head.

~

For John, the first test involving the Gaelic series was the air flight! The trip to London and then Dublin was the longest flight he had ever undertaken and he certainly didn't relish the prospect. However, the flight was *"flat and calm"* and no-one was any the wiser about his fear of flying. The potential problems of international travel materialised on arrival in Dublin, with the news that the luggage of half the tour members had gone astray, which the airlines took 24 hours to resolve, forcing players to share their training gear for the first couple of days. The squad had assembled for the first time on the plane, leaving only six days to prepare for the

Chapter 18 – Coaching the Green and Gold

first trial game, which was four days before the first Test. The initial task was to get the players bonding as a group, so on the morning after their arrival John called a 6am training session, warning everyone to be on time. For the first time in his life, he missed an alarm call and slept in, making him the only person late for the meeting! Realising this was a poor start, his mind raced on how to handle the situation and, as he took the lift down to the hotel lobby, it finally came to him. As he entered the meeting, with plenty of derisive comments being aired, he threw £20 onto the table and announced that, naturally, he was fining himself for being late and the same rules would apply for the rest of the tour. Murray Rance, to this day, believes John was deliberately late to set the tone for the tour, but in reality it wasn't a carefully crafted coaching ploy. The next day South Australia's Garry McIntosh was late, so John fined him the same amount and made him the fines master for the rest of the trip, a role he relished.

To meld the players together he had regular morning walks and games of cricket, with the Victorians usually taking on the West and South Australians – there were plenty of wagers, with the Vics usually winning the money. The tour was yet another challenge for John, who was excited about coaching a side representing the country and his State passion translated into national pride, along with team manager and selector Ted Whitten, who added all his celebrated enthusiasm for the "big V". WA team members were Steve Malaxos (captain), Ross Glendinning, Maurice Rioli, Craig Holden, Robert Wiley, Brad Hardie, Murray Rance, Allen Daniels and Peter Sartori, who had been a late inclusion despite not playing State football in 1984. A number of players withdrew from the tour and, while injuries were accepted, declining the opportunity to represent your country (as Gary Ablett did) was something John found *"extraordinary"*. Well-known Victorians in the party included Robert Flower, Mark Lee, Gary Pert, Robert DiPierdomenico, Dermott Brereton, Gerard Healy, Russell Greene, Simon Madden and Terry Daniher and the South Australians included Craig Bradley, John Platten, Stephen Kernahan, Michael Aish, Peter Motley and McIntosh, who was probably the least well known of the Croweaters, but a knockabout larrikin as tough as nails who John took an instant liking to. After being appointed fines master, McIntosh volunteered to be the team's goal-keeper, although he had no experience of Gaelic football.

1984 – The Ireland Tour. Meeting Garrett Fitzgerald, the Irish Prime Minister, with Gerard Healy (left), Russell Greene, the late Ted Whitten and Robert DiPierdomenico (right).

Only two squad members, Flower and Pert, had experience in the game, so twice-daily sessions were introduced to practise kicking the round ball and scoring 'goals' (six points for under the bar and into the net) and 'overs' (three points for between the posts, but over the crossbar). The sessions were not physically demanding, but were essential as the players struggled to kick the round ball accurately to team-mates – most players sliced or curved the ball, causing it to miss the target. The training facilities were often primitive, but John noticed that the Victorians were unfazed and generally *"just got on with it"*, while the WA and SA players often commented on the lack of amenities. He felt these respective attitudes might have something to do with Victoria's great success in State football, reflecting a more professional approach.

At training, the players practised kicking 'overs', as John felt scoring 'goals' against the Irish would be difficult. Of the other compromise rules for the series, the one that bothered him the most was the 'no tackling' stipulation. While bumping and blocking were permitted, the Aussies had real trouble in robbing the Irish of the ball when they were in possession. Tackling was a natural instinct when an opponent had the ball and John felt the Irish players, with their greater skill in using the round ball, would easily be able to step around the Australians and retain possession.

In the first trial game against a county side, the shortcomings of the Kangaroos[87] were quickly displayed – they lost by 14 points, failing to score any 'goals' and relying on 'overs' as their main scoring option. Many kicks went astray as they struggled with the round ball – the county players also kept possession easily as they ran with it, despite the Australian attempts to impede their progress by bumping. John said the team would perhaps struggle in its early games, but promised the side would be more aggressive in its approach in the first Test. They certainly were, as John orchestrated some surprises for the Irish when national pride went on the line. In a pre-match interview, a well-meaning Irish journalist suggested the oval Australian ball be used in the next two Tests, given Australia's problems with kicking the round ball. The suggestion enraged John, who told the players that *"... they were assuming we couldn't win with their ball"*. It was another reason to buck the odds and cause an upset. However, the main thrust of his tactics was to frustrate the flow of the Irish when they had the ball and he wasn't about to let the composite rules get in the way! He told the players to tackle hard, knock them over and take them to the ground as often as possible, knowing this would result in free kicks, but the interruption to their forward flow and the 'softening up' of the opposition would make it worthwhile.

The Australian intentions were made clear early, when Lee 'took out' two Irish opponents in the one play and McIntosh came off his line and 'ran through' an opponent. In addition, 'professional trips' were used when the Irish players were breaking away with the ball. The surprise tactics paid off as Australia recorded an all-the-way 70-57 win, which included two 'goals'. There were several fiery incidents, including an all-in brawl which also involved the respective coaches' benches. The Irish were seething about the rough house Australian tactics, which clearly flouted the rules, and Ireland manager Peter McDermott called for players to be sent off for similar breaches in future matches. He added – *"It really went beyond the bounds*

---

87. The team played under the name of Australia's most famous animal, also the title of Australia's national rugby league side.

of sportsmanship". John, at his diplomatic best, said – *"It wasn't a terribly physical game by Australian standards"* and that *"the crowd loved it"*, before challenging the Irish to *"play our type of game"* in the next Test.

The next day John was spared the likely media assault on the team as Robert Trimbole, the fugitive Australian crime boss, was captured in the hotel across the road, which stole the headlines. However, the tactics almost caused a minor international incident! Members of the Gaelic Athletic Association (GAA) wanted to scrap the series in response to the *"lack of Australian sportsmanship* [88]*"*. Crisis meetings between the GAA and the Australian NFL representatives led to a directive designed to prevent the same tactics being used in the next Test. The directive did not specify tackling, but made it clear the umpires would send players off for violent play and persistent fouls. If sent off, a player could be replaced, but was not permitted to take any further part in the game.

In their next county match, the Kangaroos were on their best behaviour with no deliberate tackling, partly because the match was in Ulster, in Northern Ireland, and the previous week a visiting Irish side who had won there had its team bus tipped over by irate local fans! There had also been a bomb scare near the ground two days previously and John told the side that they were not, under any circumstances, to win, but just do the right thing by their hosts so they could get out of the Province in one piece. He made certain of this by resting most of the Test team and the side lost by 50 points. He played his tall ruckmen, as he saw little need for them in the compromise-rules game, feeling that the ruck-rover types were better suited and taller players were not mobile or agile enough to be effective. To keep up the midfield pressure, John paired off his players for the Test matches and swapped them off the bench, much like the midfield rotation carried out by AFL teams today.

The second Test was again full of controversy. Although tempted, John refrained from following the winning tactics of the first match and told the side to beat the Irish at their own game, leaving them nothing to whinge about. After conceding a 20 point lead in the second quarter, the Kangaroos came home strongly, but went down 86-80, which kept the series alive. John was highly critical of the Irish referee, who grabbed and pushed Australian players when awarding free kicks to the home team, saying *"If he does it again, my boys will hit back and he can take the consequences"*. He also criticised both referees [89] for not penalising the Irish defenders, who persistently pushed the Australian forwards in the back as they attempted to mark. There was still plenty of feeling between the two camps, although the Irish grudgingly conceded an 'increase' in Australian sportsmanship. The crowd also got involved, as the Australian players were pelted with tree nuts (like honkey nuts) and roundly abused when standing on the sideline waiting to come on. Before the first Test the Irish had been very hospitable, but this had soon changed! The Australians could have wrapped up the series in this game with better scoring conversions, but failed to take several opportunities to net 'goals' so, despite heading to London for four days of sightseeing, the players continued their twice daily training sessions.

---

88. Twenty years on, little has changed. After the first Test of the 2002 series, the GAA made similar noises and Australian coach Garry Lyon defended his side's physical approach, accusing the Irish (who lost) of *"sour grapes"*.
89. The Australian representative for the series was leading VFL umpire Rowan Sawers.

The Irish win got people in Dublin talking and 40,000 fans turned out for the deciding Test. Pre-game, John said – *"National pride was the key to victory"* and he expected the Kangaroo players to rise to the occasion, as they *"did not often get the chance to play for their country"*. He told the players to *"breathe in the honour"* when *Advance Australia Fair* was played before the match. With the series on the line, the Australians adopted a physical approach, although they stopped short of applying blatant tackles. McIntosh triggered an early brawl when he 'took out' an Irish opponent who passed the ball over his head to a team-mate and that set the stance for the day – there were no backward steps from the Australians and the Irish knew they would earn their kicks. The Irish hit the front in the last quarter, but Australia fought back tenaciously and did the Green and Gold proud by winning 76-71 to take the series. An ecstatic John said to them *"You were magnificent; you fully deserved your victory"* as they received a warm reception from the Irish crowd as they ran a lap of honour.

For the Kangaroos, Platten was simply outstanding and one local reporter wrote that he was the best Gaelic footballer he had seen, while Rioli and Healy were also instrumental in the victory. Daniher was another who had a tremendous series, having some great tussles in the centre with Irish captain Jack O'Shea, who was the country's most celebrated Gaelic footballer, but the Essendon star matched him for hardness and skill as he quickly adapted to the game.

Post-match there was still more controversy, as the Irish manager McDermott couldn't contain his feelings at the official dinner and again labelled the Australians as *"unsportsmanlike"* by resorting to *"unfair tactics"* to win, whatever the cost. Fortuitously, John was armed with the perfect reply. Via the Perth media, he had received a snippet from an old *Readers' Digest* magazine where McDermott was quoted as saying he would gladly bend the rules in order to win a game if necessary. John read the brief note to the thunderous applause of the Australian contingent and the silence of the Irish. Later, McDermott ruefully conceded to John that he knew those words would one day come back to haunt him!

The series win capped off a great four week tour and the team had one day to spare to spend over £1000 in fines collected for various misdemeanours. For John, the victory wrapped up a remarkable year where he had won everything on offer for a coach. The atmosphere for the final Test was the equal (if not better) of any grand final or State match he had experienced and many of the Victorians similarly rated it favourably with a VFL grand final. To win the series for the country on such a limited preparation was a great achievement. Almost 20 years on, John is pleased that the opportunity to represent the nation is still available to the All Australian sides – *"It is something they should cherish"*.

~

John arrived back in Perth a couple of days before the Swans players left for an all expenses paid end of season trip to America, the reward for a hat trick of premierships funded by a Western Underwriters insurance premium payout of $100,000, courtesy of the foresight of the Swans board. Finance Director John Farris, with the players contributing half at John's urging, had taken out a $13,000 premium to return $100,000 for winning three in a row. However, after the long flight back from Ireland John was *"finished"* and simply couldn't face the prospect of another long air trip. Despite protests from the players and Walker, he missed the trip, preferring to visit some good fishing spots along the WA coast as he wound down from a stellar year of coaching.

Chapter 19
The Eagles land (but without JT)

John, writing in the Swan Districts annual report about the 1986 season:

"... one of the worst years I have experienced in football".

John, bluntly commenting to the directors of the fledgling West Coast Eagles in October 1986, when challenged about Swans poor season:

"You don't lose your ability in one year".

On Australia Day 1985 John's honours continued with an Advance Australia Award for outstanding contributions to the advancement and enrichment of the Australian way of life. His family, particularly mother Doris, were thrilled with the award and she greatly enjoyed the ceremony at Government House. For John, it was *"nice to be recognised"*, but he probably got more enjoyment out of seeing how much pleasure Doris got from the day.

It was also the centenary of WA football and having marked Swans 50th year in 1984 with a premiership, the challenge was to win four flags in a row to commemorate 100 years of football in the State. Since 1931, when the Page final four system was introduced, no club had managed this feat – East Perth had won a record five successive premierships (1919-23) under the old system that didn't involve four finals, while East Fremantle had achieved four flags in a row, from 1928-31.

Once again, Swans had some player turnover, with Brad Shine going to Carlton[90] and Gerard Neesham returning to East Fremantle, explaining that *"I'd had enough of Todd and he'd had enough of me"*. Neesham was a 'headstrong' player and the two had occasionally clashed over tactics, coming to a head in the 1984 grand final when Neesham surprisingly started on the bench and missed the 10 goal first quarter. John's tactic was to use Neesham as a loose man behind the play against the wind and he performed this role brilliantly in the second and fourth quarters, to be one of Swans best. John told him after the game that, without his performance, the side may not have won, but Neesham couldn't accept the decision and his frustration was clear in the victory lap of honour when he ran by himself, 10 metres away from the rest of the players. He returned to his old club, much to the disappointment of Swans, and was reluctantly swapped for Kevin Taylor, whom East Fremantle had lost patience with over off-field problems. These would continue at Swans and the Sharks certainly got the better of the deal.

On the plus side, Garry Sidebottom returned from Fitzroy and, along with stalwarts Keith Narkle, Tom Mullooly and Bill Skwirowski, were the only players left from 1977 when John

---

90. He was the 11th Swans player to go to the VFL since 1981. Coupled with retirements, the club had lost 18 players from their league team over the premiership years.

joined the club. Sadly, Narkle would only play three games before returning to Bunbury after a dispute with John over his role in the team. Narkle had won his third Swan Medal in 1984, playing as a wingman or half-forward, where he had played most of his career, but John felt his experience and speed would suit a move into a back pocket to give some much-needed run out of defence. He believed Narkle could play for two or three seasons in this role, thereby extending his career, but Narkle felt his form was good enough to play more creative roles up the ground and he decided to retire. It was an untimely and unhappy finish to a great career for the three time premiership player, the last two as captain, and John is still saddened that it ended this way as he thought Narkle was a terrific player and captain. Narkle was 50 games short of Bill Walker's club record of 305 games and John felt this tally was not beyond him, as he had been relatively injury free. Ironically, when he returned to Bunbury, Narkle played country football for several more seasons, mostly out of a back pocket! He would now also agree that his exit from league football was premature.

In the pre-season John tested the mettle of the players in a totally different way, taking them on a weekend 'survival' camping trip to the South-West, an exercise that has since been widely used with football teams. The Swans players were told to take food and camping gear but, unbeknown to them, this was all left at Bassendean Oval. When they arrived at their 'campsite' some four hours later, they were divided into groups and told to find their way through the bush to another location where there would be some food. The older and wiser heads in the group realised what they were in for... over the next two days the players slept on the ground, ate little, made clothes for themselves out of hessian bags and performed various tasks such as building shelters and rafts under the keen eye of John and Ed Blackaby, now the reserves coach and the instructors from Adventure West, who organised the camp.

As a bonding, character building and leadership exercise, it was a successful weekend, but few players would have agreed at the time! It certainly caught them by surprise and forced them to help each other to cope with adversity, which, for John, was *"what it was all about"*. Having organised many pre-season training camps over the years, he sees their one real value as being *"character tests"*... *"Finding out how players react to unexpected adversity, physical or mental, is the true benefit from a coach's point of view"*. The ability to persevere, maintain composure, be a team player and perhaps show leadership in a crisis was what he looked for, as the same requirements were needed for success when things were tight and hard in a game, especially in finals. Over the years, some players who maybe didn't have as much ability as others – Skwirowski is a good example – certainly enhanced their reputation in John's eyes because of their steadiness under pressure in testing pre-season camps. A weary, sore and hungry group got back to Bassendean late on Sunday, unpacked their camping gear from the 'forgotten' trailer and headed home to find new appreciation in a soft, comfortable bed and warm food.

In the practice games John again found himself at loggerheads with the WAFL. Sidebottom was reported against Subiaco for what John thought was a frivolous incident and, for the rest of the game, the big forward *"couldn't buy a free kick"* and was *"constantly penalised every time he went for the ball"*. At three-quarter-time John remonstrated with the umpires and later launched a blistering attack on the standard of umpiring in WA, adding that *"people bemoan the fact we lose good players to Victoria, but when we get them back they are victimised"*. At the time, the umpires were threatening strike action over pay rates, so John inflamed the situation by organising his own umpires for the next practice game, using Junior Council officials for a match with Perth, now being coached by Mal Brown who was happy to support him on the issue. Sidebottom was cleared by the Tribunal and played against Perth, but the game was marred by several brawls. No reports were made as the umpires didn't have the authority, which brought stinging criticism on both John and the WAFL. Many media people posed the question as to who was running football in the State – John or the WAFL – as the league had been strangely quiet over the issue. Certainly, they should not have allowed the game to be played without WAFL umpires, as players were not subject to the same rules for reportable incidents as players in other clubs. Further, they didn't sanction John for his attack on the umpires and their inaction was curious – whether they were reluctant to confront John because of his success as WA coach or because it was only pre-season and therefore 'unofficial' games is not clear. On John's part, he was (rightly or wrongly) incensed about Sidebottom's alleged victimisation and felt strongly enough about it to take a stand. Whether it helped the player is one of those imponderables, but Sidebottom wasn't suspended once during the year, playing every game and winning Swans goal-kicking (with 78) and the fairest and best award, the only player to achieve this double in the club's history.

Of Swans chances for four in a row, John thought there might have been enough left for a decent shot at another flag and, when queried by the media about the loss of players, he repeated the lesson he had learned in 1955 *"... if you can win without Steve Marsh you can win without anyone"*. However, as in previous seasons, the first round of qualifying fixtures saw the team play without consistency. A 79 point loss to East Fremantle in the opening game was disappointing, but wins over West Perth and East Perth provided a reasonable start before losses to Claremont and Subiaco left the side languishing. A third consecutive loss was recorded when the side returned to the VFL night competition, suffering an inglorious 91 point thumping by Fitzroy. However, wins against South Fremantle and Perth left the side third after seven games, but John could see some chinks in the armour. After a 66 point loss to the unbeaten Sharks at Bassendean, he took off the gloves publicly, labelling the side soft and questioning their hunger for further success. He said few of his current players had been *"through the grinder"* as the Swans sides of the late 1970s had been, when the players were hurt by losing regularly. Once more, the players responded, winning the next three games before heavy defeats against Claremont and South, followed by a much-needed win over bottom side Perth left the side handily placed in third position.

A hard-fought 14 point win over the Sharks, who had only lost one game, and consecutive wins again over West Perth and East Perth raised hopes for a second semi-final berth, but losses to Claremont and Subiaco ended this prospect. The side was safe in the four with two games to play, but couldn't finish better than third, as Subiaco had second spot safe. Their first semi-final opponents were confirmed the next week when West Perth, in John Wynne's first season as coach, clinched a finals berth ahead of Claremont, who missed the finals for the first time since 1978.

~

As well as chasing a fourth consecutive flag with Swans, there was the chance of a hat trick of Australian championships – planning for the State games took up a considerable amount of John's time, prompting calls from media critics that an independent State coach should be appointed in the future. While John knew this was probably the best option, he was glad to have the job as the previous two State series had been *"just terrific to be involved in"*.

After losses in 1983 and '84, the Victorians had promised a more committed approach to the 1985 championships. Coached by Kevin Sheedy for the first time, they got off to a fine start with a 54 point win over SA in Adelaide, in a physical game with all the hallmarks of Sheedy's Essendon side, which was dominating the VFL competition. However, on protest by the SANFL, the NFL took the win off Victoria, as they had played 22 players, when only 21 had been agreed on. This put extra sting into the WA-SA game in Perth, as a Croweaters' victory would, officially at least, give them the championship.

Once again John blooded many newcomers to State football [91] and the side bore little resemblance to the team that went to Adelaide in 1984. Missing were the likes of Steve Malaxos (Hawthorn), Brad Hardie and Allen Daniels (Footscray) and Robert Wiley and Peter Bosustow (injuries and form), leaving the side as one of the most inexperienced to represent the State. In contrast, the SA side was similar to the previous year, containing names like Stephen Kernahan, John Platten, Craig Bradley, Michael Aish, Peter Motley, Garry McIntosh and Malcolm Blight, as their player exodus to the VFL had been minor compared to WA's. The experience and class of these players showed as SA blitzed the home side to win 30.18 (198) to 16.15 (111), a final margin of 87 points. Blight, at age 35, kicked six goals, Kernahan got seven and Bradley won the Simpson Medal after a superb display on a wing. John blamed the player drain to Victoria, saying that WA *"didn't have much left"* and needed to be left alone for a couple of years to get the stocks back up. He predicted that the VFL talent scouts would soon plunder the SANFL ranks, as had occurred in WA [92].

Although the SA win secured them the championship for only the second time (their first was in 1911), there was still much interest in the WA-Victoria clash. The Vics were determined to win so the South Australians could only claim a 'hollow victory' in the championship and WA were out to atone for their terrible display against the Croweaters. Surprisingly, the Victorians had agreed to a WA request initiated by John for open selection of the State of Origin team for the first time and this opened the door for players such as Simon Beasley and the Krakouer brothers to be considered. With so many former WA players now with VFL clubs – Footscray and Carlton each had seven for example – picking only one player from each team had been difficult. After naming a 23 man squad of Melbourne based players and 10 from the WAFL, John went to Victoria several times to take training, taking the 10 local players with him on one occasion.

Never before had the WAFL gone to such lengths to prepare for a State clash, particularly as the championship was out of reach, and eventually the selectors settled on 17 VFL based players and five from WA; this upset several media critics who thought local talent was being overlooked. However, John felt *"the WA cupboard was fairly bare"* and had little choice but to go mostly with Melbourne-based players. Coaching against Sheedy for the first time, John began the 'mind games' as he called a 3pm training session the day before the match – the same

---

91. The State rookies were Steve Richardson, Kevin Caton and Bill Skwirowski (Swans), Murray Wrensted, Clinton Browning, Colin Waterson and Peter Wilson (East Fremantle), Dwayne Lamb and Phil Scott (Subiaco), Bryan Cousins (Perth), Mark Bairstow (South Fremantle) and Phil Bradmore (West Perth).
92. In 1986 Platten, Kernahan, Bradley and Motley would all go to the VFL.

time Victoria had scheduled their session. Despite vigorous protests from the visitors, John refused to yield and he conducted the brief session in one half of the ground, leaving the other half to the Victorians. The next day Sheedy held his team in the rooms for an extra five minutes before the game, perhaps in protest against the clash of training times the previous day – this meant the game was nearly 10 minutes late starting. When Victoria finally ran out it was just in the nick of time for WA selector and runner Grant Dorrington, who had just been instructed by John to run the WA players through the Victorian team banner! Only one goal (to WA) was scored in the opening quarter, but Victoria kicked 18 goals to nine in the next three quarters to win convincingly by 65 points. After half-time the two coaches involved in more byplay as Sheedy again kept WA waiting; when the Vics finally appeared, John ordered the WA players back into the rooms for about two minutes. When they re-appeared, the 40,000 strong crowd expressed their disapproval with a chorus of boos. John defended his actions by saying *"the Victorians were not entitled to make us wait"* and he refused to be walked over by them. The third quarter was WA's best, but the Vics responded with a 10 goal last term to leave no doubt as to who was the best State side in 1985.

The gamesmanship indulged in by the two coaches was definitely overdone as it affected the fans, but it certainly provided some talking points. Suggestions of a feud between the two coaches were aired, but in reality nothing could have been further from the truth. John had met Sheedy previously, via Brown after his days at Richmond, and the two had always got on well and still do today. They have much in common as coaches – a flair for the unexpected or unusual, hard discipline and a great passion for the game and its ongoing development. Both men never shirk an issue, often making their point of view clear to the controlling body on all types of matters within the game. They have always been keen to help those less fortunate than themselves and to pass on their knowledge about the game. John regards Sheedy as a *"great lateral thinker"* (few would argue that!) and someone who *"has been terrific for the game"*. In recent years Sheedy has often sought John's opinion on prospective WA recruits for Essendon and, on a few occasions, John has arranged for young players from South and Swans who have been overlooked in the draft to try out with Essendon in the hope of making their rookie list [93].

~

In the first semi-final Swans earned a hard-fought 32 point win over the Falcons in a high scoring match, with Sidebottom kicking nine goals and Taylor five, to give the club some tangible reward for its recruiting investments. Kimberley played the kick behind the play role to perfection when West Perth had the breeze, ensuring Swans path to the preliminary final. After the week's break they were up against Subiaco, who had narrowly lost the second semi to the Sharks. At the team meeting the night before the game, John had the players who were part of the three premierships speak to the rest of the team. Their message was two-fold – the satisfaction of seeing all the season's hard work come to fruition by reaching the grand final and the rare opportunity to win four flags in a row. Obviously, this hinged on beating Subiaco, who were also hungry for success, being back in the finals for the first time since 1974.

---

93.   Dean Rioli is one player who was assisted in getting a start in the AFL via the affiliation between the two men.

Swans started well with a three goal lead by quarter-time, but Subiaco then kicked seven goals to two as Swans lost their composure following an incident when Sidebottom *"lost the plot"* and was reported by five umpires for kicking Subiaco's Kevan Sparks. Sidebottom lost focus and John took him off as he continued to engage in undisciplined acts – no doubt the realisation he would probably miss the grand final if Swans made it weighed heavily on his mind. It takes a special type of mental strength to play well in these circumstances and, on this particular day, Sidebottom couldn't find it; he later received a lengthy suspension from the WAFL Tribunal. At half-time John bluntly told him that his undisciplined play may cost the side the game, but that he had a chance in the second half to put things right, which he owed the team.

At the last change the match was evenly poised and the dream of four flags was still alive as Swans fought back to be only two points behind. At the 15 minute mark of the last term, there was still only a few points in it, but Subiaco then powered away to win by 51 points. The Sidebottom incident hadn't helped Swans cause, but other factors such as a lack of influence from rovers Kimberley and Taylor, who were well tagged, were important reasons for the defeat. In the end, too much was left to the likes of Jon Fogarty and Don Langsford and there was simply not enough support for them. It was the end of the 'golden era' for Swans and for John. Although he would take Swans and South to other premierships and finals appearances, the six years from 1980-85 was his most sustained period of coaching success. The great Swans sides of the early 1980s had come to the end of their cycle, as had occurred with Claremont and South, the other sides that dominated this era of WA football.

The preliminary final defeat didn't really surprise John. He thought the side was *"fragile"* – the tough, relentless, uncompromising attitude that characterised the premiership teams wasn't there and the lack of steely commitment to the cause was exposed against Subiaco. He feels that possibly the toughest assignment in coaching is to keep the right attitude in place so initial success is followed by more, as it is *"... so easy to relax after reaching the top. After working your way up, particularly after a long run of outs, it's important to cash in while you can, because you can't win forever. Eventually injuries, retirements, clearances and a fall in attitude will get you. Teams that have a sustained run at the top (even without winning a lot of premierships) which is bloody tough to do, are to be greatly admired for their strength of character, because everyone else is trying to pull you down"*.

East Fremantle held on to beat a fast-finishing Subiaco in the grand final after Sandover medallist Murray Wrensted [94] and forward Andrew Lockyer missed late chances to wrap up the game. Subiaco persevered throughout and ruckman Phil Scott kicked a goal right on the final siren to see the Sharks win by five points; the closest grand final since East Perth's two point win in the wet in 1978.

The 1986 year started with John receiving another honour. Along with actor Paul Hogan, television host Ian 'Molly' Meldrum, tennis player Paul McNamee and former boxer Tony Mundine, John received the Order of Australia, which again delighted his family, although John wasn't sure what all the fuss was about. Doris again thoroughly enjoyed her trip to Government House for the ceremony and says with a good deal of pride that she has made

---

94. In 1985 the voting system was changed to 5-4-3-2-1.

Chapter 19 – The Eagles land (but without JT)

four trips to the Governor's residence – two for John's awards and two to see second son Bill receive decorations for bravery earned as a long-serving member of the WA police force.

After stumbling in the finals, most judges thought Swans faced a re-building period and would probably slide down the ladder in 1986. But John refused to entertain the thought and, while Murray Rance (Footscray), Fogarty (Geelong) and Tony Solin (East Fremantle) were gone, he believed there was still enough in the ranks to remain in finals contention. He stepped up the discipline by fining players $200 for missing a training session and put a searching endurance fitness programme in place – and told the brilliant, but erratic Taylor, to *"toe the line and do the work"* or his career would be over. He took the broom to the fringe league players, moving out 10 whom he didn't see as having a future at the club as he sought to rekindle some hunger and desire.

Personally, he withdrew from some media commitments, in particular the popular Friday lunchtime radio panel shows – *"I was tired of being the one to supply the controversial quotes and of being the bunny and getting criticised for what I say"*. Of the current WAFL coaches, there was no doubt he and Brown were always a rich source of copy for the media, as both spoke their minds on a whole range of issues and were not afraid to upset people (particularly in the WAFL) along the way. Often they would go in tandem, talking up a game by deliberately baiting each other or one of their star players in a contrived tit-for-tat exchange to attract more fans to the game. They did this often in the late 1970s and early '80s when Swans and South were forces in the WAFL and they had little competition from the other coaches, with the likes of Graham Moss, Ron Alexander and Haydn Bunton (Jnr) lacking their flamboyance. Those coaches were probably content to leave it to the outspoken pair, but John felt they could (and should) have had a bit more to say to help promote the game. For now, he decided to take a media back seat and concentrate on developing the new talent at Swans, although he still couldn't help himself on occasions.

The 1986 season proved to be a disaster and in the club's annual report John described it as *"one of the worst years I have experienced in football"*. The rot set in early – midway through the second quarter of the opening game against East Perth, Swans trailed by nearly 10 goals before fighting back to win by two points, in probably the highlight of the year. There was only one more win in the first round as the team struggled to balance up due to injuries and the absence of the suspended Sidebottom. The second round was no different, with wins in the first and last games separated by five straight losses. Four wins from 14 matches saw the club out of finals contention for the first time in six seasons, a point John had conceded a few weeks earlier. Acknowledging that Swans would miss the four, he said – *"You have to be sensible about these things. Nothing lasts forever and while it is hard to accept defeat, one has to be realistic"*. However, the third round was even worse and only one win in six games saw Swans slide to last position, a fall from grace that was much quicker and steeper than John had considered possible.

In the final game, Swans played South at Fremantle to decide who would claim the dubious honour of the wooden spoon. Facing a three goal deficit at the final change, John called for a last-ditch effort, but the spirit was flagging and South were well led by (soon to be) Sandover medallist Mark Bairstow and a young John Worsfold to win by 58 points. The player loss to the VFL had finally caught up with Swans, with the hard core of seasoned, disciplined team players steadily reduced over recent seasons. When injuries hit there wasn't the depth to cover, as had been the case in the past. Of the senior players, only captain Langsford, Kimberley, Steve Richardson and Peter Sartori managed full seasons, and the club used 42 players in the league side, with 17 first year players.

In the finals, Bunton guided Subiaco to a resounding victory over East Fremantle to take their first flag since 1973, but it was the second semi-final that created most discussion. East Fremantle scored a 50 point win, with full-forward Darren Bennett kicking a finals record of 10 goals. However, once the game seemed out of Subiaco's reach, Bunton indulged in a host of curious moves. Playmakers were left off the ground or kept out of the action as he sought to 'ambush' the minds of the victorious Sharks. In many ways, his tactics were similar to the 1961 second semi-final when East Perth easily accounted for Swans, who turned the tables in the grand final to win their first premiership. This time, Subiaco overcame Perth in the preliminary final and then completely outplayed the Sharks to win the premiership by a resounding 69 points.

~

Although he had no State team coaching duties in 1986, John was re-appointed as the Australian coach to play the visiting Irish team in another modified rules Gaelic series in October and he had several meetings with co-selectors Ted Whitten and Alan Schwab to shortlist players. Invitations were sent to 19 players each from WA, SA and Victoria to join the squad as John didn't want to be tied to the All Australian team, believing that the ruckmen and tall key-position players weren't suited to the Gaelic game. When the 45 man squad was announced, only 11 WA players were named, with 19 from Victoria and 15 from SA. Many WA players hadn't even bothered to reply to the invitation (including 1986 All Australian captain Brian Peake), which left John annoyed and dumfounded. He publicly lambasted their attitude, saying that – *"The difference is that SA and Victorian players want to represent their country. I'm a West Australian and proud of it and I fly our flag whenever possible, but I think we might be a bit soft. I used to hate Victorians but, after being involved with them over time, I can only admire their professional approach towards playing at the highest level. In Ireland in 1984 it was a tremendous feeling to stand there in front of 40,000 people before the third Test and hear the Australian national anthem. I now know what it must feel like to win an Olympic Gold Medal"*.

The players assembled in Perth in early October to prepare for the series, with John running a similar training programme as in Ireland two years earlier. Several of those players were back in the team – with stars like Maurice Rioli, John Platten, Terry Daniher, Gary Pert, Dermott Brereton, Robert DiPierdomenico, Gerard Healy, Garry McIntosh, Craig Holden and Brad Hardie selected, along with newcomers such as Gary Buckenara, Mike Richardson, Peter Wilson, Wayne Johnston, Kevin Walsh, Dale Weightman, Gary Wilson, Paul Roos, Mark Naley, Chris Langford and Sandover medallist Bairstow. The rules had been slightly modified after the controversy created by the 'no tackling' conflict of 1984, with partial tackling allowed when a player had the ball, but only to restrain him, not sling the player to the ground. The send-off rule for blatant offences was tightened, as warnings were no longer required before a player could be banished. Nevertheless, the Irish had selected a 'robust' squad, in anticipation of a repeat dose of Australia's vigorous approach to the game.

Chapter 19 – The Eagles land (but without JT)

After trial games against the Irish (in Bunbury) and a composite Swans team, Australia went into the first Test at the WACA Ground under lights – 25,000 Perth fans flocked in, with the gates thrown open 15 minutes before the start on police orders to reduce crowd congestion outside. John was confident of victory with a team that again had McIntosh in goal and lots of ruck-rovers and rovers, whom he planned to rotate regularly off the bench. He instructed the side to be physical in the first term to test the mettle of the Irish, but the rotating plans were curtailed when Pert and DiPierdomenico were sent off (along with two Irishmen) after an all-in brawl in the first quarter and Walsh was out with a dislocated shoulder. It was a bruising encounter with the fights continuing and just before three-quarter-time McIntosh was sent off for rough play, leaving Australia vulnerable in goal. However, with Daniher again starring, the players showed great spirit and character to hold off the Irish and record a stirring 65-57 win, with an emotional coach telling the players that they were *"magnificent"*.

The Australians returned to their home States for a few days before assembling in Melbourne and, as had been the case two years earlier, the coaches and players were told to reduce the rough play or future series would be put at risk. There were less fights this time around and the Aussies appeared subdued as Ireland recorded a 62-46 win to level the series, resulting in John dispensing with the niceties and stirring up a hornets' nest by labelling the Irish as *"bloody wimps"*. The Australian camp was furious with several Irish players who lay on the ground after physical clashes and John told the visiting Irish press to check the meaning of the word *"wimp"* in the dictionary, accusing some of their players of *"taking a dive"*. He added – *"Our guys accept it and we don't whinge. We just get up and play the game"*.

Irish coach Kevin Heffernan remained humble in victory, refusing to indulge in a war of words, but the battle lines had been clearly drawn for the deciding match. However, with far superior ball control and kicking skills in wet conditions, the Irish were too good, winning convincingly 55-32. With the series slipping away, half-time saw John deliver one of his trademark 'sprays' as he appealed to their national pride for a lift. Part way through his lively address, his eye caught Buckenara's and he went for him, asking him when he was going to have some impact on the game. Buckenara was taken aback at being targeted and was not prepared to let it go, which was out of character for him as he copped plenty of the same from Allan Jeans at Hawthorn. *"I might be able to do something if you put me on the ground"* was his curt retort, as he had sat on the bench for the entire first half!

Despite having a man sent off, the Irish dominated the final quarter after leading by only three points at the last break. While the game was physical, the expected fireworks didn't eventuate and John paid tribute to the tourists, saying they were *"far too strong"*. Losing the series was disappointing for him, with national pride and honour at stake, and he felt the main reason for the defeat was that Australia were the 'home' side and, by breaking camp after the Perth Test, the players lost some of their sense of unity and purpose – *"In comparison to the Ireland tour, where the players did everything together and developed a tremendous team bond, the same degree of togetherness simply wasn't there in 1986. With travelling teams, especially on a tour lasting a month or more, great benefits in team morale are normally achieved. When a team is in a slump, getting on the road together is often an important part of breaking the cycle. In the AFL today, travelling for an away game can be (and should be) a positive experience for the team. While away sides have struggled to win in the early 2000s, this hasn't always been the case and good sides, with strong attitudes, can win anywhere, as most Victorian State teams have consistently proved"*.

In August 1986, the WA football league took the momentous decision to accept an invitation for a WA side to enter an expanded Victorian football league. The issue had been steadily brewing for several years and, as early as 1975, the WANFL directors were first briefed about entering a WA side into the VFL as part of a national competition. The issue had been floated as early as 1980 when East Perth made an abortive bid to join the VFL as an individual club. By 1985 it was really a case of 'when' rather than 'if', as the groundswell of support for the concept grew, although it was not a unanimous view. When the vote was taken, several clubs, including Swans, were against the proposal, vigorously arguing that it would reduce the WAFL to 'reserves' status and destroy the financial viability of the clubs. However, the player drain from WA to VFL clubs had reached epidemic proportions by the middle of the decade and concern over declining standards in WA virtually presented the WAFL directors with a fait accompli over the matter.

John viewed the introduction of a WA team into the VFL as *"inevitable"* and felt the State was best to get in at the start, rather than hold off, as most of the leading players would have been taken by the VFL clubs in any case. At least a WA side gave players the opportunity to stay home, while still moving to the next level of football. The WAFL appointed former East Perth and West Perth player and coach George Michalczyk to 'scout' for potential players for the Perth side, both at home and in Melbourne, and they set about deciding on a coach for the new side. It was never seriously considered that an outsider from Victoria would get the job first up, as the new side really demanded a WA coach and, of the league coaches at the time, John, Alexander, Bunton, Moss and Brown were all touted as likely candidates. Brown ruled himself out of calculations, as did Bunton, who wished to stay with Subiaco, leaving the field at three. However, soon after Claremont lost the first semi-final, Moss stepped down as Tigers coach and took up an administrative position with the new side, leaving the choice clearly between John and Alexander.

Both men had good claims, with recent club premierships and State success, as Alexander had coached WA to another national championship in 1986, beating SA in Adelaide and Victoria in Perth by three points. However, John had a clear edge in experience, having coached 18 seasons of league football compared to Alexander's five. He was keen to get the job and waited expectantly for a call from league headquarters to be interviewed for the position. He never thought the job was his for the taking, as he knew Alexander wanted it as well, but he certainly expected an opportunity to put his case forward. The call never came, which really cut him to the bone, given his experience and his passion for the State and the game. One of the creeds he has lived life by is to *"never dwell on the past (or present) for long"* and to always *"move on and see what the future holds"*.

However, in this case, he felt so insulted that he fired off a stinging letter (one of the few he has ever written) to each of the WAFL directors, expressing his disgust at not at least being given an interview. The letter ruffled a few feathers at the WAFL and chairman Roy Annear and chief executive John Walker asked John to meet with them and some of the directors, but this was virtually a courtesy call at the 11th hour, as the decision to appoint Alexander had already been taken, although not made public. The meeting was short and superficial and John left knowing he had missed the job, which certainly completed a wretched 1986. Swans had finished last, the Irish had triumphed in the Test series and he had missed out on coaching the newly-formed West Coast Eagles. It was a stark contrast to 1984, when he had won everything on offer.

While there is no doubt Alexander had sufficient credentials to get the job, the way in which John was ignored was poor treatment of one of WA's greatest servants of the game. In looking for reasons why he was overlooked it's hard to go past his 'rough diamond' demeanour. He was certainly outspoken, a free spirit who regularly shot from the hip and one who wasn't afraid to confront issues and personalities and step on toes if necessary. He had taken on the VFL when he sent the Swans reserves side to play Richmond in 1982 and the WAFL in 1985 when he used junior council umpires in a practice game against Perth. Those incidents and his volatile nature probably saw him regarded as a 'loose cannon'; someone who couldn't be trusted to do the bidding of the WAFL directors, particularly in the new football environment created by WA's entry into the VFL. John believes these were reasons why he didn't get the job, but he shrugs it off matter-of-factly, saying he has *"never been afraid of the path I've travelled and there are no regrets"*. It was possible that the WAFL felt John's star was on the wane – and Alexander's on the rise – as Swans had slipped to last place on the ladder in 1986, but this would have been a short-sighted view. This point was raised in a round-about way at his brief meeting with the directors, to which he bluntly replied that *"every good coach has a bad year along the way, as so many factors are beyond your control in football... and you don't lose your ability in one year"*. Alexander's playing career in Melbourne worked in his favour, but this was balanced by John's experience. The West Coast Eagles were being floated on the share market to raise some of the $4 million licence fee demanded by the VFL and big business had a significant foothold in the game. As a 'rough diamond' from Fremantle, John had few connections and little interest in the business world. With the corporate image becoming important in the game, especially with a new side that needed to be marketed aggressively, Alexander was probably seen as a more appealing prospect.

~

The 1987 season was one where everyone more or less held their breath – no-one really knew how the Eagles would be received and what impact their formation would have on the WAFL competition. It didn't take long before the Eagles were attracting 20,000 or more fans to their games, as the WA football public quickly embraced the new team and the expanded competition. As a result, the going was tough for WAFL clubs, with crowds dropping by 50% on 1986 levels, such as at Swans, where 77,811 people watched their games compared to almost 147,000 fans the year before – and that was a season when the team played poorly. Swans lost half their members and saw their income reduced by 50%, as did most other clubs. It was the start of a struggle to survive that has been the lot of the WAFL clubs ever since.

Financial matters aside, the season was good for John and Swans as they rebounded from last place to fourth, winning 13 games. John also returned to State coaching as Bunton declined the offer, but WA were no match for SA and Victoria, losing both games in Perth by big margins. In the first semi-final, Swans played East Fremantle, now coached by Graham Melrose, who had taken over from Alexander. The Sharks proved too strong, winning by 56 points and John felt he had coached his last game at Bassendean. His contract was up for renewal and he believed it was definitely time to move on. With a coaching position in the

VFL his main goal, he thought a move to South Australia might be beneficial, as he didn't anticipate a vacancy at the West Coast Eagles for some time. Under Alexander, the side had performed creditably in the first year, winning 11 of 22 games and remaining in finals contention until the last few weeks of the qualifying rounds. John watched their games with interest and had been kept appraised of their progress by Manning, who had been appointed a selector. John thought they played well for a side in the first season of a new competition, but he had had no involvement with the Eagles throughout the season.

Towards the end of the season, John received an offer to coach Woodville, who were looking to replace the retiring Malcolm Blight, and the club fitted his criteria. After joining the SANFL in 1964, they had become the perennial battlers and were yet to win a flag. John always fancied taking on the underdog so, after discussions with Meryl and the girls, he took the job, with Meryl quite excited about the move as she was keen to see different places and liked what she had previously seen of Adelaide. Then, quite unexpectedly, the day before he was due to leave for SA, John received a phone call from Swans president Bill Walker asking him to meet with Bill Kerr, West Coast's managing director and Moss, who was the general manager, to discuss his availability to coach them! The door to the VFL, which had been slammed shut 12 months earlier, had suddenly opened.

Chapter 20
Highs and lows in the VFL

John, commenting on the West Coast Eagles first final – the elimination final in 1988:

"We lost with dignity".

John, reflecting on the isolation he felt in his worst year of football, 1989:

"It got so lonely that I had to go to the butcher's shop to buy a bone to hang around my neck so my dog would play with me".

The meeting at the West Coast Eagles with Kerr and Moss took place on October 5. It wasn't really an interview for the coaching job, simply to clarify that John was interested and available. At an afternoon press conference the next day, Kerr announced that John was taking over from Alexander *"because he is a better coach"*. John accepted the job by saying *"It has always been my ambition to coach at the highest level. I'm pleased to be part of the Eagles because I'm a loyal West Australian when it comes to football. And, when we cross the border next year to play in Victoria, it will be war!"*.

It was one of the biggest shocks in WA football history, with the changeover effected without the media having any inkling of what was about to occur. Shortly before the press conference, Alexander had been summoned to a meeting with Kerr, Moss and chairman Neil Hamilton when he was handed a brief three-line letter saying he had been replaced as Eagles coach. An understandably shocked and angry Alexander sought an explanation, but none was forthcoming and he has never properly received one. By any yardstick, the record of 11 wins in the first season was highly commendable and Alexander had no reason to think his job was in jeopardy – nor did John. It seems the Eagles management had concerns over Alexander's ability to discipline the players, perhaps stemming from a late season trip to Carrara, on the Gold Coast, to play the Brisbane Bears, after which the team stayed in the Eastern States before playing Melbourne at the MCG the next weekend. The game was vital to the team's finals prospects, but during the week several players broke curfews and, after the Melbourne game (which the Demons won easily), the players were given a free day, instead of watching their next opponents St Kilda, as originally planned. Alexander didn't go to the game either, which may have been a fatal mistake.

In the aftermath of the surprise announcement it was widely rumoured in football circles that John must have undermined Alexander in some fashion and, if not him, then John's long-time friend and current West Coast selector Bob Manning must have engineered his downfall. Neither assertion has any truth to it. John had no contact with anyone from West Coast before the October 5 meeting and was, in fact, signed and ready to leave to coach Woodville, in the

SANFL[95]. Manning's only inkling that a change might be contemplated came when Moss called him to a meeting in early October, when he was asked what he thought of Alexander as a coach. A somewhat relieved Manning, who thought he was getting his own marching orders, declined to discuss his personal views about Alexander unless the coach himself was present. Moss then asked his opinion of John, to which he replied that he was *"still WA's best coach"* mainly because he was strong on discipline, which he felt the Eagles lacked. At no other time in the year had he been asked for, or offered, any thoughts on Alexander's coaching.

It seems the Eagles were fixed on removing Alexander some weeks before the announcement, but John was not the only candidate. Moss was firmly of the view that a Victorian coach was required to provide better knowledge of the rival players and Melbourne conditions and David Parkin, coaching Fitzroy at the time, was actually signed up, but eventually decided against the shift and stayed with the Lions. John's case (without his knowledge at the time) was being pushed by Bill Walker, who sought a meeting with Kerr when he said John was the best man to coach the Eagles and that WA football could not afford to lose him. After two further meetings with Walker, Kerr asked him to arrange for John to come in for the meeting at which the decision to replace Alexander was taken. The West Coast board accepted Kerr's recommendation the same day, ironically without even speaking to John. Some of the board members were the same men who 12 months earlier had not considered John worthy of an interview for the job!

~

John wasted little time in getting started, meeting the players the next day to outline his requirements and announcing changes to the support staff line-up, including the addition of Graham Farmer and former East Perth, Claremont and South Fremantle player John 'Irish' Hayes as assistant coaches, to join Barry Cable, who had been with the team in 1987. Pre-season involved a lot of cycling, water polo and swimming sessions because John realised the players had endured a searching preparation in their first year of VFL competition and he didn't want to overload their legs with too many running workouts. Although many of the players were poor swimmers, they embraced the water workouts with gusto, appreciating the break from strenuous endurance running. For the cycling workouts, he had former world and Australian champion and Olympian Steele Bishop take some sessions. His training philosophy was simple – unless you pushed yourself to the point of being sick (vomiting), then you hadn't trained hard enough! The players soon appreciated the finer points of cycling, in particular the benefits of padded cycling pants and superior bike technology! No-one enjoyed these workouts more than Cable who had taken to cycling in a big way after his 1979 tractor accident and had all the best equipment. The players also felt a change in discipline with John's arrival and several were fined up to $1000 for pre-season breaches; trainer Wayne Davies was fined $200 when he forgot to bring the firewood for a team barbecue!

However, these incidents were a gentle prelude to his reaction to WA losing both matches at the bicentennial Australian championships in Adelaide in March. With the Eagles providing

---

95. After taking the West Coast job, he had to pay Woodville to release him from his contract.

most of the team, it was logical that John coached the side. After Victoria handed out a 10 goal thrashing in the first game, worse was to follow. Relegated to the play-off against NSW for third place, WA failed to score in the first quarter, but had drawn level by half-time. However, the NSW side contained the likes of Terry Daniher and Bill Brownless and refused to lie down, leading by 11 points at the last change. A final quarter surge by WA was too little too late and the underdog Blues triumphed by two points, consigning the Sandgropers to last place in the championships. It was the low point of John's State coaching career and he gave full vent to his feelings. In one of his most heated post-game addresses, he severely castigated the team for a sloppy and unprofessional approach to the championships, believing too many had *"short changed"* the State by not having the necessary commitment to the cause. Certainly, several players had enjoyed the social scene at the carnival – *"I hadn't imposed strict curfews on the team, but relied on the professionalism of the individual to do the right thing"*. However, the 'Hollywood factor' the Eagles had experienced in their first season was still present and there is little doubt the mindset of some players was not attuned to the job of winning against good quality opponents.

Several players individually felt the full force of a Todd 'serve', some for the first time. The two who copped the worst of it were David O'Connell and Murray Wrensted. John bluntly told O'Connell that *"if I knew then what I know now, you would never have been picked for the Eagles"*[96]. This piercing analysis was delivered in full earshot of all the players and team staff, including O'Connell's father John, the former Claremont and Geelong ruckman, who was the team manager. Wrensted got similar treatment as John accused him of *"loafing"* since his 1985 Sandover Medal win and told him he might not have much time left at the top level of football. It was an early insight into John's methods, particularly after a bad loss, and many Eagles players hadn't been exposed to him previously in either club or State football. Some West Australians with Victorian clubs, such as Gary Buckenara, witnessed the *"pay-outs"* and left Adelaide thinking how lucky they were not being part of the Eagles. When they arrived back in Perth, the Eagles players sought out Swans players and fellow squad members Phil Narkle and Don Holmes, asking how to deal with these 'serves'. Narkle's advice was simple – make yourself invisible by moving to the back of the huddle, don't make eye contact and hope you're not singled out! John's approach was definitely not the same as Alexander's, who would quietly pull a player aside and work through perceived problems, rarely berating players, especially in front of the rest of the team. The West Coast players now knew that things were very different; the Alexander approach was poles apart from John's.

During January and February of 1988, the Eagles were like a roving band of gypsies as they trained at different locations around Perth. Their lack of a football base was a serious problem and it wouldn't be until their early 1990 move to Subiaco Oval that they actually had a place to call home. Many training sessions were held at Arthur Pexton Reserve, a playing oval belonging to the private college Guildford Grammar and located close to the Swan River, thereby being soft and boggy underfoot. The facilities were basic and the players got changed out of their cars, as they had done for much of their first season, and would drive home in their gear to shower. John chose the ground for two reasons – firstly, the oval was the nearest thing

---

96. O'Connell had been added to the Eagles squad at the end of 1987.

to the boggy Melbourne conditions the players had struggled to handle in their first year and secondly because of the 'Hollywood factor'. Perth was infatuated with the Eagles and the players were receiving plenty of free gifts and enticements, particularly on the social scene. It wasn't too hard to get a little 'starry eyed' with all the attention the team was receiving and this factor concerned John greatly – *"I wanted the players to do it tough and just get on with it at training, much as I had seen the Victorians do on the 1984 trip to Ireland, where the training conditions were pretty primitive"*. He constantly worked on this theme as he fought to keep a lid on the egos of several players and also raised the issue of 'State pride' regularly, which he reminded them had been severely dented in Adelaide.

The Eagles showed encouraging form in the practice games and in late February they thrashed the Sydney Swans by 87 points in a first round Panasonic Cup match at the WACA Ground. This was the first and last pre-season Cup match be staged in Perth for several seasons, as the VFL/AFL decided this was an unnecessary 'luxury' for the Perth club. In mid-March the Eagles took their first trip east for the year, to play Essendon in the second round of the Panasonic Cup. After much discussion over travel times, John opted for a 'hit and run' approach and, to the great amusement of the Victorian media, the side went for a jog at 2am Melbourne time after flying out of Perth at 5.30pm. With daylight saving in the Eastern States, it was after 1am when the team finally arrived at their hotel. Good practice for athletes after plane travel involves some light exercise to loosen the body from the stiffness developed by sitting in cramped conditions so, despite the late hour, the players headed to the park across the road in full glare of the media and TV cameras.

Later in the year at one of these late night 'loosen ups', John caused great amusement by telling the players to each take an imaginary football with them and practise their 'skills' as they jogged around. After a few minutes John noticed that Troy Ugle was just jogging and not using his 'ball' and, when asked why, the training session came to an abrupt end as the players collapsed into fits of laughter. Ugle told John he had 'kicked' his ball towards some trees and was unable to find it in the dark! After these late night sessions the players were allowed up to 10 hours' sleep before rising the next morning and they generally stayed on Perth time while in Melbourne.

A six goal loss to the Bombers marked the end of the pre-season Cup for the Eagles, but there were plenty of positive signs. A week before the season opened, the Eagles became the first WA side to (unofficially) win at the MCG as they accounted for the Demons, 20.15 (135) to 12.12 (84). Defender Michael O'Connell kicked eight goals before the Eagles returned home to prepare for their first round match, against Geelong at Kardinia Park. The pre-season had gone well for John and the club after the turmoil of changing coaches, but two days before the Geelong game he was again in hot water.

He was a special guest on the radio 6PR panel show at a hotel in Mandurah, a holiday resort 100km south of Perth, and was sitting alongside former West Perth president Rod Brown. The two men were hardly friends, stemming from incidents in the early 1980s as part of the Swans-West Perth feud, and sparks were likely to fly, which is probably why the radio station put them together. It was perhaps another example of how the media contrived to 'set up' John to get him to do or say something controversial, given his volatile nature. Brown baited John by saying Alexander had been shafted and that he hoped John was *"up to the job"*. John took this barb as a suggestion that he and the Eagles would fail and reacted angrily by asking Brown *"What are you, a West Australian, or something else?"*. After further spirited exchanges, John grabbed Brown by the tie and *"pulled it a bit tighter"* and in the process delivered a backhander to Brown's chin, which saw him tumble from the stage. Years later John still has no regrets about the incident as he felt Brown wasn't supporting the Eagles (or the State). Brown later conceded the comment was inflammatory and, if the roles had been reversed, he might well have dished out a backhander himself. The next day John apologised for the indiscretion, but explained his actions to the Eagles management and the players by saying he was merely *"sticking up for them before things got a little out of hand"*.

The first game marked the VFL debuts of Guy McKenna and Karl Langdon and the first Eagles outing for Murray Rance, who had transferred back home from Footscray. For three quarters only a goal separated the sides, with the Eagles just in front, but a five goal effort from Michael O'Connell and a best-on-ground display from ruckman Alex Ishchenko saw the Eagles to a 21 point win. A deathly hush fell over Kardinia Park as the Geelong faithful came to terms with a first-up loss to the unwanted interlopers from the West. An ecstatic John was caught on the hop by the Melbourne media post-match as he was a little slow to react when a journalist asked when the Eagles would win a game in Melbourne. *"Where are we now?"* was his quizzical reply, at which the reporter slowly and plainly stated that *"this is Geelong, not Melbourne!"*. The Victorian press were not prepared to give West Coast any plaudits unless it was completely unavoidable.

The side really built on this win over the next two weeks, with a 99 point demolition of Essendon followed by a resounding 118 point thrashing of the Brisbane Bears, in a game that was transferred to the WACA Ground because of flooding on the Gold Coast. After three rounds, the Eagles were on top of the VFL ladder and the warning bells were sounding in Melbourne. A month later they were still there after two more home victories and two Melbourne losses, with one of the wins being a 76 point thumping of St Kilda, who could only kick three goals.

Controversy then reared its head as several players enjoyed some celebrations at a Perth nightclub after this game and word soon filtered back to John. Part of the price paid for being a VFL/AFL player is that your public actions inevitably attract attention and, in most cases, the clubs don't need to solicit this information, as the social misdemeanours of players are eagerly reported by members of the public, perhaps as a consequence of the 'tall poppy' syndrome. Regardless, John reacted savagely to the news – *"I disliked the heavy media and social attention the players received simply by being a West Coast Eagle. They were put on a pedestal that wasn't deserved and receiving all this exposure without winning anything would sap their hunger for success, which bothered me greatly"*. He had issued repeated warnings about the need to be more professional, both on and off the field, and felt now it was time to deliver a severe jolt to the side. He told the players that the whole squad –not just those who had been nightclubbing – would be fined $1000 each for bringing the club into disrepute. He explained that several players who had been fined previously for similar incidents were letting the rest of the squad down and peer pressure was now required to correct the situation so that team success could follow. The players were shocked at the size of the fine, which was large for the time, and also that innocent parties were also penalised. Holmes expressed his discontent at being fined for someone else's mistakes but, while several others thought the same thing, they were either too dumbfounded to speak out or feared the consequences of taking issue with John. What impact the fine had is difficult to ascertain, but the players were left in no doubt that their coach was not to be taken lightly!

This incident marked the start of a mid-season slump which saw the Eagles lose their next five matches, the first two being home defeats by top sides Hawthorn and Carlton followed by away losses to Richmond, Melbourne and Sydney. In the early years, two or three weeks on the road was commonplace for the Eagles, a far cry from the present situation where it is rare to have two consecutive games away, apart from finals. The Richmond defeat was particularly galling as the Tigers were last with just one victory, but the Eagles again fell victim to the MCG bogey as the opposition posted nine goals before they replied. John lamented to the press – *"Maybe we are soft. Maybe we have to hurt more before we turn things around"*. The next day the players certainly were hurting as they ran 100x100 metre sprints as John put their character to the test and reminded them they had more to give in games. The side put up a more spirited display against Melbourne, but after the Sydney loss he changed tack and put the onus back on the players by having them write an essay on the flight back to Perth on how they lost the game – *"In a slump, you need to be prepared to try anything"* – and while he received some press criticism over the ploy, the players responded well to it. Three home wins over the next month put the slump behind them and with an 8-8 record, a finals berth was still a realistic prospect as the Eagles sat in sixth place.

The next fixture was against Fitzroy at the MCG on a Friday night and the game turned into a disaster, with the finals seemingly a forlorn hope as they struggled with the heavy ground and night dew, conditions totally foreign to most of the players. The side was seven goals behind at half-time and eventually lost by 70 points. In the days after this debacle, John made a statement to the rest of the team by virtually 'sacking' defender Mark Zanotti, who was considered to be the 'party animal' of the club. He had not let the Fitzroy loss dampen his social activities on the Friday night, being involved in a late night incident at their Melbourne hotel, therefore was told to train with his WAFL club Subiaco for the rest of the season, effectively ruling him out of Eagles selection [97]. The management also made a statement by sacking Hayes as an assistant coach and runner, replacing him with former Hawthorn player and Subiaco captain-coach Brian Douge, who was Kerr's choice. Hayes was a good friend of John's and one of his appointees, and his sacking showed that John, as coach, didn't have the power and control he was used to as a WAFL club coach. This point would become more apparent to him in 1989.

The Fitzroy game was a turning point for the Eagles – to make the finals they needed to win at least four of the remaining five games and John again called on them to *"do it for the State"* and restore some of the prestige lost in Adelaide earlier in the year. They squared the ledger at 9-9 with a 44 point win over Melbourne at Subiaco and backed up with a hard-fought 31 point home win over North Melbourne, returning them to fifth place, but only on percentage, from Footscray, Essendon and Sydney. With two of the remaining three games in Melbourne,

---

97. Zanotti never played for the Eagles again. He was cleared to Brisbane in 1989 and later went to Fitzroy.

an away win was imperative; this was achieved the next week when the Eagles led all game against St Kilda at Moorabbin, surviving a last-quarter fight-back to win by nine points. With finals fever building in Perth, John had *Westside Football* editor Alan East write the story of the game from the *"inner sanctum"*, as he acted as the interchange steward for the team. West Coast's last home game was against third-placed Collingwood and a crowd of 36,000 were there to see the Eagles turn the game into a rout with a 12 goal to four second half, winning by 10 goals. After four wins in a row, the Eagles held fourth place, but Melbourne, Essendon, Footscray and Sydney were still chances, depending on the outcomes of the final set of fixtures.

The Eagles faced a trip to Western Oval to play Footscray on the Sunday, which gave them the luxury of knowing the other results before their match. A narrow loss would have been enough to secure fifth place for the Eagles, as their percentage was superior to the other sides still in the race – *"I stressed this point to the players, telling them to negate Footscray at every opportunity and to run down the clock wherever possible"*. With Footscray needing victory to have any chance of a finals berth, these tactics forced them to make the running, which wasn't really their normal style of game. In the heavy, wet conditions it was a dour struggle for three quarters, with the Eagles five points clear at the last change. Five minutes into the last quarter captain Ross Glendinning goaled and they kept the Bulldogs goal-less, adding two more to win by 21 points and claim fourth spot. It was a terrific second year effort by the Eagles; no previous 'new' side in either the VFL or the WAFL have ever made the finals in such a short time. It was all the more meritorious considering the side had won their final five games, including two at Melbourne grounds where they had never won before. In fact, over the previous two seasons, the team had only won three games outside WA – Carrara, Geelong and Melbourne – before the victories over St Kilda and Footscray.

1988 – Celebrating the round 22 win over Footscray to see West Coast make the finals in only their second season. With Geoff Miles (left), captain Ross Glendinning, John Gastev, David O'Connell and Chris Mainwaring.

The Eagles were underdogs in the elimination final, despite their powerful finish to the season and, as always, it was a position John relished. The only injury from the Footscray match was to ruck-rover John Annear, who had ruptured his pectoral (chest) muscle, but otherwise the side was reasonably settled. Glendinning was the key forward target, having played almost exclusively at full-forward in 1988, after being shuttled between defence and attack by Alexander in 1987. David O'Connell had cemented his place at centre-half-forward after several weeks in 'Siberia' following the Adelaide carnival and the midfield was shared between Dwayne Lamb, Steve Malaxos, Annear, John Worsfold, John Gastev, Wally Matera, Dean Turner and Wrensted, with Chris Mainwaring and David Hart as wingmen. Rance had centre-half-back to himself and Geoff Miles, Andrew Lockyer and Michael Brennan all had turns at full-back. Laurie Keene and Phil Scott covered the ruck duties, with Keene taking the place of Ishchenko, who had also fallen out of favour with John. Around the flanks were the likes of Langdon and Chris Lewis up forward, with Dean Laidley, McKenna and Zanotti (until banished) in the backline.

The game was at Waverley, where the side hadn't played since the pre-season Panasonic Cup. A crowd of 43,384, mainly parochial Melbourne supporters, were there – the biggest crowd the Eagles had so far played in front of. On a cold and wet day, the Eagles started well, with only goal-front inaccuracy limiting their half-time lead to 22 points. Scott had gone down with a hamstring strain, which limited John's tall options and at half-time he told team doctor Rod Moore to give him a pain-killer and get him back on the field. With the aid of heavy strapping, Scott reappeared for the second half knowing full-well that if the Eagles won, he wouldn't be fit for the next match. Melbourne hit back with six goals, keeping the Eagles to two points and the Demons led by 14 points at the last change. Not to be denied, the Eagles surged back with five goals, including three from Glendinning, which should have been four but for an 'unpaid' free kick for an obvious high tackle by Melbourne full-back Danny Hughes.

Still, with only a minute to play, the Eagles led by three points before Garry Lyon crumbed a spoilt ball and snapped truly across his body. At the centre bounce the Melbourne players swarmed onto the ball, causing another ball up, which then saw Worsfold split the pack and handball forward. It fell to Matera who tapped it across to Malaxos, whose quick left foot kick was taken by Wrensted. He played on but his shot for goal went left as the siren sounded, leaving Melbourne home by two points and on their way to an eventual grand final appearance against Hawthorn. There were no harsh words from the coach – *"I praised the players for their courageous and gutsy effort, saying it was an honourable defeat and we lost with dignity"*. It was a comment that surprised many, given his intense dislike of losing. Alan East wrote in *Westside Football* – *"Todd won back many of his critics, he handled two after match press conferences brilliantly, talking proudly about his players and being genuinely satisfied with them"*.

Apart from Scott, McKenna was stretchered off in the last quarter after a collision with Earl Spalding and O'Connell was also injured, making it unlikely that the club could have fielded a competitive side for the next final had they won. John told them all to be proud of their efforts and to build on the performance in the next season. He consoled Wrensted, telling him that *"it was one of those things"* and there were several other near-misses equally important in the context of the game. Sadly, this fact is rarely remembered in these cases and the player responsible for the final missed shot usually bears the scar of defeat. In Wrensted's case, the scar ran deep. The kick was replayed over and over for the next few weeks on Perth television, which was very unfair and John recalls that *"It should never have been highlighted the way it was"*. Wrensted never recovered from this missed opportunity, despite the best efforts of everyone at the club and he left the next year [98], convinced John didn't rate him as a player, despite the fact he had brought him into the finals side at the last minute. Wrensted played a respectable 13 games in 1988, after missing a month with injury and, unfortunately, he is probably better remembered for the missed shot on goal than for the quality of his play and his 1985 Sandover Medal.

~

The euphoria of making the finals in their second season left many giddy with success and expecting more of the same in 1989. However, it would prove to be the worst season in the club's short history (until 2001, when the side won two fewer games) and John's hardest and toughest year in football. Although he has coached teams to less victories than the Eagles recorded, the pressures on him were the worst he had experienced in his long involvement in the game.

The first and most telling setback came in October when Glendinning announced his retirement, even though John had no doubts his captain had another good year left in him. He respected the decision and didn't try to talk him around, only saying he could leave a final decision until the new year if he wished. However, Glendinning was firm in his conviction that it was time to go, as he was keen to leave the game at a time of his own choosing, not anyone else's. As John says *"... not many players get to choose their time, with the decision often made for them which is sad and unpleasant"*. Nowadays, with so much money in the game, he sees players often staying a year too long in order to make another $200,000 or more, when their performance really isn't up to it. While he accepts that money is an important consideration for a professional footballer, the result is often that *"many former greats fade sadly from the game, as they cannot command a regular league spot in their final season. Therefore, some of the accolades they are due don't come their way"*. He greatly admired Glendinning for his decision to retire when he did, as he was still the Eagles most important player and could easily have played on. His absence would leave a gaping hole in the side, but John respected his honesty.

The Perth football rumour mill soon went into overdrive with suggestions that Glendinning had retired because he didn't get on with John. Both men categorically refute this notion. While John's style of coaching was not how Glendinning would have done it himself, he was similar to Ron Barassi and John Kennedy, who had coached the Brownlow medallist at North Melbourne and John being coach played no part in his retirement decision. John is totally dismissive of the suggestion – *"If you are a champion, it doesn't matter who the coach is"*.

During pre-season the squad had to be finalised and the club was able to take part in its first national draft in November 1988, with further openings being created by John's decision to move Zanotti and Ishchenko on. Both had fallen foul of John mainly because they refused to

---

98. He joined Collingwood, but managed only 10 more games before fading from the VFL/AFL scene.

curb their social activities and he regarded them as poor role models for the younger players. They were traded to Brisbane for draft picks No. 2 and 44. Other players to depart were Matera (to Fitzroy), Wrensted (to Collingwood) and Gastev (to Brisbane); of these, Gastev was the player John really wanted to retain. It's generally believed that Gastev was also 'sacked' by John, but he actually left the club of his own accord after rejecting contract offers from the Eagles.

New players into the system were Peter Sumich, Don Pyke, Craig Turley, Stevan Jackson and Scott Watters as the pre-draft concession choices; they were joined by Todd Breman, Peter Higgins and Peter Melesso, plus seven other draftees from the Eastern States. The only one of these seven who would represent the club was Port Adelaide ruckman David Hynes, but he delayed his arrival until 1991. In the March draft, four more locals who had been listed by VFL clubs were selected to take the squad to 40 – Shane Ellis, Clinton Browning, Shane Cable and Richard Geary. The selection of these WA-based players, rather than Victorian youngsters, was John's idea and was done to save the club money on relocation costs. Quite simply, the club was several millions dollars in the red and he saw this as one way to save money. Also, the Victorian country recruits were only young and often homesick [99], therefore they represented a risky (and costly) investment. John's plan was to top up the list with WA-based VFL registered players who would be called on to play in a crisis. However, as fate would have it, injuries beset the Eagles in 1989 and John was forced to use these 'sleepers' more than he anticipated.

In February 1989, the side scored a 26 point win over St Kilda at Waverley in their first round Panasonic Cup match and two weeks later they were tied with Hawthorn at full-time, but a point kicked by Paul Peos in sudden death extra time advanced the Eagles to the semi-finals. This was a re-match of the elimination final and the result was virtually the same, with Melbourne winning by a point, 7.13 (55) to the Eagles 6.18 (54). Sumich appeared to be the logical replacement for Glendinning in front of goals, but pre-season he was used at centre-half-back as John explained – *"I told him I was fast-tracking his development as a key forward by playing him on the likes of Dermott Brereton in order to learn from the best"*. It was a tough introduction for the young Sumich, who could have played a year earlier, but after joining the squad for one training session he decided to stay at South Fremantle for another season. John attracted some media criticism for playing Sumich in defence, but answered by saying that *"... coaches can't always give players the know-how and experience they need"*. Sumich had no qualms about the tactic and readily admits that it *"did him the world of good"* and was a smart piece of coaching.

Practice match form was good and reinforced the club's optimistic view of the year ahead, but another setback disrupted the team's preparation three weeks before the first match. After the Melbourne game, the club was unable to organise any further practice matches against VFL sides, partly due to financial considerations as management didn't wish to fund a trip to Melbourne and they were unable to attract sides to Perth on a shared costs basis. In hindsight, it was a bad mistake as the team was not match hardened and this was an important factor in their poor start.

---

99. By May 1989, three of the four Victorian country recruits taken by the Eagles in the November 1988 draft had returned home.

In the week leading up to the clash with Essendon to open the season, Rance was named captain, which was a surprise as Malaxos was favoured in most quarters. It has been wrongly assumed that John's previous association with Rance at Swan Districts influenced the decision. However, Malaxos had previously been captain at both State and national level with John as coach and the choice of Rance was basically a decision by Kerr and Douge. In a radical innovation for that era, John named four vice-captains in Malaxos, Annear, Keene and Worsfold, whose leadership qualities were already well-respected despite his youth. The press again criticised John for naming four deputies instead of the traditional vice-captain and deputy vice-captain and the media made great copy out of debating how a captain for the day would be chosen if Rance was unavailable. Again John was ahead of his time as a leadership 'group' is commonly selected in AFL teams these days. He explained his decision by saying it was a simple way of expanding the leadership responsibilities and of having more designated leaders in more areas of the oval at any one time. The logic of this seemed obvious to him and he wondered at the time why no-one in the media could (or perhaps even tried) to think it through. It was an early example of how his relationship with the media would plummet to new lows in 1989.

Against Essendon, Pyke, Turley and Sumich made their debuts, with Sumich starting at full-back on Paul Salmon. West Coast kicked the first five goals, but by quarter-time the scores were level before the Eagles gradually faded, losing by 16 points, with ruckman Scott kicking seven goals playing as a forward. The next week saw the Eagles not only lose to Geelong (by 95 points), but also ruckman Keene went down with an Achilles tendon injury that would sideline him for 18 months and which marked the start of an appalling run of injuries for the club. Losses to Sydney and North Melbourne by sizeable margins left the Eagles win-less and on the bottom of the ladder and, as the pressure mounted, Rance was compelled to publicly declare that the players were fully behind the coach.

Once more, in times of crisis, John sought to pull a rabbit from the hat. Heading to Carrara to play the Bears, he told the players that he was extremely confident of victory, so he suggested they back themselves to win! He planted the seed with Geoff Miles, the team's most avid punter, and he soon had unanimous agreement from the players, especially after indicating that any winnings would go to the players' trip fund. The wager certainly lifted the enthusiasm within the ranks and, on arrival at the Gold Coast, Manning was dispatched to invest $4000 at the generous odds of 9/4.

Jackson made his debut, kicking six goals as the Eagles collected the cash with an all-the-way 52 point win. In the post-match excitement, word of the winning bet leaked out and was headline news in *The West Australian* the following Monday. The VFL expressly forbade teams or club staff betting on the outcome of matches, but unfortunately neither John nor Manning realised they were contravening the rules and with the bet now public knowledge, they were in trouble. As coach, John risked suspension by the VFL, so through Douge the club attempted a cover up. Manning offered to take the blame as he had placed the bet, but Douge didn't want any of the football staff held responsible, so eventually the 'fall guy' became Ron Lorimer, one of the unpaid club helpers who happened to be in hospital at the time. Manning telephoned him and told him the story and he cheerfully agreed to be named as the punter. A few weeks later the VFL fined the club $9000 (i.e. the winnings), leaving the players' trip fund rather short of cash.

However, the Brisbane win buoyed morale and the under-manned team put in some spirited performances over the next six weeks, but couldn't notch another win. The season was gone, with the previous year's finals appearance a fast-fading memory, but it could have been different with a little more luck. Four games were lost by eight points or less and, in a two point loss to Richmond, Turner's last-gasp shot on goal hit the post. With several players including Rance, Scott and Worsfold missing through injury, the Eagles simply couldn't balance up week to week and were forced to play rookies and 'sleepers'. After a five point loss to Hawthorn, a still-positive John said – *"In two years' time the Eagles talent will be awesome. We have 13 players aged between 19 and 21 and some of these young men are going to be great players"*. Finally, against Footscray at the WACA Ground, with Sumich scoring his first bag of eight goals, the losing streak was stopped with a 32 point win, although the three-quarter-time lead was more than 10 goals.

The next three games were all in Melbourne, which was in the midst of its wettest winter for years and, at Princes Park before the clash with Carlton, a 'Super Sopa' was used to remove surface water. After being in the game for three quarters, the Eagles faded in the heavy conditions to lose by 23 points. The next two weeks represented the low point of a bleak season and remain the worst two successive games in the club's history. Firstly, a 91 point drubbing by Hawthorn had John fuming and he delivered a stinging post-match blast to the side, who paid for the insipid display the next day with a two hour session of interval shuttle runs [100]. After a physical week of training, they ventured back to Melbourne to take on the Bombers at Windy Hill and several players (quietly) bet $1000 that they could beat Essendon, but it was a case of supremely misplaced optimism. In their darkest hour in boggy conditions, the Eagles managed one goal – kicked by Lewis in the second quarter – losing by 142 points, 25.10 (160) to 1.12 (18). This score remains their lowest and the biggest losing margin, with the total of 18 points also being the lowest score recorded by a team coached by John.

Rance remembers the dark day vividly – *"We just never got going. Essendon seemed as though they were floating on the surface, whereas we seemed to be knee deep in the bog. Nothing went right"*. And that included the messages John was sending out to the players! Half-way through the second quarter, with the Eagles 10 goals behind, he was perplexed to see runner Douge apparently giving his instructions to the wrong players. It transpired that Douge was concussed from a collision with Rance earlier in the quarter, when he had run straight into the player and virtually knocked himself out as he kept his eyes on the ball! However, he regained his senses at half-time and saw out the game. The only winner on the day was Lamb, who spotted a dollar coin on the ground, so he picked it up and put it in his sock. Lamb had a reputation for being a little 'tight with money' so none of his team-mates were the least surprised when they heard about his find. John refrained from giving the players a tongue lashing, as he had done the previous week, but, sensing they were at a low ebb and stunned by the enormity of the defeat, he urged them to use the loss to get mentally stronger so they wouldn't find themselves in this position too often. John feels the size of the defeat was also the genesis of the great rivalry between the two clubs, with due credit to the fostering role provided by Kevin Sheedy waving his jacket after a narrow Bombers victory in 1993.

---

100. As he had done in the past, the players started by running 15 times out and back over 20 metres. They then did 14 repeats, then 13 and so forth down to one.

The fallout from such a massive loss, especially after a bad defeat the previous week, was predictably severe. John arrived back in Perth to find the media *"staking out"* his home – he couldn't leave the house without a swarm of reporters clamouring around him. Meryl was also a target and she soon had enough of their unwanted attention – *"I confronted several of them, demanding to know what gave them the right to interfere in our daily lives in such an uncaring manner"*. While a few had some empathy for her, they all said they were told to be there by their editors and in the end John escaped through a back gate into his neighbours' house and used their car to give them the slip. However, this frenzied attention was only a warm-up as the media were calling for John's resignation or sacking and packed the Eagles office for the regular Monday press conference, expecting to see blood. They were disappointed as Kerr said – *"John Todd is not being sacked today. We are concentrating now on beating Sydney next Sunday"*. With his back to the wall, John defiantly said *"To resign now would be the coward's way out"* and left no doubt that he would fight through the situation with all the energy he could muster.

While he survived the press conference, he was forced to cope with a situation where Kerr now wanted to have a role in helping prepare the team for the Sydney match. Kerr's background as an administrator was in real estate and he had never been involved with top-level football – or any other sport. He had been put into the managing director's position by chairman Neil Hamilton in August 1987, when he and Murray McHenry organised a $5 million payment to secure the failing share float. Kerr was therefore the representative of the club's owners, which was a vastly different structure to what John was used to as a WAFL coach. His first instinct was to tell Kerr his assistance wasn't required (albeit in more colourful language) as he was the coach and it was his responsibility. However, he let it pass as he was very unsure of where he sat in the club power structure. This was a new environment for him, as he was used to absolute control within the WAFL club set-up.

Kerr came up with a 'P-plan' which John went along with. The 'P' was used because the Sydney game was the 16th of the season and P is the 16th letter of the alphabet. Each player was given a large 'P' to take home and were asked to write down some key 'P' words – such as pride, persistence and perseverance – which had special meaning for them. The change rooms were decorated with large 'Ps' and several players wrote 'P' on the back of their hands prior to the game. At half-time Sydney led by a point, but John gave a stirring speech, telling the players it was time to repay the public for their support and to silence the critics. The players were fortified for the second half, not only by John's words, but also by a quick nip of some traditional Slav grappa (wine) supplied by Sumich at John's request. He had reverted to the old 'sherry bottle' fix of the 1950s and '60s to ease the tension, given the closeness of the scores. He was concerned that with the build-up to the game produced by the 'P' plan and the inglorious displays of the past two weeks, the players might have become *"suffocated"* by the pressure of needing to win. Having a swig from the bottle may or may not have helped to relax the players, but in any case they swamped Sydney with a 12 goal to five second half. After the 42 point win John said *"This was a win the Eagles owed the WA public. Everyone in the club made a contribution"*. In a curious coincidence, the 'P' plan was seemingly reflected in the Eagles score – 16.16. The game marked the start of a strong finish to the season as the Eagles won five of their last seven matches to rebound courageously from the Windy Hill debacle.

Unfortunately for John, the Sydney victory and the apparent success of the P plan emboldened Kerr, who now wanted to speak to the players at team meetings the day before a game. This sat badly with John, as it compromised his own authority but, feeling isolated within the club power structure, he felt his hands were tied. The players found it quite odd and could sense the coach's unease and John recalls feeling so lonely and isolated that *"... I had to go to the butcher's shop to buy a bone to hang around my neck so my dog would play with me"*. While Kerr never wanted a match day role, his weekly attempts to provide a motivational spur certainly indicated to the players that John's position as coach was under threat. He had no illusions about this and, after a Friday night game at the WACA Ground late in the season, despite beating Geelong by 44 points, he said to Meryl – *"I'm gone, they are going to get rid of me"*. Despite winning well, not one club director made any effort to speak to him in the rooms, which he felt confirmed his perception of where he stood. Manning recalls that in this period, particularly in Melbourne on the night before games, John would often receive crank phone calls, where the anonymous caller would gleefully tell him he was going to be sacked.

The next week, the Eagles produced their best form of the season in beating Carlton by 76 points but, even with the dramatic improvement in the team over the previous six weeks, the press speculation about his future continued unabated. Many times he was forced to repeat his position – yes, his contract was up for renewal at the end of the season; no, he wouldn't be resigning and yes, he would like to continue as coach next year – *"What really irked me about the media was that they concentrated almost solely on the negatives of the situation and on me, ignoring the team and the positives which were the good form of many younger players such as McKenna, Worsfold and Sumich"*.

The regular Monday press conferences at the Eagles offices were, win or lose, the bane of John's week. The former Premier of Queensland, Joh Bjelke-Petersen, once described holding a press conference as *"feeding the chooks"* but, in John's situation, this was more like *"feeding the lions"* and he was the only dish on offer! Being tactful or cunning with the media was never one of his strong points and, with little or no support coming from the club in this regard, he was often easy meat for the press gallery. When backed into a corner (which was often), his basic instinct was to fight and he invariably took them on, often questioning their loyalty to the State as one negative question after another was asked. The incessant questioning about his future and indeed, his ability to coach at this level, naturally made him bristle and several times the conferences degenerated into slanging matches as the press played on his volatility. On one occasion he simply couldn't contain his anger at a question from local television journalist Peter Ensell, so he stood up, unbuttoned his sleeves and invited Ensell to join him in the adjoining room where the matter could be further discussed in private! Cooler heads prevailed and no punches were thrown and he then challenged Ensell to do a positive human interest story on the *"Magnificent Seven"* – McKenna, Worsfold, Waterman, Lewis, Peos, Watters and Sumich – who were all now playing with West Coast after being members of WA's victorious 1985 Teal Cup (under 18s) side. Ensell eventually did the story and won a media award for it, but John is still waiting for his thank you for the suggestion.

The final game of the season was against Collingwood, at Victoria Park but, with about 10 players missing through injury and suspension, the undermanned Eagles put up a brave display before eventually losing by 49 points. The game is remembered by many at the Eagles for the terrific 'screamer' taken by Melesso, who 12 months later would be fighting for his life (successfully), after being diagnosed with cancer. As John walked across the ground after the game, all the players shook hands with him, signalling the end of a tough season, but their gesture also had a sense of finality to it. They knew the situation (as he did) and thought it unlikely they would see him again as coach. Some were no doubt content with this prospect. Mid-season, with the club at its lowest ebb, John had perhaps lost the faith of some players, especially those who bore the brunt of his frustrations with the team performances. He believes that this is *"part and parcel of a tough season and I never felt I had lost the players to the point where it would be pointless to continue as coach"* – as he knew was the case at East Fremantle at the end of 1976. Early the next week John asked Hamilton and Kerr *"to put their cards on the table"* and told them that *"if you want to change direction, then fine, let me know and we can all walk away friends"*. However, they weren't about to rush the decision and wouldn't rule him in or out. With West Coast not taking part in the finals, most of the press attention in Perth was focused squarely on the coaching position.

~

Although in only their third season, 1989 was a watershed year for the Eagles. By year's end many important changes to the structure, finance and operations of the club had been put into place, which paved the way for future stability and success. The Western Australian Football Commission had been established and, after protracted negotiations with the principal Eagles shareholders, assumed a 75% control of Indian Pacific Limited, the Eagles parent company. Much of the impetus for this development came from the State government who provided financial assistance to the WA football system, which was some $10 million in debt. A new board was appointed to administer the Eagles – Brian Cook, who had experience as a player, coach and administrator, replaced Kerr as chief executive and Trevor Nisbett, an experienced and respected football administrator (and now the club's CEO), was appointed football manager with a clear brief to run the football operations. Lastly, and perhaps most importantly, agreement was reached for Subiaco Oval to become the training and administrative base of the Eagles. The 'gypsy' days were over and the Eagles were taking on the look and feel of a traditional football club, the importance of which cannot be overstated. The 'hard yards' necessary to get the new team established had been completed and the one big decision remaining was who would coach the side.

There were a few obvious reasons why the Eagles struggled in 1989. First and foremost was the loss of Glendinning; Collingwood coach Leigh Matthews (later to be the Brisbane triple premiership mentor), summed up the significance of his loss by saying – *"Ross Glendinning is of more importance to the Eagles than any other player is to any other club"*. Rance says of his absence – *"In 1988 we could bomb the ball forward with confidence because he was there and probably a 75% chance to get it. We certainly missed this in 1989"*. John knew the side lacked a focal point up forward, although by the end of the season with 45 goals from only nine games at full-forward, Sumich was ready to blossom.

Secondly, the side had a terrible injury run – in 1988 two players lined up in all 23 games and six played 20 or more; in 1989 not one player appeared in every game and only three notched 20 or more. As a result, the squad's depth was sorely tested and found to be wanting, as the 'sleepers' had to be used and they simply weren't quite up to the job. John's 'money saving' plan hadn't quite worked out. The side only became stabilised late in the season, coinciding with the team's solid finish.

Thirdly, the lack of hard match practice in the three weeks before the first game got the side off to a poor start which was difficult to recover from, particularly when injuries hit. While John agrees with this analysis of the season, at the time he preferred to emphasise the *"positives"* of the situation. In his coach's report for the year, he commended the players on their ability to *"rally in the crisis"* (after the Windy Hill loss), adding that *"the capacity of the players to survive these critical times was an excellent indication that the club can move forward successfully in 1990 and beyond"*. He continued – *"The Eagles have developed a quality hard core of young players between 19 and 22 years of age, headed by John Worsfold and Guy McKenna and I'm confident the Eagles will rebound strongly in 1990"*. Certainly, the crop of young Eagles was probably better than at any other club at the time and, despite the poor results in 1989, they seemed set for a bright future. As Essendon ruckman Simon Madden said after the Eagles record Windy Hill loss – *"It's not the end of the world for the Eagles. The one thing they have is youth. With youth and a long term plan they can be a future force"*. Rance expressed a similar sentiment at the end of the season when he told the West Coast directors that *"... it doesn't matter who the coach is. With the kids coming on, the side will be successful in 1990"*. He made the comment in support of John as coach, although he felt a change was *"probably more likely"*. Bill Walker also sprang to John's defence, telling Kerr that he would be *"a successful long-term coach if you give him some time"*. However, the board wanted to assess the options available and spoke to several Victorian candidates including Sheedy, Wayne Schimmelbusch, Alan Joyce, Robert Walls and Michael Malthouse.

In the week leading up to the VFL grand final, the directors interviewed Walls and Malthouse in Melbourne, after deciding against the others. John was also in Melbourne for the club's grand final breakfast and, according to Kerr, *"still very much in the mix"* although John thought otherwise. He had been invited to go to the game by Hamilton, but just *"didn't feel a part of it"* as he felt he was being given the *"cold shoulder"* by the board members. He rang Meryl to ask what she thought and her advice was simple – *"If you want this job, then fight for it, don't make it easy for them"* as she encouraged him to go to the game. This was the first (and perhaps only) time she has seen John hesitant and uncertain, instead of his normal confident and decisive self. It indicated to her how much the strain of the season had taken out of him. Despite her repeated urgings, he decided against going and flew back to Perth on the day of the game. Later that day Mal Brown rang her to say he had seen Hamilton with Malthouse at the game, telling her to get John to *"watch his back"*.

However, it was a bit late for this. On the following Monday the Eagles directors met to discuss the coaching position and it was obviously between John and Malthouse. According to Kerr, there was a strong chance of John being reappointed right up to the finish, but after six hours of vigorous discussion, the board voted to give Malthouse the job. While it was accepted that the Eagles had been made tougher and were more disciplined under John, it was felt the knowledge of Victorian conditions, players and teams that Malthouse offered added an important *"extra dimension"* to the club and there is no doubt this swung the vote his way. Nevertheless, it was a close thing. One factor which concerned the board was the possibility of a financial backlash from the WA public for appointing an 'outsider'; ironically, the Eagles had beaten Malthouse's old side Footscray twice in 1989 and finished above them on the ladder – 11th versus 13th. Hamilton rang Malthouse to give him the good news, but didn't call John. The next morning John picked up *The West Australian* and, for the second time in his career, read that he had been replaced as coach without being officially informed. The press were again hounding him as they staked out his house on the day the announcement was made, but again he escaped through the back gate and his neighbours' car.

The formal announcement that afternoon was something of an anti-climax and the reason given by Kerr and Hamilton for not telling John was that they wanted to confirm flight times for Malthouse to come to Perth for the press conference. However, as John says – *"The first person told should be the outgoing coach, so there is no chance of him hearing it on the news or reading it in the paper. Why the game, in general, can't get this right is something I just cannot understand".* When interviewed, he said – *"I can assure you I have no axe to grind against the Eagles administration about their decision to appoint Michael Malthouse. I'll be a supporter of the Eagles for many years to come and wish Malthouse all the best".* However, he was less than impressed about the way the decision was kept from him, saying it *"lacked professionalism".* Even now, this oversight still rankles him and Kerr and Hamilton are afforded little respect as a result. In a 2001 interview, when asked about the Eagles and Kerr, he replied *"Bill who? What's his legacy to football?".* He also reflects that *"... without a football structure in place to help me, I paid the price. After 1990, when the coach and the football manager were given control of running the team, whoever followed me was going to be successful and that's no reflection on Mick Malthouse, who did a super job".*

The real reason for not telling John the decision on the previous night should be put on record – even though it has never been told to him officially. According to board member Murray McHenry, the directors decided on Malthouse around 5pm and wanted to inform John then, but public relations consultant Chris Codrington, who had sat with John two years earlier as he waited to be announced as the new Eagles coach, advised against this. He feared John would react badly and because of his (perceived) association with Robbie Burns, of *The Daily News*, would give him the scoop. Codrington felt there was a good chance the news would break in the late evening edition of the paper and he persuaded the board to take his view, although they were uncomfortable with it. Arrangements were made to fly Malthouse to Perth the next morning (under an assumed name), but things went awry as Greg Denham, of *The West Australian*, chased down the story in Melbourne by discovering that an unsuspecting Nanette Malthouse (Mick's wife) had called friends to tell them Mick had the job. Denham punted that he had the scoop he wanted and it was headline news in *The West* the next morning, much to the chagrin of the board. Sadly, the bad blood between John and the board over the handling of the decision could have been easily avoided. If they had enough faith in John to keep it to himself, which he would have done, then he would have left the club on better terms. Why they didn't have this faith and follow their first instincts rather than accept Codrington's view is hard to fathom. All John had ever asked of the board was to be *"up front and honest"* and it disappointed him greatly that this wasn't the case.

Despite the bad taste left by the botched disclosure of his removal from the job, he has great memories of coaching the Eagles – *"To have been involved was fantastic"* – and his two year coaching stint went some way towards satisfying his previous ambition to play in the VFL, denied to him by his knee injury. While he certainly would have liked a longer tenure, he never saw himself as *"holding up"* for several years, principally because of the air travel involved – *"The regular flights to the east and back were hard to handle and on many occasions I never felt myself again for two or three days after returning to Perth. In some weeks, when the Eagles had two consecutive away games, I was back on the plane three days later!"*. The regular interstate flights had exacerbated, rather than cured, his fear of flying.

Chapter 21
Football in the 1980s

WAFL president Vincent Yovich in 1981, when calling for a two year deferment of VFL plans to introduce a draft system to regulate the spiralling transfer fees that WA clubs were asking from Melbourne clubs for their players:

> "*Our policy must be to expose the VFL for what it is doing to Australian Rules Football. We watch VFL replays every Sunday night* (The Winners) *and most of the stars are from interstate. It's a condemnation of the VFL really. They can't support their own product*".

WAFL chairman Roy Annear in 1986, when discussing the implications of WA's possible entry into the VFL:

> "*WA football will be set back at least three years if the State does not join the proposed national competition next year, as over 20 players are likely to head to Victoria at the end of the season*".

The formation of the West Coast Eagles dramatically changed the face of football in Western Australia, probably forever. The status of the WAFL competition was immediately and severely challenged, with the clubs drastically revising operating budgets, as many traditional sources of income dried up. Entering a team into the expanded VFL remains the most acrimonious, divisive and hotly debated issue football in WA has ever confronted. Many diehard fans and club administrators still rue the decision, firm in their view that it destroyed football in this State. For them, WA football now exists in two distinct phases – pre-1987, when the WAFL was king and post-1987, when the WAFL was reduced to poor relation status by the VFL/AFL, who hijacked State league football throughout the country. However, the flipside of this view is that the football industry has since grown into a multi-million dollar enterprise providing employment to thousands of people, including fully professional players and coaches, and is an important part of the economy of the respective States and the country. It is doubtful these opposing points of view will ever be reconciled. Certainly, the halcyon days of the WAFL being the State's premier football competition appear over, but ironically, the early 1980s were a time of great excitement and success. The years before 1987 saw some wonderful players and teams grace the arena and WA had its best run of interstate victories, with three national championships in four years. It was very much a decade of boom (on the field) and bust (off the field).

The early 1980s saw most clubs increase their annual turnover to $750,000 or more, up from about $500,000 at the end of the previous decade. Player payments were as high as $250,000 a club and, in the two years from 1979, Swans had almost doubled this outlay from $105,000 to $200,357. Top players were receiving $15,000 or more a season, with incentive payments for individual and team success. However, several clubs reported financial losses for 1980 and two – Subiaco and East Perth – were in dire straits. Subiaco sent out an SOS to members to renew their membership quickly (including a $50 levy) or the club would close its doors as it grappled with a $154,000 debt. East Perth were slightly worse off, with an accumulated deficit of $207,000. Quite simply, clubs were living beyond their means as the membership, sponsorship and bar trade could not keep pace with escalating costs.

In 1979, attendances for qualifying round matches, State games and finals topped the one million mark for the first and only time; in 1980 and '81 numbers were down to around 930,000 and by 1984 had dipped to about 800,000 due to lower qualifying round attendances. This decline obviously reduced club income and it was becoming apparent that clubs were surviving on transfer fees by clearing star players to the VFL. In 1982 Swans received $245,000 in transfer fees and in 1983 it was $356,000. John remembers this time *"as being absolutely crazy, as clubs got ahead of themselves and failed to secure their future as they quickly spent this income"*. There was no way the gravy train could last, as WA's stocks of quality players grew less year by year, but also the VFL clubs couldn't continue paying such massive amounts. At the end of 1983, East Perth president Mal Atwell said the club could not pay its players and launched a 'Save East Perth' fund. In 1984, both East Perth and West Perth announced that 25-30% pay cuts for their players were necessary *"for survival"* and the WAFL took out a loan which it distributed to help the clubs pay their debts. It was against this backdrop that the push for a national competition became almost irresistible as the decade wore on.

Despite the court ruling in the 1978 Brian Adamson clearance case, clubs on both sides of the country still played hard-ball on interstate transfers. The courts were regularly used to either win, refuse or delay clearances as clubs haggled over a fair price. The decade began with Adamson using the courts and the NFL Appeals Board to win a clearance from Norwood back to West Perth, providing some perfect symmetry for the ructions he created in 1978 over the restraint of trade issue. In early 1981, East Perth pair Phil Kelly and Peter Spencer took out Supreme Court writs against the VFL as the club haggled with North Melbourne, with the dispute soon resolved and the players cleared for a reported $200,000. Shortly afterwards, South Fremantle took Supreme Court action to prevent ruckman Derek Shaw from playing with Collingwood in 1981, claiming he had agreed to remain with them.

With many other disputes between clubs in progress, the NFL changed its appeals process so players could appeal to the NFL after only one (instead of two) clearance refusals, allowing the NFL to also set the transfer fee. While this reduced legal costs for clubs, it also limited their income as the price set by the NFL was usually less than that negotiated between the two parties. In any case, the VFL did not subscribe to the NFL process and came up with its own solution to limit the spiralling transfer fees – the introduction of a draft system for 1982. Eligibility for WA players was being able to satisfy two of three criteria – aged 24 years or older, having played 110 games or more, or having played for five years and at least 50 games. Transfer fees were capped at $40,000, which had the WA clubs up in arms. In June 1981 WAFL president Vincent Yovich called for a two year deferment of the draft, because of the *"ludicrous"* standard clearance fees. There was also the problem that 26 WA players had signed Form Fours (a contract indicating a willingness to play with a VFL club) and these players were to be exempt from the draft.

With 12 VFL clubs permitted to draft one player each from WA, a mass player exodus loomed. Yovich said – *"Our policy must be to expose the VFL for what it is doing to Australian Rules Football. We watch VFL replays every Sunday night* (The Winners) *and most of the stars are from interstate. It's a condemnation of the VFL really. They can't support their own product"*. It made no difference to the VFL. In October 1981 the draft went ahead, with reigning premiers Carlton springing the biggest surprise by drafting former Claremont forward Ross Ditchburn, who had played country football in WA in 1981 [101]. However, the mercenary nature of the VFL clubs was soon displayed as North Melbourne attempted to recruit East Perth forward Grant Campbell, who had just been drafted by St Kilda! Hawthorn also ignored the draft rules as they initially demanded $30,000 to clear Peter Murnane to West Perth, when VFL players coming West were exempt from transfer fees.

The draft was soon scrapped, then re-invented in April 1984 when the VFL and the WAFL agreed on new clearance criteria – 23 years of age (instead of 24), five years' service or 110 games or more, with two of the three criteria being met. The transfer fee was increased to $65,000 for a contracted player and $45,000 if uncontracted. A month later, possibly due to pressure applied by the VFL in light of the new agreement, St Kilda settled out of court with Swans and West Perth for clearances for Phil Narkle and Phil Cronan, who had both been played by the Saints without a clearance. However, despite the new agreement, messy and protracted disputes would continue for virtually all of the decade, culminating in the exorbitant transfer fees demanded by the VFL clubs for their WA players recruited by the West Coast Eagles in 1987 and 1988 [102].

The player drain to Victoria remained the greatest concern of local clubs and the WAFL and, although transfer fees were a major source of income, losing top players did little for the sustained success of clubs, which affected membership, attendance, sponsorship and bar trade. It was a vicious circle and a problem with no real solution apparent. Approaches to the State government to introduce football betting and receive a share of TAB revenue were rebuffed. By the middle of the decade, with attendances declining and clubs experiencing severe financial problems, many critics saw the only way to stem the flow of players to Victoria was to provide a higher level of competition at home and embrace the proposed national club competition.

The first shot had been fired in October 1980, when East Perth (despite their financial problems) made a formal application to join the VFL. President Jim Leahy explained the move by saying *"Our prognosis of the future of WA football is that it's destined for second grade status because of the continued loss of players to Victoria"*. The WAFL reacted quickly, with president Jim Davies adamant that *"The success of East Perth's application would ruin football at the grass roots in WA"*. The VFL rejected the application without seriously entertaining the prospect, but the die was cast and in 1984 the WAFL said it wanted to be part of a national competition by 1986, fielding two composite sides. In the same year East Fremantle received an approach from North Melbourne to consider joining a national competition. In 1985 Dr

---

101. Ditchburn took up the Carlton offer and, with 61 goals, was their leading goal-kicker in 1982 and also played in their premiership side.
102. Almost $600,000 was outlaid on seven players, the most expensive being inaugural captain Ross Glendinning, whose clearance from North Melbourne cost $135,000. The Eagles were also forced to pay Hawthorn $35,000 for Steve Malaxos, as he had been retained on their playing list despite returning to Claremont for the 1986 season.

Geoffrey Edelsten bought the Sydney Swans for $6.3 million and former East Perth and Geelong full-back and Perth radio star John K Watts and local businessman Alan Delaney announced plans to buy a VFL club and relocate it to Perth. At the end of this year, the VFL revealed plans to expand their competition to 14 teams for 1987, including one team from both WA and SA.

In February 1986, WAFL chairman Roy Annear declared his stance – *"I see the national competition as an essential addition to football in Australia. WA simply has to be represented in this competition and the only way to be represented is by one composite team"*. A VFL report revealed that several Melbourne clubs were in financial trouble and an expansion of the competition (with a large up-front licence fee for the new teams!) was essential. In July, Annear warned that *"WA football will be set back at least three years if the State does not join the proposed national competition, as over 20 players are likely to head to Victoria at the end of the season"*. At club level West Perth said they would seek to join the VFL if the WAFL decided against such a move and Claremont went the same way.

An expanded VFL competition now seemed inevitable and, if the WAFL deferred a decision, there was a real prospect that one of the clubs, or a private consortium, would take the lead and ignore the WAFL; a move likely to be backed by the VFL. The prospect of not having control over the new team could not be entertained and probably helped increase the margin of the vote. On August 22, 1986 a 12-2 vote by the eight club delegates and the WAFL executive accepted an invitation to join the expanded VFL competition. But the VFL's vote to accept a WA club was 8-4, only just satisfying the two-thirds majority needed. The $4 million licence fee, to be paid within a month, had been too good to pass up for the financially stricken Melbourne clubs. It certainly prevented at least a couple of them going to the wall.

~

Unfortunately for WA football (and Annear), 14 players were signed by Melbourne clubs in the frenzied recruiting period that followed the 1986 season and only four former WA players – Ross Glendinning, Phil Narkle, Dean Turner and John Annear – were recruited back from Victoria to help form the 35 man Eagles squad. With the player drain again enormous, despite this being a prime reason for joining the VFL, the critics were quick to express disgust – a vocal minority, headed by former South Fremantle captain John Colgan and one-time East Fremantle and Perth player Brian Lawrence, formed the *"Fight for Football"* lobby group, which called for the scrapping of the West Coast Eagles.

The early years of the Eagles produced an acrimonious relationship with the WAFL clubs; the first major issue was the transfer fee for players recruited by the new team. Subiaco were incensed when Mark Zanotti's price was set at $27,500 when they were expecting $50,000, as he had just played an outstanding 1986 finals series, winning the Simpson Medal in the grand final. Many other fees raised the ire of the WAFL clubs who saw their star players being taken by either the Eagles or VFL clubs for much less than expected. Despite missing the West Coast coaching job, John was dismayed by the bad blood between the WAFL clubs and the Eagles and, in February 1987, he called for more unity and cooperation so football could prosper. He arranged for the Eagles to play Swans in a practice game at Bassendean Oval, their first outing as a team, but as the year wore on there were few other supporters of the Eagles in WAFL ranks.

Unsure of how to best fixture the WAFL games to fit in with Eagles matches, the WAFL initially opted for double-headers; almost 24,000 people saw West Coast win their first game against Richmond (with a nine goal last quarter), but the West Perth-East Perth game that followed was marred by the sight of thousands of fans leaving the ground. The WAFL quickly scrapped further double-headers and the impact of the Eagles on local crowds was quickly evident. About 15,000 fans attended the first full round of WAFL fixtures a week later (with the Eagles away in Melbourne); that compared dismally to the comparative 1986 figure of 35,000 fans. As the WAFL juggled games between Friday nights, Saturdays and Sundays, 311,678 people attended the qualifying rounds and, with the 289,364 fans who saw the 11 Eagles home games, a total of just over 600,000 people saw senior football in the West, almost 20,000 less than in 1986. With the WAFL crowds halved from the previous year, a severe drop in income was accompanied by big decreases in sponsorship and bar trade, causing reductions in office and bar staff and serious difficulty in paying players. Not surprisingly, there was a good deal of resentment towards the Eagles, which soon flowed over into football matters. At one stage, Subiaco announced that their players would not be permitted to be called up by the Eagles at the last minute after Glenn O'Loughlin replaced an injured Malaxos on the morning of a match, while East Fremantle played full-forward Darren Bennett in their reserves side when he returned from injury, rather than disrupt their league side.

When John took over as coach of the Eagles, little changed. In fact, the 1988 crowd total fell by about 40,000, mostly due to lower attendances at Eagles games. The WAFL clubs were further rocked when the VFL aired proposals for the Eagles to expand their list from 35 to 52 players, enter a reserves side in 1989 and also reinstitute a draft to include WA players after agreeing to a two year moratorium. Swans president Bill Walker said the Eagles should withdraw from the competition if these proposals went ahead, sentiments echoed by the Fight for Football lobby, and, while the clubs were united publicly in their opposition to the VFL, privately it was a different matter. In August 1988, VFL Commissioner the late Alan Schwab revealed that East Fremantle and South Fremantle had made enquiries about entering another WA side if this happened and a day later it was revealed that six of the eight WAFL clubs had actually done so.

These proposed changes largely didn't come in, with the draft watered down, the Eagles list growing to 40, not 52 and no reserves side eventuated. But calls for the Eagles to be disbanded and the WAFL reinstated as the premier football competition became louder in 1989 as they struggled to win games and the WA football system found itself $10 million in debt. Indian Pacific Ltd, the Eagles parent company, was broke and the WAFL and the clubs had crushing debts [103]. However, thoughts of withdrawing from the VFL were never seriously entertained by the WAFL or the Eagles. In particular, the five key shareholders who guaranteed the West Coast share float by putting up $1 million each in 1987 were not about to see the castle fall over.

With State government assistance and the establishment of the WA Football Commission, which repurchased the Eagles sub-licence from Indian Pacific shareholders, football dragged

---

103. After almost folding at the start of the decade, Subiaco were now financially secure, helped by a sponsorship deal returning $200,000 for winning the 1986 flag and lucrative seating and signage deals at Subiaco helping record a profit of $442,000 for 1988.

itself back from the brink. The Commission received 75% of the Eagles annual surplus (in 2003 it was 80%[104]) and the control of Subiaco Oval was vested in it by the government, which represented a considerable annual cost saving. By the end of 1989 the financial crisis had eased, although times were still tough for the WAFL clubs, as illustrated by the fate of the pre-season competition. This had begun in 1982 with the Red Rooster carnival, which became the Kresta Blinds Cup in 1987, with $100,000 prize money. By 1988 there was only $10,000 on offer and in 1989 the series disappeared completely. In 1990, a salary cap of $100,000 per club was set by the Commission, a reduction of $50,000 from 1987, but with the on-field success of the Eagles in 1990, calls for the club to be disbanded slowly faded. The new landscape for WA football had been consolidated.

~

Although things were going bust off the ground for much of the decade, there were many exciting developments in the game – the quality of football played, especially in the first half of the 1980s, was outstanding. In 1981 the initial stage of Subiaco Oval's redevelopment was completed, with the opening of the $4 million two-tier stand. All clubs gave up one home game each so more fixtures could be staged at league headquarters to make use of the facilities and in 1982 a $200,000 electronic scoreboard was added. The raised profile of the VFL was acknowledged in 1981 as Swans and South played their preliminary final on a Sunday to avoid a clash with the VFL grand final, telecast live into WA on the Saturday. In future seasons the WAFL scheduled the grand final a week before the VFL and the match was promoted more aggressively, with the introduction of a Friday lunchtime city parade for the competing sides. Pre-season national club competition matches arrived in 1982 and Sunday games increased as the WAFL sought to maximise crowds and exposure. In 1983 live TV coverage of Sunday matches was trialled, but quickly shelved after disappointing attendances.

In 1984 the Sandover Medal count was moved to the Perth Entertainment Centre and thrown open to the public but, while well-attended, the occasion was demeaned with loud booing by sections of the audience in response to the awarded votes and this experiment was quickly discontinued. In 1987 the redevelopment of the WACA Ground saw football return to the home of cricket for the first time since Perth left for Lathlain Park in 1959. The Demons and East Perth played most of their 1987-89 home games at the arena, but the move was unpopular with members and by 1990 the Eagles were left to it, with Friday night football proving popular, with many sell-out crowds. In 1982, it cost $4 to get into the football; by 1987 when the Eagles arrived, WAFL admission had increased to $5.50 and it cost a minimum of $7.50 to watch VFL games in Perth.

The decade saw more experiments with new rules, but most were discarded. In 1986, the line across the centre circle to keep opposing ruckmen separated at the bounce was dropped (only to return in 1994) and the send off rule was introduced to the colts, but never used and subsequently deleted the next year. However, this would also reappear in 1991, but not in the AFL. In 1988 a player had to kick, rather than handball, when disposing of the ball from a

---

104. The Eagles have since contributed more than $50 million to WA football as a result of this arrangement and returned a profit every year since 1989.

free kick and, when kicking in after a behind was scored, a player couldn't kick to themselves and play on from the goal-square. These changes were also dropped after one season and have not resurfaced.

Also noteworthy in 1988 was an early-season strike by the umpires, which led to former players such as Ron Alexander, Noel Carter, Paul Mountain and Greg Brehaut officiating as field umpires on the weekend of April 24-25. Alexander added to his playing and coaching achievements by being the only umpire to lodge a report, citing Peter Worsfold (South Fremantle) for striking Tony Papotto (Perth), with the Bulldog receiving a suspended sentence.

The important tactical innovation in the WAFL for the '80s was the use of players in tagging roles to negate star opposition players. When John played in the '50s and '60s and similarly in the '70s, star players in the same positions usually opposed each other directly. However, at the start of the '80s John instigated the role of the tagger; a hard running and hard tackling, but perhaps less skilled player whose job was to run with an opposition star and nullify his influence. This role often saw the tagger not gaining any significant possessions himself as long as he kept the key opposition player quiet. John pioneered this role with the likes of Bill Skwirowski, Craig Holden and Jon Fogarty at Swans, initially using this tactic with good effect against the Krakouer brothers from Claremont. In the 1980 *Football Register*, editor Peter Poat marked the arrival of tagging by reporting that *"Swans coach John Todd succeeded in a tactical masterstroke when he found a way to curb the Krakouers, and in doing so, effectively restricted Claremont's firepower"*. Geoff Christian, in *The West Australian*, reported on the new strategy by saying – *"That tactic by coach John Todd provided some of the best talking points of the weekend, but left Jim Krakouer in particular, unamused and spoiling for satisfaction"*. Colin Hopkins added to the story by saying *"Todd's ploy of playing Bill Skwirowski on Jim Krakouer and Craig Holden on Phil Krakouer worked perfectly"*.

John explains the role by saying – *"The star opposition players would take Skwirowski and co. to where the ball was. Then they had to try and nullify them in the one-on-one contests"*. The use of taggers who changed with their opponents when they went off the ball had the additional effect of *"freeing up the forward line"*. He adds – *"It was then possible to have five or six mobile forwards, who could run up the ground and apply more midfield pressure, instead of having two players who were resting in pockets or on flanks after coming off the ball"*. John always viewed the half-forward flank and forward pocket as potential *"graveyards"* for smaller players. In his teams, *"these players were instructed to get up the ground and into the action and not make it comfortable for their opponents by sitting in a pocket or on a flank waiting for the ball to arrive"*.

The Swans premiership sides of the early '80s contained several players who could perform the tagging role and Skwirowski was the player best remembered for this, making the WA team in 1985 as tagging entered the State arena. However, he disliked the label, telling the press in 1980 that *"I'm no tagger"* when his new role came under notice. Other coaches to make good use of the tactic were Haydn Bunton (Jnr) in Subiaco's 1986 and '88 premiership sides and Mal Brown, both at South Fremantle and Perth. By the end of the decade it was a well-accepted tactic and remains so to this day. The notion of getting the right match ups across the ground, as is prevalent in current times, was a natural development of this tactic as the defensive aspects were emphasised more as the decade wore on. As a result, the 'cricket scores' top sides regularly kicked early in the decade became less frequent. The other new tactic from the early '80s was the 'huddle' at kick-ins after a behind was scored, first introduced by Robert Walls at Fitzroy. WA and VFL coaches were perhaps a little cautious about trying these kick-in innovations and it wasn't until the last few seasons of the decade that they became regular features of WAFL and VFL/AFL matches.

~

Before the arrival of the VFL in WA, the State enjoyed its golden era in interstate matches, with four national championships from 1979 and three in four years from 1983-86, an unprecedented run of success. The '84 and '86 victories required wins over SA in Adelaide, making them all the more meritorious. In each of these championship wins WA players took out the Tassie Medal for the carnival's best player – Brian Peake in '79, Stephen Michael in '83 and Brad Hardie in '84 and '86, the only dual winner in the award's history. However, his impressive record in State football counted for little in 1987 when John left him out of the State of Origin side to play Victoria. Hardie had transferred from Footscray to the fledgling Brisbane Bears after falling out with Mick Malthouse and had struggled to re-gain form, but he felt his record as a big game player should have been sufficient for his selection – and he said so. But for John reputations have never guaranteed a right to be picked, particularly for the State where he has always been keen to blood enthusiastic newcomers. WA's dominance of State football was of concern to the VFL in the lead-up to the expansion of their competition in 1987. The Melbourne clubs felt they would be confronting a WA side each week and this fear almost swung the vote against the inclusion of the Eagles. To placate their clubs, the VFL allowed two extra Form Fours per club to sign WA players at the end of the 1986 season – hoping to dilute the State's depth before a two year recruiting moratorium came into effect in WA.

The birth of the Eagles marked the end of this golden era for WA and between 1987 and '89 the only victory was in 1988 by a WAFL side coached by Gerard Neesham against the VFA in Perth. Seven other interstate defeats – four against Victoria, two at the hands of South Australia (who hadn't joined the VFL yet) and the embarrassing defeat by NSW in Adelaide in '88 – completed a bleak period. However, the exciting new level of competition provided by the Eagles softened the blow, at least for the public, as interstate crowds dipped markedly from the 40,000-plus attendances of the early '80s. In 1989, only 21,000 fans attended the WA-Victoria State of Origin clash, and interstate football, at least in WA, was on a downward spiral to redundancy as the success of the Eagles captured the hearts of the fans in the early '90s.

~

Apart from the great interstate clashes in the '80s, there were also some outstanding team and individual performances. Team-wise the decade belonged to the 'Cinderella' sides of the WAFL, Swans, Claremont and Subiaco, who had for so long been the poor relations of the competition. At the start of the '80s Swans had only three flags, Claremont four and Subiaco five. Next was Perth with seven premierships. By the end of the decade Claremont and Subiaco had joined the Demons, while Swans had doubled their tally to six. Swans made the finals seven times (1980-85 and '87) for four grand finals (1980, 82-84) and three flags (1982-84), Claremont missed the finals just once, in 1985, for six grand finals (1981-83 and 1987-

89) and three premierships (1981, '87 and '89) and Subiaco four times (1985-88) for four grand finals and two flags (1986 and '88); easily the most successful decade in the respective club histories. The other flags went to South (1980) and East Fremantle (1985), with the Perth clubs not winning a flag between them for the decade, for the first time in their histories. Perth only made the finals once (1986), West Perth three times (1982, '85 and '89) and East Perth four times (1980-82 and '84).

Swans earned the title of the best side of the decade for achieving a hat trick of premierships and only losing one grand final. Claremont and Subiaco played in three and four consecutive grand finals respectively, but could not achieve either back-to-back or triple success. However, in two of their three premiership years, Claremont produced outstanding seasons. In 1981 under Graham Moss, Claremont lost only two games and finished the qualifying rounds with the staggering total of points scored of 3352 (the WAFL record) and a percentage of 157.5. In 1987 under Neesham, the Tigers lost only one game and drew another and, while their total points scored were only 2692, their percentage slightly exceeded the 1981 figure, being 158.8.

Neesham had been an immediate success as Claremont captain-coach, taking them to a resounding victory over Subiaco in the 1987 grand final. In fact, he holds a unique record in WA football as from 1983 to '91 he was involved as a player, coach or both in every grand final, spread over three clubs – 1983 and '84 at Swans, 1985 and '86 at East Fremantle and 1987-91 at Claremont, for a total of six premierships. He would add another as coach of Claremont in 1993 before stepping down midway through the 1994 season to prepare to coach Fremantle in the AFL. In his seven seasons as Claremont coach they missed the finals only once (1992). His success as a coach was no surprise to John, who saw from the start of his career at East Fremantle in 1975 that *"he had a fine head for the game and was tactically aware and very shrewd"*. He also had a fierce desire to win and was not adverse to using *"fair means or foul"* to get an advantage on an opponent, a characteristic that saw him visit the Tribunal several times. At Swans, he was a team organiser on the ground, always having plenty to say and John knew he was a coach in waiting.

However, the decade belonged to John in regard to coaching achievements. Four grand finals for three premierships, seven finals with Swans in eight seasons, successive national championships as State coach, twice national coach with a series win (away) over Ireland and taking the Eagles to their first finals appearance in only their second season was an imposing record for a decade of coaching; by far the most successful era of his long career.

Many records which still stand today were also set in the 1980s. The WAFL's highest team score in open competition of 40.18 (258) was kicked by South Fremantle against West Perth on September 5, 1981 when South rover Noel Carter kicked 11 goals, the most by a player other than a full-forward in WAFL history. The hapless Cardinals scored 12.6 (78) and lost by a massive 180 points. In 1986 and again in '87, the record for the most goals kicked by a player in a final was set and equalled when Darren Bennett (East Fremantle) and Warren Ralph (Claremont) posted 10 goals in winning second semi-finals.

In the 1981 Sandover Medal, Stephen Michael recorded the highest votes polled[105] when he received 37 to win his second successive medal, polling votes in 15 games with nine best-on-

---

105. The previous record of 34 votes was set in 1937 when South Fremantle's Frank 'Scranno' Jenkins won the medal.

ground performances. Second was 1982 winner Phil Narkle, whose 25 votes would have won him the medal in all but three seasons since 1955, when John won his Sandover, with that tally. In 1984, the first (and only) three-way tie for the Sandover Medal was recorded, ironically in the first season since the WAFL had dropped the countback system after the 1983 tie between John Ironmonger and Bryan Cousins. Steve Malaxos, Michael Mitchell and Peter Spencer all received their 1984 medals on the night, but Cousins had to wait 14 years for his until the WAFL awarded medals retrospectively for all countback losers.

In 1985 Murray Wrensted won the first medal decided by a 5-4-3-2-1 voting system when he polled 46 votes (still the record) to win from Mitchell. Unfortunately for Wrensted, it was the year Channel 7 discontinued their $20,000 sponsorship of the medal. In 1987, Derek Kickett (Claremont) also polled 46 votes, 16 more than Perth's Mark Watson, but he was ineligible, having been suspended for striking former Subiaco, Richmond, Footscray and East Fremantle player and future West Coast Eagles selector and runner, Tim Gepp. Mid year John caused a stir when he left Kickett out of the State side to play SA, saying he thought *"the tempo of State football would be beyond him"*, which enraged Claremont and Neesham, who sprang to Kickett's defence. While he missed State selection in 1987, Kickett would eventually play State of Origin football for WA – winning the Leon Larkin Medal introduced by weekly football newspaper *Westside Football* for WA's best player against Victoria and he went on to play with distinction for North Melbourne, Essendon and Sydney.

In John's view, the outstanding players of the era were South Fremantle's Michael and Maurice Rioli and Swans duo Phil Narkle and Leon Baker – *"Michael thoroughly deserved his two Sandover Medals as he had great ability to lift the side, either by skill or physical strength. He was really a knock ruckman who was also a great ruck-rover because of his mobility around the ground. Rioli was similar, just a smaller version, as he could get the side moving with a brilliant piece of skilful play, or stem the opposition flow with a superb, hard defensive effort"*. His three Simpson Medals in the early '80s are testament to his class in big games [106]. There were few better tacklers in the game than these two players and in tandem they were a large part of the reason why South had Swans measure in 1980-81.

Narkle was nicknamed 'Magic' at Swans and it was an apt description, as John remembers his skills as *"being as good as anyone he has seen. While not an overly physical player because of his small stature, he had cat-like agility and could take a strong overhead mark. His disposal on both sides of his body was usually immaculate, which allowed him to evade most opposition attempts at tackling"*. Unfortunately, serious ankle and knee injuries suffered while playing for St Kilda hampered his career and WA fans didn't see him at his best when he returned to play for the Eagles in 1987.

Baker was *"one of the best players I had the privilege to coach. He could virtually play anywhere, was good in the air and on the ground, had great skills and loved to tackle"*. Despite starting his league career late at 24, he left an indelible impression at both Swans and Essendon, where he was highly-rated by coach Kevin Sheedy, playing in successive VFL premierships (1984-85) after two in a row at Swans (1982-83) to complete a remarkable four

---

106. He won Simpson Medals in the 1980 and '81 grand finals and in the '83 State of Origin game against Victoria.

years. However, but for that fickle change of weather in early 1982, Baker could have been lost to the game after only one season.

Inaugural Eagles captain Ross Glendinning, who John coached in several State games as well as in 1988, is also highly regarded, as confirmed by his Brownlow Medal victory with North Melbourne in 1983. He was *"difficult to counter as he had great poise and strength, both in marking contests and in the packs, and would often leave the opposition standing in his wake as he won the ball with seemingly effortless ease"*. While probably past his prime in 1988, he was *"a terrific spearhead"* for the Eagles, kicking 73 goals for the season.

John Worsfold, the Eagles club champion in 1988, is also well remembered by John – *"He was always going to be a great leader, but people perhaps forget how good a player he was"*. In 1988 and '89 John used Worsfold as the player to give the side a lift, putting him into the centre for bounce-downs or pushing him forward to create a goal when the side was in trouble. He rarely let the team down and it was Worsfold who gave the Eagles their final chance to win the elimination final against Melbourne in 1988 as he *"crashed the pack at the centre bounce and just forced the ball forward with his sheer physical presence"*.

Lastly, one player John feels was prevented by injury from really leaving his mark on the game in the 1980s was Swans centreman Mike Smith, a brilliant left-footer who suffered a serious knee injury at the start of 1981. While he made it back to play in Swans 1983 premiership side and then went to Carlton, he never regained the heights of his play in 1979 and '80, as the knee injury continued to dog him. John remembers a game at Fremantle Oval when Smith and Rioli engaged in an epic battle, with honours probably even – *"He had uncanny skills and with better luck with injury he would have become one of WA's great players"*. Smith retired in 1987 after only 78 games with Swans.

The 1990s

Chapter 22
Bouncing back

John, speaking after Swans 1990 premiership win and what it meant to him personally:

"It gave me great joy, not just for the players and the club, but for my own personal ego and satisfaction. You can never rest on your laurels in this game. People can forget quickly, they remember your last game and often forget the rest, so it was good to remind them".

The formalities of John's departure from the Eagles had been made official at a meeting with Neil Hamilton and Bill Kerr a few hours before the announcement of Michael Malthouse's appointment. Hamilton had apologised for the leak, John had expressed his disgust at their *"lack of professionalism"* and little else had been said as he departed to contemplate his next chapter in the game.

However, despite having just endured his worst season in football, John's passion for the game remained undiminished. Leaving the sport was not something he had given the slightest consideration to. The time-honoured sporting adage that you are only as good as your last game – which he preached often to his players – now loomed large in his own situation. His last game (and last season) hadn't been good and he was desperate to atone, quickly declaring that he was *"more determined than ever to remain in football"*. Not keeping the Eagles job was another setback in his long career and had seriously pricked his pride, but he was fixed on proving his (many) critics wrong. Many times throughout the season, sections of the media had questioned his coaching ability, so the challenge to answer these critics was a driving motivation and it didn't take long for an opportunity to present itself. Ed Blackaby's two year appointment as Swans coach (he was John's recommended successor) was up for renewal and he definitely wanted to retain the job, but Bill Walker was quick to move on John when the Eagles announced their decision. To Blackaby's dismay, Walker told him the job was John's if he wanted it, but otherwise his contract would be extended.

For John, the chance to return to Swans was appealing; they had finished out of the finals in the past two seasons, so there was the challenge of resurrecting the club's fortunes. This also extended to their off-field financial security, as the club, like most others in the WAFL, was mired in debt and battling to survive, requiring the launch of an SOS (Save Our Swans) appeal to raise $150,000 for debt reduction. After learning of the club's financial woes, it was an easy decision to make – Swans held a special place in his heart after they had *"stuck with me in the late '70s and early '80s before the premiership successes"*. Ten days after reading the morning newspaper telling of his loss of the Eagles job he was appointed coach of Swans for the next five years.

A five year contract was testimony to the respect John commanded at Swans and also reflected the uncertain times WAFL clubs faced. Walker proudly stated that the club now had *"Australia's best coach"* back with them and there is little doubt John was seen as a potential saviour of the club as well. His lofty profile was important in helping attract sponsorship and financial support as the administration grappled with existing liabilities of close to $500,000. Securing John for five years was seen as a sound long-term investment, but the unfortunate downside was that it left Blackaby out in the cold; for him, losing the coaching position was a bitter blow, especially after quitting his job in mid-1988 to concentrate full-time on coaching. However, as John Cooper said – *"It was a case of a seasoned thoroughbred up against a two-year-old and it was a logical choice"*. John understood Blackaby's disappointment and was not surprised when he left the club and never really returned; this was an unhappy side-effect made all the more difficult because of John's great admiration for Blackaby as a player and coach. Blackaby followed John's example of some 20 years earlier by coaching in the Sunday league, with instant success in taking Osborne Park to the 1990 premiership, but he didn't return to the WAFL scene.

John was soon made more aware of Swans financial troubles and, at a pre-season sponsors' function, he was besieged by local businessmen about the team's prospects. When asked if a premiership was possible, he naturally said yes, although his initial assessment of the squad probably told him no. Keen to help the club out of its financial predicament, a sponsorship deal was negotiated by the businessmen which offered Swans $150,000 for winning the flag. It was a financial lifeline, but the tricky part of the deal was yet to come.

In 1990, the WASFL [107] was on a *"hiding to nothing"*, with the WA Football Commission imposing a $100,000 salary cap on the clubs, who were given the year to prove their financial viability or risk not having their licence renewed. These were desperate times and John traded on this theme to inspire the players – *"I urged them to just get on with it, to shoot for the top and prove to everyone that Swans were in the competition to stay and would not be rolling over without one hell of a fight"*. These sentiments equally applied to him as well, as he strove to put the disasters and disappointments of 1989 behind him.

One of John's first moves was to get old friend John Cooper back to the fold. In August 1989, the members' area at Bassendean Oval had been officially named the John Cooper/John Todd Pavilion, so John prevailed on Cooper to return as chairman of selectors in order to (with tongue in cheek) *"earn the right to keep your name up there next to mine"*. Cooper was only too pleased to help out his old mate and readily accepted the role. On field, there was a small core of players who had experienced premiership success with John in the early '80s such as Don Holmes (who came back mid-season after retiring), Brent Hutton, Don Langsford and Brad Shine, with Phil Narkle and Murray Rance still on the Eagles list. Swans also had Troy Ugle on the Eagles list, but only Narkle would play regularly with the Black and Whites in 1990. There were also several promising youngsters blooded by Blackaby and, after just missing the 1989 finals and with John back at the helm, Swans were expected to improve.

---

107. In 1990 the competition was re-named the WA State football league, but this was dropped the following year.

Chapter 22 – Bouncing back

The season started well, with six wins in the first round leaving Swans on top of the ladder; a position they held at the end of the second round with an 11-3 win/loss record. They stamped themselves as genuine premiership contenders, along with Claremont and South Fremantle, who had 10 and nine wins respectively. Their form then dipped – four losses in the next six weeks and a home loss to East Perth in the second last qualifying game saw Swans slip to third spot. In the final set of fixtures, Swans got up in time-on to beat league leaders Claremont by seven points and East Perth downed South, allowing them to regain second spot and the double chance. They met the Tigers again in the second semi-final two weeks later, a day after the Eagles fought out a thrilling draw against Collingwood in the AFL qualifying final. The WASFL game was billed as the battle of the coaches as Gerard Neesham tackled his former mentor for the first time in a final. Swans held the edge over the Tigers during the season, winning all three games, but two were by narrow margins and the second semi was seen as an even-money contest. However, Claremont were well on top for three quarters, holding a 3-4 goal break before Swans found some spark and rattled on five goals. But the Tigers steadied and reversed the result of two weeks earlier, winning by seven points.

With the Eagles in the AFL finals, the media attention on the WASFL finals was sparse – John now had no need to impose a media ban on his players, as they were unlikely to see any press at training. This became even less likely on the Tuesday after the game when *The Daily News* closed its doors, leaving Perth without an afternoon newspaper. In the preliminary final against South, the chances of securing the $150,000 premiership bonus seemed remote, with the Bulldogs in control at half-time, leading by 22 points. However, the opportunity was resurrected with a six goal to two third quarter by Swans, leaving them just ahead at the final break. A further six goals in the last term saw them win by 27 points to secure a grand final berth.

Much of the pre-game build up again centred on the coaches, with John likely to tag the Claremont midfield and how Neesham's 'possession' game would stand up to close physical attention from their opponents. This was John's main thrust for the game – *"By putting enormous physical pressure on their opponents and having one-chase-one while everyone else stayed with their man, I was convinced Claremont would eventually give the ball up, by being forced into error as they tried to keep possession"*. He felt their chip-and-run style always *"gave you a chance to pinch the ball back, providing you were disciplined on manning up and hard at the ball"*. Once Swans had possession, they played long and direct to further catch their opponents out of position, as they had often run wide to receive. He also had a perfect rallying point for the team to provide that *"little bit of an extra motivation"*. Club captain Brad Shine had endured a terrible year with injury, managing only three games and was unfit for the grand final. However, at John's request, he led the side out and tossed the coin before watching the game from the bench. To add to the moment, Brent Hutton shed his normal No. 10 guernsey to wear Shine's No. 2 jumper, providing a visual and constant reminder of their captain who couldn't be out there.

Claremont had an early ascendency, but goal-front inaccuracy cost them and they led by only seven points at quarter-time. A seven goal second term on the back of Swans midfield dominance saw them lead by 19 points at half-time. Five further goals in the third quarter, as Claremont frequently turned the ball over when forced into error, extended the lead to a match-winning 45 points at the last change. Inaccuracy again plagued the Tigers as they kicked

2.8 in a last-ditch fight-back but, despite not goaling in the term, Swans had enough control to run out 26 point winners.

Swans had their seventh flag and John his fifth, joining Haydn Bunton (Jnr), John Leonard and Jerry Dolan as the coaches with the most WAFL premierships since the Page system of finals was introduced in 1931. On receiving his premiership medallion at the on-ground presentation, John called Shine to the stage and gave it to him to recognise his contribution to the club, not only on the day, but over the past 10 years. Another record went Swans way when rover Greg Walker won the Simpson Medal to follow father Bill [108] and become the only father-son combination to win the award.

For John, the premiership win was very satisfying, but had a little more personal feeling than before, as he felt he had silenced the critics in the best possible way – *"It gave me great joy, not just for the players and the club, but for my own personal ego and satisfaction. You can never rest on your laurels in this game. People can forget quickly, they remember your last game and often forget the rest, so it was good to remind them"*. Fittingly, he received the JJ (John) Leonard Medal for Coach of the Year in 1990. However, both then and now, he reflects that this premiership was different to the other four because of the impact of the AFL. Only 26,000 fans watched the match, well down from crowds of up to 50,000 in the pre-Eagles grand finals. But, despite the lower WAFL profile, the achievement of the players should not be underrated in any way, as *"they created their own piece of history, which can never be taken away from them"*. While this is certainly true, the reality is that post-1986 WAFL achievements are seen in a different light. At Swans, the 1990 premiership is, in many respects, the 'forgotten flag' as supporters will readily rattle off the 1961-63 and 1982-84 hat tricks, but often overlook that triumph. Similarly, the 1990 players aren't as well remembered as those in the '60s and '80s teams, as John readily acknowledges.

The other aspect of the 1990 victory which greatly pleased John was the $150,000 bonus; a terrific financial boost. It gave the club much-needed breathing space, helping reduce their debt. But the situation was accompanied by a loss of over $100,000 for the season. Despite the premiership win, in the harsh economic climate of the 1990s, on field success for the WAFL clubs was no guarantee for off field prosperity.

~

After several weeks of fishing and relaxing, John returned for the 1991 campaign and, with Swans previous premierships coming in threes, there was great expectation that the pattern would continue in the '90s. Veterans Langsford and Holmes had retired, sharing a club record four premierships, but Narkle was now full-time after retiring from the Eagles and Mike Richardson and Kevin Caton had returned from Brisbane and Fitzroy respectively. Rance and Ugle would have fairly complete seasons at Bassendean as they faded from the AFL scene, so the team had gained, rather than lost, experience and John felt that back-to-back flags was a realistic prospect.

---

108. He won the Simpson Medal against SA in 1967.

Chapter 22 – Bouncing back

However, it was not to be. As in 1985, Subiaco and Bunton ended the dream with a 32 point win in the preliminary final after Swans had put together good patches and bad throughout the season, finishing third with 12 wins, but failing to beat Claremont or Subiaco in the final two rounds. The Lions proved their masters in the qualifying[109] and preliminary final, but were no match for Claremont in the grand final, with the Tigers winning by 77 points. For John, the season was a frustrating and disappointing one, as he acknowledged in Swans 1991 annual report – *"On paper we had as good a side as any in the competition, but we failed to carry that onto the field. Our attitude lacked desperation, enthusiasm and, probably what was the biggest factor of our demise, the lack of closeness and team work which we had created over previous years"*. The highlight of the year for John was seeing one of his favourite players, Narkle, have an injury-free season, finishing runner-up in the Sandover Medal[110], two votes shy of repeating his 1982 win. As he says, *"To win Sandover Medals 10 years apart would have been a great feat and it would have been terrific for him to get up. It really would have capped off a great career"*. Only Barry Cable (1964 and '73) has achieved this honour, with Peter Spencer (1976 and '84) the next best.

The next three seasons really mirrored the Swans year of 1991 as the side was always well-placed to make the finals – third in '92 with 13 wins, second in '93 with 13 wins and fifth in '94 with 12 wins. However, the side departed the finals in 'straight sets' in '92 and '93 and lost the elimination final in '94. In '92 Mal Brown again proved John's finals nemesis, coaching South to a resounding 92 point win in the qualifying final. John's only finals win out of six clashes against Brown was the '83 preliminary final. In '93 and '94, former charges Neesham and Tony Solin (coaching Subiaco) ended Swans finals chances. In all, 15 of his former players have gone on to coach at senior level in the WAFL or the AFL[111], not an especially high number given the many hundreds of players he has coached, although many more have coached at lower levels. John's reason for this is simple – *"Why would you want to coach? It's a tough and lonely job. Playing the game is much more fun!"*.

1990 – Swans four time premiership coach and players. With Don Langsford (left) and Don Holmes.

109. The WAFL introduced a final five for the 1991 season.
110. Subiaco's Ian Dargie won the first of his two medals in 1991.
111. They are Gerard Neesham, Tony Solin, Tom Mullooly, Graham Melrose, Colin Beard, Ken Judge, Tony Micale, Andrew Lockyer, Geoff Miles, Shane Cable, John Worsfold, Don Pyke, Peter Sumich, Dean Laidley and Guy McKenna.

These four seasons were a frustrating time for John. There were plenty of injuries which didn't help the cause, but the inability of the side to win finals contests indicated to him a weakness in the character of the players. He could only conclude that, after so many final round opportunities, *"not enough wanted it badly enough and it's difficult, almost impossible, for a coach to put that hunger into players. They have to really want it themselves"*. As in 1968 and '76, he knew it was time to leave, as he didn't see himself able to get any more out of the current crop of players. It was either leave or clean out players who he felt hadn't measured up in finals and re-build the team, but his instincts told him it was time to give someone else a go *"to see if they could put the icing on the cake"*. Reluctantly, president Walker accepted his view, although he was keen for John to continue. After 16 years at Swans, he had left an indelible mark on the club, not just in premiership flags, but also on the culture and philosophies of the place. His passion for the game, refusal to yield and to push on and persevere when circumstances were difficult had left its imprint and this legacy helped keep the club afloat as it struggled to control mounting debt problems. In 1994 income had fallen about $70,000 short of budget projections, further compounding their financial troubles and Swans now faced an uncertain future without one of the most influential figures in the club's history.

~

In the wash up after the 1990 grand final, John McGrath in *The West Australian* quite aptly described John as *"one of the great survivors of WA football"*. He puts his own longevity down to two things – *"firstly, my enthusiasm for the game which never wavered despite all the ups and downs and, secondly, I was an 'underdog' coach, one who liked to build and develop a team from scratch. This took time and instant success was never expected when I took over a team"* – apart from perhaps West Coast in 1988. There is no doubt John was also able to move with the times as a coach. He was flexible and accommodating (to a point) of the social, family and employment circumstances of his players, but also to the changing face of football in WA.

Many people commented that, when he returned to the WAFL in 1990 after two seasons with the Eagles, he was a changed man. In comparison to his persona in the 1970s and '80s, he certainly seemed more at peace with both himself and the world. By necessity, he dropped the level of his demands on the players, as he recognised the reduced profile of the WAFL, and he admits to having *"mellowed a fair bit"* across the '90s, as his family, Walker, Rance and Mullooly, who coached the Swans colts in 1991-94, all readily agree. Gone were the irate outbursts against officialdom over seemingly trivial matters (the WAFL had enough to worry about!) and he was less likely to confront people and issues, at least in public. The umpires probably had an easier time of it, as did his players who noticed that the frequency of his vitriolic 'serves' were reduced, but not quelled completely. Bad losses no longer required an all-night drive to search out the reasons, and he was more understanding of a player's failings and weaknesses, providing they were still prepared to put in extra time and effort to improve.

Partly these changes were due to experiencing the VFL; it satisfied a long-held ambition that the knee injury had denied him. As a result he was more content with himself and more at ease with others. In addition, his changing mood was a reflection of where he saw the WAFL was at. With the great changes wrought in society by new technology and 'throw-away lifestyles', he quickly assessed that his old methods would not go far in the 1990s – *"With so many different work, social and sporting options available, people would often just walk away when things got too hard"*. He saw this type of attitude in many players and, with the financial rewards of playing in the WAFL drastically slashed, often it was easier to go and play in the country. He sums up the situation in the '90s by saying – *"If I coached now the way I coached in the '70s and '80s I would have had a mutiny on my hands and no players!"*.

Over this period John sustained his enthusiasm for the game from the satisfaction of seeing his players improve and graduate to AFL ranks, telling them (as always) how much the game had to offer. His eye for talent remained second-to-none. As a judge of ability, potential and character in young players, both Cooper and Walker *"have seen none better"*. At Swans from 1990-94 he introduced 45 first year players to league ranks, including the likes of Stephen O'Reilly (Geelong, Fremantle and Carlton), Jason Ball (West Coast and Sydney), 1999 AFL Coleman medallist Scott Cummings (Essendon, Port Adelaide, West Coast and Collingwood) and Craig Callaghan (Fremantle and St Kilda).

He was also a keen student of the AFL over this time; his WAFL life membership in 1991 gives him the opportunity to watch Eagles home games and he remains a strong supporter of West Coast. In 1992, he watched (on TV) with great joy as they took the AFL premiership cup for the first time – *"I was really proud of them, it was fantastic. They did the State proud. Most people rated them as a State team when they began and expected success to come easily, but few understood how difficult the early years were. With no home and no club structure it was very hard, plus breaking down the old WAFL club barriers and getting the players to unite as one took time"*. As a proud and passionate West Australian, he was delighted to see the cup taken from Victoria. For him to have coached the first side to achieve this feat would have been a crowning glory on his long career, but at the time he had no thoughts of *"what might have been"*. He has never dwelt on the past and is not interested in hypotheticals about whether the Eagles would have won a flag under his direction – *"Worry about today and tomorrow and about things you have some control over. Yesterday and last week are ancient history"*.

In the mid-1990s he became unwittingly embroiled in an incident involving West Coast which disappointed him greatly and left him threatening legal action for the first and only time in his life. It came about through the media (as was typical in his view) having *"no respect for individuals and no regard for the facts when they smell a chance to make something out of nothing"*. A Channel 7 camera crew spotted him talking with the Footscray coaching staff a few hours before a Friday night clash with West Coast at the WACA Ground. The vision was aired with a story line accusing John of plotting the Eagles downfall and questioning his loyalty to the State, a theme Eagles coach Malthouse also raised when shown the film.

In reality, he had been invited to the Perth hotel where the Bulldogs were staying by former Swans player Gordon Casey (now a member of their coaching panel) to catch up on old times, which the two did whenever Casey was in town. Casey introduced John to the other Footscray coaches as they walked past in the lobby just before the camera crew arrived. And that was all there was to it! John bristled at the suggestion he was passing information to the enemy and, as an extremely passionate and loyal West Australian, saw red when he was accused of being disloyal to the State. He recalls the incident – *"Over the years I gave out plenty of criticism and copped plenty in return, which was OK, but I was enraged when my loyalty to the State was questioned. I couldn't let this go, so for the first and only time, I sought the advice of a solicitor and fired off a letter to the station threatening legal action"*. The accusations also incensed daughter Debbie, who rang the Perth radio stations who carried the story on their sports programs to express her disgust at the treatment of her father. John also vented his spleen on Eagles general manager Brian Cook, but there was no dialogue with Malthouse; he probably tried to exploit the situation to spark the side, but the Eagles lost anyway! The incident blew over in a few weeks and John didn't pursue any action against the station, but he was *"very pissed off"* that it happened at all. It also certainly did nothing to endear Malthouse to Meryl, Debbie and Kylie.

As the Eagles success grew in the early '90s, Malthouse's profile in Perth followed. He was in great demand as an after-dinner and motivational speaker, for which he was usually well paid, often receiving $500 or more for his time. However, when he was unavailable, the next 'cab off the rank' was usually John and he did many of these engagements, mainly for charity which he generally found enjoyable and rewarding. Often though, he would 'forget' to ask for a fee, especially when it was a business lunch or dinner, and he often returned home with a bottle of wine or a set of glasses for his trouble. Many times Meryl, Bob Manning and other friends told him to ask for payment and that he should get a manager (as Malthouse had) to coordinate these speaking engagements. It could have been a lucrative sideline for him, but he never did. It just wasn't him. For a boy who had grown up in the bush and at Fremantle when times were pretty tough and who had never had (or missed) much in the way of material possessions, he just wasn't comfortable asking people for money to hear him speak. He was happy to tell his story, liberally dosed with humorous anecdotes about his life, but generally his advice was free, much to the resigned annoyance of Meryl. She enjoyed the wine, but had to give away plenty of wine glasses!

In 1993 the push for a second AFL team out of Perth began in earnest and in May 1994, Neesham was announced as the Fremantle coach for their first season in 1995. John had no contact with the people organising the new club and was not under consideration for the coaching position, which surprised many people given his experience at putting teams together from scratch, plus his time at West Coast. However, he was not disappointed and really had no interest in returning to the AFL; he was content with his lot and made no effort to sell himself to the new club. The West Coast experience in 1988 and '89 had satisfied his desires to coach at the highest level and he was proud of taking the Eagles to their first final. He was now happy to take a back seat and develop youngsters with potential in the WAFL. He thought Neesham's appointment was well-deserved given his great record with Claremont from 1987-93 (six grand finals and four premierships), although he wasn't sure his game plan would stand up to the pressure of AFL matches.

Chapter 23
Heading back home (twice)

John, remembering the night of South Fremantle's 1997 grand final win over arch rivals East Fremantle:

> "It [the derby] wasn't something I raised before the game, but it became important afterwards. It was great to see the older supporters who had followed the club in the 1950s, '60s and '70s keep up the derby traditions".

John Cooper, on John's efforts to help resurrect Swans from financial ruin in 2000:

> "If Toddy hadn't have returned to coach Swans, the club probably would have folded. He worked absolutely day and night for the club and, with all his flair and contacts, we got there. I give him as much credit as the board for getting the club over the line".

As John was deciding it was time to leave Swans, he was contacted by South Fremantle officials enquiring about what he was doing in 1995. South had only won six games in 1994 after making the finals in the previous two seasons and were looking for a new coach, having decided not to renew Mark Watson's contract. Once again, as in 1985, they were keen to get their most famous prodigal son back to Fremantle Oval. This time, with no opposition, they found the task relatively easy. The South Fremantle roots forged in the 1950s were still intact, despite no involvement with the club for 22 years. John saw it as the perfect place to end his coaching career and returning to where the journey started 40 years earlier as a 16-year-old had great appeal and symmetry to him. Not having played in a premiership at league level with South was an additional spur – perhaps he could coach them to a flag, the last of which had been in 1980 when they beat Swans.

In addition, there were two other motivating factors. Coaches, particularly after long careers, need to set goals for themselves the same as players do and John set himself to achieve two further coaching records. A sixth flag would make him the most successful coach in WA since the final four system was adopted in 1931 and a premiership with South would give him flags at three different clubs – a feat achieved by only one other WA coach, the late Sir Ross Hutchinson. Both men came from Deanmill, in WA's South West, and John had great admiration for Sir Ross, following his career (via Doris) as a player and coach, along with his exploits in the Air Force during the war and as a Liberal Member of Parliament, Cabinet Minister and Speaker of the House in the 1950s and '60s. Back in 1974 he could think of no-one better to address the East Fremantle players before the grand final and now he could think of nothing better than to emulate his coaching feat. He told the South board that a premiership was possible within three years as some team building was needed, to which they readily agreed. The prodigal son of 1955 had finally returned home.

In reality, while nothing can ever be taken for granted in sport, John really wanted to finish his career at South. Both he and Meryl had Fremantle roots and, despite the almost daily 45 minute drive to Bassendean Oval, they never contemplated moving from the district. In the year or two before rejoining South, Meryl recalls that often when going to the movies they would walk past Fremantle Oval and John would pause to watch training. She recalls John expressing dismay at the general state of the place, as *"it looked a bit run down"*, but more so at the presentation of the players, dressed in an assortment of shorts, jumpers, socks and T-shirts which he never liked. *"They need some discipline"* was his assessment of the situation, which Meryl took as the first sign of the seed to return being planted.

One of John's first actions as coach was telling the players that a new club uniform, at a personal cost of $240, was compulsory. This was a considerable sum for players to outlay as most would only receive $50-100 for a league game. However, he wanted to test their commitment and he followed with a decree that only a full South playing strip (supplied) could be worn at training, the same as when he last coached South in 1966. He organised a 'busy bee' involving the players to clean up the change rooms and surrounding facilities. For some players it was time to move on voluntarily, while others were moved out as he put his stamp back on the club, promising ample opportunities for younger players.

Much had changed at Fremantle Oval since he was last there. The oval precincts were now a council car park, which made access for training nights difficult. The Fremantle Dockers used the ground for training and South, to some degree, had to fit around this and negotiate with the WA Football Commission about the club's rights to retain its presence at Fremantle Oval. However, much of the old Fremantle spirit remained – the mixture of stoicism and knockabout humour he had first seen as a boy and then experienced as a player and coach in the 1950s and '60s was still there and it felt good to be back. He approached the new season with the same enthusiasm as any of his previous 26 seasons as a coach.

By mid-season the Bulldogs were fourth when the WAFL went into recess as the State side went to Brisbane to play Queensland, with John appointed coach in the absence of 1994 premiership mentor Ken Judge, who had left East Fremantle to join Carlton as an assistant coach. John was always pleased to lead WA into battle and on this occasion there was more than the usual amount of State pride at stake. Two weeks before the Queensland game, WA's State of Origin side, coached by Gary Buckenara, had lost in Perth to the Allies[112], the AFL's latest initiative in interstate football. For the WAFL State side to lose to Queensland, a rugby state where football only had a toehold, would complete a dismal year on the interstate scene.

Apart from emphasising the need to uphold State pride, John impressed upon the squad that *"it was a wonderful opportunity to show your wares and put your case forward to be drafted, as all the AFL talent scouts would be at the game"*. He used his old ploys to break down club ties and get the players together, such as training with imaginary footballs, which created plenty of humour. He also got them to appreciate the importance of communication with their team-mates by pairing them up with one wearing a blindfold and the other talking his partner

---

112. The Allies were made up of players who originated from the minor football states – NSW, Queensland, ACT, Northern Territory and Tasmania.

Chapter 23 – Heading back home (twice)

safely through some obstacles. These old tricks were well received by the players and they duly delivered victory by 27 points, with a side that included future AFL players such as Craig Treleven (who won the Simpson Medal), Daniel Chick, Fraser Gehrig, Todd Curley and Phil Matera (five goals).

After the State game South continued to improve and looked set to finish second, but then inexplicably lost their last three games against bottom sides to finish third on the ladder. It was an opportunity missed. In the first semi-final South were 38 point losers to East Fremantle, now coached by John's brother-in-law, Tony Micale, which presented a mild quandary for John's mother Doris, but her first loyalties were always with her son.

The 1996 year saw South fail to build on the relative success of '95 and, in an up and down season, could only manage sixth place, with injuries to senior players restricting their impact – losing six matches by seven points or less left them two games adrift of fourth spot. The plus in John's view was the 16 first year players blooded and he remained optimistic that success wasn't too far away, given a better run with injury. In 1997, his youth policy came to fruition as he found the right blend between the senior players and those nurtured over the previous two seasons. In particular, for three younger players he saw the opportunity to carve a special niche in the club's history. In South's last premiership in 1980, Stephen Michael, Maurice Rioli and Basil Campbell were key members of the side and now, 17 years and a generation later, Michael's son Clem, Rioli's nephew Dean[113] and Campbell's son Warren had the chance to emulate family feats and bring a premiership to the port. With a sense of history perhaps made more acute because he was on the losing side in 1980, John played up this opportunity to the three youngsters, because *"if I could get them playing well and chasing glory to match their fathers and uncles, that would put the icing on the cake as they all had wonderful talent"*. He didn't publicise this slant, as he didn't want too many people raising the prospect with the players. Instead, he spent additional time with them, doing one-on-one sessions at the club and swimming at the beach, talking to them about the game in general as well as the 1980 grand final deeds of their fathers/uncle to firmly plant the seed in their minds.

The side began the season with a thumping 104 point win over the fledgling Peel Thunder, the Mandurah-based club playing in the WAFL for the first time. The Bulldogs won seven of their first eight games to head the ladder, then lost three in a row before a strong second half of the season saw them finish on top, six points clear of the Sharks. A derby second semi-final created plenty of interest, although not as loud and deep as in the good old days before 1987. As so often happens, teams opposed in the last qualifying match end up playing each other in the finals and the Saturday night Fremantle Oval derby to finish the season gave South a 16 point victory. However, the tables were turned a week later[114] as Micale coached East Fremantle to a 25 point second semi-final win by successfully blanketing the influence of veteran full-forward Jon Dorotich, who had kicked 107 goals for the season. Dorotich bounced back with five goals to help South beat Perth by 37 points in the preliminary final and earn another crack at the Sharks.

---

113. Dean is the son of Sebastian Rioli, who played 48 games with South in the 1970s.
114. The WAFL played the first and second semi-finals as a double header so the finals were concluded a week before the AFL grand final.

John's three year plan was on course, but the biggest test was still ahead of them as family loyalties were put to the test as he and Micale squared off for the flag. It was Micale's first grand final and he admits it *"was strange coaching against John, who was my mentor and had been instrumental in starting my coaching career"*. In this case he found it difficult to *"hate the opposition"* as he normally would when preparing for a big match. Also in the South camp was John's brother Bill, who performed the role of player advocate at Tribunal hearings, while for Doris, Meryl, Debbie and Kylie, as well as Diane Micale, it wasn't about taking sides and wanting John or Tony to win, it was more about the fact that one was going to lose which made it difficult. No-one wanted to see either man suffer the pain of defeat. For Doris, with so much family involvement, the grand final is remembered as *"the best day of my life"*. For John though, it was very much *"business as usual"*.

In the lead up, John monitored closely the fitness of veteran Eagles pair David Hart and Peter Sumich, who were both injured in the preliminary final. In the end, he went with both players, particularly because it was Hart's last game before retiring, although he knew they weren't 100% fit. The gamble failed with Sumich, who limped off after only 10 minutes with a recurrence of a thigh strain, but Hart was an important contributor and saw the game out.

A Fremantle derby ensured the best grand final crowd for four years (32,371) and the match was a tight, hard fought and scrappy contest. South seemed a little *"off the pace"* and were three to four goals behind for most of the first three quarters, hanging in with great persistence – the Sharks were unable to deliver the knockout blow. Midway through the third term the margin reached 29 points, but two late South goals trimmed the deficit to 17 points at the last change. At this point, John rallied the players in order to change their mindset. He made them believe they could still win as long as they persisted for the whole quarter and never gave up. Predictably, as you would expect at three quarter-time in a grand final, he urged them to *"go for broke"* and be *"totally focused on winning the ball"*.

In the first 30 seconds of the final term, the Sharks stretched the lead to 23 points, but that was their last goal for the game. John sensed South were building some momentum and swung Hart to the centre, who found something extra to kick two goals, Rioli swooped on the crumbs from a Campbell tackle on an unsuspecting opponent and kicked his fourth and future Fremantle Docker Brad Bootsma, who played the second half with a broken bone in his leg, snapped truly to put South a point in front. The game closed up for 10 minutes as both sides fought for the advantage, then, with two minutes remaining, Campbell marked 70 metres from goal, under fierce pressure from Scott Spalding. Umpire Trevor Garrett deemed the challenge from Spalding to be late and signalled a 50 metre penalty. At the time John thought it was *"definitely on"* and Micale grudgingly conceded that *"it probably was"*. Campbell duly goaled from 20 metres out and South hung on to win by six points, 13.7 (85) to 11.13 (79).

Amid a sea of red and white flags, John soon found himself trapped in a Hart bear hug and, as Gary Stocks later wrote in The West Australian – *"As thousands of Bulldog supporters streamed onto the ground to celebrate the end of a 17 year drought at the expense of arch rival East Fremantle, Hart was hugging his coach like a long-lost father. In future years that is the image which will flood into the minds of anyone who saw it"*. John said – *"I never lost hope because I have always maintained that 30 points in the modern game is not enough. At 50 points you are normally safe, but with 30 you're not and all we had to do was turn it around a little. We

Chapter 23 – Heading back home (twice)

1997 – the last flag. On the premiership dais with the South Fremantle players. Captain Peter Worsfold is holding the cup. Ex West Coast premiership players David Hart (front row, second from right) David Hynes (back row, extreme right) and Peter Sumich (third row, second from left) were in the team.

Football wise, the WAFL used him as a mentor for junior coaches on a part-time basis and he watched the Eagles and Dockers regularly. In fact, in early 1999, at the urgings of his family who felt he was too young to retire, he offered his services to Fremantle as a selector and he had talks with chief executive David Hatt and coach Damian Drum. John felt he could help Drum cope with the corporate pressures of the job, drawing on his own experiences at West Coast and told him *"... sooner or later, the corporate wheelers and dealers behind the scenes will bring you down unless you learn to work with them"*. However, nothing eventuated, probably because Drum saw him as a threat to his authority, although John had no desire to fill a coaching role.

During 1999 he saw few WAFL games, as he was happy to *"mess around on Saturdays"* without any commitments, but one match was a must – a South-Swans clash at Fremantle Oval. They were playing for the John Todd Cup in recognition of his grand service to both clubs and he was to present the cup to the winning side. South, one of the top sides, were coached by Micale and it was the club's centenary year, so every effort had been made to make it a successful season. Swans were coached by former East Fremantle, Richmond and West Coast player Peter Wilson and (almost as usual) were doing it tough. South dished out a terrible hiding to Swans, which moved John to seek out Wilson after the game to offer some encouragement, but also find out what was happening at the club. Wilson didn't paint a rosy picture – the club was on its knees financially, so there were few resources he could call on to help attract or keep players and he couldn't see himself continuing next season. Dismayed and alarmed, John sought more information from John Cooper, who confirmed that the club was in dire straits and there were serious doubts about their ability to continue in the WAFL competition, as a pressing debt of $175,000 simply could not be serviced.

The only way out was a rescue operation involving an appeal to members and supporters to pledge donations to save the club and who better to head up the project than John, the longest serving and most successful coach in their history! After meeting with the Swans board and other club stalwarts such as Cooper, Bill Walker, Keith Slater and Haydn Bunton (Jnr), he decided to see what he could do. John felt obliged to lend a hand because *"I was indebted to the club for sticking with me through the hard times before the premiership successes of the 1980s, when they could easily have changed direction and cut me adrift"*. Swans hold an equal place in his heart with South, so he couldn't stand by and watch the club fall without personally fighting for its survival.

Initially he was happy to *"get out and beat the drum"* to raise money. Then Cooper suggested he come back as coach; with Wilson stepping down, the coaching role wasn't a terribly attractive proposition for prospective applicants. It wasn't something John had considered before Cooper's remark – he certainly didn't have *"itchy feet"* in 1999 and was content he had coached his last game. Cooper's suggestion got him thinking, especially when he was approached by Peel Thunder to coach them in 2000. In many respects, their approach solidified his thinking; if he was going to come out of requirement to coach, then it was only going to be with Swans, where he had some history and passion for the place and not with a new and struggling club. At 61, he was fit and healthy enough to handle the job, taking heart from the fact that Bobby Robson, at age 68, had just returned to the English premier league to manage Newcastle United.

Chapter 23 – Heading back home (twice)

He went to the Swans board with a plan to put some much needed continuity back into the football department and the team – the club had used three different senior coaches in the five years[116] since he had left in 1994 and the league side had not made the finals. Off ground, the administration was also disjointed, with three presidents and five general managers over this period. He said he would coach the side and help set things up to stabilise the club for the future by putting in place assistant coaches and support staff who knew the club and had passion and feeling for the place and could carry on when he stepped back from coaching for the final time. One of the unfortunate side-effects of changing coaches in football clubs, particularly in the WAFL these days where money and resources are tight, is that a lot of additional knowledge and expertise also departs. Most incoming coaches adopt the 'new broom' approach, with support staff also going, and often it can take 12 months of a new appointment to stabilise things. John's vision was that this would be avoided so the club had stability in the long term – *"I was happy to put blocks on blocks and do the hard yards and try to build Humpty Dumpty up again so there would be something there for the future long after I'm gone"*. In the club's bleak situation at the end of 1999, his plan, as well as his passion and reputation, represented both hope and salvation and he was speedily re-appointed as coach.

When he returned to Bassendean Oval, he found the club in a terrible state. The grounds were untidy and overgrown with weeds, the clubrooms dirty and run down, pictures of the premiership sides of the 1960s, '80s and 1990 lay in suitcases gathering dust and the players' lockers had been vandalised. The place reeked of neglect, with no respect given to the work of those who had built the club and brought it success in the past 65 years. In part, this was due to financial woes as the club was operating on a skeleton staff of paid workers and relying heavily on unpaid volunteers. Dismayed, but not deterred, he simply rolled up his sleeves and got to work.

Firstly, he became the public face of the fund-raising drive to save the club, working with the board to raise awareness of the club's plight; he called on many businessmen and women from the 1980s to explain the position and ask for help. Secondly, with the board's approval, but without money to spend, he embarked on a revamp of the players' change rooms to lift the appearance and spirit of the place. As at South in 1995, he organised the players in busy bees to clean up the rooms and their surrounds and prevailed on his many contacts in the business community to get the building materials to re-model the area. He had 6000 bricks donated, along with cement and labour to build some new walls, and new hot water systems provided free of charge. Few others at the club could have pulled this off for no cost, but John had tremendous respect within the Swans community and his passion for the cause was infectious. No job was beneath him; he vacuumed the floors and cleaned the toilets because there was no money for cleaners and, wherever there was a shortfall, he picked up the slack. He worked full-time for part-time wages and, with the help of many others, turned things around. By the end of 2000, Swans were back in the black and the $175,000 debt all but covered. The final word on the rescue mission belongs to Cooper – *"If Toddy hadn't returned to coach Swans, the club probably would have folded. No-one knows the work he did to get the finances right. He worked absolutely day and night and, with all his flair and contacts, we got there. I give him as much credit as the board for getting the club over the line"*.

---

116. Graham Melrose in 1995-96, Phil Cronan in 1997 and Peter Wilson in 1998-99.

considered – the survival of the club. This was his first priority and he wanted to provide a solid foundation for the future but, having done the *"hard yards"*, he feels somewhat let down that a *"new broom"* swept away much of what he tried to put in place. While he now shrugs and says *"that's footy"*, at the time his disappointment at the turn of events was obvious.

While the board and the club will be eternally grateful to John for his efforts in 2000-02 in helping resurrect Swans financially, the reality is that his mid-season retirement announcement got them off the hook. The board didn't want him to continue as coach in 2003, but faced the considerable dilemma of how to tell their most successful coach – and one who had just been instrumental in saving the club – that his services were no longer required. His retirement saved face on both sides. For John, the aftermath of season 2002 was an unsavoury way to conclude his long career, but he bears no scars – *"Waking up tomorrow is always more important than what happened yesterday".*

Chapter 24
Football in the 1990s and the new millennium

John, reflecting on the changes in the game in the 1990s:

"If people like Ron Boucher were playing today, he would never survive with trial by video, but the game needs talking points and personalities. It's far too clinical. What sort of folklore is being established in today's game?".

For the two tiers of West Australian football, the 1990s were a mix of contrasting fortunes. AFL premierships in 1992 and 1994 and finals appearances in every year of the decade saw the West Coast Eagles go from strength to strength. Their membership approached 40,000 in the new century, sponsors queued up and crowds were strong; even in their worst season in 2001 attendances still averaged almost 33,000. That these levels of membership, sponsorship and attendances could be maintained by West Coast bode well for the rest of the football industry. With 75-80% of their annual profit flowing back to the WAFC, the Eagles effectively bankroll the game in WA and the industry would be in dire straights without this arrangement. While Fremantle operates under the same agreement, they have struggled to return a profit in eight years and have not contributed anywhere near the anticipated revenue to the WAFC. With the WAFC paying for the final stage of the Subiaco Oval redevelopment [117], the flow-on effect to the WAFL and the other levels of football has seen continual belt-tightening, with budget projections regularly revised as grants to the WAFL clubs fall below that expected. Swans were certainly not the only club to experience severe financial problems in the 1990s.

The 1995 formation of the Dockers was achieved with far less acrimony than for the Eagles, but it provided something of a double-whammy for the WAFL clubs. Eight years on from 1987, most clubs had stabilised their operations and lived within the financial constraints now existing in WA football. The Dockers meant an AFL game in Perth each week, instead of every fortnight, and there was further competition for members and supporters. Total WAFL attendances for the 1995 qualifying rounds dropped by 83,000 to just under 157,000 and have since remained around this level. In the 1990-94 period, qualifying round attendances were between 240,000 to 290,000 per year and, by the end of the '90s, gate receipts for WAFL clubs were about half of what they were at the start of the decade and could no longer be relied on as a major source of income. In 1990, the home ground attendance of 35,553 provided gate receipts of $84,823 for Swans, but by 2000, the respective figures had fallen to 17,558 and $32,732.

---

117. Lights were added in 1997 and redevelopment was completed in 2000, but in 2003 the WAFC still owed $32 million on loans to fund this work.

During the '90s, the WAFC ran a tight financial operation, certainly out of necessity because of loan repayments but, largely because of this, relations with the WAFL clubs were often strained. Salary cap limits of around $100,000 remained in force over the decade, despite overtures for increases to bridge the gap with the SANFL, where the cap was around $300,000 – players were regularly tempted across the border, in addition to the AFL drain.

An on-going problem for WAFL clubs was their inability to retain senior players, especially those returning from the AFL, and having the financial resources to adequately recompense their better players and prevent them being poached by other clubs, or lured to country leagues, was a constant challenge. At the end of 2003, only 12 players had notched up 200 or more WAFL/AFL games – Ryan Turnbull, Paul Symmons, Jeremy Barnard and Russell Thompson (East Perth), Marty Atkins and Tommy Bottrell (jnr) (South Fremantle, both now retired), Daniel Metropolis and Matt Connell (Subiaco), Travis Edmonds (Swans), Derek Hall and Stephen Pears (Peel Thunder, both now retired) and Craig Treleven (East Fremantle, now retired).

In John's view, keeping these veterans around the clubs to *"give something back to the game and help more players reach 200 games is an important aspect of maintaining a viable competition"*. Expanding the salary cap would certainly help in this respect, *"but the game must be able to afford it and the players have to be worth it. At present, neither is probably the case"*, he says. The other option available is obviously 'under the table' – sponsor payments to players or their family in breach of the salary cap rules. There is little doubt this happens, as it does in the AFL, but there is one important difference in the accounting procedures adopted by the two controlling bodies – independent AFL auditors go through the clubs' books while, in the WAFL, the clubs appoint their own auditors. The cash-strapped WAFC does not have the financial resources to pay independent auditors to conduct surprise spot checks on the WAFL clubs, which would help stamp out salary cap rorts. No WAFL club has been charged with salary cap fraud, although several have voluntarily reported breaches, but it is a widely held view that breaches are commonplace.

Two other controversial WAFL issues in the 1990s were the introduction of a ninth team, Peel Thunder, in 1997 and the 'host club' arrangements instituted for the benefit of the Eagles and Dockers in 1999. The genesis for the WAFL expansion came from a 1992 *Football 2000* review prepared for the WAFC as a blueprint for the development of the game. In brief, the paper recommended 10 WAFL teams, with two country clubs added to the existing eight city based teams, with most clubs relocating to more populous areas within the metropolitan region. At various times during the decade it was mooted that teams from Kalgoorlie, Bunbury, the South-West and even the Northern Territory might join the WAFL and in 1994 West Perth[118] made the long-anticipated shift to Joondalup. In 1996, the WAFL presidents agreed to admit a Mandurah-based side, but the vote was only won at the 11th hour when Perth president Nick Catalano changed his mind and voted for their admission after being instructed by the Perth board to oppose the move. In the absence of any mergers between existing clubs (which the WAFC wanted), the admission of Peel created a nine-team league and a bye in the weekly fixtures. The disjointed weekly playing schedule became a source of discontent between the WAFL clubs and the Commission, in addition to financial grants to the clubs being split nine ways instead of eight.

---

118. More than 20,000 fans attended West Perth's final game at Leederville Oval in 1993.

Since 1997 Peel Thunder has struggled to win games and are yet to make the finals, and the 2003 season was perhaps their worst to date. By the end of the decade, the eight established clubs wanted them out of the competition, but a legal dispute over their licence agreement saw them survive with a new five year licence granted in 2002.

The 2000 *Fong Report* called for a return to an eight-team WAFL competition, with Peel the most likely victim, but mergers remained a preferred WAFC option. John's view is that *"Peel isn't such a bad thing for the competition, although expanding the WAFL in 1997, when the football system was not financially healthy, seemed a crazy move"*. He is not opposed to Peel staying, but would go a little further than suggested by the *Fong Report*, having only six WAFL teams rather than the established eight, allowing the available resources to be poured into two fewer clubs and less players, which should improve the quality of football. He firmly believes that Swans should merge with another club and that South and East Fremantle should eventually do the same. While he understands the feelings of traditionalists (he is one himself!), he feels football must move on, with the current structure unable to survive much longer in its present form. *"Something is better than nothing and if you had told me 10 or 20 years ago that East Perth would celebrate premierships at Leederville Oval*[119] *instead of Perth Oval, then I would have laughed at you. Nothing stays the same now – the world is moving too quick"*.

The host club arrangements created much division between the WAFC and the WAFL clubs, particularly the Eagles, with the Dockers seeming ambivalent. In the absence of a West Coast reserves side, the next best option was to have all their players based at one WAFL club, similar to the structure of the minor and major league teams in American baseball. The Eagles believed that having the players together when not playing in the AFL would be a big advantage, but rival WAFL clubs were wary of the proposal for fears the team would dominate. The WAFC was caught in the crossfire. The Eagles were their 'cash cow'; they felt some obligation to support the club, which injected so much money into the State's football system, but were also mindful of the WAFL clubs. After the system had been mooted for several years, a full host-club arrangement[120] was introduced in 1999, with Claremont hosting the Eagles and South Fremantle the Dockers, but this format lasted for just one year. Claremont, coached by former Eagles midfielder Don Pyke, experienced a severe player backlash about the arrangement. With up to 10 or 12 Eagles available each week, home-grown players struggled for league games and the club faced a mass exodus of players at the end of the season. The system was modified to a semi-host club arrangement[121], which ran for seasons 2000 and 2001 with East Perth now hosting the Eagles, but the death knell for the system was sounded when East Perth and South Fremantle played off for the 2001 grand final. The connection between being a host club and a grand final appearance proved irresistible for the other WAFL clubs and the arrangement was abandoned in 2002, much to the annoyance of the Eagles.

A major rule change saw an expansion of the number of interchange players to three in 1994 and four in 1998 (AFL) and 2000 (WAFL). The increases resulted from sustained calls for more

---

119. East Perth boosted their income in the late 1990s by leasing Perth Oval for training and playing purposes to Perth Glory, WA's national soccer league side, and trained at Leederville Oval before making the move permanent in 2002 after the members endorsed the change of headquarters.
120. All Eagles and Dockers players, regardless of their WAFL club of origin, played for Claremont and South Fremantle.
121. Only interstate recruits with no prior link to a WAFL club were allocated to the host club.

players to avoid keeping injured players on the ground, with Eagles coach Mick Malthouse a passionate advocate for the change. However, as is often the case with rule changes, coaches exploit them in different ways and one effect of the interchange expansion has been the rotation of players (especially midfielders) at pre-set times, a system John dislikes *"as it interrupts the flow of the players"*. Ironically, the change has probably increased the likelihood of injury as the regular rotations keep players fresher for longer, increasing the speed of the game; a factor associated with higher rates of injury, as borne out in recent research by Professor Kevin Norton, at the University of South Australia.

The other rule change entrenched – though sparingly applied – in the WAFL, but not in the AFL, is the send-off rule, which was introduced in 1991. Swans player Steven Handley gained the dubious distinction of being the first player sent from the ground under the new rule, when he was removed by umpire Phil O'Reilly in the 1991 preliminary final after being reported for unnecessary rough play. However, under the laws in place at the time, O'Reilly erred as this was not a send-off offence. In the 2002 WAFL second semi-final, the send-off rule again created controversy when Subiaco's Richard Maloney was sent off after being reported for a second time. He had been reported in the first quarter for wrestling (under the much criticised 'melee' rule) and in the second term for charging, incurring an automatic send off. The charging report was later withdrawn by the umpires before reaching the tribunal and it was confirmed that a melee report was not intended to count towards a send-off sanction. This anomaly in the rules was quickly amended the next week amid fears that unscrupulous coaches might exploit the rule to get a star opponent removed from the ground.

Other major changes and interpretations to the laws of the game were the introduction of the three umpire system (1994), the controversial 'blood' rule (1995), the issue of 'prior opportunity' in holding the ball decisions (1996) and the slow, but steady, rise in the number of video reports laid by umpires and investigators. Racial vilification laws were also added to the rule book in June 1995 after a much publicised AFL incident between Essendon's Michael Long and Collingwood's Damian Monkhurst in 1994.

John's general view of these changes is that most represented unwarranted intrusions into the game – *"While I accept the need for a mediation system for racial abuse, I'm disappointed the game (and society) can't sort these issues out privately, man on man, without resorting to a public and semi-legal hearing. The three umpire system, the melee rule and many of the tinkerings with the laws have sanitised the game and deprived it of some colour and characters. If people like Ron Boucher were playing today, he would never survive with trial by video... but the game needs talking points and personalities. It's far too clinical. What sort of folklore is being established in today's game?"*. It would be easy to dismiss these laments as the gripes of a man from a bygone era who refuses to accept change, but that is not the case. He is very accepting of the need for change as society and the world continues to evolve. He had to embrace changes in the game to survive for so long, but he firmly believes that today's football is *"over policed"* and is being robbed of much of its previous spectacle and unique character.

The '90s also saw the passing of an era in WA football. By the end of the decade, all players who had started their careers before 1987 – and therefore played in the WAFL when it was the no. 1 competition before the advent of the Eagles – had retired. Gone were stalwarts such as Brian Peake (402 games) [122] in 1990, Steve Malaxos (375 games) in 1998, Dwayne Lamb (350 games) in 1996, Darrell Panizza (354 games) in 1995 and Mike Richardson (314 games) in 1994. It's problematic whether any more players will achieve 300 games in the WAFL, or in combination with an AFL career, especially as the majority of seasoned AFL players don't usually return to WAFL ranks, preferring to retire. Again, John feels *"it would be terrific to see more of them return to the WAFL for a few seasons, to give something back to the game, help the kids and give the competition more profile"*.

The other sad change in the game was the demise of State of Origin football, with WA's last fixture in 1998, when South Australia were too good at Football Park in Adelaide. In the early 1990s, with the Eagles dominating the AFL with a mainly home-grown squad, they formed the majority of the State of Origin sides, but this became a concern for the club from an injury-risk situation. By mid-season players with niggling injuries had the chance for a week's break, particularly before heading into the finals, which was appealing for players and coaches. In several instances, it's fair to say players with injury concerns that probably wouldn't have kept them out of an Eagles match, were 'encouraged' to miss the State game, although no player who was fit and keen to play was ever removed from the squad. For many Eagles players, especially after winning premiership flags in 1992 and '94, State football was no longer the pinnacle of the game; they were playing and beating the Victorians on an almost weekly basis. Under these circumstances State footy was doomed.

However, John believes this mood may be changing and he hopes State of Origin football can be resurrected, as *"it can add another chapter to a player's career. To represent the State and then perhaps your country is an opportunity to be cherished and can really put the stamp on your time in the game"*. With WA players spread across the AFL and a fair percentage of the Eagles and Dockers squads coming from other States, the selection of a State of Origin side would not compromise the two WA teams, as was the case in the early '90s. John adds – *"We now have two Brownlow medallists* [123] *with other AFL clubs and WA fans see them play perhaps once a year. Interstate football would provide another opportunity to local fans to see these guys in the flesh, against the best the other States have to offer. It would be great to have a carnival again, as occurred in my playing days, but even those great mid-week battles with Victoria at Subiaco Oval in the early 1980s tell me this could work again. These players came off Saturday games to play again on Tuesday and they managed it pretty well. Surely Friday night or Saturday AFL games could be scheduled for the round before a State of Origin clash so the players had time to recover. Every State now has a floodlit stadium, so Tuesday night games could be programmed to avoid school and work clashes in the afternoon"*.

The two West Coast premierships and regular finals appearances throughout the decade made it a great era for WA from an AFL perspective and, although Fremantle didn't enjoy a lot of success in their early years, making the finals for the first time in 2003, the Western derbies quickly captured the Perth public's interest. It became evident that the rivalry between the two clubs was just as intense as it was for the Fremantle derbies in years past – the Eagles jealously guarded their turf as the State's No. 1 AFL team by winning the first nine contests before Fremantle broke through for their first win in 1999, on the occasion of Chris Mainwaring's 200th Eagles game.

---

122. These figures include all senior games in the WAFL, VFL/AFL, SANFL and State matches.
123. Shane Woewodin (Melbourne and Collingwood), was the 2000 winner and in 2002 Simon Black (Brisbane) won the medal; both were drafted from East Fremantle.

In 2001, the fortunes of the two AFL sides plummeted dramatically, with Fremantle finishing last with only two wins, while the Eagles fared slightly better, taking 14th position with five victories. For both clubs it was their worst season on record and coaches Damian Drum and Ken Judge were replaced. In 2002 the Eagles, under favourite son John Worsfold, bounced back to make the finals in his first year as a senior coach and Fremantle, guided by former Hawthorn assistant coach Chris Connolly, improved to finish 13th with nine wins. In 2003, both sides made the finals, but went out in the first week, Fremantle losing at Subiaco Oval to Essendon and West Coast losing to Adelaide in Adelaide.

In the 1990s WAFL premierships were shared among five clubs, with East Fremantle (1992, '94 and '98) and Claremont (1991, '93 and '96) each winning three flags, West Perth two (1995 and '99) and Swans (1990) and South Fremantle (1997) one apiece. East Perth have since joined that rare group of clubs to win a hat trick with the 2000-02 premierships, with West Perth adding another flag in 2003, beating Subiaco, who have been regular finalists and were also runners up in 1991 and '95. Perth are the only traditional team missing a grand final in this era (1978 was their last), although they made the finals in '91 and '97, and Peel Thunder are yet to play a finals match. In the Sandover Medal, all clubs except Claremont and South Fremantle had winners, with history being made in 2002 when Allistair Pickett became Peel Thunder's first medallist. Of the medallists, perhaps East Fremantle's 1995 winner Craig Treleven, who went on to play successfully with Hawthorn before returning to East Fremantle in 2002, and Ryan Turnbull, who won his medal in 2001 after a 1994 premiership with West Coast, are best known. Subiaco's Ian Dargie was a dual winner of the award (1991 and '94) and had brief stints in the AFL with both West Coast and Brisbane.

~

As football makes its way into the new century, it is appropriate to see how John, as the elder statesman of the sport in WA, views the state of the game. He has always held strong and forthright views on football and, despite not being directly involved in the AFL for over 10 years, remains well placed to comment on both tiers of the game. In brief, with football now a full-time profession at AFL level, the game offers great financial rewards for those who make it. Successful players should be able to set themselves up for life financially with a 10 year career and while this is a *"big positive"*, John is alarmed by what he sees as exorbitant salaries paid to players and coaches in the AFL – *"With many clubs in real financial difficulty, the increasing wages bill is sending the game broke. Annual salaries to play or coach of $500,000 or more are quite simply a joke and the game cannot afford these costs for much longer. Clubs will fold or merge, or the AFL will have to 'lock out' the players, as has occurred in American baseball in order to reduce salaries. Either way the game will suffer. This grab for more money by player managers is fast destroying the game, because not only is it sending the clubs broke, it is also damaging the loyalty factor within the game. Trading players against their will for salary cap reasons, as happened to Brownlow medallist Shane Woewodin at the end of 2002, is a disgrace and will cost the club members and fans, as they want to see their favourite players stay with their team, not be horse traded against their wishes. The fans remain loyal to their club, no matter what the situation and in return they expect the players and club to be loyal to each other. In cases like Woewodin's, the fans have every right to feel bitter".*

"One way of maintaining loyalty in the system would be to set up AFL zones for each club, with WA divided into WAFL club zones with half allocated to the Eagles and the other half to the Dockers. Then the AFL and WAFL clubs could work together in their respective zones to foster and promote the game and junior players would have a clear career path ahead, firstly through their WAFL club and then to their respective AFL team". His sentiment is clear – *"Let's get back to some State versus State rivalry. Let the Vics keep their kids and we'll keep ours, then we won't have situations like the Jeff White* [124] *and Des Headland sagas"*.

The other aspect of the high player and coach salaries that greatly concerns John is that they will become seduced by the money and lose sight of the pure essence of what sport is all about. For him, it will always be *"to win at all costs and be the best you can possibly be"*. John hopes that in a *"crunch situation"* the only thoughts in a player's head concern these sentiments and are not clouded, even slightly, by thoughts of *"self preservation"* and *"next week"*. Guaranteed money, rather than incentive and match payments for games played, can certainly see players lose their competitive edge, especially in the first season of a new and lucrative contract – *"Based on their relatively poor performances in a season, many players should be paying money back to the clubs"* is his blunt assessment. He sees the money and the structure of the football system stifling the initiative of players to improve themselves. Mostly, *"they wait to be told they have a problem by one of the coaches, then wait for the coach or one of his many assistants, to organise a practice session for them. Why don't they just get down to the park with a footy and work on their game, instead of waiting to be told?"*.

This comment particularly refers to first year rookies drafted into an AFL club, often at the tender age of 17. In John's view, this is at least two years premature; at 19 school and growing are finished and the player should have made it into a WAFL league side for a season or two. He advocates a return to the type of qualifying criteria used by the WAFL in the 1980s for interstate clearance purposes – perhaps aged 19, with 20 or so league games or two seasons of service to the club might be trialled as draft entry criteria – *"Expecting them to step out of colts footy (in many cases) straight into the AFL is a big ask. Then two years later, if they don't make a quick impact, they could be on the scrap heap when still only 19 or 20 and many are lost to the sport, scarred by the experience"*. The money paid to the rookies in their first year is also *"staggering"*... *"what other profession pays a first year apprentice $50,000 a year to learn the trade? It's too easy for them. The money seduces them and they fail to develop the attitude and work ethic they need to succeed"*.

Lastly, he laments that the *"corporatisation"* of the game has taken it out of the reach of many grass roots supporters. In 1987 it cost $7.50 to watch the Eagles in their first season; by 2002 this admission charge had risen to $16 and often just getting a ticket to a game is impossible, particularly for Eagles fans, with almost as many members as the current seating capacity of Subiaco Oval. Recent proposals to return a section of the ground to 'standing room' are welcomed by John, *"as this might bring a bit of noise and colour back to the game and get some of the grass roots people back to the footy"*. However, he fears the corporate business elements of the clubs are having too much influence over football decisions. – *"The marketing implications might sway a judgement or colour an approach taken on a football matter, such that the football decision isn't the No. 1 priority. If we go too far down this path then you become an entertainment club, rather than a football team"*.

---

124. White, a Victorian, left the Dockers in 1997 after three seasons to return to his home State, while Headland reluctantly spent four years in Brisbane before achieving his wish to return to WA when traded to the Dockers at the end of 2002.

Therefore, in many areas, John sees the game at a low ebb and at a critical point in its history. The excessive payments to players and coaches must be reined in, otherwise the industry will be in real trouble and clubs will fold or merge. WA zones for the Eagles and Dockers would be great for football in the State, as would raising the AFL draft age to 19. Less corporate influence and tampering and tinkering with the rules of the game would also help the spectacle of the sport. For the WAFL to prosper, an increase in the salary cap is needed, thereby helping senior players stay in the game after their AFL careers are over, giving it some much needed profile. Mergers to get back to six clubs would also assist the viability of this important second tier of WA football.

Finally, it is John's fervent hope that State of Origin football can be resurrected – *"I have great memories of my State games, both as a player and coach, and the careers of current AFL players will always be somewhat incomplete without the opportunity to play for their State. Our young stars deserve the chance to represent the State and this equally applies to the WAFL, as it is important to also provide this incentive for the players at the second tier of the game".*

Chapter 25
A football legacy

John, reflecting on his long career:

> "I have no regrets about anything. I can walk away knowing that I gave everything my best shot and, as long as I wake up tomorrow, I'll be happy".

Since 1955, the name John Todd has been synonymous with WA football. As a player or a coach he has been involved in the sport at senior level for 41 seasons – no-one has seen the game change and evolve like he has while still remaining an active participant in it. His achievements span virtually his whole career and they are briefly summarised below, separated into playing and coaching.

Playing career

- 132 games for South Fremantle (1955-66)
- Sandover Medal 1955 (youngest winner in open competition)
- Club fairest and best 1955, '58 & '61
- *Daily News* Footballer of the Year (1958)
- 13 State games (1955-62)
- All Australian selection (1961)

At State training in 1959.

Coaching career

- *South Fremantle* 1959, 1966-68, 1995-98
  172 games – 83 wins, 88 losses and one draw. Premiership 1997
- *East Fremantle* 1973-76
  87 games – 45 wins, 41 losses and one draw. Premiership 1974
- *Swan Districts* 1977-87, 1990-94, 2000-02
  417 games – 217 wins and 200 losses. Premierships 1982, '83, '84 & '90
- *West Coast* 1988 & 89
  45 games – 20 wins and 25 losses. Club's first final in 1988.
- *Total* 721 games – the third highest tally in Australia and the most in WA football
- *Wins/losses* 365 wins, 354 losses, two draws, for a winning percentage of 50.6%.
- *Premierships* Most premierships (6) for a WA coach since 1931,
  when the final four system was introduced.
- *WA coach* 1975, 1983-85, 1987-88, 1995 & 1998
  13 games – five wins and eight losses.
  National championship wins in 1983 and 84.
- *Australian composite rules side vs Ireland* 1984 & 1986
  Six games – three wins and three losses and a series win in 1984.
- Youngest coach in WA history in 1959, aged 20 and the oldest in 2002, aged 64.

Emphasising a point at three quarter time in the 1988 elimination final. Karl Langdon is the player in the background.

Chapter 25 – A football legacy

Holding the cup aloft after three flags in a row – 1984.

Awards and honours

As a predictable consequence of this imposing record, John has received many awards and honours, which are briefly summarised below:

- 1973 Life Member of South Fremantle
- 1985 Advance Australia Award
- 1986 Order of Australia
- 1987 Life Member of Swan Districts
- 1989 Members' pavilion at Bassendean Oval named the John Cooper/John Todd Pavilion
- 1990 JJ Leonard Medal for Coach of the Year
- 1991 Life Member of the WAFL
- 1997 Western Australian Hall of Champions
- 1997 Fremantle Dockers Hall of Legends
- 1997 City of Fremantle Hall of Fame
- 1999 The John Todd Cup introduced for matches between South Fremantle and Swan Districts
- 2000 The John Todd Entrance opened at Subiaco Oval
- 2001 The John Todd Medal introduced for the WAFL premiership coach
- 2002 Named as coach of Swan Districts *Team of the Century*
- 2003 AFL Hall of Fame (coaching)
- 2004 WAFL Hall of Fame (player and coach)

Induction into the AFL Hall of Fame was a fitting tribute for him – *"It's been a long journey. You don't start off to accumulate accolades, but at the end of the day it's great to be recognised – it's just terrific"*.

Chapter 25 – A football legacy

2003 – After being inducted into the AFL Hall of Fame.
With the WA contingent, including fellow Hall of Famers Graham Farmer (second row, extreme left), George Doig (third row, extreme right), Ross Glendinning (back row, second from left), Merv McIntosh (front row, extreme right), Stephen Michael (third row, second from right), Bill Walker (back row, third from right), Haydn Bunton (back row, second from right) and Jack Sheedy (second row, extreme right). Meryl Todd is in the front row, the other lady is Beryl Cooper, wife of John, who is standing on the right.

What then is John's lasting legacy to the game that he has served so well and devoted his life to? There is no doubt he has been good for the game, just as football has been good to him. He is one of those lucky people who considers that they have not actually worked for a living, rather being able to indulge his passion for the sport across six decades, making a tidy living along the way. At age 65 he can settle into retirement knowing that his colourful, sometimes chequered, but always passionate career has enriched football in WA.

As a player he was a boy wonder, set to be *"the greatest player the game had ever seen"* until a cruel twist of fate curtailed and almost took away his gift forever. His left knee is probably the most famous knee in the State's sporting history and, when it is eventually replaced with an artificial one, it should be preserved and put on display, perhaps in the Western Australian Hall of Fame. It's a shame that his trusty old knee brace has been lost and cannot be displayed alongside it. For now though, when the pain in his knees[125] gets worse, he rides his bicycle for that little bit longer or spends extra time in the pool, working the legs against the water. The disciplines learnt and practised so many years ago continue to serve him well and he will not submit to the surgeon's knife easily. The game has also left its mark on his hands, with most of his middle knuckles permanently enlarged and the top section of the middle finger on his right hand bent at a 45-degree angle from the rest of the digit. The bone became set in this position after he broke the finger on the eve of a State match in 1957. There was no question of him not playing and he saw a dentist friend who made him a rudimentary cast which he used in the match and for the rest of the season, by which time the bone had set at the awkward angle. In later years, when John *"pointed the finger"* at an under-performing player, many were uncertain as to exactly who was in the firing line, unless they were named by the coach!

After the knee injury, coaching was always on the agenda, particularly as he had not played in a league premiership side or been able to take his talents to Melbourne and the VFL. As a coach he was the hardest of taskmasters, at least until the 1990s when he mellowed somewhat on returning to the WAFL after coaching West Coast. In John's early days the verbal lashings players received were his trademark and that was how the public characterised him. It has long been suggested that his (perceived) highly volatile and cantankerous nature stemmed from the knee injury and that he carried a large chip on his shoulder because his playing career had been cut so short. His perceived intolerance towards those who couldn't (or wouldn't) meet his demanding standards was taken to reflect his bitterness at not being able to play football.

Being portrayed in this way by the media (whom he admits to never having a good relationship with) has always made good copy, but has presented a false image of him to the public. As he says – as a 'half' lament – *"If you did a street survey about me, 90% of the people wouldn't be able to give you a correct assessment"*. Rarely mentioned is his wicked and lateral sense of humour or his considerable empathy for those suffering with illness, injury or disability. Usually the report is, as he describes it, *"... about one of my angry shots which aren't all that frequent"*.

---

125. His right knee is arthritic also.

Chapter 25 – A football legacy

To put the record straight, the source of the vitriolic outbursts was not his knee injury (he had the potential well before that happened), but his absolute passion to be the best he could be; something he developed and honed at a tender age. This translated into a fierce love of winning and a deep hatred of losing. As a coach, he simply needed every player to be the best they could be in order to achieve the same, which is why *"playing was so much easier than coaching"* as he only had himself to worry about. In addition, he hated to see talent go to waste, *"as the game has so much to offer, even more so in current times"* and, most importantly, *"the team was being let down by a selfish individual"*. In these situations, the player was also letting himself down by not being the best he could be, which invariably earned them a hefty serve. It was his way of trying to get more out of the individual. He readily agrees it wasn't the only way to do it, but it was the way for him.

John's career has brought him in touch with literally thousands of people and his enthusiasm and passion have been such that he could never be easily forgotten. Most people he has had something to do with could tell you a story about John Todd, whether funny, angry, happy or sad. As a coach he has given hundreds of players their first games of league football and, for most, a rich source of memories and lessons in life. Many players he played with or has coached have also touched him. In 2001, when former South ruckman Fred Seinor was diagnosed with a brain tumour, John was quick to pay him a visit and was deeply saddened by his rapid and untimely demise.

Similarly, in 2002 he was shaken by the sudden death of East Fremantle great Norm Rogers, who had coached the colts and reserves in John's time at the club in 1973-76. At the funeral, former team-mate Trevor Sprigg delivered a eulogy, part of which included this quotation – *"Loyalty is important in football, as in all other walks of life. With this in mind, I pay tribute to East Fremantle reserves coach and my right hand man, Norm Rogers. Anyone who saw Norm play any of his 234 games for Old Easts would not doubt his loyalty to his club. He was tough and relentless as an opponent and deserves to be ranked as one of the club's all time greats. Since his playing days ended, Norm has continued to work hard for the club and, whether it be in coaching or helping select league teams, I have found his knowledge invaluable. But it has been his undivided loyalty that has made the biggest impression on me over the past three years. When things go wrong as they often do, you can bet Norm will stick by you through thick and thin. A rare person, Norm Rogers"*. The words were John's, borrowed from 1975 when he spoke about Rogers at the trophy presentation night. He laments the fact that loyalty today is no longer what it used to be and the game is the poorer for it. A favourite story of his which typifies the enormous changes that football has undergone through the eras from the 1950s concerns Rogers. In the early 1960s Footscray were keen to entice him to Melbourne and, as an inducement to sign, he was offered a pair of club socks! Not surprisingly, it wasn't enough to sway him and he stayed with East Fremantle for his entire career.

In John's 721 games as a coach he pitted himself against 102 different opposition coaches, going head to head most against Mal Brown (48 games for 23 wins), followed by Ken Armstrong (38 games for 27 wins) and Graham Moss (35 games for 14 wins). As society and football evolved, John certainly changed with it, introducing several new strategies and styles of play which have become entrenched in the theory of the game. In the 1950s and '60s it was considered sacrilege to kick the ball across goals in defence because it was too risky. In the 1970s he introduced the switch-of-play style which encouraged players to move the ball across goals into space on the other side of the ground, turning this long-held football maxim upside down. Switching play has since been an accepted tactic.

In the 1970s John freed up the game by moving from tall to small ruck-rovers and changed them on half-forward or half-back flanks as well. The modern running style of game, as opposed to the mark and kick pattern of the 1950s and '60s, was thus commenced. In the early 1980s, he instituted the tagging role and had flexible key position players who could play forward and back equally well, providing extra dimensions to match tactics which remain a common element of the game today. His long tenure of coaching across six decades certainly left an indelible mark on the way football changed over the years and is played today.

With all these achievements on record, what legacy does John see himself leaving behind? After a brief pause for contemplation, he answered with, *"I guess maybe the value of persistence, instilled into me so many years ago by my mother. My story is really one of perseverance, first to get back playing after hurting my knee, but also then in my coaching. It took me 20 years before I won my first flag. In sport and life there are always going to be highs*

1989 – with mother Doris, who is holding the first trophy John ever won, as best player for the Warren Association team, in a carnival held in 1949.

and lows and unexpected twists and turns. A setback is not and should never be the end of it. Never say die, never say never, never give up. Great things are often just around the corner if you get more determined and persevere. Showing and feeling disappointment is a waste of time and gets you nowhere. If you are prepared to make sacrifices and really persist, even when the odds are against you, then you will normally get through". His family all echo these sentiments saying that, above all else, he demonstrated to them what can be achieved with passion and 100% commitment.

He recaps on his career as *"very enjoyable and rewarding. I think I managed to give something back to the game along the way. I'm glad my mother got so much pleasure from my career. It might have helped keep her alive"*. When asked if there were any regrets, he quickly replied – *"I have no regrets about anything. I can walk away knowing that I gave everything my best shot and, as long as I wake up tomorrow, I'll be happy"*. He will not say it, because it is *"ancient history"*, but if John had the power to change just one thing it would be his injured left knee, as he just loved to play football. With two good knees, he might still be turning out in the veterans' competitions that operate today.

So what of the future for John Todd? He has always joked that he wouldn't be far away from the training track *"with my dark glasses on and my white cane"*. At present he has no plans for any formal football involvement, media or otherwise, but coaching at senior level is firmly off the agenda. He figures that his bones have *"earned a rest from cold, wet and bleak training nights in the middle of winter"*. He plans to watch Eagles and Dockers games regularly (using his WAFL life membership admission pass) and hopes both clubs can do well, but in Western Derbies he remains an Eagles man. He will keep an interest in the WAFL, particularly with Swans and South, but will pick the games he attends, keeping his Saturday afternoons largely free. When moved to do so, John will continue as the elder statesman of WA football and present his views on the state of the game.

Seeing the north of the State and the rest of the country (preferably by car or train!) with Meryl is also likely and there will be plenty of fishing and gardening to keep him occupied. He will gladly spend more time with his grandchildren, who have certainly added an extra dimension to his life; recently he has been teaching seven-year-old Olivia how to ride a bike. Often the two ride off together to the river, or John sets up a few markers in the driveway for Olivia to weave in between. On more than a few occasions Meryl has had cause to semi-cringe as she hears John's booming voice instructing and correcting the youngster in the finer points of cycling. Old habits, especially those accumulated over nearly 50 seasons of playing and coaching, die hard.

Epilogue

2003 was a year of general contentment for John (and Meryl). He certainly didn't miss the grind of training nights and having to concern himself with player issues or team performances. His football fix was more than satisfied by watching the Eagles and Dockers regularly and by attending the John Todd Cup game between South and Swans and the WAFL finals. Being part of the pre-match AFL grand final motorcade (as an AFL Hall of Fame inductee) was *"a great experience, although I felt a bit awkward being treated like royalty. But it was great to be a part of the occasion and the crowd were terrific"*.

In late October, however, he was feeling a *"bit washed out"*. For the first time in his life he found himself falling asleep during the day when he sat down to watch TV or read. After some mild prodding from Meryl, he eventually went to the doctor for a check up, which included a blood test. The results came back to show a slightly elevated PSA level, an indicator of prostate abnormality, and the doctor ordered further tests, including an ultrasound examination and biopsy. A few days later they met the specialist to get the biopsy results; the enlarged prostate had several tumours on it, some were benign, but some were cancerous. Meryl felt her jaw drop and the blood drain from her face, John received the news without any overt emotion, just that uncomfortable feeling that arises in the pit of your stomach. It was confirmed – he had prostate cancer. After a brief discussion about the treatment options, he decided on the spot to have an operation to remove the prostate as soon as possible.

~

Over the next few weeks, while waiting for the operation, he learnt a lot more about prostate cancer. Statistics such as that approximately one in eight men will get it, that regular blood testing and rectal examination should occur from the age of 50 onwards (40 if there is family history of the disease), but that only about one in 10 men are PSA tested, compared with about seven out of 10 women for the female equivalent, breast cancer. Further, that common problems after treatment are incontinence and erectile difficulties and that some surveys estimate that up to 40% of Australian men are either ignorant about prostate cancer or afraid to be tested. He fitted this mould perfectly. He was blissfully unaware that he should be having annual check-ups (he had undergone one or two rectal examinations in the previous 10 years) and knew little about the disease, believing, like most other men, that *"I was pretty invincible to this sort of thing – it wouldn't happen to me"*. He also had, as is natural, fleeting thoughts about his own mortality, *"but not many"*. *"As I learned more about it, I got more confident that I would beat it, as I felt that I had a good deal of control over it and I would give it my best shot. It had been picked up early, so I figured the odds were in my favour and, with a positive attitude, there was no way it was going to get me"*. In his usual fashion, he confronted the problem head on and dealt with it, exercising his own control over it as much as possible. Two years previously he had an episode of kidney stones so he *"went back to nature"* and decided to drink nothing but water, which he has done ever since (with no recurrence of kidney problems).

He also related the circumstances back to the time of his knee injury – *"To be told at age 18 that I couldn't play footy again was the worst time of my life... the cancer news was a relative 'stroll in the park' compared to that. Probably because sport has more lows than highs associated with it, it toughens you up to life's knocks. It makes you persevere and move beyond any self doubts, which just can't help you. Plus, I knew I had more control over this than I did with my knee".*

While in hospital he took a call from Haydn Bunton who had recently had the same procedure done and had heard that John was in for the same reason. They discussed their respective test results and operations, during which John planted the seed with Bunton that *"we need to put our faces out there and see if we can raise awareness about prostate cancer, as so many people seem to be afraid to deal with it. Men are so much more self-conscious than women; they don't like to talk about these issues but they need to be more up-front and open about it. If we could be role models and act as someone to talk to about it, then we might be able to help overcome that fear of the unknown and get people to confront it and deal with it, not hide from it".*

Bunton was initially a little reluctant but, with John's urging, has 'come around' and is now happy to take on a more public role with him to try to raise awareness about the condition. For John, this is just *"one more challenge"* to be met and a project that, via the Cancer Council,

2001 – With Swan's greatest ever player, Bill Walker (left) and the club's only other premiership coach, Haydn Bunton. By the end of 2003, both Bunton and John were recovering from prostate cancer operations.

he hopes will *"make a difference"*. *"Both 'Bunt' and I defied the odds to play again after injury so I think we can help people beat prostate cancer, by getting them to deal with it and think and act positively"*. In fact, there are many remarkable similarities about the two men's lives and careers. As players, both suffered serious leg injuries early on and were not expected to play again, but both made it back. As captain (Bunton) and vice captain (John), they led WA to the 1961 ANFC Championship. Both won a Sandover Medal, coached Swans to a hat trick of flags and were in charge for over 700 games. They started their coaching careers early – Bunton at 19 (the Australian record) and John at 20 (the WA record). Bunton won three early flags at Swans (1961-1963) but then had to wait 23 years for his next (1986 and 1988) at Subiaco. John did the reverse, waiting 20 years for the first flag (1974), then winning the remaining five over the next 23 years. Then, in 2003, both fell victim to prostate cancer within a few weeks of each other.

~

John woke from the operation to find his left knee bandaged, as it was supporting the drain, which would stay in place for several days – *"I'm glad it was my left knee – it's used to being taped up"*. By January 2004 he was pretty much back to his normal routine, save for not being able to ride his bike.

He has been inundated with phone calls and visits from friends and strangers who have passed on their best wishes, but also sought his help to speak to people they know who have recently been diagnosed with cancers of various sorts, a role that he has enjoyed greatly.

Although John still requires regular blood tests over the next 12 months before he is officially 'cleared' of the problem, he has no doubt that *"it is beat"* and looks forward to *"banging the drum in public"* about the disease. It is one more challenge, like so many met previously, that you sense he is going to relish.

Appendix

John Todd's great teams that he played in or coached

Other than his six premiership sides, the following five teams are afforded special status for their great achievements.

- The 1961 WA Carnival team – ANFC Champions.
- The 1980 Swan Districts team that won 13 games straight.
- The 1983 WA State team that defeated Victoria to become Australian champions.
- The 1984 WA State team that again defeated Victoria to become (back to back) Australian champions.
- The 1984 Australian team that toured Ireland, winning the first official Test series, 2-1.

WESTERN AUSTRALIAN NATIONAL FOOTBALL LEAGUE
Australian Championships – Brisbane
15th – 23rd July, 1961

Back Row: D. Marshall, N. Beard, K. Holt, R. Gabelich, J. Clarke, K. Slater, K. Bagley, L. Cook, J. Turnbull
Centre Row: F. Fuhrmann (Selector), T. Cross (Head Trainer), E. Holdsworth (Selector), D. Barron, M. Atwell, G. Farmer, J. Gerovich, N. Rogers, R. Mellowship (Selector), J. Hampton (Property Man), J. Sheedy (Coach)
Front Row: R. Graham, C. Regan, R. Sorrell, J. Fanchi, H. Bunton (Captain), J. O'Dea (Manager), J. Colgan, L. Mumme, J. Todd (Vice-Captain), D. Chadwick
Absent: D. Williams, J. Dethridge, B. Metcalfe

The 1961 WA Carnival team – ANFC Champions.

The 1980 Swan Districts team that won 13 games straight.
Back row (from left): Phil Narkle, Brad Shine, Mike Richardson, Graham Melrose, Jeff Davidson, Gordon Casey, Ian Williams, Ross Prater, Craig Holden, Keith Narkle.
Middle row (from left): Peter Chidlow, Tony Solin, Steve Gillespie, Ross Fitzgerald, Simon Beasley, Alan Sidebottom, Craig Hoyer, Brian Hemming, Mike Smith, Don Holmes.
Front row (from left): John Cooper (President), Bill Skwirowski, Gerard Neesham, Stan Nowotny (Captain), Jon Fogarty, Don Langsford, John Todd (Coach).

Western Australia vs Victoria
Perth 12 July 1983

Back Row: W. Blackwell, P. Bosustow, K. Hunter, P. Cronan, G. Malarkey, G. Buckenara, A. Solin, L. Baker, D. Panizza, M. Rioli, M. White

Centre Row: S. Brown, B. Smith, D. Langsford, M. Rance, R. Boucher, P. Harding, A. Purser, G. Sidebottom, W. Ralph, M. Aitken, R. Griffiths, E. Doherty

Front Row: M. Richardson, R. Barrett, R. Glendinning (Vice-Captain), J. Todd (Coach), S. Michael (Captain), A. Johnson, K. Taylor, A. Buhagiar

The 1983 WA State team that defeated Victoria to become Australian champions.

**1984 Australian Champions
Western Australia vs Victoria
Perth, July 17, 1984**

Back Row: H. Gloede (Propertyman), W. Blackwell, A. Daniels, P. Cronan, D. Langsford, M. Aitken, L. Baker, P. Bosustow, B. Peake, S. Satti, T. Bottrell (Trainers)

Centre Row: Dr. R. Moore, S. Ellis, G. Carter, G. Sidebottom, P. Harding, A. Purser, R. Baynes, J. Dorotich, M. Rance, B. Hardie, R. Griffiths (Team Manager)

Front Row: M. Richardson, D. Warwick, R. Wiley, S. Malaxos (Captain), J. Todd (Coach), R. Glendinning (Vice Captain), C. Holden, M. Rioli, K. Taylor

The 1984 WA State team that again defeated Victoria to become (back to back) Australian champions.

Appendix

The 1984 Australian team that toured Ireland, winning the first official Test series, 2-1.
Back row (from left): K Goddard (Trainer) Maurice Rioli, Allen Daniels, Garry McIntosh, Michael Aish, Craig Bradley, Peter Motley, Dermott Brereton, Robert DiPierdomenico, Terry Daniher.
Third row (from left): J Bennett (President, TNFL) Ross Glendinning, Gerard Healy, Murray Rance, Gary Pert, Russell Greene, Peter Sartori, Mark Lee, Simon Madden, Stephen Kernahan, Ted Whitten (Selector), D Cooper (Team Doctor).
Second row (from left): Vince Yovich (WAFL President), G Clarke (Trainer), Rowan Sawers (Umpire).
Front row (from left): Robert Wiley, David Ackerly, John Platten, Allen Aylett (NFL and VFL President), Steve Malaxos (Captain), John Todd (Coach), Ed Biggs (Team Manager), Robert Flower, Brad Hardie, Craig Holden, Max Basheer (SANFL President).

A

Abernethy, Bruce 23
Ablett, Gary 205, 213
Adamson, Brian 148, 150, 171, 179, 248
Ainsworth, Don 84
Aish, Michael 213, 220
Aitken, Ian 125
Aitken, Mike 198
Alexander, Ron 190, 207, 211, 223, 226-232, 236, 253
Allen, Chris 203
Allen, Frank 72
Allen, Graeme 190
Amaranti, Peter 47, 101
Annear, John 190, 236, 239, 250
Annear, Roy 226, 247, 250
Arbon, Roy 156
Argent, Laurie 205
Armstrong, Ken 49, 174, 293
Ashworth, Graham 152
Atkins, Marty 272, 280
Atwell, Mal 79, 81, 104, 109, 119, 123, 130-131, 202, 248
August, Ashley 84
Avery, Noel 140-141, 144
Aylett, Allen 64, 81, 191

B

Badham, Stan 47, 84, 88, 92
Bagley, Ken 193
Bairstow, Mark 220, 223-224
Baker, Leon 183-184, 189, 193, 195-196, 201-202, 205, 210, 256
Baldock, Darrell 122
Ball, Jason 265
Ball, Mike 204
Barassi, Ron 80-81, 121, 140, 172, 237
Barker, Tim 29
Barnard, Jeremy 280
Barron, Dennis 81
Bartlett, Kevin 156
Bauskis, Eddie 165
Baynes, Rhett 204
Beard, Colin 62, 67, 84, 106, 110, 113, 115, 121, 158, 263
Beard, Neville 80, 83
Beasley, Simon 161, 168, 177-179, 181, 184-185, 187, 195, 205
Becu, Bob 130-131, 144, 146, 151
Beecroft, Barry 193
Bellos, Tony 71, 76
Bennett, Darren 224, 251, 255
Bennett, Robert 128
Bentley, Ron 138, 141, 144-145, 151, 153
Bewick, Ron 127, 180
Bishop, Steele 230
Bjelke-Petersen, Joh 242
Black, Simon 283

Blackaby, Ed 177, 179-181, 184-186, 193, 195, 209, 218, 259-260
Blackwell, Wayne 205
Blair, Dennis 134
Blight, Malcolm 220, 228
Bond, Eileen 76
Book, Fred 119-120
Boot, Colin 26
Bootsma, Brad 270
Bosustow, Peter 178, 204, 220
Bottrell, John 15
Bottrell, Tom (Jnr) 280
Bottrell, Tom (Snr) 15, 76, 87, 106
Boucher, Ron 157-158, 161, 165, 168, 175-176, 180-181, 184-185, 189, 192-194, 197, 199-201, 207, 209-210, 279, 282
Bow, Glen 84-85, 88, 91-92
Bowe, Ron 62, 67, 84, 88
Bowe, Ross 84, 92
Bowler, Peter 174
Bradley, Craig 198, 213, 220
Bradman, Don 24
Bradmore, Phil 220
Brehaut, Greg 121, 253
Breman, Todd 238
Brennan, Michael 236
Brenton, Leigh 203-204
Brereton, Dermott 213, 224, 238
Brewer, Ian 97
Brindley, John 84
Brown, Mal 112, 119, 133-134, 147, 149, 152, 158, 170, 172-173, 175, 182-183, 186, 190, 198, 204, 211, 219, 221, 223, 226, 244, 253, 263, 293
Brown, Rod (SD) 162
Brown, Rod (WP) 232-233
Browne, Richard 131
Browning, Clinton 220, 238
Brownless, Bill 231
Bucat, Bob 67, 108
Buckenara, Gary 167, 199, 224-225, 231, 268
Buckley, Nathan 100, 119
Buhagiar, Tony 132, 139, 143-144, 149, 205
Bukevich, George 83
Bull, Ned 58
Bunton, Haydn (Jnr) 16, 60, 79-83, 85, 87-88, 113, 115, 123, 130, 155-156, 175, 193, 204, 208, 223-224, 226- 227, 253, 262-263, 272, 274, 291, 298-299
Bunton, Haydn (Snr) 43
Burns, Robbie 205, 211, 245
Burton, Peter 172
Buttsworth, Fred 72
Byfield, Dan 56, 59, 61-64, 84
Bygraves, Gary 10
Byrne, Ray 190

C

Cable, Barry 23, 97-99, 108, 111, 116, 119, 121-123, 128, 160, 165, 168, 175, 184, 230, 263
Cable, Shane 238, 263
Cahill, John 80
Callaghan, Craig 265
Campbell, Basil 269
Campbell, Graham 147, 175, 179
Campbell, Grant 174, 249
Campbell, Warren 269-270, 272
Carbon, Harry 19-20, 22, 26, 29, 31, 37, 39, 47-48, 54, 63
Carson, Bob 108
Carter, Dan 47-48, 50, 53
Carter, Gavin 204
Carter, Graeme 151
Carter, Noel 182, 186, 190, 253, 255
Casellas, Cyril 95
Casey, Gordon 158, 160, 162, 165, 168, 183, 195, 265
Castledine, Fred 111, 155, 163, 193
Catalano, Nick 280
Caton, Kevin 207, 220, 262
Cerutty, Percy 156
Chadwick, Derek 81
Charleson, Alf 187
Chick, Daniel 269
Christian, Geoff 96, 98, 142, 144, 172, 196, 204, 253
Ciccotosto, Brian 109, 111
Clarke, Jack (Vic) 36, 77
Clarke, Jack (WA) 71-72, 77-79, 81, 83
Clarke, Sammy 31
Cloke, David 192
Close, Brian 162
Clune, Kevin 101, 200
Coates, Kerry 138, 141-142, 144-145, 151, 172
Codrington, Chris 245
Coleman, John 99
Colgan, Bill 40, 98, 110
Colgan, John 35, 47, 54-56, 59, 61, 63-64, 67, 75, 78-79, 85, 100, 250
Collingwood, Ted 105
Collins, Bill 21, 25, 30-31, 61, 106
Collins, Brian 42
Colreavy, John 152
Coleman, John 99
Coleman, John 99
Conigrave, Noel 67, 87-88
Connell, Matt 280
Connolly, Chris 284
Conway, Jim 31, 72, 103, 118
Cook, Brian 243, 266
Cook, Lorne 111, 198
Cooper, Beryl 291
Cooper, John 154-156, 158-163, 165, 172, 177, 180, 187, 191-192, 194, 196, 198, 204, 209, 260, 265, 267, 274- 275, 277, 291
Corbett, Roy 52
Couper, Murray 144, 160

Index

Cousins, Ben 119
Cousins, Bryan 206, 220, 256
Cowan, Merv 125, 128-129, 131, 133, 138, 140-142, 144, 146-147, 151, 153, 155, 191
Cox, Greg 31
Cox, Norm 109, 111-112
Crabbe, Lenny 19, 21
Cransberg, Alan 194, 196, 202, 210
Crawford, Ray 27, 41-42
Cribb, Bob 104
Cronan, Phil 205, 249, 275
Cronin, Mick 117
Cummings, Scott 265
Curley, Todd 269

D

Dale, Stroud 156
Dalton, Pat 122, 175
Daly, George 126
Daly, Pat 46, 63
Daniels, Allen 205-206, 213, 220
Daniher, Terry 213, 216, 224-225, 231
Darcy, Don 41-42, 54, 56
Dargie, Ian 263, 284
Davidson, Jeff 192
Davidson, Ron 50, 87
Davies, Jim 169, 173, 249
Davies, Wayne 230
Davis, Craig 190
Daw, Rowley 109, 113
Day, Barry 151
de Gruchy, Bill 60
Delaney, Alan 250
Dempsey, Bill 119, 172, 175
Denham, Greg 245
DiPierdomenico, Robert 213, 224-225
Ditchburn, Ross 249
Dobson, Mal 132
Doig, Charlie 141
Doig, George 291
Doig, Ron 46, 67, 84, 92
Dolan, Jerry 16-17, 262, 272
Doncon, Keith 112
Donnes, Eddie 130, 133, 138, 144, 146, 151
Dorotich, Jon 269, 272
Dorrington, Grant 184, 221
Dougan, Peter 108, 110, 114
Douge, Brian 234, 239-240
Doust, Wally 18, 21, 38, 72
Drum, Damian 274, 284
Durnthaler, Glen 141-142, 144, 149
Dyer, Jack 17, 20, 23

E

Eakins, Peter 121
East, Alan 170, 235-236

Edelsten, Geoffrey 250
Edmonds, Travis 280
Elliott, Herb 137, 156-157, 159, 277
Elliott, Laurie 137-138, 143, 145, 156, 165, 167, 189
Ellis, Shane 238
Ensell, Peter 242
Ensor, Jack 154-155
Eriksson, Eric 21
Evans, Ron 64
Evans, Vic 115
Everett, Tom 36, 52, 60

F

Fanchi, Joe 81
Farmer, Brett 186, 193, 195, 203, 210
Farmer, Clinton 130, 132
Farmer, Graham 23, 30-31, 37, 39, 42, 53, 58, 64-66, 72, 78-81, 85, 99, 101, 113, 119-120, 123, 127-128, 160, 172, 174
Farris, John 216
Featherby, Peter 170-171
Fenner, Gary 128, 131
Ferguson, Neil 131, 144, 147, 149, 151, 172
Fitzgerald, Garrett 213
Fitzgerald, Ross 189, 196, 210
Fitzmaurice, Jim 117
Fitzpatrick, Mike 172
Flower, Robert 213-214
Fode, Lenny 107
Fogarty, George 50
Fogarty, Jon 181, 189, 193, 204, 210, 212, 222-223, 253
Foley, Brian 50, 64, 66, 72, 78, 119
Fong, Neale 281
France, Brian 111, 122
Frazer, Kevin 97
Freemantle, Terry 112
French, Ray 26
Frost, Greg 156-157
Fuhrmann, Frank 29, 37, 50, 57, 65, 79, 86

G

Gabelich, Ray 79-81
Gairdner, Charles 32
Gallop, Geoff 276
Gardiner, Don 106, 108
Garrett, Trevor 270
Gastev, John 235-236, 238
Gates, Frank 12
Gates, Roger 12
Geary, Richard 238
Gehrig, Fraser 269
George, Max 148-149, 162
Gepp, Tim 256

Gerovich, John 22, 26, 30-31, 35, 38-39, 50, 55-57, 62-67, 77-79, 83, 85-86, 91-92, 100, 103, 105-108, 110, 112-117
Gibellini, Gary 130, 132, 143-144, 147-148, 151, 172
Gillan, Don 15, 34, 56, 60
Gillespie, Steve 158, 162, 168, 195
Glass, Don 47, 55
Glendinning, Ross 99, 151, 206, 213, 235-238, 243, 249-250, 257, 291
Glucina, Ivan 104-105, 108-109, 112, 116, 122
Gorman, Eric 108
Goulding, Steve 198, 206
Graf, Steffi 24
Graham, Bob 148
Gray, Brian 164
Green, Doug 130, 133, 139, 141, 144, 147-149, 175
Green, Laurie 21, 25
Greene, Russell 213
Greer, Gary 92, 107-108, 110-113, 116
Grljusich, Don 108, 110
Grljusich, George 76, 118, 144
Grljusich, John 144, 149
Grljusich, Tom 76, 79, 83-84, 97, 113-114, 116, 144, 175
Grose, Eric 41-42, 76
Guthrie, Tom 101

H

Hadfield, Tom 50
Hafey, Tom 190
Hall, Derek 280
Hamilton, Neil 229, 241, 243-245, 259
Handley, Stephen 282
Hank, Bob 161
Hardie, Brad 204, 206, 213, 220, 224, 254
Harding, Paul 198-199
Harper, Keith 64
Harper, Roy 76
Harrison, Frank 38, 41-42, 48, 54
Hart, David 204, 236, 270-272
Hatt, David 274
Hawke, Steve 53, 101
Hayes, John 230, 234
Head, Lindsay 36
Headland, Des 285
Heal, Stan 117
Healy, Gerard 205, 213, 216, 224
Hebbard, Colin 17
Heffernan, Kevin 225
Henfry, Ern 27, 60, 104, 119
Hetherington, Kim 203, 206
Hickman, Colin 47
Hicks, Chris 139, 144, 149, 157
Higgins, Peter 238
Hillier, Cliff 39, 41-42, 56, 61, 63, 66

Hindes, Charlie 10, 12-13, 58
Hindes, Lucy 9-10, 58
Hindes, Ron 11-12, 22, 29, 37
Hird, James 119
Hogan, Paul 222
Holden, Craig 168, 184, 186-187, 189, 195, 213, 224, 253
Holdsworth, Ted 161
Hollins, David 130, 133, 139, 144, 148, 172, 175
Holmes, Don 162, 179, 189, 204, 209-210, 231, 233, 260- 261, 263
Holt, Bill 40
Hopkins, Colin 145, 253
Hopkins, Ted 121
Howard, Harry 82
Howard, Ray 13, 31
Hoyer, Craig 179, 183
Hughes, Bill 48
Hughes, Danny 236
Hunter, Ken 205
Hutchinson, Gwen 10
Hutchinson, Ross 9, 14, 19, 142-143, 212, 267, 272
Hutton, Brent 204, 260-261
Hyde, John 30
Hynes, David 238, 271

I

Idle, Don 26
Ingraham, Doug 19, 61
Ironmonger, John 206, 256
Ischenko, Alex 233, 236-237

J

Jackson, Stevan 238-239
Jackson, Syd 93, 112-113, 121
Jakovich, Glen 44
Jancey, Max 104, 123
Jeans, Allan 210, 225
Jenkins, Frank 31
Jenzen, Graham 104
Jez, Mick 148
Jinman, Laurie 49
John, Graeme 120
John, Griff 46
Johns, Michael 200-201, 203, 207
Johnson, Bob 104, 106, 108, 110, 129
Johnson, Frank 84
Johnson, Percy 60, 158
Johnston, Wayne 224
Jones, Dennis 130
Joyce, Alan 128-129, 153, 155, 211, 244
Judge, Ken 263, 268, 284
Junner, Colin 76, 103

K

Keane, Mervyn 192
Keene, Laurie 204, 236, 239

Kelleher, Max 163
Kelly, Des 21, 25
Kelly, Harry 169
Kelly, Paul 44
Kelly, Phil 165, 168, 171, 248
Kennedy, John (Snr) 129, 153, 237
Kennedy, Laurie 18
Kenny, Peter 195-197, 202, 210
Kerley, Neil 80, 174
Kernahan, Stephen 198, 213, 220
Kerr, Bill 228-230, 239, 241, 243-245, 259
Kettlewell, Laurie 79
Kickett, Derek 256
Kiernan, Max 200
Killigrew, Alan 110
Kilmurray, Ted 38, 57, 66, 72
Kimberley, Barry 203, 207, 210, 221-222, 224
Krakouer, Jim 186, 193, 196, 253
Krakouer, Phil 186, 193, 196, 253

L

Lacey, Jack 14, 20
Laidley, Dean 236, 263
Lamb, Dwayne 220, 236, 240, 282
Langdon, Don 71
Langdon, Karl 233, 236, 288
Langford, Chris 224
Langsford, Don 162, 181, 189, 198, 205, 210, 222, 224, 260, 262-263
Larkin, Leon 174, 256
Lawrence, Brian 250
Leahy, Jim 249
Lee, Mark 192, 213-214
Legena, Frank 97, 104
Leonard, John 16, 262, 272
Lewington, Clive 19, 21-22, 25-27, 29-32, 34-35, 40-41, 46-48, 50, 55-56, 59-60, 66, 97, 118-119, 182
Lewis, Chris 236, 240, 242
Lewis, Fred 121
Lincoln, Merv 157, 277
Lockyer, Andrew 222, 236, 263
Long, Michael 282
Lorimer, Ron 239
Lyon, Gary 215, 236

M

MacDonald, Murray 67, 84, 108, 110, 113-115
Mackellar-Hall, Mr 43
Madden, Simon 213, 244
Maffina, Joe 91
Maffina, Sonny 148
Magee, Stuart 154-155
Magro, Stan 149, 171
Mainwaring, Chris 235-236, 283

Malaxos, Steve 184-186, 193, 195-196, 206, 210, 213, 220, 236, 239, 249, 251, 256, 282
Maloney, Richard 282
Malthouse, Michael 192, 203, 244-245, 254, 259, 265-266, 282
Malthouse, Nanette 245
Manea, Ernie 54-55
Mann, Hassa 116, 126, 148, 187
Manning, Bob 164, 166, 173, 178, 200-201, 205, 228-230, 239, 242, 266
Marinko, Don 35, 50, 60
Marinko, Ray 101
Marsh, Steve 15, 19, 21-23, 25-27, 29-33, 35-37, 42, 46- 47, 52-54, 57, 60-61, 67-68, 72, 78, 83, 94, 99, 117, 122, 129-130, 141, 143-144, 219
Marshall, Denis 79, 88, 94, 120
Marshall, Ken 203
Martinovich, Kris 34, 40-42, 98
Matera, Phil 269
Matera, Wally 236, 238
Matson, Phil 273
Matthews, Leigh 128, 243
Maynard, Colin 155-156
McAullay, Ken 198
McCormack, John 84
McDermott, Peter 211, 214, 216
McDiarmid, Norm 18
McDonald, Archie 84
McDonald, Gary 162
McDonnell, Marty 68, 75-78, 84, 87-88, 91-92, 111, 117-118
McGill, Kevin 18, 72
McGilvray, Bill 47
McGrath, John 264
McHenry, Murray 241, 245
McHenry, Russell 130-131, 141-142, 149
McIntosh, Garry 213-214, 216, 220, 224-225
McIntosh, John 121
McIntosh, Merv 28, 30, 32, 35, 72, 291
McKay, Joe 182
McKenna, Guy 233, 236, 242, 244, 263
McKenna, Peter 128
McNamee, Paul 222
Meldrum, Ian (Molly) 222
Melesso, Peter 238, 243
Melrose, Graham 129-131, 133, 137-141, 143-147, 149, 153, 172, 175, 177, 179-181, 184-185, 194-195, 197, 209-210, 227, 263, 275
Menzies, Robert 69
Meredith, Harry 32
Merifield, Kevin 127
Merillo, Joe 107
Metropolis, Daniel 280
Micale, Tony 111, 126, 132, 134, 137-138, 143, 146, 263, 269-270, 272, 274, 276-277

Index

Michael, Clem 269, 272
Michael, Stephen 99, 181-182, 186, 199, 254-256, 269, 291
Michalcyzk, George 190, 226
Miles, Geoff 235-236, 239, 263
Miller, Bob 84, 119
Miller, Des 47
Miller, Ian 165, 175, 211
Miller, John (J.J) 164
Miller, Ken 117, 119-120
Miller, Kevin 108, 110, 112-113, 116
Mills, Bert 47-48, 53
Mills, Jim 96
Mitchell, Bill 126
Mitchell, Michael 198, 206, 256
Moiler, Tom 127
Moloney, George 50, 64
Monkhurst, Damian 282
Monteath, Bruce 170
Montgomery, Ray 76-77, 83
Moore, Rod 236
Morgan, Harry 211
Morris, Bill 17
Mosconi, Warren 204
Mose, Bill 58
Moses, Stan 155
Moss, Graham 99, 152, 160, 171, 174, 192, 198, 206, 210, 223, 226, 228-230, 255, 293
Motley, Peter 213, 220
Mountain, Paul 156, 181, 253
Mulloolly, Tom 155, 158, 162, 168, 175-176, 184, 194- 195, 197, 200, 209-210, 217, 263-264
Mumme, Les 17, 64-65, 79-81
Mundine, Tony 222
Murnane, Peter 249
Murray, Dan 79
Murray, Jack (SD) 10
Murray, Jack (SF) 71
Murray, Kevin 109, 120-121

N

Naley, Mark 224
Narkle, Keith 159, 168, 175-176, 179, 184, 194, 196, 206- 208, 217-218
Narkle, Phil 162, 168, 179, 184, 193-196, 202, 231, 249- 250, 256, 260, 262-263, 266
Naylor, Bernie 20-21, 23, 25-26, 29, 61, 64, 115, 177
Neesham, Gerard 147, 165, 168, 177, 179, 181, 184-185, 187, 189, 195, 197, 206-207, 210, 217, 254-256, 261, 263
Neesham, Harry 129
Nesbit, Tony 155, 193
Nicholas, Ross 152
Nicholls, Paul 139-140, 145, 149
Nisbett, Trevor 243

Norton, Kevin 171, 282
Nowotny, Stan 141, 151, 155-156, 158-159, 161-162, 164- 168, 172, 175-176, 178, 181, 183-184, 186-187, 190- 192, 194, 196, 200-202, 207, 209-210

O

O'Connell, David 231, 235-236
O'Connell, John 231
O'Connell, Michael 232-233
O'Donoghue, Mark 112
O'Loughlin, Glen 251
O'Reilly, Phil 282
O'Reilly, Stephen 265
O'Shea, Jack 216
Olliver, Arthur 76, 118
Olsen, Mark 159, 167-168, 177
Osmetti, Charlie 104-105, 112
Owens, Len 31, 35-36

P

Page, Bob 116, 123
Panizza, Darrell 206, 282
Papotto, Tony 253
Parentich, Tony 46-47, 56, 61, 63, 67, 76, 84, 100
Parkin, David 147, 230, 277
Parkinson, John 111, 122
Pavy, Len 17
Peake, Brian 99, 130, 139, 142-144, 148-149, 155-156, 160, 171-172, 175, 224, 254, 282
Pears, Stephen 280
Peos, Paul 238, 242
Perkins, Lance 168
Pert, Gary 213, 214, 224-225
Picken, Billy 190
Pickett, Allistair 284
Pitter, Eddie 112
Platten, John 213, 216, 220, 224
Poat, Peter 170, 253
Potts, Colin 22
Powell, Ron 140
Preen, Alan 36, 57
Pretty, David 144
Prosser, Alan 130, 133, 139
Purser, Andrew 203, 205
Pyke, Don 238-239, 263, 281
Pyke, Frank 93, 104

Q

Quartermaine, Alan 151, 175

R

Raines, Geoff 192
Ralph, Warren 186, 193, 195, 205, 210, 255

Rance, Murray 178, 184, 189, 192, 195-196, 198, 209- 210, 213, 223, 233, 236, 239-240, 243-244, 260, 262, 264, 277
Randall, Neil 181
Rawlings, Barry 192
Read, Mick 67
Regan, Con 79
Regan, Michael 76
Rehn, Shaun 44
Reid, Alan 144
Reid, Russell 273
Reilly, Graeme 97, 104, 116, 140, 147
Reilly, Jack 19
Richards, Ray 9, 12, 22, 27, 36-37, 45, 52, 55-56, 59-61, 64, 66, 94, 110
Richardson, Max 109, 111, 116, 121
Richardson, Mike 162, 179, 181, 184, 186, 189, 197, 210, 224, 262, 282
Richardson, Steve 210, 220, 224
Richardson, Wayne 109, 121
Rioli, Dean 221, 269-270, 272
Rioli, Maurice 182, 186, 192, 213, 216, 224, 256-257, 269
Rioli, Sebastian 269
Roach, Michael 192
Roberts, Neville 205
Robertson, Austin (Jnr) 20, 110, 114-115, 119, 132, 175
Robertson, Austin (Snr) 35, 50-51, 55, 63-64
Robinson, Mary 30-31
Robson, Bobby 274
Rodriguez, Pat 70, 79, 81, 119
Roe, Willie 198
Rogers, Norm 62, 64, 79, 81, 97-98, 120, 129-130, 141, 293
Roos, Paul 224

S

Salmon, Paul 44, 239
Sarich, Eric 129
Sartori, Peter 192, 201, 207, 210, 213, 224
Sawers, Rowan 215
Schimmelbusch, Wayne 244
Schofield, Ray 60
Schrader, Jim 34
Schwab, Alan 224, 251
Schwartz, David 44
Scott, Don 177
Scott, Gary 62-63, 84-85, 92, 96-97, 104, 106, 110-111, 116-117, 119, 122
Scott, Graham 104, 106, 108, 114, 116
Scott, Phil 220, 222, 236, 239-240
Scott, Ray 31
Seal, Paul 72

Seinor, Fred 84-85, 92, 96, 104, 110-113, 119, 293
Sergeant, Rod 183
Sewell, Jim 151
Shaw, Derek 248
Shaw, Gary 193
Shaw, Tony 190
Sheedy, Jack 27, 31, 37-38, 60, 66, 69-70, 79, 81-82, 88, 99, 106, 175, 291
Sheedy, Kevin 220-221, 240, 244, 256
Shepherd, Barry 17
Sheppard, Vicki 198
Shields, Bob 119, 127
Shine, Brad 189, 201, 210, 217, 260-261
Sidebottom, Alan 158, 180, 189, 195, 197
Sidebottom, Garry 158-159, 161, 217-219, 221-223
Simms, John 151
Skehan, Charlie 10, 12, 27, 32, 36, 64
Skilton, Bob 15, 64-65
Skwirowski, Bill 186, 189, 194-196, 210, 217-218, 220, 253
Slater, Keith 79, 87, 110-111, 119, 193, 274
Smith, Bradley 168, 172, 175
Smith, Don 61, 63
Smith, Graeme 110
Smith, Keith 84, 105, 112
Smith, Len 80
Smith, Mike 162, 179, 184-186, 189, 195, 202, 210, 257
Smith, Norm 35, 42, 55
Smith, Phil 134
Smith, Ross 130, 147, 175
Solin, Tony 177, 184, 198, 223, 263
Sorrell, Ray 36, 52-53, 63-65, 79-81, 83, 85, 92, 94-97, 99, 103, 119-120
Spalding, Earl 236
Spalding, George 212
Spalding, Scott 270
Spargo, Bob 113
Sparks, Kevan 222
Sparrow, Frank 117
Spencer, Peter 151-152, 206, 248, 256, 263
Sprigg, Trevor 107, 119, 151, 293
Stannage, Tom 200-201
Steward, Peter 130
Stewart, Don 13, 27, 31, 35, 47, 55, 63, 84
Stockden, Barry 156
Stocks, Gary 270
Stooke, Wally 48
Sumich, Jack 62-63, 67, 77-79, 94
Sumich, Peter 188, 238-243, 263, 270-271
Sutton, Daryl 183-185, 187
Symmons, Paul 280

T

Taylor, Brian 192
Taylor, Jim 30
Taylor, Kevin 168, 199, 217, 221-222
Thompson, Russell 280
Thorne, Peter 198
Thornley, Bert 110, 120, 129
Throssell, Michael 53
Titus, Jack 122
Todd (Booth), Meryl 84, 88, 90, 93-95, 97-98, 105, 109, 127-128, 130, 135,153, 160, 163, 167, 228, 241-242, 244, 266-267, 270, 273, 276, 291, 295, 297
Todd (Micale), Diane 17, 22, 52, 72, 111, 270
Todd, Bill (Jnr) 13-14, 18, 29-30, 34, 72, 223, 270
Todd, Bill (Snr) 10-11, 13, 15, 17-18, 30, 37, 40-42, 98
Todd, Debbie 90, 95, 97, 109, 128, 266, 270, 273, 276
Todd, Doris 9-18, 21-22, 25-27, 29-30, 33, 37-40, 42-43, 48, 52, 55, 57-58, 60, 71-72, 129, 217, 222, 267, 269- 270, 294
Todd, Kylie 105, 109, 128, 266, 270, 273, 276
Tomka, Franz 97, 104, 108, 116, 137
Towers, Bill 17
Townsend, Rex 130
Treasure, Frank 21, 30, 35, 47, 55
Treleven, Craig 269, 280, 284
Trimbole, Robert 215
Turco, Mario 142
Turley, Craig 238-239
Turnbull, John 79, 193
Turnbull, Ryan 280, 284
Turner, Dean 236, 240, 250
Turner, Steve 277
Tyson, Charlie 23, 35-36, 54, 60, 66, 84, 94
Tyson, Ted 132

U

Ugle, Troy 232, 260, 262
Uittenbroek, Bob 139, 147

V

Verstegen, Hans 112
Voss, Michael 119

W

Walker, Bill 23, 83, 95, 98-99, 108, 111, 116, 119, 121- 122, 141, 155, 158, 163, 175, 180, 183, 193, 198, 203, 212, 216, 218, 228, 230, 244, 251, 259-260, 262, 264-265, 274, 291, 298
Walker, Dick 30, 84, 87
Walker, Greg 262
Walker, John 226
Walls, Robert 244, 254
Walsh, Kevin 224-225
Ward, Murray 211
Ware, Peter 204
Wares, Don 18-19, 71
Warren, Ron 59, 87-88
Washbourne, Jim 71
Waterman, Chris 242
Waterson, Colin 220
Watson, Laurie 143
Watson, Mark 256, 267
Watters, Scott 238, 242
Watts, John 26, 64, 250
Weightman, Dale 192, 224
Werner, Paul 200
Whinnen, Mel 96, 151, 160, 175
White, Barry 26-27, 31-32, 35, 47, 56, 59, 62-63, 76, 84, 106, 128
White, Jeff 285
White, Merv 151
Whitten, Ted 50, 56, 72-73, 80-81, 213, 224
Wiley, Robert 144, 160, 171, 192, 204-205, 213, 220, 273
Wilkinson, Col 56, 87, 96
Wilkinson, Greg 204
Williams, Don 79, 81
Williams, Fos 30, 80
Williams, Ian 168, 174, 180-181, 185, 189, 195
Williams, Kerry 139, 141-143, 147, 149, 151
Williams, Mark 190
Wilson, Barry 138
Wilson, Gary 224
Wilson, Noel 116
Wilson, Peter 220, 224, 274-275
Woewodin, Shane 283-284
Wood, Graeme 152
Woods, Fred 117
Worsfold, John 44, 223, 236, 239-240, 242, 244, 257, 263, 284
Worsfold, Peter 253, 271
Worthington, Kevin 190
Wrensted, Murray 220, 222, 231, 236-238, 256
Wynne, John 219

XYZ

Yovich, Vincent 247-249
Zanotti, Mark 234, 236-237, 250
Zeuner, Reg 50, 76